16 M 23
17 T 24
18 W 25
19 T 26
20 F 27
21 S 28
22 S 29

CONTINUING

KOREAN

CONTINUING

KOREAN

by Ross King, Ph.D. and Jae-Hoon Yeon, Ph.D.,
with Insun Lee

Tuttle Publishing
Boston • Rutland, Vermont • Tokyo

First published in 2002 by Tuttle Publishing, an imprint of Periplus Editions (HK) Ltd., with editorial offices at 153 Milk Street, Boston, Massachusetts 02109.

Distributed by:

USA
Tuttle Publishing
Distribution Center
Airport Industrial Park
364 Innovation Drive
North Clarendon, VT 05759-9436
Tel: (802) 773-8930
Tel: (800) 526-2778

Japan
Tuttle Publishing
RK Building, 2nd Floor
2-13-10 Shimo-Meguro
Meguroko-ku
Tokyo 153 0064
Tel: 81-35-437-0171
Fax: 81-35-437-0755

Southeast Asia
Berkeley Books Pte. Ltd.
130 Joo Seng Road
#06-01/03 Olivine Building
Singapore 368357
Tel: (65) 280-1330
Fax: (65) 280-6290

First edition
06 05 04 03 02 01 00 99   10 9 8 7 6 5 4 3 2 1 Printed in the United States of America

Contents

Preface

This book is the follow-on volume to *Elementary Korean*, published by Tuttle Publishing in 2000. For detailed background about the making of this two-volume textbook series, please refer to the preface in *Elementary Korean*.

Like *Elementary Korean*, *Continuing Korean* owes much to the comments and criticisms of several cohorts of students at the School of Oriental and African Studies (SOAS), University of London, and at the University of British Columbia (UBC), during the years 1990–2001. Likewise, *Continuing Korean* has benefited from valuable feedback on the part of numerous colleagues in Korea, Great Britain, the United States, and Canada. We have acknowledged most of these debts in the preface to *Elementary Korean* but would like to take this opportunity to record our gratitude to the following UBC Teaching Assistants (TAs) and Sessional Lecturers who have contributed in numerous ways to the making of *Continuing Korean*: Jee-Weon Shin (TA, 1996–1997 academic year); Soowook Kim (academic years 1997–1999; 2000–2002), Dafna Zur (1999–2000). In addition, Sunah Park Cho made numerous helpful criticisms during the years 1998–2000 while working as webmaster for the UBC Korean Language Program Web sites, Susie (Yunju) Cho and Victoria Wilding helped compile the glossaries and exercise answer key and Mookyung Kim, Soowook Kim, and Victoria Wilding proofread the manuscript several times. Finally, we are grateful to Sunah Cho, Sun Hyang Jung, Ilsung Lee and Soowook Kim for providing their voice talents for the audio CD, and to Frank Ludwig and Al Farrell of Quantum Sound Studio and Frank Talk Publishing, Ltd., for their expert assistance in producing and editing the audio recordings.

We would be delighted to hear more feedback, positive or negative, from future users of this book. Please contact us at the addresses below:

Ross King
Dept. of Asian Studies, UBC
Asian Centre
1871 West Mall
Vancouver, B. C. (Canada)
email: jrpking@interchange.ubc.ca
fax: (604) 822-8937

J. H. Yeon
Centre of Korean Studies
SOAS, University of London
Thornhaugh Street, Russell Square
London WC1H OXG (U.K.)
email: jy1@soas.ac.uk
fax: (171) 323-6179

About This Book

Preliminaries: Assumed Knowledge

This book is the sequel volume to *Elementary Korean* (Tuttle Publishing, 2000) and assumes a thorough knowledge of the patterns and vocabulary introduced in that book. For the vocabulary introduced in *Elementary Korean*, please consult the glossaries in that book; in principle, any word in this book not to be found in the glossaries here was already introduced in *Elementary Korean*. Likewise, a detailed list of the Korean patterns covered in *Elementary Korean* can be found in the English-Korean and Korean-English Pattern Glossaries in that book, but for the convenience of learners and instructors alike, we summarize the main points covered in *Elementary Korean* below:

<u>Speech Styles</u>
- Polite Style (해요)
- Formal Style (합니다)

<u>Particles</u>
- 까지 (as far as; by; until; up to)
- 께
- 께서(는)
- 도 (also; even; too; [not] either)
- 들
- 마다
- 만
- 부터
- 씩
- 에 (at [Static Location]; to [Direction Particle]; in [Static Location])
- 에게(서)
- 와/과
- 으로/로
- 은/는
- 을/를
- 의
- 이/가
- (이)나 (about; any/every; approximately; generalizer; or; or something)
- (이)랑

- 쯤
- 처럼
- 하고 (and; with)
- 한테(서)

General Verb Mechanics

- all regular verbs, including:
    - w - ㅂ verbs
    - ㄹ - ㄷ verbs
    - ㅅ - Ø verbs
- irregular verbs 하-, 되-, and the copula -이-
- long and short negation (안 해요, 못해요; 하지 않아요, 하지 못해요)
- the pattern in **NOUN** 밖에 + **NEGATIVE** meaning "only"
- honorific -(으)시-

Verb Endings

ONE-SHAPE ENDINGS	
past marker	-ㅆ-
suspective	-지
suppositive	-지요
"but"	-지만
future-presumptive	-겠-
rhetor. retort	-잖아요
고-form	-고 (싶-, 있-)
dictionary form	-다
"as soon as"	-자 마자

TWO-SHAPE ENDINGS		
	After vowel	After consonant
honorific	-시-	-으시-
honorific polite	-세요	-으세요
sequential	-니(까)	-으니까
purposive	-러	-으러
formal decl.	-ㅂ니다	-습니다
formal imper.	-십시오	-으십시오
formal propos.	-ㅂ시다	-읍시다
formal interrog.	-ㅂ니까	-습니까
suggestions	-ㄹ까요	-을까요
consider doing	-ㄹ까 하-	-을까 하-
"wanna"	-ㄹ래요	-을래요
prob. future	-ㄹ 거에요	-을 거에요
immed. future	-ㄹ게요	-을게요

Introduction

Like other Korean language textbooks on the market, this textbook has its strengths and weaknesses. The authors have tried to write a book that will appeal to a broad range of learners, including individuals working on their own, professional people working with a tutor, and university students in a classroom setting. The remarks here are aimed primarily at teachers contemplating using the textbook with learners of the latter type.

Main Objective

The main objective of the two volumes comprising *Elementary Korean* and *Continuing Korean* is communicative competence in contemporary spoken Korean through a systematic and streamlined introduction to the fundamental patterns of the language. Most lessons in *Continuing Korean* (this, the second volume) also contain a "Reading Passage," and both volumes introduce a small number of patterns more relevant to written language than spoken. In such cases, the student is advised as to the spoken vs. written language status of the pattern in question. Thus, these textbooks do not aim at oral competence alone.

In terms of the ACTFL Proficiency Guidelines, the authors believe that the two volumes together provide enough material for a student to attain Intermediate-Low to Intermediate-Mid proficiency level. Of course, this is also dependent on the number of contact hours and the quality of "act"-related (as opposed to "fact"-related) instruction provided.

Basic Methodology

This textbook is unabashedly structuralist and eclectic in its philosophy and methodology. Some teachers versed in the latest task-based and proficiency-oriented approaches to language teaching may find the book's structuralist approach reminiscent of the "grammar translation method" and the "audio-lingual method." Such teachers should remember one point: the book does not teach the course in the classroom.

The authors believe the textbook is amenable to any number of language teaching approaches and styles in the classroom and see it primarily as an out-of-class reference tool to ready the students for whatever activities their teacher has prepared for them in class. The grammar notes here are richer (though still concise, we hope) than those in other textbooks for at least two reasons:

      1) to help those students working on their own without recourse to a teacher, and

      2) to reduce the amount of class time needed for "fact" (as opposed to "act").

About the Exercises

The exercises at the end of each lesson are designed primarily as *written* homework, not as oral exercises for the classroom. We have deliberately omitted oral pattern drills from the lessons because we feel such drills are easily constructed by the teacher and take up unnecessary space. Thus, one major shortcoming of the two volumes is the lack of a teacher's manual with ideas and guidance for both task-based classroom activities and pattern drills. The lack of a teacher's manual or activity book places an additional burden on the teacher, but in this respect our textbook is no different from other Korean textbooks currently available. Insun Lee is now preparing such a volume for both *Elementary Korean* and *Continuing Korean*, and it should appear in the near future. Insun Lee has also prepared an excellent series of Web-based exercises (with extensive audio) to accompany the materials in both volumes. The materials for *Elementary Korean* can be found at UBC's Korean Language and Literature Web site (http://www.asia.ubc.ca/korean/) and should be available on CD-ROM some time in the next year or two. In the meantime, we encourage teachers using the book to share their ideas and supplementary materials with us.

About the Dialogues: Themes and Situations

The dialogues were written after the authors had determined which patterns were to appear in which sequence in the course. This introduces the danger of producing dialogues that become mere vehicles for the structural items being introduced. Keeping this danger in mind, we have tried to write dialogues that succeed at once in illustrating each new structural point in the lesson and in introducing tasks and situations likely to be of immediate use to a beginner in the language. We have tried to keep the conversations natural and colloquial, and where possible, humorous.

The dialogues cover the themes of daily academic life in Korea and business and travel. Most of the dialogues center around two middle-aged foreigners (Chris and Eunice Murphy) and their two university-aged children (Eric and Sandy). The authors hope this will enhance the functional range and potential market for the book.

Situations and functions covered in the two volumes include greetings and leave-takings, classroom expressions, identifying things and introducing people, existence, location and possession, asking for directions, buying tickets and other travel-related situations, discussing one's studies and one's language abilities, telling time, ordering at a restaurant, asking for people on the telephone, shopping, and social drinking. Though our treatment of situations is by no means comprehensive, most situations and tasks necessary for attaining basic proficiency are covered.

About Contact Hours

Most university Korean courses in the United States, Canada, the United Kingdom, Australia and New Zealand meet four or five hours per week. At this pace, the authors would recommend covering one lesson every eight to ten classroom hours, where the students have at least a thirty-minute quiz at the end of every other week. But the authors recognize that different students and different courses proceed at different paces; thus, anywhere from six to ten hours per lesson is possible, depending on the circumstances. The authors believe the book is particularly well-suited for an intensive course of eight to ten contact hours per week, in which case it would be possible to finish both volumes in one academic year.

About Vocabulary

This textbook introduces a lot of vocabulary, some one thousand items in each volume. The authors are skeptical of statistical "frequency list" approaches to introducing vocabulary, since these frequency lists are never based on the vocabulary needs of university students, businessmen, or travelers learning Korean. Thus, our book includes many sophisticated adult, intellectual vocabulary items — the sorts of words that mature adults would like to be able to say early in their Korean learning career. Furthermore, since Korean does not give the English speaker as many shortcut vocabulary "freebies" as French or Spanish or German, it is a hard fact of life that students need to spend more time on vocabulary building.

It is also the view of the authors that some vocabulary items "cost" more than others to learn. This view is reflected in the layout of the vocabulary sections, where certain words are indented beneath others to indicate that these items are related to the main vocabulary item in question, and thus "cost less" to learn.

Other features of the vocabulary sections to be born in mind are these: (1) all verb bases are given in the special notation that students learn in Lesson Seven in *Elementary Korean*; (2) processive and descriptive bases are distinguished from each other by their English glosses — descriptive verbs are always preceded by *be* (*blue, sad*, etc.), while processive verbs are not; (3) vocabulary is broken up into sections according to part of speech — verbs, nouns, adverbs, and so on (although the classification of verbal nouns is often arbitrary); (4) we have tried to provide more exemplification of the vocabulary items than is typical of other textbooks. Example sentences using a particular vocabulary item in context are indented below the main word. Note also that in *Continuing Korean* we have adopted the new tactic of listing new vocabulary items in alphabetical order within their part-of-speech category (usually "Noun," "Verbs," and "Adverbs").

About Orthography

Some teachers are finicky about spelling and conforming to the latest official orthographic guidelines. We are not. Whether one writes 할 거예요 or 할 거에요, for instance, seems to have little or no bearing on how well students assimilate this pattern. Our book uses the latter spelling, even though it is now "non-standard" orthography, because (1) this is how it is actually pronounced; indeed, *Continuing Korean* continues to write -에요 everywhere for the Polite Copula after vowel-final forms, as in *Elementary Korean*. And (2) students have already learned the simple rule for the copula that the -이- drops regularly in colloquial speech after a vowel. However, we have made a few minor orthographic changes in this volume: (1) we now write -(으)ㄹ게요 instead of -(으)ㄹ께요, and (2) we have tried to be more consistent with word spacing rules (e.g., 이분 vs. 이 분 *this esteemed person*, etc.). Still, the authors maintain that students can learn about the vagaries and idiosyncrasies of official Korean orthography at a later stage in their learning, once they actually know the patterns.

About the English Translations and Glosses

Many of the English translations of Korean expressions and patterns are structured to resemble as closely as possible the Korean meaning. In some cases, students and teachers may feel that certain English renditions are not typical English usage. For example, the authors are well aware that "wanna" is not considered good English. However, this contracted form is used for pedagogical reasons (the form in question is also a contraction in Korean), and seems to work as a mnemonic device, too. The same goes for other less-than-typical English usages in the book, and the authors ask for indulgence on this matter.

About Linguistic Symbols

Both primary authors received their doctoral training in linguistics, and this background is reflected in the analyses in the book and in the use of certain linguistic symbols. Our use of linguistic symbols amounts to a special kind of code that is designed to streamline the learning process for the student and to streamline the book's presentation. Once the teacher and students have mastered the few simple symbols below, they should have no trouble following the exposition in the book.

Symbol	Comments
- (Times), - (Apple Myungjo)	The hyphen is used to demarcate boundaries and bound forms. Because the abstract Korean verb stems (we call them bases) to which students must attach endings are all bound forms (that is, they cannot be used and do not occur in real speech without some ending), verbs in each lesson's Vocabulary List are listed as a base,

that is, as a bound form, followed by a hyphen to its right (e.g., 사-ㄹ- *live*). The same goes for all verb endings in Korean—they are abstract notions that only occur in Korean when attached to a verb base; they are bound forms and always appear in the book with a hyphen to their left. We continue to refer to verb bases and endings in the grammar notes in this way, too.

+ (Times), + (Apple Myungjo)	The plus sign means "plus" "added to" "in combination with."
/ . . . / vs. [. . .]	Phonemic notations are enclosed by slash brackets and phonetic notations by square brackets. Most examples of slash brackets have been purged from the book, but we often use square brackets to indicate the phonetics, that is, actual pronunciation of a Korean form when this is not indicated in the Korean orthography. Another usage of the square brackets is to indicate optional material.
*	The asterisk is used to mark grammatically unacceptable utterances.
→	This arrow sign means "becomes," "gives," "yields," "produces."
←	This arrow sign means "comes from," "is a product of," "derives from'."
~ (Times), ~ (Apple Myungjo)	The tilde is used to represent an alternation, and means "in alternation with."

Note also the following abbreviations:

sb	somebody
s.th.	something

Cast of Characters

The Murphy Family:

Christopher Murphy, a middle-aged British businessman in charge of the Seoul office of a Yorkshire textiles firm; **Eunice**, his Australian wife who teaches piano at an International School in Seoul; **Eric** and **Sandy**, their twenty-one-year old twins, both attending the International Division at Korea University.

The Kim Family:

Mr. Ch'ang-gi Kim, Chris Murphy's Korean teacher, a middle-aged Korean; **his wife**, a full-time housewife active in their local church; **Chin-yŏng**, their twenty-one-year-old daughter, and **Chin-sŏp**, their twenty-year-old son, both attending Korea University.

Others:

Miss Lee, Christopher Murphy's secretary, a woman in her mid-twenties.

할머니 (halmŏni), the "grandmother" living across the hall from the Murphys.

Mr. Kang, a middle-aged man who is a long-time business associate of Chris Murphy and senior employee of Han'guk Sŏmyu, a Korean textiles firm based in Pusan.

Mr. Nam, another business associate of Chris Murphy.

Yŏngch'ŏl, a friend of Eric's from Korea University.

Sŏngman, a friend of Sandy's from Korea University.

Miss Kwak, a waitress befriended by Eric.

송 선생님, Eric and Sandy's Korean teacher at Korea University.

Yuko, a Japanese friend Sandy has met at Korea University.

보희 and 경숙, two of Chin-yŏng's high school friends from Inch'ŏn.

The list above is given to clarify the gender, age, status and interrelationships of the various characters in the book, since this affects the style of Korean that they use in addressing each other.

Lesson 16

늦어서 죄송합니다.

In this lesson we see Eric apologizing to his Korean teacher for being late to class and explaining the circumstances behind his tardiness. The lesson introduces ways to combine two or more sentences with -고 meaning *and* or *and then*, and the important ending in infinitive -아 ~ -어 plus 서 for causes and sequences. The lesson also introduces two ways to say *about*, and the new explanatory ending in -거든요.

Korean Dialogues

Dialogue 1

Eric has arrived late to his Korean class and is about to apologize to his teacher, Mr. Song, a graduate student at Korea University.

에릭	늦어서 죄송합니다.
송 선생	괜찮아요. 어서 들어와요.
	그런데, 왜 늦었어요?
에릭	어제 밤에 술을 마시고 늦게 잤거든요.
	아침에 늦게 일어나서 버스를 놓쳤어요.
송 선생	날마다 술을 마셔요?
에릭	아니오, 매일 마시지 않아요. 비싸고 건강에 나쁘거든요.
송 선생	숙제는요?
에릭	시간이 없어서 못 했어요. 죄송합니다, 선생님.
송 선생	어제 숙제 하지 않고 술만 마셨어요? ~~gov't/politics~~
에릭	네, 술집에 가서 한국친구들하고 정치에 대해서 이야기했거든요. *of course* 물론 한국말로요.
송 선생	학생들이 다 이렇게 게으르니까, 속상해서 죽겠어요!

게으르다
to be lazy

Korean Text - A Monologue

나는 아침 8시에 일어납니다.

먼저 세수를 하고 아침을 먹습니다.

9시쯤 한국말을 배우러 학교에 갑니다.

한국말 수업이 끝나고 5시까지 도서관에서 공부합니다.

그런데 오늘은 토요일이라서 수업이 없습니다.

저녁에는 보통 한국 친구들을 만나서 술을 마시러 술집에 갑니다.

그 친구들은 영어를 잘 못하지만 언제나 재미 있게 놀고 이야기합니다.

요즘 그 친구들 덕분에 한국의 정치에 관해서도 많이 배우고 있습니다.

한국말 연습도 많이 하고요.

나는 지금은 한국말을 조금 밖에 못하지만, 빨리 잘 하고 싶습니다.

내일부터 열심히 공부하겠습니다.

Vocabulary

New Adverbs

거의	nearly, almost, well-nigh
거의 다 왔어요.	We're almost there.
거의 다 했습니다.	I'm almost finished.
수영을 거의 매일 합니다.	I swim almost every day.
드디어	finally, at last
또한	moreover, furthermore, what's more
의사이고 또한 교수에요.	She is a doctor and (what's more) a professor.
돈도 있고 또한 머리가 좋아요.	He has money, and he's also smart.
어서	right away, quickly (usually limited to commands and suggestions)
오래	for a long time
오래 기다리셨습니까?	Have you been waiting a long time?
오래간만에	after a long interval, for the first time in a long while
오래간만에 영화를 봤어요.	I saw a film for the first time in a long while.
오랫동안	for a long time
이리	this way, this direction, here
이리 오십시오.	Please come this way.
그리	so, to that extent, in that way
그리 어렵지 않아요.	It's not so/that hard.
저리	that way, that direction, over there
저리 가요!	Go away!
하루종일	all day long

New Nouns

갈비	ribs
김치	*kimchee*
미용실	beauty parlor; hairdresser's
병원	hospital
빨래	laundry, dirty clothes
빨래(를) 하-	wash laundry, do the laundry
욕조	bathtub
육교	a pedestrian overpass
컴퓨터	computer

| -후 | afterwards, later, later on |
| 그 후에 | afterwards, later, subsequently |

New Verbal Nouns

Personal Grooming

머리(를) 하-	do one's hair (used by women)
머리(를) 자르-	cut one's hair, get one's hair cut
머리(를) 깎-	cut one's hair, get one's hair cut
면도(를) 하-	shave
면도칼	razor blade
칼	knife
면도크림	shaving cream
면도기	electric shaver
목욕(을) 하-	have a bath
목욕탕	public bath; bathroom
세수(를) 하-	wash face
이발(을) 하-	get a haircut (usually used by males)
이발소	barbershop
이발사	barber
파마(를) 하-	get a perm
화장(을) 하-	put on one's makeup

Using Words

강의(를) 하-	lecture, give a lecture
강의	lecture (in a regular series or part of a course)
강연	lecture (a special lecture)
말씀(을) 드리-	tell someone (humble for 말(을) 하-)
설명(을) 하-	explain, give an explanation
설명	explanation

선생님은 시험에 대해서 설명하셨습니다.

The teacher explained about the exam.

약속	an appointment; a promise
약속(을) 하-	make an appointment; promise
약속했지요?	You promise, right?
오후에 약속이 있습니다.	I have an appointment in the afternoon.

Other

식사(를) 하–	eat a meal
식사를 하셨습니까?	Have you eaten?
연습(을) 하–	practice, do exercises
연습	practice
운전(을) 하–	drive, operate a vehicle
위험하–	be dangerous
위험하니까, 천천히 가세요.	It's dangerous, so please slow down.
준비	preparations
준비(를) 하–	prepare, make preparations
준비가 다 됐습니까?	Is everything ready?

New Verbs

Verbs That Take Objects

갈아타–	change (transport, lines, etc.)
시청에서 갈아타세요.	Change [buses/trains] at City Hall.
감–	wash (hair)
머리(를) 감았어요?	Did you wash your hair?
건너–	cross [the street]
자, 길(을) 건넙시다.	OK, let's cross the street.
나누–	share, divide
나눠서 먹읍시다.	Let's share it [eat it together].
낳–	give birth to; have (baby)
애기를 낳았어요.	She had a baby.
놓치–	miss (bus, plane)
늦어서 기차를 놓쳤어요.	I was late, so I missed the train.
모으–	gather (it), collect
빌리–	borrow (use with 한테); rent (a car)
도서관에서 책을 빌렸어요.	I borrowed a book from the library.
만호 씨한테 돈을 빌렸어요.	I borrowed money from Manho.
LA에 가서 차를 빌릴 거에요.	We're going to go to LA and rent a car.
씻–	wash
손(을) 씻고 올게요.	I'll just go and wash my hands.
어기–	break (a promise)
약속을 어겼어요.	He broke his promise.
약속을 잘 지켜요.	She's good at keeping her promises.
지키–	keep (appointment/promise); abide by, stick to

Descriptive and/or Sensory Verbs

게으르-	be lazy
귀찮-	be a pain in the neck, be a nuisance, be annoying
기쁘-	be happy, content
뜨거w-	be hot to the touch
뚱뚱하-	be fat, chubby
마르-	dry up; be/get dry
목(이) 마르-	be thirsty, feel thirsty
목	throat
배(가) 고프-	be hungry, feel hungry
배가 고파서 죽겠어요.	I'm starving. (lit.: I'm so hungry I could die.)
부지런하-	be hard-working, diligent
속(이) 상하-	be distressing; feel distressed
슬프-	feel sad, sorrowful
시원하-	be refreshing, reviving; fresh, cool; feel relieved
차가w-	be cold to the touch

Intransitive Verbs (Processive Verbs That Cannot Take Objects)

막히-	get/be blocked, congested
길이 많이 막혔어요.	The roads are really congested [with traffic].
우-ㄹ-	cry, weep
웃-	smile; laugh

Lesson Notes

16.1. Verbs: The -고 Form

16.1.1. How to Make -고 Forms

The -고 form is a one-shape ending like -지 or -겠-; it is the same regardless of whether it comes after a vowel or a consonant. You have already learned it in part when we covered the -고 싶어요 (*wants to do*) construction (Lesson Nine).

As seen in Lesson Nine, one-shape endings that begin with voiceless consonants (ㄷ, ㅅ, ㅈ, ㄱ) are all attached to bases in much the same way, so that the -고 form is formed very much like the -지 form.

주의

Here are some rules to help you with the pronunciation of gerunds:

a.   Consonant-base verbs like 들- that end in ㄹ change the final consonant to ㄷ before another consonant, and the ㄷ is pronounced as 〔ㄱ〕 before ㄱ or 〔ㅈ〕 before ㅈ.

들-, 듣다   *listen*   →   듣고   〔드꼬〕; 듣지 〔드찌〕

b.   Bases that end in ㅅ, ㅆ, ㅈ, or ㅊ change their final consonants to an interim ㄷ.

벗-   *removes*   →   벗고   (→ 벋고)   〔버꼬〕
있-   *there is*   →   있고   (→ itko)   〔이꼬〕
찾-   *seek*   →   찾고   (→ čʰatko) 〔차꼬〕

Naturally, this includes **all** past-tense gerunds:
-었고 (→ -얻고) 〔-어꼬〕

c.   Consonant bases like 구w- *broil* that end in w change the w to ㅂ before another consonant:

가까w-   *be near*   →   가깝고   〔가깝꼬〕
             (가까워요)   →   가깝지   〔가깝찌〕

---

d.   For bases that end with more than one consonant (other than ᆭ and ᆰ — see Rule f below) you pronounce only one of the consonants when you attach an ending that starts with a consonant.

없-	*there isn't*	→	없고	(→ 업-고)	〔업꼬〕
읽-	*read*	→	읽고	(→ 일-고)	〔일꼬〕
				or (→ 익-고)	〔이꼬〕

e.   Bases that end in ㅁ (including ᆱ), ㄴ (including ᆬ), and an ㄹ that is a reduction of a cluster (like ᆰ in *read* above) double a following voiceless consonant.

신-	*wear on feet*	→	신고		〔신꼬〕
앉-	*sit*	→	앉고	(→ 안-고)	〔안꼬〕
젊-	*be young*	→	젊고	(→점-고)	〔점꼬〕

f.   Notice how final -ㅎ aspirates the following ㄱ in examples like these:

좋-	*be good*	→	좋고	〔조코〕
많-	*is much*	→	많고	〔만코〕
싫-	*be disliked*	→	싫고	〔실코〕
낳-	*give birth to*	→	낳고	〔나코〕

g.   The ending -고, like -지, is attached to the EXTENDED bases of L-extending vowel verbs.

| 파-ㄹ- | *sell* | → | 팔고 |

There are tenseless (plain) -고 forms, made by attaching the ending -고 to the plain base of the verb (가- *go*: 가고), and past-tense -고 forms, made by attaching -고 to the past base.

Plain Base	가-		*go*
Past Base	갔-		
Past -고 form:	갔고 〔가꼬〕		*went and . . .*

Lesson Sixteen / 8

In actual speech, however, past base plus -고 forms are uncommon; they appear only in the first usage described below (section 16.2) in the meaning . . . *and* . . . to anticipate a past-tense verb at the end of the sentence; even here, they are used only in long sentences and could still be replaced, just as correctly, by a plain base plus -고.

You can add -고 to an honorific base in -(으)시-.

Plain Base	가-	*go*
Honorific Base	가시-	
Honorific -고 form	가시고	[someone esteemed] *goes, and*

In the past tense, you add -고 to the past honorific base:

Plain Base:	가-	*go*
Honorific Past base:	가셨-	
Honorific Past -고 form:	가셨고 〔가셔꼬〕	[someone esteemed] *went, and*

16.1.2. The Meaning of -고 Forms

The Korean -고 form is used for joining sentences, and can take on two meanings.
    a.   *does* or *is* [so-and-so], ***and*** . . . [i.e., ***and also***]
    b.   *having done* or *been* [so-and-so], ***and*** . . . [i.e., ***and then***]

16.1.3. Uses of the -고 Form: *And*

A -고 form is a way of breaking a sentence into parts and linking the parts with *and*. The implication may be that the separate actions happen more or less alongside each other [. . . ***and also***], as in:

1.   나한테는 책을 줬고, 어머니한테는 꽃을 드렸어요.
    He gave me a book and gave my mother some flowers.

You could also do this sentence without the past base in the first clause.

2.   나한테는 책을 주고, 어머니한테는 꽃을 드렸어요.
    He gave me a book and gave my mother some flowers.

Or it may imply that one action happens necessarily in sequence after/later than the other [. . . *and then*], as in:

3.   나는 세수하고 면도했어요.
     I got washed up and (then) shaved.

4.   옷을 입고 머리를 빗어요.
     I get dressed and (after that) comb my hair.

When a -고 form is used in the middle of a sentence we have a situation that is common in Korean: a word or phrase that is a compact unit in Korean corresponds to things that in English may be separated from each other. For example, a noun with the particle 도 must be pronounced as a unit—나도 *I, too*—though the English equivalent may place these parts at opposite ends of the sentence: *I* [do so-and-so], *too.* Another example is the -지만 construction you have learned: 가지만 *goes, but* . . . , for example, is an indivisible unit in Korean that may however be translated in widely separated English equivalents: *He **goes** to the movies every evening in the week, **but** . . .*

The same is true of Korean -고 forms, and as you will see, it is true also of nearly every other Korean verb form that is used in the middle of sentences.

> # 주의!
> ATTENTION!
> **The -고 form has no tense of its own.**

The -고 form gets its tense meaning from the next verb in the sentence that carries any tense—usually the verb at the end of the sentence.

5.   A.   어제 뭘 했어요?
          What did you do yesterday?

     B.   아침을 먹고 학교에 갔어요.
          I ate breakfast, and [then] went to school.

6.   A.   언제 학교에 가요?
                When do you go to school?

    B.   날마다 아침을 먹고 학교에 가요.
                Every day I eat breakfast, and [then] go to school.

In a similar way, a final command or suggestion usually carries through onto any preceding –고 forms.

7.   아침을 먹고 학교에 갑시다!
      Let's eat our breakfast and [then] go to school!

16.1.4. Negative –고 Forms

To make a –고 form negative, you attach the –고 ending to the negative verb (or you just use the short negation pattern with 안).

사고 *buys, and . . .*	사지 않고	or	안 사고	*doesn't buy, and . . .*
	사지 못 하고	or	못 사고	*can't buy, and . . .*
팔고 *sells, and . . .*	팔지 않고	or	안 팔고	*doesn't sell, and . . .*
	팔지 못 하고	or	못 팔고	*can't sell, and . . .*
많고 *many, and . . .*	많지 않고	or	안 많고	*aren't many, and . . .*

Since the copula does not normally take the long negation pattern, we find only:

내 책이고   내 책이 아니고
It is my book, and . . .   *It is not my book and (nor) . . .*

> ### 주의!
>
> Negative –고 forms in this use have flexible English equivalents
> and tend to translate as *instead of . . . ing*, or *without . . . ing.*

8. 공부하지 않고 잡지를 읽었어요.
    I didn't study — (but) I read a magazine instead.   or:
    Instead of studying, I read a magazine.   or:
    I read a magazine without doing my studying.

If the final verb is a command or proposition, you use -고 on the auxiliary 말아요 *desists.*

9. 사지 말고, 파세요!
    Don't buy; (instead) sell!

10. 팔지 말고, 삽시다!
    Let's not sell; [instead] let's buy!

11. 책만 읽지 말고, 운동을 좀 하세요.
    Don't just read—do some exercise!

Here are more sentences showing the usage of -고 forms.

12. 저녁에는 책을 읽고 자요.
    In the evenings, I read books and then go to sleep.

13. 언니는 머리를 감고 나갔어요.
    My older sister washed her hair and went out.

14. 술을 마시고 운전하지 마세요. 위험하거든요.
    Don't drink and drive—it's dangerous.

15. 선생님은 연구실에 계시고, 학생은 교실에 있어요.
    The teacher is in her office and the students are in the classroom.

16. 옷도 없고, 돈도 없어요.
    I have no clothes and no money.

17. 나는 어제 나가지 않고 하루종일 집에 있었어요.
    Instead of going out yesterday I stayed home all day.

16.2. Verbs: More on the Infinitive Form -어 ~ -아

As seen in Lesson Seven, Korean infinitives are obtained by removing the polite particle 요 from the polite-style present tense form (i.e., from the 해요 form). In that lesson we went through the way in which the infinitive is formed for each of the different types of Korean verb bases. If you have any doubts or are unclear about the formation of the infinitive from a certain kind of verb base, then you should go back and review Lesson Seven. We are going to learn many new patterns based on the infinitive, so it is important that you understand it clearly. We now look at some further types of infinitive we have not yet studied explicitly.

The past infinitive is also formed by dropping the 요.

Past Polite		Past Infinitive
기다렸어요	*waited*	기다렸어
먹었어요	*ate*	먹었어
왔어요	*came*	왔어

Past Honorific Polite		Past Honorific Infinitive
하셨어요	[sb esteemed] *did*	하셨어
들으셨어요	[sb esteemed] *listened*	들으셨어
파셨어요	[sb esteemed] *bought*	파셨어

From honorific polite present-tense forms (하세요), to find the honorific infinitive, you change 세 to 셔 (하세 → 하셔). To put it another way, you add the infinitive vowel -어 to the honorific base (하시- + -어 → 하셔).

Honorific Present Polite		Honorific Infinitive
앉으세요	[sb esteemed] *sits*	앉으셔
하세요	[sb esteemed] *does*	하셔
읽으세요	[sb esteemed] *reads*	읽으셔

16.2.1. Uses of the Infinitive I: Review of Polite Style

POLITE-STYLE verb forms, those forms you use at the end of your sentences when speaking with someone you are on polite-style terms with, are based on the infinitive. The present-tense polite style is the plain infinitive with 요 added to it (해요). The past-tense polite style is the past infinitive plus 요(했어요). This much you know already.

16.2.2. Uses of the Infinitive II: with the Particle 서

16.2.2.1. Two Kinds of 서

Observe the following sentences.

18.　백화점에 가서 신을 살까요?
　　　Shall we go to the department store and buy some shoes?

19.　늦어서 택시를 타고 갈래요.
　　　It's late, so I think I'll go by taxi.

In the middle of a sentence, the particle 서 after an infinitive (or sometimes an infinitive all by itself, with no 서) can have two different meanings:

I.　**Cause and Result**

Usually, it has the general meaning *so*. The first half, ending with -어서, gives a cause, and the second half gives a result.

CAUSE:　　돈이 없어서 . . .　　　　*I have no money , so . . .*
RESULT:　　. . . 가지 못 하겠어요.　　. . . *I won't be able to go.*

II.　**Sequence**

The 서 can take on a meaning of *so as to . . .* or *[did], and then . . .* —a purpose-and-result flavor that emphasizes a tight link in the **sequence** of events, usually with verbs of direction like 가- *go* and 오- *come*.

PURPOSE:　상점에 가서 . . .　　　　　　*I went to the store . . .*
RESULT:　　. . . 담배를 샀어요.　　　　*. . . (so as) to get some cigarettes.*

It is usually the case that when using the construction with this meaning the subject of the first and second clauses will be the same. It is certainly advisable for you to stick to that as a rule for your own use.

The difference between the constructions with -고 and those with -어서 can be seen in part from the following two examples.

20.　술을 마시고 늦게 잤어요.
　　Having had a drink, I went to bed late. or *I had a drink and then went to bed late.*

21.　술을 마셔서 늦게 잤어요.
　　I went to bed late because (or *since*) *I had (had) a drink.*

Here again we are faced with a unified Korean construction that corresponds to a separate English construction: sometimes the *so* or *and* is separated from the verb only by a slight pause, and sometimes a number of words may intervene.

22.　날마다 가게에 가서 담배를 사요.
　　I go to the store every day and buy some cigarettes.

23.　늦어서 택시로 갔어요.
　　It was late, so I went by taxi.

Note that in example (23) above, the verb 늦- *be late* has no tense of its own. In this respect, infinitive + 서 is like the pattern in -고: it has no inherent tense of its own, and speakers must infer the tense from the verb at the end of sentence or else from time adverbs or context.

16.2.2.2. -어서 좋아요 I'm glad that . . . ; Good thing that . . .

There is a special English translation when –어서 is followed by 좋아요 in the second half of the sentence. Such sentences, which mean literally [so-and-so happens], *so it's good,* are generally rendered by some such English pattern as *I'm glad (that) . . .* or *It's a good thing (that) . . .* For example:

24.   새 신을 사서 좋아요.
       I'm glad I bought new shoes.

25.   아들을 낳아서 좋아요.
       I'm glad we had a son.

26.   수진 씨가 와서 좋아요.
       It's nice that Sujin is here or *I'm glad Sujin came.*

27.   수진 씨가 와서 나는 좋아요.
       I'm glad Sujin is here. [= *Sujin came, so, as for me, it's good.*]

Now observe these examples.

28.   학교에 와서 강연을 하셨어요.
       He came to school and gave a lecture.

29.   넥타이를 하나 사서 김 선생님께 드렸어요.
       I bought a tie and gave it to Mr. Kim.

In the 서 constructions in these sentences, you **cannot** use a past-tense infinitive; if the verb at the end of the sentence is past, the infinitive also usually carries a past-tense meaning.

16.2.2.3. -(이)라서 Copula + 서

The copula infinitive has a variant form –이라 that exists alongside the regular form in –이어. Colloquial Korean prefers to attach the 서 form to this variant. Thus, -(이)라서 is more common in colloquial Korean than the more predictable –이어서 (which is also acceptable, but less common in spoken language) For example:

30.   오늘이 일요일이라서 기차에 사람이 많아요.
       The train is crowded because it is Sunday.

Here are some more examples of infinitives with 서 in sentences.

31.   날마다 목욕탕에 가서 목욕을 해요.
       He goes to the public bath every day and bathes.

32. 너무 많이 먹어서 배가 부릅니다.
I ate so much [that] I'm full.

33. 안 비싸서 좋아요.
I'm glad it's not expensive.

34. 시간이 없어서 준비를 못 했어요.
I couldn't prepare—I didn't have time. [There wasn't time, so . . .]

35. 영화가 너무 슬퍼서 끝까지 못 봤어요.
The movie was so sad I couldn't watch it to the end.

36. 배가 별로 안 고프니까, 1인분만 시켜서 나눠서 먹읍시다.
I'm not particularly hungry, so let's order one serving and share ["share and eat"] it.

37. 꽃을 주셔서 감사합니다.
Thank you for the flowers. [= You gave me flowers, so thank you.]

38. 버스가 늦어서 비행기를 놓쳤어요.
The bus was late, so I missed the airplane.

39. 집에 와서 빨래를 했어요.
I came home and did the laundry.

주의!

Another way to say *go to do something*, you will recall, is to use the infinitive followed by - (으)러.

> 물건을 사러 상점에 갔어요
> *went to the store (with the purpose) to buy things.*

Compare:

> 상점에 가서 물건을 샀어요
> *went to the store and bought things = went to the store to buy things.*

The first expression does not tell you whether the mission was actually accomplished. The expression 가서 사요 emphasizes the ***buying***, the expression 사러 가요 emphasizes the ***going***.

16.2.2.4. The Difference Between -어서 and -(으)니까

You have already learned another ending that can express both a reason or a kind of sequence, namely -(으)니까. How, then, are -어서 and -(으)니까 different? The difference can be summarized as follows.

-어서

Clause A -어서, Clause B

> Related sequence, i.e., *Clause B after Clause A and with some relation to it.*
> As a logical formulation, -어서 is **assertion of cause**.

-(으)니까

Clause A -(으)니까, Clause B

> Discovery, i.e., *When Clause A, one finds that Clause B.*
> As a logical formulation, **-** 으니까 is **argumentation**.

Clauses in -(으)니까 also tend to have a more friendly, less coldly rational feel to them, and have the effect of involving one's interlocutor more intimately in the event or argumentation being discussed. Here are some sentences contrasting these two endings:

40. 봄이 됐으니까, 꽃이 피고 있어요.
    The flowers are blooming because it's spring, i.e., *Now that spring has come, the flowers are blooming,* or *The flowers are blooming—no wonder, it's spring.*

41. 봄이 돼서, 꽃이 피고 있어요.
    The flowers are blooming because it's spring, i.e., *Spring has come and so the flowers are blooming,* or *Spring is making the flowers bloom.*

42. A. 왜 이렇게 늦었어요?
        Why are you so late?

    B. 버스가 안 와서 늦었어요.
    B'. * 버스가 안 왔으니까 늦었어요.
        I'm late because the bus didn't come

The answer in B' is inappropriate, because it assumes that A *knew* that the bus hadn't come.

16.3. Unfinished Sentences and Afterthoughts with -서요 and -고요

43.   시간이 없어서 못 했어요. 머리도 아프고요.
       I couldn't do it because I didn't have time. And I had a headache, too.

Koreans, like other people, don't always think ahead and organize what they are going to say. Most of the sentences in this book are well organized and constructed as if they had been well planned in advance; the verb, for example, always comes at the end. But in unguarded speech, people will often blurt out the verb (or some larger part of the sentence), and then—as an **afterthought**—add one or more of the phrases that they should have put in earlier.

44.   벌써 오셨어요? 손님들이요.
       Are they already here—the guests?

As you have learned, a sentence whose final verb is turned into a -고 form *and . . .* is normally put **before** some other sentence it joins to make a compound sentence. But as an afterthought you can add the -고 form **after** you have said the other sentence. The afterthought sentence will have the normal intonation (statement, question, command, etc.) you would expect of it if it were an ordinary sentence, and if you are talking in the Polite Style you will add the polite particle 요.

Examples with 서요 are often unfinished sentences, more of a lazy way to get around saying a whole sentence. Here are some more examples of afterthoughts and unfinished sentences.

45.   표는 어디서 사요? - 또, 값은 얼마고요?
       Where do we buy the tickets? And how much are they?

46.   비빔밥은 이리 주세요. – 냉면은 저리 드리시고요.
       The pibimpap here, please, [waiter]—and the naengmyŏn there, please.

47.   가서 주무세요. 기다리지 마시고요.
       Go to bed; don't wait up.

48.   이것은 수진 씨 모자이고, 저것은 수진 씨 책이고요.
       This is your hat, [Sujin] and that is your book.

49. A. 빨리 가고 싶어요.
I want to go right away .

B. 왜요?
Why?

A. 배가 너무 고파서요.
Because I'm so hungry.

50. A. 김치는 왜 안 먹지요?
Why aren't you eating any kimchee?

B. 너무 매워서요.
Because it's too spicy.

51. A. 사과를 왜 안 사 왔어요?
Why didn't you buy (and bring) the apples?

B. 너무 바빠서요.
Because I was too busy.

16.4. Descriptive Verb + -어서 죽겠어요: *so . . . I could die*

You can use the infinitive plus 서 pattern in combination with a descriptive verb (usually one describing a mental state or physical sensation) and 죽겠어요 *I think I'm going to die* to create a lively, colloquial pattern meaning: *I feel so . . . I could die* or *I'm incredibly . . .*, and so on. Here are some examples.

52. 배가 고파서 죽겠어요.
I'm starving ["so hungry I could die"].

53. 머리가 아파서 죽겠어요.
I have an incredible headache.

54. 어머니가 보고 싶어서 죽겠어요.
I miss my mother terribly.

55. 기분이 나빠서 죽겠어요.
I'm in a foul mood.

16.5. NOUN - 에 대해서, NOUN - 에 관해서:
about, concerning

The postpositional phrase -에 대해서 means *about, with respect to, concerning*, etc. The postpositional phrase -에 관해서 means the same thing, but is somewhat more formal and bookish. Here are some examples.

56. 만호 씨는 컴퓨터에 대해서 많이 알고 있어요.
     Manho knows a lot about computers.

57. 영국사람들은 언제나 날씨에 대해서 이야기를 합니다.
     English people always talk about the weather.

58. 어제 문 박사님은 한국경제에 관해서 강연을 하셨습니다.
     Yesterday Dr. Moon gave a lecture about the Korean economy.

16.6. - 거든요: . . . , you see?

The verb ending in -거든요 is a one-shape ending and can occur with any base, though usually you will encounter it on Plain and Past bases more than on Future bases. L-extending bases appear in their extended form before this ending: 사-ㄹ- → 살거든요.

The ending in -거든요 is used to offer a kind of follow-up explanation to what has just been said (or implied). A literal translation of its effect might be: *I hasten to give you an explanation or rationale for what I just said (or implied) in perhaps too crude, obscure or blunt a fashion.* In other words, the ending in -거든요 also functions as a sort of politeness strategy or "grease on the skids" to keep conversational exchanges moving. It performs the latter function by inviting a response (notice that is usually has a rising, question-like intonation)—usually just an understanding 네 or a nod—from the person you are talking to. Often the only crude way to approximate the flavor of this ending in English is with the tag . . . *you see?* Here are some examples:

59. 나는 김치를 못 먹어요. 너무 맵거든요.
     I can't eat kimchee. It's too hot.

60. 머리가 아파서 죽겠어요. 어제 술을 너무 많이 마셨거든요.
    I have an incredible headache. Last night I drank too much.

61. 요즘 연 선생님은 아주 기분이 좋으세요. 지난 달에 아들을 낳았거든요.
    Mr. Yeon is in a really good mood lately. Last month they gave birth to a son.

62. 내일 다시 오세요. 준비가 아직 안 됐거든요.
    Please come again tomorrow. It's not ready yet.

Exercises

Exercise 1: Using -고

Each of the following items contains two sentences connected with 그리고 *and*. Combine these into a single sentence by using –고, and then translate. For example, the first will be: 진섭 씨는 한국사람이고 에릭 씨는 영국사람이에요. *Chinsŏp is Korean, and Eric is English.*

1. 진섭 씨는 한국사람이에요. 그리고 에릭 씨는 영국사람이에요.
2. 1사람은 도서관에 갔어요. 그리고 또 1사람은 기숙사에 돌아 갔어요. [dormitory]
3. 아침에 일어나서 먼저 세수를 해요. 그리고 머리를 감아요.
4. 옷을 입어요. 그리고 아침을 먹지요.
5. 식사 후 이를 닦아요. 그리고 버스 정류장으로 나가요. [complete]
6. 학교에 와서 도서관에서 숙제를 마쳐요. 그리고 수업에 들어 가요. [lesson]
7. 오후에는 피아노를 연습해요. 그리고 운동장에 나가요.
8. 옷을 갈아 입어요. 그리고 운동을 좀 하지요.
9. 저녁에는 집에 와서 쉬어요. 그리고 부엌에서 저녁식사를 준비해요.
10. 공부를 조금 더 해요. 그리고 자요.
11. 나는 이발소에 가요. 그리고 그분은 목욕탕에 가요.
12. 나는 면도를 했어요. 그리고 우리 집사람은 화장을 했어요. [mfc]
13. 이것은 싸요. 그리고 저것은 비싸요.
14. 비행기는 빨라요. 그리고 자전거는 빠르지 않아요.
15. 중국음식은 싸요. 그리고 맛이 있어요.
16. 여름에는 더워요. 그리고 비가 많이 와요.
17. 겨울에는 추워요. 그리고 눈이 많이 와요.

Exercise 2: Using -고 with Long Negatives

Each of the following items contains two sentences. Combine these into a single sentence by using -지 않고 so that it means *didn't do this—did that instead*. For example, the first will be: 나는 공부하지 않고, 부엌을 청소했어요. *I didn't study—I cleaned the kitchen instead.*

1. 나는 공부하지 않았어요. 부엌을 청소했어요.
2. 나는 이발소에 가지 않았어요. 목욕탕에 갔어요.
3. 나는 수진 씨를 만나지 않을 거에요. 그 동생을 만날 거에요.
4. 우리 아들이 밖에 나가지 않아요. 집에서 책만 읽어요.
5. 우리는 여기서 살지 않아요. 우체국 옆에 살아요.
6. 우리는 버스를 서울역에서 갈아 타지 않았어요. 시청에서 갈아 탔어요.
7. 숙제를 하지 않을래요. 다방에 갈래요.
8. 이 옷을 입지 않을래요. 다른 옷으로 갈아 입을래요.
9. 테레비를 보지 않을래요. 피아노 연습을 할래요.
10. 지하철을 타지 않아요. 걸어 왔습니다.

Exercise 3: Using -고 with Negative Commands

Each of the following items contains two commands, the first a prohibition. Combine these into a single sentence by using -지 말고 so that it means *Don't do this—do that instead*. For example, the first will be: 자지 말고 공부나 하세요. *Don't go to sleep—study or something instead.*

1. 자지 마세요. 공부나 하세요.

2. 그냥 놀지 마세요. 일 좀 하세요.

3. 내일 가지 마세요. 오늘 가세요.

4. 공부하지 마세요. 주무세요.

5. 식사를 하지 마세요. 그냥 가세요.

6. 일만 하지 마세요. 좀 쉬세요.

7. 옷을 벗지 마세요. 입으세요.

8. 아직 가지 마세요. 나하고 같이 좀 더 있어요.

9. 도서관에 가지 마세요. 술집에 가서 술이나 마십시다.

10. 지하철을 타지 마세요. 택시로 오세요.

11. 혼자만 먹지 마세요. 나눠서 먹읍시다.

12. 걸어 가지 마세요. 지하철로 갑시다.

13. 나한테 물어 보지 마세요. 선생님한테 물어 보세요.

Exercise 4: Fill in the Blank

In this exercise, fill in the blank with an appropriate -어서 form. E.g.: 늦어서 미안합니다, and then translate: *Sorry I'm late*. (Remember—-어서 ~ -아서 is compatible only with plain bases!)

1. 기분이 _____ 노래를 부릅니다.

2. 시간이 _____ 택시를 탔습니다.

3. 책을 많이 _____ 눈이 아픕니다.

4. 오래간만에 친구를 _____ 기분이 좋습니다.

5. 공부를 많이 _____ 피곤합니다.

6. 술을 많이 _____ 배가 아픕니다.

7. 하루종일 _____ 피곤합니다.

8. 비가 _____ 야구를 못 했습니다.

9. _____ 미안합니다.

10. _____ 기분이 좋습니다.

11. _____ 반갑습니다.

12. 점심을 못 _____ 배가 고파요.

13. 영화가 너무 _____, 끝까지 못 봤어요.

14. 사과는 이것만 있으니깐, _____ 먹읍시다.

Exercise 5: Using Infinitive + 서

Each of the following items contains two sentences. Connect them into a single sentence by using –서, and then translate. (Remember––어서 ~ –아서 is not compatible with past or future bases!) For example, the first will be: 편지를 써서 우체국에 갔습니다. *I wrote a letter and then went to the post office.*

1. 편지를 썼습니다. 우체국에 갔습니다.

2. 집을 팔았습니다. 미국에 갔습니다.

3. 도서관에 가겠습니다. 친구를 찾겠습니다.

4. 교실에 들어 가세요. 선생님한테 물어보세요.

5. 나오세요. 잠깐 기다리세요.   나와서

6. 공원에 가시지요. 운동을 하시지요.

7. 밖에 나가세요. 담배 피우세요.

8. 일어나세요. 아침을 잡수세요.

9. 여기 앉으세요. 기다리세요.

10. 일어나세요. 노래를 부르세요.

11. 누우세요. 좀 쉬세요.

12. 선생님을 만나요. 말씀 드리지요.

13. 머리가 아파요. 죽겠어요.

14. 더워요. 죽겠어요.

15. 피곤해요. 죽겠어요.

16. 배가 고파요. 죽겠어요.

17. 어제 우리 집 개가 죽었어요. 좀 슬프지요.

Exercise 6: Using -거든요

Each of the following items contains two sentences. Change the verb in the second sentence to the -거든요 ending, and then translate.

1. 어제 하나도 못 잤어요. 언니하고 밤 늦게까지 남자들에 대해서 이야기 했어요.

2. 배가 고파서 죽겠어요. 점심을 못 먹고 왔어요.

3. 빨리 오세요. 준비가 다 됐어요.

4. 교수님은 지금 안 계십니다. 강의를 하러 들어 가셨어요.

5. 요즘 너무 바빠서 죽겠어요. 지난 주에 개학을 했어요.

6. 다음 주에 못 가겠어요. 우리 할아버님이 돌아가셨어요.

7. 손이 아파서 죽겠어요. 어제 다쳤어요.

8. 일요일은 안 되겠어요. 그 날 친척이 와요.

9. 나는 바다에 가지 않고, 산에 갈래요. 수영을 못 해요.

10. 손이 차갑지요? 밖이 추워요.

11. 걱정하지 마세요. 시간이 아직 있어요.

12. 거기 가지 마세요. 위험해요.

13. 기다리지 마세요. 아직 멀었어요.

14. 못 먹겠습니다. 방금 뭘 많이 먹고 왔어요.

15. 요즘 매일 수영을 해요. 수영장이 우리 집에서 가까워요.

Exercise 7: English to Korean Translation

Translate the following English sentences into Korean.

1. Yesterday I went to the market and bought apples.
2. This morning I went to the department store and bought a present for my mother.
3. My father knows a lot about cars.
4. I'm glad my younger brother came yesterday.
5. Last Tuesday I went downtown and watched a movie.
6. Yesterday my friend came to our house and ate supper with us.
7. How about going to a *tabang* and having a cup of coffee?
8. I'm glad I drove for the first time in a long while.
9. Lately I'm learning a lot about Korean politics.
10. I feel good now that I've shaved.
11. My hand and arm hurt, so I won't be able to play tennis with you.
12. I shaved and washed my face, so I feel refreshed now.
13. Let's do the preparations first and then rest.
14. Our house is near [from] the bookstore.
15. A. I can't solve this problem.

    B. Then tell Professor Kim.
16. Let's ask the teacher about the exam.
17. I'll go home quickly now and prepare our meal [Immediate Future].
18. That professor lectures very well, so many people come.
19. Don't get off here—change at the next station instead.

 # Lesson 17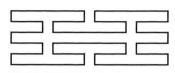

육개장이랑 김치도 잡숴 보셨어요?

In this lesson we see Eunice Murphy and Miss Lee discussing Korean foods and their food likes and dislikes. In addition, we observe Chris Murphy going through the check-in procedures at a hotel on Cheju Island with his family. The lesson introduces a number of new patterns built on the infinitive in -아 ~ -어: use of sensory verbs in the third person, compound verbs of *going* and *coming*, resultant states in -어 있-, the exploratory pattern in -어 보-, and doing favors with -어 주-. Finally, the lesson introduces the "nominalizer" ending in -기 and three patterns based on it: *begin to do . . .* in -기 시작하-, *because* in -기 때문에, and *before . . .ing* in -기 전에.

Korean Dialogues

Dialogue 1

Eunice Murphy is chatting with her husband's secretary, Miss Lee, at the office.

미스 리	한국음식을 좋아 하세요?
유니스	네, 특히 갈비와 비빔밥을 좋아해요.
	한국에 오기 전에 많이 먹어 봤거든요.
미스 리	그럼, 육개장이랑 김치도 잡숴 보셨어요?
유니스	먹어 봤지만, 별로 안 좋아 해요.
미스 리	너무 매워서, 먹기가 어렵지요?
	그럼, 우리 언제 한번 삼계탕이나 먹으러 갈까요?
유니스	그러지요.
미스 리	그런데, 내일은 선약이 있으니까 모레쯤 어떠세요?
유니스	그래요. 우리 남편도 한국 음식을 언제나 먹고 싶어 하니까 내가 물어 봐서 날을 정하지요.

Dialogue 2

The Murphy's have flown down to Cheju Island for a short holiday. Chris Murphy is just about to check in with the family at their hotel.

크리스   안녕하십니까? 예약했는데요.

아가씨   성함이 어떻게 되십니까?

크리스   크리스 머피입니다. 지난 달에 2인용 방 둘을 예약했습니다.

아가씨   (checking the computer) 예, 찾았습니다. 304호하고 305호
         되겠습니다. 3층에 있습니다.

크리스   발코니 있지요?

아가씨   그럼요. 발코니도 있고, 전경도 아주 좋습니다.

크리스   그리고, 식사도 다 포함돼 있어요?

아가씨   아니오, 아침 식사만 포함돼 있습니다.

크리스   참, 학생할인이 있습니까? 이 애들은 대학생이거든요.

아가씨   네, 할인해 드릴게요. 이 숙박부에 먼저 기입해 주시고, 올라 가
         보시지요. 열쇠는 여기 있습니다.

크리스   감사합니다.

Reading Passage

오늘 친구의 형님이 결혼을 했습니다.

나는 결혼식장에 가기 전에 목욕을 하고 이발소에 갔습니다.

이발사가 내 머리를 다듬어 주고 무스를 발라 줬습니다.

결혼식장에 가서 신랑과 신부에게 인사를 했습니다.

신부가 아주 아름다웠기 때문에 모두 신랑을 부러워 했습니다.

친구의 아버지도 아들이 결혼을 해서 아주 기뻐하셨습니다.

나는 친구 형님에게 결혼 선물로 책을 한 권 사 줬습니다.

나도 연애를 한번 해 보고 싶었습니다.

Vocabulary

Nouns

Hotels and Travel

난방 장치	heating
냉방 장치	air-conditioning
독방	single room
발코니	balcony
숙박	lodging
숙박(을) 하-	lodge at, put up at
숙박부	lodging [registration] form
여행	travel; a journey
여행(을) 하-	travels
열쇠	key
요금	fee; fare
욕실	bathroom, room with a bath
유럽	Europe
유럽공동체	the European Community
전경	the view
(차)키	(car-)key
체크인	check-in
체크인(을) 하-	check in
할인	discount
할인(을) 해 주-	give a discount
할인(을) 받-	get/receive a discount
휴가	holiday, leave from work

Restaurants and Food

삼계탕	Korean ginseng chicken soup
서비스	service (e.g., in a restaurant); s.th. unexpected you get for free as part of a transaction
육개장	spicy chopped beef soup
한턱	a treat, a feast
한턱(을) 내-	treat, stand treat, give as a treat to
한턱 낼게요.	I'll treat./Let me treat you.

Weddings

결혼식	wedding ceremony
결혼식장	wedding venue
신랑	the groom
신부	the bride

Other

네거리	crossroads; intersection
저 네거리에서 내려 주세요.	Please let me off at that intersection.
대답	answer, response
대답(을) 하-	answer, respond
비서	secretary
선약	a previous appointment or engagement
선약이 있어서, 못 가겠어요.	I have a previous appointment, so I won't be able to go.
성명	full name, surname + given name [used on official forms]
소식	news, word of/from somebody

  수진 씨한테는 소식을 오래 못 들었어요.

I haven't heard from Sujin for a long time.

시계	watch, clock
얼굴	face
우표	postage stamp
인사	greeting, a formal hello or good-bye
교수님한테 인사 드렸어요?	Did you say hello/good-bye to your professor?
자, 인사 하시지요.	Please meet so-and-so. (said to the junior of two people when introducing them)
정신	spirit, mind, nerves
정신(이) 없-	be preoccupied with s. th. such that one is unable to cope with other things
키	height
키(가) 크-	be tall
태도	attitude
저 학생은 태도가 좋아요.	That student has a good attitude.
저 학생은 태도가 나빠요.	That student has a bad attitude.

Verbs

Verbs That Take Objects

기입(을) 하-	fill in (a form)
다듬-	trim, spruce up; give final embellishments to
도w-	help
도와 드릴까요?	Shall I help you?
대접(을) 하-	treat somebody (to a meal), host somebody
제가 대접(을) 하겠습니다.	I'm buying. or This one will be on me.
바르-	apply, smear it (e.g., mousse, cream)
무스	mousse for hair
약을 발랐어요?	Did you put on/apply the medicine?
무스를 바르세요?	Do you use mousse?
보이-	show it
사진을 좀 보여 주실래요?	Do you mind showing me some photos?
할아버지께 보여 드려요.	Show it to grandfather.
빌려 주-	lend (use with 한테)
세우-	bring it to a stop
여기서 차를 세워 주세요.	Please stop [the vehicle] here.
연애(를) 하-	fall in love [with = 하고, etc.]; "date"
잡숴 보시-	[sb esteemed] eat something, try something
정하-	settle upon, decide upon, fix
시간을 정했어요?	Have you decided upon a time?
포함(을) 하-	include it
포함(이) 되-	be/get included

Related Transitive~Intransitive Pairs

깨-	wake up (intransitive)
보통 몇시에 깨세요?	What time do you usually wake up?
깨우-	awaken sb, wake sb up
애기를 깨우지 마세요.	Don't wake the baby.
나-	exit, come out, appear
해가 났어요.	The sun has come out.
내-	hand in, turn in
숙제를 냈어요?	Did you hand in your homework?
내리-	get off (a bus, train, etc.); to let sb off/out

(1)	종로에서 내립시다.	Let's get off at Chongno.
(2)	육교 밑에서 내려 주세요.	Please let me off below the overhead footbridge.

Descriptive and/or Sensory Verbs

궁금하–	be/feel curious about [descriptive]
부끄러w–	feel embarrassed, ashamed
부끄러워하지 말고...	Don't be shy—[eat up!]
부러w–	be envious
섭섭하–	feel sad and/or empty about, feel wistful about [usually about somebody's absence or imminent departure]
아름다w–	be beautiful
지루하–	be boring, tedious
그 강의는 지루했어요.	That lecture was boring.

Intransitive Verbs (Processive Verbs That Cannot Take Objects)

낙제(를) 하–	fail, flunk
시험에 낙제 했어요.	She failed the exam.
닫히– [다치-]	get closed/shut
문이 닫혀 있어요.	The door is shut/closed.
도–ㄹ–	turn, spin; make a round; go around
시작(이) 되–	it begins
열리–	open, be opened
문이 열려 있어요.	The door is open.

Adverbs

대단히	very
상당히	quite
특히	especially, in particular

Other

모든 NOUN〔들〕	all NOUNs
[NOUN] 없이	without NOUN (adv.)
정신없이	with a mind for nothing else, absorbed totally
요즘 정신없이 지내고 있습니다.	Lately I don't know whether I'm coming or going.
–짜리	-'s worth [always used as a modifier for denominations or prices]
2백 원짜리 우표	a 200-wŏn postage stamp
2만 원짜리 표	a 20,000-wŏn ticket

3 살짜리 아이	a 3-year-old child
-호	number ___ (of rooms, journals, etc.) (used with Sino-Korean numerals)
뉴스위크 3월호	the March issue of *Newsweek*

Lesson Notes

17.1. Uses of the Infinitive III: Turning Descriptive Verbs into Processive Verbs with -어해요

1. 모두 신랑을 부러워했습니다.
   Everyone was jealous of the groom.

2. 선생님도 좋아하세요.
   The teacher is glad, too.

3. 읽고 싶어하세요.
   He wants to read [it].

The Korean language does not ordinarily allow a speaker to state flatly what another person feels or thinks: such inner processes can be known only secondhand, and Korean grammar requires a separate, more indirect pattern for those occasions when one needs to refer to them.

One way of doing this is to combine descriptive verbs that refer to emotions and feelings ("sensory verbs") like *dislikes* and *is glad* with 해요. This combination externalizes the emotion and, in grammar, **changes the descriptive verb into a processive one**. Observe the list of such sensory verbs on the next page.

All of the expressions in -어해요 in the second column are transitive: they take as direct objects a noun expression with the particle 을 ~ 를. Here is an illustration of the difference in usage between describing your own emotions and those of someone else.

4. 진호 씨가 와서 좋아요.
   It's nice that Chinho has come or *I'm glad that Chinho is here.*

5. 진호 씨가 와서 좋아해요.
   [Someone else] is glad that Chinho has come or *Chinho is glad to be here.*

6. 진호 씨가 와서 〔나는〕 좋아요.
   I'm glad Chinho is here.

7. 진호 씨가 와서 복동이는 좋아해요.
   Poktong-i is glad that Chinho is here.

1st & 2nd Person	3rd Person	English
좋아요 →	좋아해요	*is good, is liked* *likes*
싫어요 →	싫어해요	*is disliked* *dislikes*
싶어요 →	싶어해요	*wants to, would like to* [sb else] *wants to* or *would like*
기뻐요 →	기뻐해요	*is happy* or *glad* [sb else] *is happy* or *glad*
고마워요 →	고마워해요	*is thankful* or *grateful* *is grateful for, is thankful about;* [sb else] *is thankful* or *grateful*
부러워요 →	부러워해요	*is envious* or *jealous* *is envious of, is jealous of;* [sb else] *is envious* or *jealous*

Here are some more examples of sensory verbs in first- (I, we) and non-first-person usage.

8. a. 나는 냉면이 싫어요.
        I don't like naengmyŏn.

    This could also be expressed as:

    b. 나는 냉면을 싫어해요.
        I don't like naengmyŏn.

9. 진호 씨는 냉면을 싫어해요.
Chinho doesn't like naengmyŏn.

10. 나는 형님이 부러워요.
I'm envious of my older brother.

11. 동생도 형님을 부러워해요.
My younger brother is envious of my older brother, too.

These sensory expressions are made honorific by changing 해요 to 하세요.

좋아하세요   싫어하세요

기뻐하세요   고마워하세요

싶어하세요

In other words, you cannot say *싶으셔 해요 or the like.

주의! Honorifics

From the expression –고 싶어요 you can make honorifics in two different ways.

–(으)시고 싶어요?   or   –고 싶으세요?

and from the expression –고 싶어 해요 you also have both possibilities.

–(으)시고 싶어해요   or   –고 싶어하세요

But the latter is more common, and it is even possible to have a double-honorific form like:

–(으)시고 싶으세요   or   –(으)시고 싶어하세요.

To make the sensory verb-expression negative you change 해요 to 하지 않아요.

좋아하지 않아요   싫어하지 않아요

기뻐하지 않아요   고마워하지 않아요

–고 싶어하지 않아요

17.2. Uses of the Infinitive IV: Compound Verbs

The expressions discussed in Section 17.1, just above—좋아해요 *likes*, 고마워해요 *is grateful for*, and so on—are compound verb expressions. They are made by joining to an infinitive—a verb that names the action—some form of another verb (해요 *does* in these two cases).

주의!

Note that it is always this *second* (auxiliary) verb that does the rest of the work: it shows the tense and whether the expression is affirmative or negative, question or statement, and so on. This pattern is a general one with Korean verb expressions: the *first* (main) verb merely tells what action or quality is under discussion—*goes, eats, walks; is good, is large, is late*—and is otherwise frozen; the *second* (auxiliary) verb completes the expression and fits it into the sentence with appropriate endings. The honorific and negative expressions are usually built on the auxiliary verb, not on the infinitive.

17.2.1. Compound Verbs with 가- and 오-

Some of the compound expressions you have learned involve the verbs 가요 *goes* and 와요 *comes* used as auxiliaries to show direction.

도-ㄹ-	turn (round)	돌아가요	goes back
		돌아와요	comes back
드-ㄹ-	enter	들어가요	goes in
		들어와요	comes in
나-	exit	나가요	goes out
		나와요	comes out
걸-	walk	걸어가요	walks (there)
		걸어와요	walks (here)
오르-	ascend	올라가요	goes up
		올라와요	comes up
내리-	descend	내려가요	goes down
		내려와요	comes down

Here are some more examples of compound verb expressions with 가- *go* and 오- *come* in sentences.

12. 아버님이 내일 미국에서 돌아오세요.
    Father is returning from the United States tomorrow.

13. 장 선생님은 언제 한국으로 돌아가셨어요?
    When did Mr. Chang go back to Korea?

14. 그 영화관에 사람이 너무 많아서 나오고 싶었어요.
    There were too many people in the movietheater, so I wanted to come out.

15. 걸어 갈래요, 버스 타고 갈래요?
    Would you rather go on foot or take the bus?.

16. 나는 1달 동안이나 밖에 나가지 않았어요.
    I haven't been out fora whole month.

17.2.2. Compound Verbs: Resultant States with 있-

Another kind of compound verb expression involves the verb 있어요 *is, stays* used as an auxiliary to show resultant states. This is a very important usage, which you should observe carefully.

Base	English	Resultant State	English
앉-	*sit*	앉아 있어요	*is seated*
		앉아 있지 않아요	*is not seated*
누w-	*lie down*	누워 있어요	*is lying down*
		누워 있지 않아요	*is not lying down*
서-	*stand up*	서 있어요	*is standing*
		서 있지 않아요	*is not standing*
열리-	*be opened*	열려 있어요	*(door) is open, ajar*
		열려 있지 않아요	*is not open*
닫히-	*be shut*	닫혀 있어요	*is shut, closed*
		닫혀 있지 않아요	*is not shut, closed*
포함되-	*be included*	포함돼 있어요	*is included*
		포함돼 있지 않아요	*is not included*
드-ㄹ-	*go into*	들어 있어요	*is contained*
		들어 있지 않아요	*is not contained*

Here are some more examples of resultant state compound verb expressions in sentences.

17. 서비스는 포함돼 있어요?
Is the service included?

18. 나는 누워 있지도, 앉아 있지도 않았어요. 서 있었어요.
I was neither lying down nor sitting. I was standing.

19. 저 창문이 열려 있어요?
Is that window over there open?

20. 난방, 냉방 장치가 다 돼 있습니다.
Heating and air-conditioning installations are all in place.

Note that verbs denoting wearing behave somewhat differently and do not take this construction. Instead, they use the -고 있어요 pattern, which is ambiguous between the two meanings of *is wearing* [i.e., *is in the state resulting from having put on*], and *is in the process of putting on*.

21. 만호 씨는 넥타이를 매고 있어요.
Manho is wearing a tie. or *Manho is putting on a tie.*

22. 수진 씨는 청바지를 입고 있어요.
Sujin is wearing blue jeans. or *Sujin is putting on blue jeans.*

17.3. The Exploratory Pattern in -어 봐요

Observe the following sentences.

23.　회사에 전화를 걸어 보세요.
　　　Try making a call to the company.

24.　김치를 먹어 봤어요?
　　　Have you tried eating kimchee?

The verb 봐요 ordinarily means *looks, sees, reads*. As an auxiliary verb following an infinitive, however, it means *tries doing*—not *attempts to do* but *tries doing*—samples the act to see what it's like, *does it to see* (just how it will be, how it will turn out, etc.)—an exploratory construction. Some actions are by their vary nature exploratory. You have learned the base 물- *ask*, but this almost always occurs with 보- as 물어보- *ask (and see what answer you get)*. Here are some more examples.

25.　한국말로 편지를 써 봤어요.
　　　I tried writing a letter in Korean.

26.　일본 신문을 읽어 봤어요.
　　　I glanced through a Japanese newspaper.

27.　영국에 가 보셨어요?
　　　Have you ever been to England [to see how you'd like it]?

28.　한국에서 여행해 보셨어요?
　　　Have you traveled in Korea?

29.　새 옷을 입어 볼까요?
　　　Shall I try on the new clothes?

30.　새 신을 신어 보고 있어요.
　　　I'm trying on some new shoes.

31.　새 모자를 써 볼게요.
　　　I'll try on my new hat.

32.　한국에서 살아 보고 싶어요.
　　　I wish I could live in Korea (to see what it would be like).

17.4. Doing Favors with 줘요 (주어요)

To tell about a favor done for someone, you use a compound consisting of the infinitive plus a word for *give*—either 줘요 *gives* (to anyone) or 드려요 *gives* (to someone esteemed). Though it need not be present in a sentence, if you wish to specify the person **for** whom the favor is done, this person is treated as the indirect object and takes the particle 한테 (or 에게) or its honorific equivalent 께.

33.   택시를 불러 주시겠어요?
      Would you please call me a cab?

always. (언제나.)

34.   그 친구는 나를 많이 도와 줘요. 부모님도 늘 도와 드리고요.
      That friend helps me a lot. And he's always helping his parents, too.

35.   그 친구는 지난 주에 책 1권을 나한테 사 줬고, 어머니한테 꽃을 사 드렸어요.
      Last week he bought a book for me and (bought) some flowers for my mother.

36.   내일 7시까지 깨워 주실래요?
      Would you mind waking me up by 7 tomorrow?

37.   오늘은 제가 점심값을 내 줄게요.
      Today I'll treat you to lunch.

38.   옆집 아주머니가 우리 아이를 좀 봐 주고 있어요.
      The lady next door is looking (after) my child for me.

39.   어머니한테 결혼 사진을 보여 드렸어요?
      Did you show mother the wedding photos?

40.   할아버님께 선물을 부쳐 드렸어요.
      I sent Grandfather a present.

41.   힘 드시지요? 그럼 제가 도와 드릴게요.
      That task is difficult, isn't it? Then let me help you.

42.   잠깐 기다려 주시겠어요?
      Will you wait for me a moment, please?

43.   와 주셔서 감사합니다.
      Thanks for coming.

17.5. Verbs: Nominalizer Form -기

The one-shape nominalizer ending -기 is attached to bases in exactly the same way as is the -고 form (see sections 9.5. and 16.1.) Thus, L-extending verbs attach in their extended form: 파-르- → 팔기 *sell*, etc. You can make past forms by attaching it to past bases, and future forms by attaching it to future bases.

Base Type	Nominalizer	Pronunciation
Present/Plain	하기	
Past	했기	해끼
Future	하겠기	하게끼

The resulting forms are nounlike words; they mean *the act of doing* if processive, and *the state of being* if descriptive. Past forms mean *the act of having done*, *the state of having been*; and future forms mean *the act of going-to-do*, *the state of going-to-be*. Sometimes the forms translate *to do/to be*.

These nounlike forms are used in all of the four positions that regular nouns are used in—most commonly these three:

    a.   Followed by a particle
    b.   Modifying a following noun
    c.   In absolute (adverbial) position—in constructions where a particle has optionally been dropped

It is rarer to find a -기 form in the remaining noun use.

    d.   Before the copula

44.   이렇게 하기에요.
       (It is [a matter of] doing it this way=) Let's decide to do it this way.

Nominalizer forms enable you to take an entire sentence; convert it into one big noun; and then use this noun as the subject, object, or some other part of a larger sentence.

-기-Conversion

45.   여행을 해요.   →   [여행을 하-기]_{NOUN}
       I travel.

46.   〔여행(을) 하기〕를 싫어해요.
       I hate to travel.

Sentence (42) neatly contains two direct objects: one within the -기 clause, and one that is the -기 clause itself. You can, of course, drop either particle 을 ~ 를 — or both of them.

47.   a. 〔여행을   하기〕를   싫어해요.

       b. 〔여행을   하기〕   싫어해요.

       c. 〔여행   하기〕   싫어해요.

Another example:

48.   가수가 나오기를 기다리고 있었어요.
       We were waiting for the popstar to appear.

17.6. Other Nounlike Uses of -기 Forms

Observe the following examples.

49.   모든 것을 다 잘하기(가) 어려워요.
       It's hard to do everything well.

50.   공부만 하기가 재미 없잖아요?
       It's no fun to do nothing but study, don't you think?

51.   수영하기를 좋아하세요?
       Do you like swimming?

52.   밖에서 놀기가 참 좋아요.
       It's very nice to play outside. or *I really like playing outside.*

53.   혼자서 술 마시기를 싫어해요.
       He hates drinking alone.

In each of these six sentences, a -기 form appears as subject or object, and in each case, the subject or object particle (as usual) is optional, so the -기 form without the particle is left in an absolute, or adverbial, construction.

Note that the class of verbs that can pattern with –기 in this way is limited; one cannot, for example, say:

54.　　 *이 김치는 먹기가 너무 매워요.
　　　　This kimchee is too hot to eat.

Of the verbs learned so far in this course, the following are compatible with this pattern.

재미(가) 있–/없–　　　귀찮–
좋–　　　　　　　　　　싫–
쉬w–　　　　　　　　　 어려w–
힘(이) 드–ㄹ–　　　　　어때요?

Thus, all are descriptive verbs, and (with the exception of 어때요) all are sensory verbs that participate in the –어해요 pattern for third persons. But it is not the case that *all* sensory verbs can be used this way, so be wary of trying out new verbs until you have heard them from a Korean yourself.

Here are some more examples of this kind of sentence.

55.　　 한국말 배우기(가) 쉬워요?
　　　　Is it easy to learn Korean?

56.　　 한국말 배우기(가) 어렵지요?
　　　　It's difficult to learn Korean, isn't it?

57.　　 책을 읽기(가) 재미있어요.
　　　　It's fun to read books.

58.　　 A.　서울에서 살기는 어때요?
　　　　　　What's it like to live in Seoul?
　　　　　　[I.e., As far as living in Seoul (Topic)—what's it like?]

　　　　 B.　살기는 좋지요.
　　　　　　It's good, of course!

59.　　 이 집에는 방이 하나 밖에 없어서 살기가 쉽지 않지요.
　　　　It isn't easy to live in this house, because it has only one room.

60.　　 할머니는 너무 말씀을 많이 하셔서, 듣기가 싫어요.
　　　　Grandmother talks so much I hate to listen.

The expression 듣기 싫어요 *I hate to listen* is often used where we would say things like *Ugh!, I don't want to hear about it!, Must you say such things?!, What an awful thing (to hear)! Stop talking!* Likewise, the expression 보기 싫어요 means something like *How disgusting (to see).* or *That (or he, she, etc.) makes me sick.*

17.7. Plain Base + -기 시작하-: *Begin to ...*

Another -기 pattern is the construction with 시작해요 *begins*, in which the -기 form is, optionally, the direct object of the phrase 시작해요. To say *begins to do* or *begins doing* you use a plain base + -기 form (with or without the direct object particle 를) and 시작해요 *begins*.

61.　사람들이 버스에서 내리기(를) 시작했어요.
　　The people started to get off the bus.

62.　비가 오기 시작해요.
　　It's beginning to rain.

63.　해가 나기 시작했어요.
　　The sun has started to come out.

64.　한국말은 언제부터 배우기 시작하셨어요?
　　[Since] When did you start learning Korean?

65.　무스를 바르기 시작했어요.
　　I've started to use mousse.

> ## 주의!
>
> This construction is used with processive verbs only.

For adjectives—*begins to be*—you use an infinitive in -어 ~ -아 with the auxiliary verb 져요 *begins [to be]* (see section 18.6).

66.　더워져요.
　　It's getting hot [= It's beginning to be hot].

17.8. Any Base + -기 때문에: *Because . . .*

After a regular noun, 때문에 means *because of the NOUN*.

67.   우리 동생 때문에 못 가겠어요.
      I won't be able to go because of my brother.

68.   날씨 때문에 방학이 별로 재미 없었어요.
      My vacation wasn't much fun because of the weather.

A -기 form (on any of the three kinds of base) followed by 때문에 *by reason of, because of* means *because one does/is* or *did/was* or *will do/will be*.

69.   점심에는 다른 약속이 있기 때문에, 저녁을 사 줄게요.
      Because I have another engagement for lunch, I'll treat you to supper.

70.   오늘 시험에 합격했기 때문에, 한턱 낼게요.
      Because I passed the exam today, I'll treat you.

71.   내일 떠나기 때문에 결혼식에 못 가겠어요.
      Because I'm leaving tomorrow, I won't be able to go to the wedding ceremony.

When the because sentence has 너무 *overly, too* plus adjective, it is sometimes better to translate it with *so ADJECTIVE that*.

72.   이 모자가 너무 좋기 때문에 샀어요.
      This hat was so ["too"] nice I bought it. [Because this hat was so nice, I bought it.]

73.   김 선생님 댁이 너무 멀기 때문에 자주 못 가요.
      Mr. Kim's house is so far away, I can't go often.

74.   날이 너무 더웠기 때문에, 수영장에 사람이 아주 많았어요.
      It was such a hot day that there were lots of people at the swimming pool.

You can also do this with the somewhat weaker form of *because*, expressed by -어서.

75.   너무 비싸서 못 샀어요.
      It was so expensive I couldn't buy it.

17.9. Plain Base + -기 전에: *Before . . .*

Processive plain bases in the -기 form enter into phrases with 전에 *before* to mean *before* [someone] *does.* Regardless of the time of the English—*before* [he] *does* or *before* [he] *did* or *before* [he] *will do*—the Korean -기 form remains constant, so the meaning of the phrase is *before doing . . . .* In other words, past, present, and future tense are all handled at the end of the sentence—the ending in -기 always attaches to a plain base.

76.   A.   나가기 전에 머리를 빗어요.
                I comb my hair before I go out.

        B.   나가기 전에 머리를 빗었어요.
                I combed my hair before I went out.

        C.   나가기 전에 머리를 빨리 빗을게요.
                I'll just comb my hair quickly before we go out.

77.   손님들이 오기 전에, 내가 식사 준비를 정신 없이 했어요.
       Before the guests came, I prepared supper in a daze.

78.   방학이 시작되기 전에 마치고 싶어요.
       I want to finish it before vacation begins.

79.   상점에 가기 전에 은행에 먼저 갈래요.
       I want to go to the bank (first) before I go to the store.

Exercises

Exercise 1: *I'm glad that . . .*

Each of the following sentences mean *someone does or did something.* Change each so that it means *I'm glad someone does or did something.* For example, the first sentence will be: 선생님이 오셔서, (나는) 좋아요. *I'm glad the teacher came.* Be sure to translate the complete sentence. It is not necessary to include the 나는 to mean *I am glad,* but without it the sentence might also be translated *It's good that . . .* or *It's nice that . . .*

1.   선생님이 오셨어요.
2.   아버지가 자동차를 파셨어요.
3.   시험이 너무 어렵지 않았어요.

4. 오늘은 바쁘지 않아요. *music concert.*
5. (음악회) 표를 샀어요.
6. 음식이 아주 매워요.
7. 네거리에서 차를 갑자기 세웠지만, 애기가 안 깼어요.
8. 동생이 시험에 합격했어요.
9. 아내가 아들을 낳았어요.
10. 우리 딸이 좋은 사람하고 결혼했어요. (좋은 사람: nice person)
11. 내일부터 휴가가 시작돼요.
12. 저 학생의 태도가 좋아요.
13. 오늘 해가 드디어 났어요.

Exercise 2: Practice with Sensory Verbs

The following sentences begin with (or are understood to be about) 나는, and express a psychological state about *me*. Change them into sentences about 수미 씨.

1. 나는 냉면이 좋아요.
2. 나는 삼계탕이 안 매워서 좋아요.
3. 나는 오빠가 유럽으로 자주 여행을 가서 부러워요.
4. 나는 어제 파티에서 교수님 옆에 앉아 있어서 좀 어려웠어요.
5. 나는 무스를 바르고 싶지 않아요.
6. 나는 친구가 도와줘서 그 친구한테 고마워요.
7. 나는 방학이 돼서 좋아요.
8. 나는 내 친구가 외국어를 많이 해서 부러워요.
9. 나는 애기때문에 정신이 없어서, 나가고 싶어요.
10. 나는 다른 사람한테 부탁하기 싫어요.

Exercise 3: Practice with - 기 때문에

Each of the following items contains two sentences, the second beginning with 그렇기 때문 에 *because it's like that.* Combine them into a single sentence meaning *Because [this] happens, [that] happens.* For example, the first will be: 수진 씨가 일찍 오지 않았기 때 문에, 나는 수진 씨를 못 만났지요. *I couldn't see Sujin, because she didn't get there early.*

1. 수진 씨가 일찍 오지 않았어요. 그렇기 때문에, 나는 수진 씨를 못 만났지요.

2. 나는 돈이 조금 밖에 없어요. 그렇기 때문에, 컴퓨터를 사지 못 하고 있어요. *fiancée*

3. 어제 날씨가 너무 추웠어요. 그렇기 때문에, 나는 집에 있었어요.

4. 약혼자가 꽃을 좋아해요. 그렇기 때문에, 나는 꽃을 많이 사 줘요.

5. 나는 그 영화가 너무 좋아요. 그렇기 때문에, 두 번이나 봤어요.

6. 그 안경이 비싸요. 그렇기 때문에, 나는 못 샀어요.

7. 우리는 내일 저녁에 약속이 없어요. 그렇기 때문에, 음악회에 가서 음악을 들을 거에요.

8. 오늘은 피곤해요. 그렇기 때문에, 운전하지 않겠어요.

9. 내일 밤에 손님이 오세요. 그렇기 때문에, 어머니가 음식을 많이 준비 하고 계세요.

10. 내일 아침에 수업이 8시부터 시작해요. 그렇기 때문에, 오늘 밤에 일찍 잘래요.

11. 집에 400원짜리 우표가 없었어요. 그렇기 때문에, 200원짜리 2장을 사서 편지를 부쳤어요.

Exercise 4: The Exploratory Pattern

Each of the following sentences means *someone **does** or **did** something*; change each so that the meaning is *someone **tries** or **tried** doing something*; *someone **did** something **to see** (how it would be)*. For example, the first will be 만호 씨가 일본에 가 봤어요. *Manho tried going to Japan. Manho went to Japan to see. Manho went to see Japan.* Be sure you know what each of your sentences means.

[Note: Be careful to make the changes in the *first* verb expression, not in the auxiliary verb. For example, don't change 않아요 or 싶어요.]

1. 만호 씨가 일본에 갔어요.
2. 나는 한국 음식을 먹었어요.
3. 나는 서울에 기차를 타고 가고 싶어요.
4. 한국 목욕탕에 갈래요.
5. 버스를 한번 운전했어요.
6. 나는 이 책을 읽고 싶어요.
7. 유럽 여행을 했어요.
8. 나는 시내를 구경하고 싶어요.
9. 사무실에 올라 갔어요.
10. 나는 안경을 쓰고 싶어요.

Exercise 5: Practice with - 기 전에

Each of the following sentences means *[something] happens*. Change them so that they mean *[this] happens before [that]*. For example, the first will be: 김 선생님을 만나기 전에, 표를 2장 샀어요. *I bought two tickets before I saw Mr. Kim.*

1. 김 선생님을 만나요. 표를 2장 샀어요.
2. 박 선생님 부인이 오셨어요. 박 선생님이 벌써 오셨지요.
3. 아이들은 밥을 먹었어요. 놀았어요.
4. 선생님이 방에서 나가셨어요. 그 학생이랑 이야기 하셨어요.
5. 할아버지한테 사진을 보여 드렸어요. 어머니한테 보여 드렸어요.
6. 수업 시간이 끝났어요. 영어로 말하지 마세요.
7. 한국을 떠날 거에요. 박 교수님께 인사를 드리고 싶습니다.
8. 집 안으로 들어 가요. 어머니하고 같이 이야기를 좀 해 주세요.
9. 옷을 입어요. 세수하고 면도를 빨리 하세요.
10. 주무세요. 창문 좀 닫아 주세요.
11. 아버지가 집에 돌아 오세요. 저녁 준비를 합시다.
12. 택시에서 내렸어요. 돈을 냈어요.

Exercise 6: English to Korean Translation

Translate the following sentences into Korean.

1. Don't show mother those magazines!
2. It's raining, so let's wait under that footbridge a while.
3. Have you tried [eating] Korean ginseng chicken soup?
4. Could you give me two 200-*wŏn* stamps, please?
5. Father had already left before Mr. Kim came.
6. I want to buy six 300-*wŏn* stamps.
7. Please give me 3 tickets at 10,000 *wŏn*.
8. Do you collect stamps?
9. Grandfather is lying down upstairs.
10. Would you wake him up [for me] first, please?
11. Could you send this letter to Korea [for me]?
12. Before I travelled in Europe, I hadn't tried speaking any foreign languages.
13. This book is really difficult. Could you read it [for me], please?
14. Yesterday I bought a $2,000 computer.

15. Have you ever been to China?

16. I bought the tickets for tomorrow's concert before we saw that movie.

17. I like listening to the radio.

18. We can't go because there aren't any tickets.

19. Mr. Lee's nephew wants to travel in Europe.

20. He began to write that book last year, but hasn't finished it yet.

Exercise 7: Korean to English Translation

Translate the following sentences into English.

1. 일본어 시험들은 너무 길고 어려워서, 낙제하기가 쉬워요.

2. 동생한테 소식이 없어서 어머니가 궁금해 하세요.

3. 〔호텔에서〕 이 요금에 아침도 포함돼 있습니까?

4. 수진: 아직도 빵과 콜라만 먹어요?
   토마스: 아니오, 요즘 한국음식도 자주 먹기 시작했어요.

5. 영진: 수진 씨, 시계가 너무 멋이 있어요! 생일 선물이에요?
   수진: 네, 아버지가 사 주셨어요.

6. 〔리셉션-파티에서〕
   진호: 음식이 맛이 있지요?
   수진: 네, 그런데 의자가 없어서 먹기가 불편해요.

7. 우리 7살짜리 애는 드디어 학교에 다니기 시작했어요.

8. 현철: 중국말 배우기가 어때요?
   수미: 말하기는 쉽지만, 읽고 쓰기는 아주 힘들지요.

9. 〔차 안에서〕
   철호: 어느 길이 더 빠를까요?
   만호: 이쪽 길은 막히기가 쉬우니까, 저쪽 길로 갑시다.

10. 내가 영어로 "헬로" 하니까 애는 울기 시작했어요.

11. 철호: 왜 이렇게 늦을까요? 그 사람이 약속을 잘 지킵니까?
    수진: 네, 그런데 비 때문에 좀 늦을거에요.

12. 우리 16살짜리 애는 요즘 운전을 배우기 시작했어요.

13. 철호: 10,000원만 빌려 주실래요?
    수진: 지난 주에도 만원 빌려 줬잖아요?!

14. 수진: 머리 스타일이 너무 예뻐요! 어디서 했어요?
    미나: 엄마 친구가 잘라 주셨어요. 멋 있지요?

Exercise 8: Vocabulary Drill

Here are a number of short sentences, each having a blank space. Express them in Korean
—filling the blank each time with one of the expressions listed below the sentence.

1. I'm glad that _____.

    a. my friend is coming.
    b. my brother is getting married.
    c. I've got a 약속 tomorrow.
    d. it's Sunday.
    e. my mother isn't busy now

2. Manho has on _____.

    a. a necktie.
    b. glasses.
    c. new shoes.
    d. his hat.
    e. new clothes.

3. I walked _____.

    a. to the store.
    b. in the park.
    c. up to the third floor.
    d. from the post office to the bank.
    e. from home to school

4. Manho wants to _____.

    a. brush his teeth.
    b. get a haircut.
    c. wash his face.
    d. wash his hair.
    e. shave.

5. Eric is trying on _____.

    a. some shoes
    b. his shirt.
    c. gloves.
    d. new clothes.

    e. new glasses.

6. 숙희 _____ for me.

    a. looked after my children.
    b. bought a hat.
    c. waited two hours
    d. bought some tissues and
        towels

    e. posted the letter

7. Sangho _____ for my parents.

    a. bought a watch
    b. went to the bank and
        got some money
    c. called a cab
    d. filled in the lodging form

8. I'd like to _____.

    a. buy lots of hats.
    b. sell my car
    c. go home now.
    d. see Japan and Korea.
    e. travel in Europe by train.

Lesson 18

자동차는 어디서 빌릴 수 있습니까?

In this lesson we observe Eric discussing his health problems with his Korean teacher, and we watch Chris Murphy go through the procedure of renting a car at the hotel on Cheju Island. This lesson introduces some more new patterns built on the infinitive in -어 ~ -아, including the pattern for *have to~ought to* in -어 ~ -아야 돼요 and that for *even though* in -어 ~ -아도. These patterns are useful for expressing obligation and for asking and giving permission. The lesson also introduces another infinitive-based pattern, that in -어 + 지- for *get/become* . . . Finally, the lesson introduces *can do* and *cannot do* in -(으)ㄹ 수 있어요/없어요, the somewhat bookish conjunction (*and*) in -(으)며 and NOUN(을) 통하 (서) *through (the agency of) NOUN*.

Korean Dialogues

Dialogue 1

Eric is complaining about his health to his Korean teacher, Mr. Song.

에릭	요즘 술을 너무 마셔서 건강이 나빠졌어요.
	날마다 술을 먹고, 늦게 일어나서 아침을 못 먹거든요.
송 선생	아무리 술을 마셔도 아침을 꼭 먹어야지요.
	그리고 잠도 제대로 자야 돼요.
에릭	선생님, 오늘 좀 일찍 집에 가도 괜찮아요?
송 선생	그래요. 그리고 학교 병원에 한번 들러 봐요.
에릭	가고 싶어도 오늘은 돈이 없어서 갈 수 없어요.
송 선생	그럼, 병원에는 가지 못해도, 약국에나 가서 약을 좀 사서 먹어요.

Dialogue 2

Chris Murphy wants to rent a car for the duration of their stay on Cheju Island. He goes to the front desk to ask about the procedure.

크리스	자동차는 어디서 빌릴 수 있습니까?
아가씨	저희가 해 드릴 수 있습니다. 설명서는 여기 있습니다.
	(Chris looks over the brochure)
크리스	여기에 마일수도 포함돼 있습니까?
아가씨	마일수는 포함 돼 있지만 휘발유값이랑 보험료는 따로 내셔야 합니다.
크리스	보증금도 내야 합니까?
아가씨	저희 호텔을 통해서 빌리시니까, 보증금은 안 내셔도 됩니다. 운전 면허증만 보여 주세요. 그러면 제가 서류를 다 준비해 드리지요.
크리스	감사합니다.

Reading Passage

한국말은 어렵기 때문에 하루에 적어도 3시간씩은 공부해야 하며 매일 공부해야 합니다. 한국사람은 한국어 문법을 따로 공부하지 않아도 문법을 자연스럽게 이해하며 자연스럽게 이야기할 수 있지만 외국사람은 문법을 제대로 알아야 한국말을 잘 배울 수 있습니다. 처음에는 사전을 보지 않아도 괜찮지만 단어를 많이 외워야 합니다. 어떤 사람은 문법은 잘 알아도 단어를 많이 모르기 때문에 말을 잘 하지 못 합니다. 그리고 물론, 한국사람들하고 자주 어울려야, 한국말 연습이 되며 텔레비젼을 통해서도 많이 배울 수 있으니 텔레비젼도 자주 보십시오.

그렇게 해야, 한국말 공부하기가 재미있어집니다. 한국말이 좀 어려워도 열심히 공부하십시오.

Reading Passage Notes

어떤 사람   *some people.* The word 어떤 means *which? what kind of?* But like other question words in Korean, 어떤 can also function as an indefinite. Hence the meaning *some . . . , [a] certain . . . .*

그래야   [Literally: only if you do so, only if you do it that way; only then.] This form is from the base 그러-, 그래요, about which you will learn more in Lesson Twenty-two.

Vocabulary

Adverbs

당장	immediately, straight away, on the spot
지금 당장	immediately, right now
따로	separately
따로 따로	[each] separately
점심값은 따로 따로 냅시다.	Let's pay separately for lunch.
몹시	very, awfully
오늘은 몹시 무더워요.	Today is extremely hot and muggy.
아무리 〔 . . .-어도〕	however much [one VERBs]; at the very [(ADJ-est)]
유창하게	fluently
자연스럽게	naturally; fluently, freely
점점	gradually, little by little, by degrees
점점 나아 지고 있습니다.	I'm gradually getting better.
제대로	as it should/ought be done, properly, in proper fashion

숙박부에 제대로 기입을 안 했기 때문에 다시 써야 했습니다.

Because I didn't fill in the lodging form correctly, I had to write it again.

즐겁게	enjoyably, happily

Nouns

School and Language Learning

–과	lesson
제1과	Lesson One

제2과	Lesson Two
제3과	Lesson Three (etc.)
-과	department
무슨 과에 다니세요?	Which department are you in?
과장(님)	Head of Dept., department chairman
단어	word; vocabulary item
동창	classmate, graduate of same school
동기동창	classmate (graduate of same school, same year)
동창회	alumni society; club for graduates of same school
문법	grammar (pronounced〔-뻡〕)
사전	dictionary
한영사전	Korean-English dictionary
영한사전	English-Korean dictionary
사전에서 찾아보세요.	Look it up in the dictionary.
동양	East Asia
동양학	East Asian Studies
동양학과	Department of East Asian Studies
서양	the West; Western countries; Western (as modifier)
선배	senior from school
한자 〔한짜〕	Chinese character
한자어 〔한짜어〕	Chinese character word
후배	junior from school

Cars, Driving and Travel

거리	street
길거리 〔-꺼리〕	main road, thoroughfare
공항	airport
기름	oil; gasoline, petrol (more colloquial than 휘발유)
기름(을) 넣-	get gas, put in gas
차에 기름을 넣어야 돼요.	I need to put gas in the car.

마일	mile
마일수 〔-쑤〕	mileage (lit.: number of miles)
면허증 〔-쯩〕	license, certificate
운전면허증	driver's license
보증금	deposit
보험	insurance
보험료 〔-뇨〕	insurance fee, insurance charge
보험(을) 드-ㄹ-	take out insurance, insure
서류	document
설명서	a brochure, pamphlet, piece of explanatory literature
주유소	gas station
택시요금	taxi fare
휘발유 〔-발류〕	gasoline, petrol

Other

기타	guitar
기타(를) 치-	play the guitar
모임	gathering, meeting
내일 모임에 못 가겠어요.	I won't be able to go to tomorrow's meeting.
몸	body
소용	a use; utility, usefulness
소용(이) 없-	be useless
약국	pharmacy, drugstore
약사	pharmacist, chemist
오해	a misunderstanding
오해(를) 하-	misunderstand something
오해하지 마세요.	Please don't misunderstand/take it wrong.
이해	understanding
이해(를) 하-	understand something
이해(가) 가-	one understands it; it is understandable
이해가 안 가요.	I just don't get it.
자리	seat, place
제-	ordinalizer (makes ordinals like "first," "second," etc., for Sino-Korean numbers

| 하느님 (Catholic), 하나님 (Protestant) | God |
| 하늘 | heaven; sky |

Verbs

Verbs That Take Objects

결정	decision
결정 (을) 하-	decide it
그만하-	quit, stop doing it
그만해요!	Stop it!
그만두-	quit, stop doing it
아직도 골프를 배우세요?	Are you still learning golf?
아니오, 그만뒀어요.	No. I stopped.
때리-	hit, strike, beat
만나 뵈w-	meet [with] sb. esteemed; see sb. esteemed
바꾸-	(ex)change it, trade it
이것을 새 것으로 바꿉시다.	Let's exchange this for a new one.
자리를 바꿉시다.	Let's trade seats.
뵈w-	humbly see or meet; have an audience/interview with. Note that the spelling of this verb is irregular: 뵈도 or 뵈어도 for expected *뵈워도, 뵐 for expected 뵈울, etc.
처음 뵙겠습니다.	How do you do [on being introduced].
그럼, 내일 뵐게요.	See you tomorrow, then.
야단 (을) 맞-	be/get scolded [for "from" use 한테]
야단 (을) 치-	scold, give a scolding to [use 한테 or 을 ~ 를]
어울리-	spend time with [= 하고], hang around with, associate with
외우-	memorize it
단어를 외우고 있어요.	I'm memorizing words.
찾아 가-	call on; visit, go calling on
찾아 뵈w-	call on sb. esteemed; visit, come calling on sb. esteemed
만나 뵈w-	meet [with] sb. esteemed; see sb. esteemed
찾아 오-	call on; visit, come calling on

Descriptive and/or Sensory Verbs

기-ㄹ-	be long
가난하-	be poor, indigent
따뜻하-	be warm

Lesson Eighteen / 58

오늘은 따뜻하고 좋아요.	Today is nice and warm.
무더w-	be hot and muggy
복잡하-	be complicated; crowded
이 문제는 참 복잡해요.	This problem is really complicated.
어제는 지하철이 아주 복잡했어요.	Yesterday the subway was very crowded.
불쌍하-	be pitiful; "poor thing"
쌀쌀하-	be cool, chilly
유명하-	be famous
이르-	be early
조용하-	be quiet
조용히	quietly
조용히 하세요!	Please be quiet!
짧-	be short
편찮으시-	be ill, not well (honorific)
흐리-	be cloudy, overcast
날이 흐려요.	It is overcast.

Intransitive Verbs (Processive Verbs That Cannot Take Objects)

들르-	drop in, drop by

내일 1시쯤에 사무실에 좀 들러 볼래요?

Would you mind stopping by the office tomorrow around 1 o'clock?

없어지-	disappear

Lesson Notes

18.1. Uses of the Infinitive V: with 야 *Only if*

To express obligation—*have to, must, should, ought to*—you use an infinitive for the main verb, and attach to it the particle 야 *only if* plus a form of 하- or 되- *becomes*; -어야 해요 or -어야 돼요 gives the meaning of *have to* to the main verb. Literally, the pattern means *only if (someone) VERBs will it do* or *become,* but in practice this is merely the normal Korean way of saying that *someone is compelled* or *has to do something.*

1. 오늘 저녁에 친구를 만나야 해요.
    I have to meet a friend this evening.

2.   이 구두를 바꿔야 하겠어요.
     I'll have to exchange these shoes.

3.   교회 안에서는 조용히 해야 돼요.
     You have to be quiet inside the church.

4.   머리가 너무 길어서 이발을 해야겠습니다.
     My hair is so long I'll have to get a haircut.

Occasionally –어야 is followed by some verb other than the auxiliary 해요.

5.   1,000원이 있어야 들어가요.
     You have to have 1000 wŏn to get in. (lit.: *Only if you have 1000 wŏn do you go in*).

6.   선생님한테 물어봐야 알아요.
     We will only find out by asking the teacher.
     or *We won't find out unless we ask the teacher.*

Be careful about trying to use negatives for this type of expression. The genuine opposite of these, in English, is *doesn't have to; needs not*. But the Korean opposites are made by an altogether different construction, discussed in Section 18.2.4.

Must not—which appears on the surface to be the negative of *has to*—is actually a denial of permission; it is the opposite of *may*, which gives permission. The denial of permission, again, is an entirely different Korean construction that will be taken up later.

Here are some more examples of –어야.

7.   오늘 밤까지는 이 과를 마쳐야 해요.
     I must finish this lesson by tonight.

8.   나는 오후 5시까지는 약국에 들러야 해요.
     I have to drop by the pharmacy by 5 PM.

9.   내일 선배 한 분을 찾아 가야 해요.
     I have to look up one of my seniors tomorrow.

10. 보증금을 따로 내야 합니다.
     You have to pay a deposit separately.

11. 고기는 그 가게에 아침 일찍 가야 사요.
     You'll get meat only by going to that shop early in the morning.

In some forms it is common for the auxiliary verb 하– to be abbreviated. In colloquial Korean, this happens most often in these two patterns.

해야[하]지요 → 선생님도 오셔야지요!
. . . should do it, you know. *You should come, too!*

해야[하]겠어요 → 빨리 가야겠어요.

. . . will have to do it. *I really must hurry along.*

12. A. 이 문제를 꼭 풀어야 돼요?
   *Do we **have** to solve this problem?*

   B. 그럼요, 풀어야지요!
   Of course you have to solve it!

13. 자동차를 빌려야겠어요.
   We'll have to rent a car.

Finally, note that you can use the particle 야 on a past infinitive, in a construction meaning *should have done*, i.e., *only if one had done.*

14. 어제 밤에 숙제를 했어야 됐지만, 못 했어요.
   I should have done my homework last night, but I couldn't.

18.2. Uses of the Infinitive VI: with 도 *Even though*

18.2.1. -어도: *Even though . . .*

An infinitive with the particle 도 has the basic meaning *even though* [so-and-so happens].

15. 수진 씨는 돈이 많지 않아도, 늘 쇼핑을 해요.
   Even though Sujin hasn't much money, she's always shopping.

16. 상점이 멀어도 자주 가요.
   Even though the stores are far away, I go there often.

On a past base:

17. 돈이 조금 밖에 없었어도 늘 즐겁게 살았어요.
   Even though he hadn't much money, he always lived happily.

Again, with this construction, it is not necessary to use a past-tense infinitive before the 도, even when the meaning is past, unless ambiguity would otherwise result; the past-tense verb at the end does all the work.

Notice the basic similarity between this construction and the –지만 *but, although* construction you have learned. Both constructions mean *though* [so-and-so happens] . . . but, –어도 is stronger. It means *even though . . .* or *in spite of the fact that . . .* ; if we want to switch its force to the next part of the sentence, we can give it some such translation as *. . . but even so.*

> *I haven't much money, **but even so** I'm always buying things.*
> *The stores are a long way off, **but in spite of this** I go there a lot.*
> *He had no money at all, **but nonetheless** he was always happy.*

Constructions with –지만 (*although . . .* or *. . . but*) are not this strong, but the fundamental meaning is similar.

18.2.2. Special Copular Form -(이)라도

Just as the copula can take the special shape –이라 before 서 (Lesson Sixteen), it can assume this shape before 도: –이라도 alongside –이어도 *even though it be.*

18. 하루에 반 시간씩이라도 단어를 외워야 돼요.
     You should memorize vocabulary for at least (lit.: *even though it be*) *half an hour a day.*

The special copular form –이라도 *even though it be* (as in the sentence above) means about the same thing as the particle 도 *even* by itself; sometimes *at least* is a good translation. Here are two more examples.

19. 다른 것이 없으니까, 이것이라도 좋아요.
     This one will be all right, since you haven't got any others.

20. 저는 못 가겠으니까, 유진 씨라도 갔다 오십시오.
     As I won't be able to go, at least you go (without me), Yujin.

Here are some more examples of -어도.

21. 할아버지는 돈이 많으셔도 나한테는 안 주세요.
     Even though granddad has lots of money, he doesn't give me any.

22. 나는 나이는 많아도 마음은 젊어요.
     Even though I am old in age, I am young at heart.

23. 나는 매일 공항에서 일을 해도 비행기를 한번도 타 보지 못 했어요.
     Even though I work at the airport everyday, I haven't even once flown on an airplane.

24. 어젯밤에 비가 그렇게 왔어도 파티에는 300명이나 왔어요.
     Even though it was raining last night, some ["as many as"] 300 people came to the party.

25.   나는 아무리 아파도 병원에 한번도 가보지 않았어요.
      No matter how sick I might be, I've never gone to the hospital.

18.2.3. Asking and Giving Permission with -어도

To ask for permission in Korean you use a construction with the literal meaning *even though I [do it], is it all right?* or *even if I [do it], does it matter* or *make any difference?* This corresponds to English *may* or *can I [do it]* or, much more closely, *is it all right if I [do it]?* You may use any of three verbs for the final one in the sentences, as the examples show. The three verbs are 돼요, 좋아요 and 괜찮아요.

26.   오늘 새 옷을 입어도 좋아요?
      Is it all right for me to [= May I] wear my new clothes today?

27.   새 신을 신어도 괜찮아요?
      May I wear my new shoes? [Even though I wear . . . does it make a difference?]

28.   오늘 밤에 집에 늦게 들어 와도 돼요?
      Is it all right for me to [= Do you mind if I] come home late tonight?

18.2.4. *Doesn't have to . . .* with -지 않아도

To say *I have to . . .* in Korean, you use the construction -어야 해요 (Section 18.1.). The negative of this — *I don't have to . . .* — is a permission construction, meaning literally *even though I don't [do it], it's all right* or *it doesn't matter if I don't [do it].* You may use either the long or short negative for this pattern, either 안 가도 or 가지 않아도. For the *it doesn't matter, it's all right*, etc., you can use 괜찮아요, 돼요 or 좋아요. Here are some examples.

29.   일찍 돌아오시지 않아도 괜찮아요.
      You don't have to come back early.
      [= Even though you don't come back early, it doesn't matter.]

30.   운전면허증을 안 보여 주셔도 좋아요.
      You don't have to show me your driver's license.

31.   차를 빌리지 않아도 괜찮아요.
      You don't need to rent a car.

32.   오늘 모임에 가도 좋고 안 가도 좋아요.
      It doesn't matter whether I go to the meeting today or not.
      [= If I go to the meeting today it's all right, and if I don't go it's all right.]

33. 그 서류는 지금 쓰지 않아도 되지만, 이 편지는 당장 써야겠어요.
   I don't have to write that document now, but this letter I'll have to write immediately.

18.3. Some Idiomatic -어도 Expressions

There are a few descriptive verb infinitives with the particle 도 that have a special maximum-minimum meaning (alongside their usual meaning, in other contexts, of *even though it's ...*) like these.

늦어도   *at the latest [even though it's late]*

적어도   *at least [even though it's few or small]*

Here are some examples of these in sentences.

34. 여기서부터 학교까지 적어도 1시간은 걸리겠어요.
   From here to the school it must take at least one hour.

35. 오빠 자동차는 빨라도 1시간에 80킬로 밖에 못 가요.
   At the fastest, my older brother's car won't do over eighty kilometers an hour.

36. A. 지금 몇 시에요?
   What time is it now?

   B. 왜요?
   Why?

   A. 늦어도 10시까지는 집에 들어 가야 하거든요.
   We have to return home by 10 o'clock at the latest.

18.4. Infinitive -어 + 져요 (지-): *Get/Become*

The auxiliary verb 져요 (an abbreviation of 지어요 from the base 지-) means *begins to be . . .* or *gets (to be)*. It follows the infinitives of descriptive verbs (adjectives) to form processive verb compounds, like these.

추워요	*is cold*	→	추워져요	*gets cold, cools off*
더워요	*is hot*	→	더워져요	*gets hot, warms up*
좋아요	*is good*	→	좋아져요	*gets better*
나빠요	*is bad*	→	나빠져요	*gets worse*
흐려요	*is cloudy*	→	흐려져요	*gets cloudy, clouds up*
피곤해요	*is tired*	→	피곤해져요	*gets tired*

(Notice that natural English often uses a phrase to translate such compounds: *warms **up**, cools **off***, etc.).

> # 주의!
>
> Note that Korean spelling requires that the auxiliary verb 지- be written flush with the preceding infinitive form, without any intervening space: 추워져요 and not 추워 져요 for *gets cold, cools off*.

Verb phrases with the auxiliary descriptive verb 싶어요 *wants to, would like to* can also enter into such compounds.

(하)고 싶어요	*wants to [do]*
(하)고 싶어져요	*gets so that one wants to [do]*

As is usual for compound expressions, the infinitive remains changeless. It is the auxiliary 지- that adjusts to fit the sentence by adding an appropriate ending:

더워요	*is hot*
더워져요	*gets hot*
더워졌어요	*got hot*
더워질 거에요	*will get hot*
더워지지만	*gets hot, but . . .*
더워질까요?	*Do you suppose it will get hot?*

The auxiliary 지- is usually inseparable from the infinitive; it is tacked right on to the -어 in pronunciation.

37.   요즘 낮에는 더워지고 밤에는 추워져요.
      Lately, it gets warm in the daytime and gets cool at night.

38.   날이 갑자기 흐려졌어요.
      It got cloudy suddenly.

39.   여름 방학 동안에 머리가 길어졌어요.
      My hair got long over the summer vacation.

40. 째즈 음악이 좋아졌어요.
    I've come to like jazz music.

41. 과일 값이 비싸졌어요.
    The price of fruit has gotten expensive.

42. 내 우산이 없어졌어요.
    My umbrella has disappeared.

Finally, note that whereas it is impossible to use adjectives like 더워요 directly in the construction with -기 시작해요, you can first put it in the -어져요 construction and then use it like any other processive expression.

43. 더워지기 시작했어요.
    It started getting hot.

44. 숙제가 점점 어려워지기 시작해요.
    The homework is gradually beginning to get (more) difficult.

18.5. *Can/Cannot Do* : -(으)ㄹ 수 있-/없-

You have already seen a few patterns that incorporate the prospective modifier -(으)ㄹ: -(으)ㄹ까요? -(으)ㄹ 거에요 and -(으)ㄹ게요. The noun 수 means *case, circumstance; way, means* and 수(가) 있어요 means literally *a means exists*. Following the prospective modifier this pattern conveys possibility and/or ability.

Expressions meaning *can* and *can't* are made in Korean by attaching -(으)ㄹ 수 (pronounced -(으)ㄹ 쑤) plus 있어요 or 없어요 to any plain base. The way in which this is done is exactly the same as you learned for attaching the probable future form in section 13.3 and the *wanna* form in -(으)ㄹ래요 in section 12.7. That is because the first ㄹ of all those endings is the same—the prospective modifier that we look at in its own right later on. So, for example, L-extending bases attach the ending to the unextended base.

살 수 없어요	*can't live*	(base 사-ㄹ-)
애기가 걸을 수 있어요?	*can the baby walk?*	
쓸 수 없어요	*can't use*	
볼 수 있어요?	*can [we] see?*	
따뜻할 수도 있어요	*(you never know, it) can also be warm*	
구울 수 없어요	*can't broil*	(base 구w-)

Lesson Eighteen / 66

Expressions with 수(가) 없어요 correspond to one of the meanings of negative forms with 못: 갈 수 없어요 = 못 가요 or 가지 못해요 *can't go*. Here are some more examples of this construction.

45.　사장님을 잠깐 뵐 수 있을까요?
　　　Do you suppose I could see the company president for a moment?

46.　오늘 밤에 우리 집에 오실 수 있어요?
　　　Can you come to our house this evening?

47.　시간이 없어서, 준비를 다 끝낼 수 없었어요.
　　　I couldn't finish the preparations—I didn't have time.

48.　오늘은 비가 와서, 이발하러 갈 수 없었어요.
　　　It was raining today, so I couldn't go for a haircut.

49.　오늘은 거리가 조용하지만, 그 길은 복잡할 수도 있어요.
　　　Today the street's quiet, but this road gets [can be] crowded, too.

18.6. Expressing *and* with -(으)며

This two-shape ending can attach to any type of base and means simply *and* (sometimes also *while*, i.e., *and [simultaneously/at the same time]*). Thus, -(으)며 has the same function as one of the usages of the one-shape ending -고. But there are two differences to keep in mind:

> A. -(으)며 is a literary, bookish form, rarely used in spoken language,
> 　　　whereas -고 is widely used in colloquial Korean.
> B. -(으)며 does <u>not</u> have the *having done . . . ; does, and then . . .* meaning of -고.
> 　　　Its one and only meaning is *and*.

Note that L-extending bases keep their ㄹ before -며: 사-르- → 살며 *live, and . . .* Here are some examples.

50.　동양학과 과장님은 한국말 문법을 가르치시며 다른 강의도 가끔 하세요.
　　　The Chair of the Department of East Asian Studies teaches Korean grammar and sometimes gives other lectures, too.

51.　어제는 무더웠으며 내일도 날이 덥고 흐릴 겁니다.
　　　Yesterday was hot and muggy, and tomorrow it will be hot and cloudy, too.

52.　숙박부에 기입하셔야 하며 면허증도 보여 주셔야 합니다.
　　　You have to fill in a lodging form and show your driver's license, too.

18.7. NOUN(을) 통해(서) *through the agency of NOUN*

Dialogue Two and the Reading Passage in this lesson contained the following phrases:

텔레비젼을 통해서도 많이 배울 수가 있으니 . . .
Since you can learn a great deal through television, too, . . .

저희 호텔을 통해서 빌리시니까, . . .
Since you're renting [the car] through our hotel, . . .

This pattern is based on a verb you learned already in *Elementary Korean* (Lesson Thirteen): 통하- *get through to, make contact with*. Following a noun (optionally marked with the object particle 을/를), the verb phrase 통해(서) or 통하여(서) (the latter in more bookish, written language), this pattern means *through; by way of*. This pattern is typically used with nouns indicating sources of information (persons, media sources, institutions, activities, etc.). Here are some more examples:

53. 이번 여행을 통해서 많이 배웠습니다.
     I learned a lot through this past trip.

54. 수진: 상호 씨를 어떻게 알아요?
     Sujin: How do you know Sangho?

     만호: 친구를 통해서 만났어요.
     Manho: I met him through a friend.

55. 만화를 통해서도 한국에 대해서 많이 배울 수가 있지요.
     Of course, you can learn a lot about Korea through comics, too.

56. 수진: 그런 한국 비디오를 어디서 받아요?
     Sujin: Where do you get Korean videos like that from?

     만호: 한국 영사관을 통해서 받을 수가 있어요.
     Manho: You can get them through the Korean consulate.

18.8. *Decides/agrees to do* with -기로 하-

This pattern involves a summative form in -기 followed by the particle (으)로, but the resultant meaning is not so easily deduced. Processive verbs in the -기 form plus 로 해요 mean *decides to do* or *agrees to do* or *promises to do*. Notice that the -기 form remains fixed; it is the form of 해요 that contains any past or future markers. Instead of 하-, you may also use the following expressions.

약속(을) 하-   *promise*
결정(을) 하-   *decide*

Here are some examples.

57.   숙제는 다음 시간에 내기로 했어요.
      I've decided to hand in my homework next hour.

58.   음식점에 가서 먹기로 결정했어요.
      We decided to go eat at a restaurant.

59.   10시 반에 만나기로 약속했어요.
      I promised to meet him at 10:30.

60.   집에 있기로 했어요.
      I decided to stay home.

61.   그 그림을 여기에 걸기로 했는데, 어떻게 생각하시지요?
      We've decided to hang the picture here, but how do you think that would be?

62.   김 선생님은 다음 월요일에 부산에 가시기로 하셨어요.
      Mr. Kim has decided to go to Pusan next Monday.

Exercises

Exercise 1: Practice with - 어도

Change the -지만 clause in each of the following sentences into the -어도 pattern and translate the new sentences into English.

1. 비가 오지만 가고 싶습니다.
2. 한국말이 어렵지만 재미있어 질 거에요.
3. 멀지만 꼭 가야겠습니다.
4. 바쁘지만 모임에 가야 합니다.
5. 그 분이 찾아 오지 않으시지만 나는 찾아 가야지요.
6. 돈은 있지만 사지 않을래요.
7. 한국말이 재미없지만 열심히 공부하세요.
8. 이 책을 읽고 있지만 이해가 안 갑니다.
9. 영국에서 5년 살았지만 영어를 잘 못 합니다.
10. 할머니는 좀 편찮으시지만, 꼭 오실 거에요.
11. 하늘이 흐렸지만, 비는 안 올 거에요.
12. 한국학 전공이지만, 말은 아직 잘 못 합니다.
13. 약은 먹지만, 소용이 없어요.
14. 병원에 들러 봤지만, 소용이 없었어요.

Exercise 2: More Practice with - 어도

Each of the following sentences means *someone does something*. Change each so that it means *it's all right for someone to do something* or *someone may do something*. Or, if the sentence is negative, make it mean *someone need not do something* or *it's all right if someone doesn't do something*, *someone doesn't have to do something*. For example, the first sentence will be 한국에서도 이 구두를 신어도 좋아요? *Is it all right (for me) to wear these shoes in Korea, too?*

1. 한국에서도 이 구두를 신어요?
2. 내가 아기한테 이 음식을 줘요?
3. 애들이 개와 같이 놀아요.
4. 언니의 친구가 오늘 점심 먹으러 와요.

5. 선생님이 학생을 야단 치세요.

6. 문을 닫지 않아요?

7. 지금 전화하지 않아요?

8. 보증금을 내지 않아요.

9. 약국에 들르지 않아요.

10. 과장님을 잠깐 뵈요.

11. 호텔을 통해서 차를 빌리지 않아요.

12. 기타를 쳐요.

13. 동창회 모임에 가지 않아요.

Exercise 3: *Need not/Don't have to*

Each of the following sentences means *someone* **has to do** *something, someone* **must do** *something*. Change each one so that it means *someone* **need not do** *something, someone* **doesn't have to do** *something*. In some of your sentences, use 좋아요 and in others use 괜찮아요 for *it's allright*. Then translate the sentence. For example, the first will be: 내일 아침은 우리가 일찍 일어나지 않아도 좋아요 (or 괜찮아요). *We don't have to get up early tomorrow morning.*

1. 내일 아침은 우리가 일찍 일어나야 해요.
2. 과장님을 찾아 뵈야 해요.
3. 양복을 입고 가야 해요.
4. 딸이 그 남자와 결혼해야 해요.
5. 오늘은 넥타이를 매야 해요.
6. 숙박부에 기입해야 돼요.
7. 이발을 해야 해요.
8. 라디오를 들어야 해요.
9. 전화를 걸어야겠어요.
10. 불고기를 더 구워야 되겠어요.

Exercise 4: *Has to/Must do*

Each of the following sentences means *someone **need not do** something, someone **doesn't have to do** something*. Change each one so that it means someone **has to do** something, someone **must do** something. Then translate the sentence. For example, the first will be: 우리는 친구를 기다려야 해요. *We have to wait for our friends.*

1. 우리는 친구를 기다리지 않아도 좋아요.
2. 방학 동안에 아르바이트를 안 해도 괜찮아요.
3. 떠나기 전에 교수님한테 인사를 안 드려도 좋아요.
4. 어머니는 아기와 같이 많이 놀지 않아도 좋아요.
5. 선생님은 이 의자에 앉으시지 않아도 좋아요.
6. 친구한테 결혼 선물을 주지 않아도 좋아요.
7. 혼자 살지 않아도 좋아요.
8. 병원에 들르지 않아도 좋아요.
9. 내일 날씨가 덥지 않아도 돼요.
10. 라디오를 듣지 않아도 괜찮아요.

Exercise 5: *Can(not) do*

Each of the following sentences means either *someone **does** (or **did**) something* or *someone **doesn't** (or **didn't**) do something*. Change each so that it means either *someone **can** (or **could**) do something* or *someone **can't** (or **couldn't**) do something*. Then translate the sentence. For example, the first will be: 호텔을 통해서는 차를 빌릴 수 없어요. *You can't rent a car through the hotel.*

1. 호텔을 통해서는 차를 못 빌려요.
2. 한국에서도 미국음식을 많이 먹어요?
3. 형님이 영어를 가르쳐요?
4. 수영을 잘 해요.
5. 나는 외국에서 살아서, 한국음식을 못 먹었어요.
6. 우리 남편이 운전해요.
7. 담배를 피우지 못 했어요.
8. 아이들이 저 공원에서 놀아요.
9. 우리가 택시를 불러요.
10. 어제는 제가 모임에 오지 않았어요.
11. 기타를 쳐요.

Exercise 6: Practice with - (으) 며

Each of the following items contains two sentences connected with 그리고 *and*. Combine these into a single sentence by using -(으)며, and then translate. For example, the first will be: 진섭 씨는 내 선배이며 만호 씨는 내 후배에요. *Chinsŏp is my senior, and Manho is my junior.*

1. 진섭 씨는 내 선배입니다. 그리고 만호 씨는 내 후배입니다.
2. 한 사람은 병원에 갔습니다. 그리고 또 한 사람은 동창회 모임에 갔습니다.
3. 아침에 일어나서 먼저 단어를 외웁니다. 그리고 아침을 먹습니다.
4. 수진 씨는 노래를 잘 부릅니다. 그리고 기타도 잘 칩니다.
5. 이 호텔 방은 난방장치가 돼 있습니다. 그리고 발코니도 있습니다.
6. 크리스 씨는 차를 빌려서 갔습니다. 그리고 우리는 기차로 갔습니다.
7. 보증금을 안 내도 됩니다. 그리고 휘발유 값은 따로 내야 됩니다.
8. 오늘은 하늘이 좀 흐립니다. 그리고 몹시 무덥습니다.
9. 오늘은 대단히 춥습니다. 그리고 눈이 옵니다.

Exercise 7: Practice with -기로 해요

Complete each of the answers to the following questions using the pattern in -기로 하- (약속하-, 결정하-). For example, the first might be: 네, 이제부터 한국말을 열심히 배우기로 했거든요.

1. 만호: 한국어 테이프를 샀어요?
   크리스: 네, _____.
2. 만호: 여름 방학 때 어디 놀러 안 가요?
   크리스: 네, _____.
3. 만호: 다음 주말에 동창회에 갈 거지요?
   크리스: 네, _____.
4. 만호: 아니, 기타를 샀어요?
   크리스: 네, _____.
5. 만호: 골프를 계속 배울 거에요?
   크리스: 아니오, 너무 비싸서 _____.
6. 만호: 남 사장님한테 연락을 했어요?
   크리스: 아니오, 그런데 _____.
7. 만호: 어머님한테 편지를 자주 쓰십니까?
   크리스: 아니오, 그런데 _____.

8. 만호: 휴가 때 가족이랑 같이 어디 놀러 안 가세요?

   크리스: 네, _____.

9. 만호: 수진 씨 결혼 선물을 사셨어요?

   크리스: 네, _____.

10. 미스 김: 사모님이 세 시계를 사 주셨어요?

    크리스: 네, 그런데 마음에 안 들어서 다른 것으로_____.

11. 미스 김: 렌트카는 어떻게 하실 거에요?

    크리스: 호텔을 통해서 _____.

12. 만호: 그 사실은 사장님도 알고 계세요?

    크리스: 아니오, 내일 말씀 _____.

Exercise 8: Practice with NOUN (을) 통해(서)

Make up complete sentences using each of the phrases below:

1. 대사관을 통해서   _____.
2. 친척을 통해서   _____.
3. 도서관을 통해서   _____.
4. 교회를 통해서   _____.
5. 은행을 통해서   _____.
6. 텔레비전 뉴스를 통해서   _____.
7. 학생회관을 통해서   _____.
8. 외국어 공부를 통해서   _____.
9. 선생님의 설명을 통해서   _____.
10. 운동을 통해서   _____.
11. 이번 모임을 통해서   _____.
12. 음악을 통해서   _____.

Exercise 9: English to Korean Translation

Translate the following sentences into Korean.

1. Is it all right if I visit you this evening? [once normally, once humble-honorific]
2. You must go to the station immediately to meet the guests.
3. You needn't do your homework tonight.
4. This car goes too slow, so I'll have to change it.

5. Even if you find this lesson uninteresting, you still have to learn it!
6. I feel great, despite it being so hot and muggy.
7. Even though I come home late every night, my parents don't scold me.
8. Grandmother is not well, so I'm going to buy her some flowers.
9. It's probably going to get hot this afternoon.
10. In Korea, even if the weather is hot and muggy, you can't take off your shirt.

Exercise 10: Korean to English Translation

Translate the following sentences into English.

1. 내일 교회에 나가야 됩니다.
2. 비가 와도 꼭 만나 뵙고 싶습니다.
3. 날이 좀 흐렸어도 비가 안 올거니까 우산은 사지 않아도 돼요.
4. 한국음식을 아무리 많이 먹어 봐도 더 먹어 보고 싶거든요.
5. 결혼식에 가기 전에 머리를 잘라야겠습니다.
6. 그렇게 유명하셔도 사람은 아주 좋습니다.
7. 저희 집에서 선생님 댁까지 멀어도 3시간밖에 안 걸릴겁니다.
8. 이 일이 별로 어렵지 않아도 동생은 그리 똑똑하지가 못해서 좀 어려워 할거에요.
9. 아무리 속상해도 밥은 먹어야지요.
10. 그 사람은 밥을 아무리 많이 먹어도 배가 안 나와서 부러워요.

Exercise 11: Vocabulary Drill

Here are some sentences, each having a blank space. Express the sentence in Korean aloud—filling the blank each time with one of the expressions listed below the sentence.

1. I have to _____.
   a. go to hospital
   b. finish my homework
   c. buy a Korean-English dictionary
   d. exchange these clothes
   e. shave

2. It's all right not to _____.
   a. have a lot of money
   b. go by taxi
   c. phone me tonight
   d. take off your shoes now
   e. drop by the pharmacy tomorrow

3. You must _____ now.

    a. comb your hair

    b. put on your socks

    c. get dressed

    d. tie your necktie

    e. wash your hands

4. I can _____.

    a. play tennis

    b. swim

    c. drive

    d. rent a car

    e. visit you tomorrow

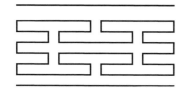 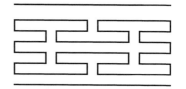

Lesson 19

지금 듣는 음악이 뭐에요?

In this lesson we observe Eric discussing Korean pop music with his friend, Yŏngch'ŏl. Then we watch Chris Murphy buy a ticket to Pusan at the train station. This lesson introduces the important new category of modifier—the past/adjectival modifier in -(으)ㄴ, the processive modifier in -는, and the retrospective modifier in -던. Modifiers are an essential building block for other patterns in Korean, and this lesson discusses modifier clauses as well as new postmodifier patterns in -는 길이에요 *is on the way to . . .* , -(으)ㄴ 일/적(이) 있어요 /없어요 for past experiences, and modifier plus 것 *the fact or act of doing*. Finally, the lesson includes the new particle 보다 for comparisons, and a section on words for *young* and *old*.

Korean Dialogues

Dialogue 1

Eric's Korean friend 영철 spots Eric on campus listening to his Walkman.

영철	에릭형! 지금 듣는 음악이 뭐에요?
에릭	우리 한국어 선생님한테서 빌린 한국 팝송 테이프에요.
영철	어디 봅시다. 아이구, 이건 옛날 거잖아요!
	10년 전에 유행하던 노래에요.
에릭	나야 그 전에 들어 본 적이 없어서 잘 모르지요.
	그러면 이 노래를 부른 가수는 인제 인기가 없어요?
영철	뭐, 10년 전에 대학 다니던 중년들에게는 인기가 있겠지요.
	갑시다 – 내가 요 앞에 좋은 가게를 아니까, 이것보다 훨씬 최근
	테이프를 사 줄게요.

Lesson Nineteen / 77

Dialogue Notes

어디 봅시다.	*Let's have a look. Let's take a look. Let me take a look.*
나야	Lit.: *if it be only me*, i.e., *I, for one* . . .
요 앞에	요 is the diminutive version (or "light isotope") of 이 *this*. Here it has the force of *just right in front here*.

Dialogue 2

Chris Murphy is at the train station again and needs to book himself on a train to Pusan.

크리스	다음 부산행 열차는 몇 시에 있습니까?
아가씨	부산 가는 열차는 4가지인데요. 어떤 걸 원하십니까?
크리스	글쎄요. 뭐뭐 있습니까?
아가씨	속도에 따라 다 다릅니다. 비둘기호는 완행이고, 통일호는 그거보다 좀 빠르고, 예약석도 있습니다. 무궁화호와 새마을호는 급행이고, 제일 비싸고 편한 것은 새마을호입니다.
크리스	사실, 대구로 연결되는 열차를 원하거든요. 통일호로 해야겠지요?
아가씨	네, 맞습니다. 다음 통일호는 3시에 떠나는 것이 있지만, 좀 지연됐습니다. 괜찮으시겠어요?
크리스	상관 없습니다. 그걸로 하지요, 뭐.

Dialogue Notes

4가지인데요.	*There are four types [and I am about to elaborate on them if you wish].* You will learn in more detail about the Imminent Elaboration form in -(으)ㄴ/-는데요 in Lesson Twenty-three. For now, just memorize this form as part of the dialogue.
뭐뭐 있습니까?	The reduplicated form 뭐뭐 here has the force of *What all?* Compare also 어디어디? *Where all?* 누구누구? *Who all?*, etc.

NOUN에 따라	*In accordance with NOUN, depending on NOUN.* Here: *depending on the speed it's going at . . .*
그걸로 하지요, 뭐.	*Well, then, I'll take that one.* or *Well, then, let's decide on that one.* The particle (으)로 (here with its ㄹ expanded or doubled in colloquial pronunciation) can replace the object particle 을~를 when the noun in question represents a deliberate choice from among two or more options.

Reading Passage

오늘은 어제보다 별로 바쁘지 않아서 샌디와 에릭이 시내로 놀러 나갔습니다. 샌디는 아무 영화나 보고 싶어했으며, 에릭은 한국 영화를 본 적이 없었기 때문에 한국 영화를 보고 싶어했습니다. 극장에는 기다리고 있는 사람들이 대단히 많았습니다. 신문을 읽고 있는 사람, 팝콘을 먹는 사람, 친구들과 이야기하는 사람, 워크맨을 듣고 있는 사람들로 극장은 몹시 복잡했습니다. 샌디와 에릭은 같이 로비에 있는 의자에 앉아서 영화가 끝나기를 기다렸습니다. 지루한 영화였지만 음악은 아름다웠습니다. 영화가 끝나고 2사람은 극장 근처에 있는 식당에 가서 맛있는 음식을 먹고 집에 돌아 오는 길에 노래방에도 들렀습니다.

Vocabulary

Verbs
<u>Verbs That Take Objects</u>

기억(을) 하-	remember
기억(이) 나-	remember
저를 기억하시겠어요?	Do you remember me?
기억이 안 나요.	I can't remember.
버-ㄹ-	earn, make (money)
부(ㅅ)-	pour it
조금 더 부어 주세요.	Please pour a little bit more.
너무 많이 붓지 마세요.	Don't pour too much.

부-르-	blow
바람이 많이 불어요.	The wind is blowing hard.
불어 보세요.	Try blowing on it.
뽑-	take out, extract
이를 하나 뽑아야 돼요.	I have to have one of my teeth pulled.
싸우-	quarrel, argue with [= 하고]
지(ㅅ)-	build (house); make (rice)
작년에 집을 지었어요.	They built a house last year.
미소(를) 지(ㅅ)-	smile
만호 씨는 미소를 짓고 있어요.	Manho is smiling.
지나가-	pass by
진찰(을) 하-	examine sb medically
원하-	want, desire, wish for
헤어지-	separate from, part with, split up with [= 하고]
여자친구랑 헤어졌어요.	I've broken up with my girlfriend.

Descriptive and/or Sensory Verbs

귀여w-	be cute
깊-	be deep
낮-	be low
높-	be high, tall [but not about people, which is 키가 커요]
높은 건물	a tall building
느리-	be slow
더러w-	be filthy, dirty
상관(이) 없-	not to care, not to be concerned; be of no concern
그건 나하고 상관 없어요.	That has nothing to do with me.
새로w-	be new
시끄러w-	be noisy, loud
얕-	be shallow
얕은 지식	shallow/superficial knowledge
얕은 개울	shallow stream, shallow brook
인기(가) 있- 〔pron. 인끼〕	be popular, well-liked

친하-	be close (e.g., with a friend)
저희 어머님은 저분하고 친하세요.	My mother is close to that person.
틀리-	be different; be wrong, incorrect
이게 틀렸어요.	This is wrong.
이것하고 저것은 틀립니다.	This is different from that. (The meaning "different" is considered substandard but is widespread.)

Intransitive Verbs (Processive Verbs That Cannot Take Objects)

〔-에〕 걸리-	catch (a sickness, disease)
암에 걸렸어요.	He [has] caught cancer.
나타나-	appear, put in an appearance; show up
낡-	get old (things)
낡았어요.	It's old.
남-	remain, be left over
돈이 얼마 안 남았어요.	There isn't much money left.
늙-	get old (people)
늙었어요.	he's old.
서-	stop, come to a stop
서 있을래요.	I prefer to stand.
연결(이) 되-	be/get connected with
연착(이) 되-	be/get delayed [train, plane, etc.]
비행기가 연착이 됐습니다.	The plane has been delayed.
지연(이) 되-	be/get delayed [time or date]
날짜가 지연됐습니다.	The date has been delayed.

Nouns

Trains and Train Travel

급행	express (train, bus)
급행버스	express bus
급행열차	express train
도착시간	arrival time
무궁화	Rose of Sharon (Korean national flower)
비둘기	pigeon

새마을	New Village (name of a rural development movement in the 1960s)
속도	speed
식당차	dining car
예약석	reserved seats
완행	stopper (train, bus); the local (train, bus)
완행버스	slow bus, stopping bus
완행열차	slow train, stopping train
2호선	Line 2 (on Seoul subway)
출발시간	departure time
통일	unification

People and Their Ways

나이 드신 분	old person, oldster [respectful]
늙은이	old person, oldster [somewhat disrespectful]
애인	steady girlfriend/boyfriend
어린 아이	small child, infant
어린이	a young one, child
젊은이	young person, a youth
중년	middle age
중년들	middle-aged people

Noun Modifiers

그런 NOUN	such a/that sort of NOUN
이런 NOUN	such a/that sort of NOUN
저런 NOUN	such a/that sort of NOUN
헌 NOUN	old/used NOUN
헌책방	secondhand bookstore

Other

로비	lobby
멋	(good) taste, elegance, style
멋지-	be stylish, cool, elegant
멋(이) 있-	be stylish, cool, elegant

무식하–	be ignorant
유식하–	be learned, knowledgeable, refined
바람	wind
바람(이) 불어요.	The wind blows.
병	sickness, disease
병(이) 나–	get sick
눈병 〔눈뼝〕	eye disease
샴푸	shampoo
생각	thought, idea
생각(이) 나–	it comes to mind; think of something
생각(이) 안 나요.	I can't remember.
갑자기 어머니(의) 생각이 났어요.	I suddenly thought of mother.
시절	time, era; days when . . . ; a time in the past
학생시절	one's student days
암	cancer
우리 할머니는 암으로 돌아가셨어요.	Our grandmother died of cancer.
옛날	old days, ancient times; in the past
옛날, 옛날에	Once upon a time . . .
오페라	opera
유행	something popular, something in vogue
유행하–	be popular, in vogue
유행이–	be the vogue, the fashion
작가	writer, author
지식	knowledge
NOUN 중(에서)	among NOUNs . . .

한국가수들 중에서 제일 인기가 있어요.

Is most popular among Korean pop singers.

최근	[as modifier] latest, most recent
최근 것	the latest, most recent thing
최근에	recently, lately
팝콘	popcorn

Adverbs

훨씬	much (. . . -er). by far

한국말은 중국말보다 훨씬 어렵습니다. Korean is much more difficult than Chinese.

Lesson Notes

19.1. The -(으)ㄴ Modifiers

Korean has a way to take a simple sentence and turn it into a clause that modifies some noun or noun phrase. This is done by changing the final verb to a modifier form and putting the sentence in front of the noun to be modified (which may or may not be lifted from the original sentence). This lesson contains a number of verbs and adjectives in two of the modifier forms.

One kind of modifier has the two-shape ending -(으)ㄴ, pronounced 은 after consonants and ㄴ after vowels (and added to the unextended form of L-extending vowel bases). You have already learned the forms 다른 *different*, the modifier form of the descriptive verb 다르- *be different,* and 지난 *last* (week, etc.), from 지나- *it passes, goes by.* Here are more examples of modifier forms.

After Consonant		After Vowel	
앉은	*sit*	만난	*meet*
좋은	*be good*	선	*stand*
적은	*be little/few*	기다린	*wait*
걸은	*walk*	본	*see*
찾은	*look for*	배운	*learn*
신은	*wear on feet*	한	*do*
입은	*wear*	준	*give*
벗은	*take off*	-인	*copula*
닫은	*close*	모른	*not know*
젊은	*be young*	논	*play* 〔노-ㄹ-〕
들은	*listen* 〔들-, 듣다〕	산	*live* 〔사-ㄹ-〕
도운	*help* 〔도w-〕	든	*lift* 〔드-ㄹ-〕
구운	*broil* 〔구w-〕	연	*opens* 〔여-ㄹ-〕
더운	*hot* 〔더w-〕	안	*know* 〔아-ㄹ-〕

This simple modifier has two different meanings, as follows.

A. With adjectives and the copula, it means *that is* ADJECTIVE, *that is* or *equals* NOUN.

| 큰 집 | *house that is large* |
| | (from 집이 커요 *the house is large*) |

| 은행원인 김 선생 | *the Mr. Kim who is a banker* |
| | (from 김 선생이 은행원이에요 *Mr. Kim is a banker.*) |

B. With processive (action) verbs, it has a past meaning—*that did* or *has done* **or** *that [someone] did* or *has done*.

| 떠난 사람 | *person who left* or *who has left* |
| | (from 사람이 떠났어요 *the person left*) |

| 쓴 편지 | *the letter that [I] wrote* or *have written* |
| | (from 편지를 썼어요 *wrote the letter*) |

Because the -(으)ㄴ modifier on a processive base already carries past tense meaning with it, it is impossible to put this modifier on a past base. Thus, one would never encounter an expression like *썼은 편지 for *the letter that [I] wrote* or *have written*.

19.2. The Processive Modifier -는

In addition to the simple forms just described, processive verbs have another modifier form made with the one-shape ending -는 (added directly to consonant and vowel bases and to the unextended form of L-extending vowel bases). You have already seen the forms 오는 *next* (week, etc.), literally *that is coming* from 오- *come*. Here are more examples.

Base	Gloss	Processive Modifier	Pronounced
만나-	*meet*	만나는	same
서-	*stand*	서는	same
기다리-	*wait for*	기다리는	same
보-	*look at*	보는	same

Base	Gloss	Processive Modifier	Pronounced
가-	*go*	가는	same
주-	*give*	주는	same
모르-	*not know*	모르는	same
아-ㄹ-	*know*	아는	same
드-ㄹ-	*lift; cost*	드는	same
들- (듣다)	*listen*	듣는	든는
받-	*get*	받는	반는
찾-	*look for*	찾는	찬는
벗-	*remove (garment)*	벗는	번는
넣-	*put into*	넣는	넌는
입-	*wear*	입는	임는
구w-	*broil*	굽는	굼는
먹-	*eat*	먹는	멍는
읽-	*read*	읽는	잉는
나(ㅅ)-	*get better*	낫는	난는

주의!

As its name suggests, the processive modifier ending in -는 is not used with adjectives (descriptive verbs)—only with processive verbs.

The verbs 있어요 and 없어요 are peculiar in that they sometimes behave like processive verbs (especially 있어요) and sometimes behave like descriptive verbs (especially 없어요). With respect to the processive modifiers, they both usually behave like processive verbs.

책이 있어요	*has a book*	→	있는 책	*the book that [one] has*
책이 없어요	*lacks a book*	→	없는 책	*the book that [one] lacks*

The processive modifier -는 has a present meaning—*that is doing* or *that (someone) is VERBing*:

먹는 사람   *the person who is eating*

읽는 신문   *the newspaper that [he] is reading*

After descriptive verbal nouns, 해요 functions as a descriptive verb and has only the modifier form 한.

(그) 사람이 유명해요   *the man is famous* →

유명한 사람
a man who is famous, i.e., *a famous man*

방이 깨끗해요   *the room is clean* →

깨끗한 방
a room that is clean, i.e., *a clean room*

After processive verbal nouns, 해요 functions as a processive verb and has the processive modifier form 하는 (*. . . that [one] does*) as well as the ordinary 한 (*. . . that [one] did*).

산보해요   *takes a walk*

산보하는 사람   *the person who is taking a walk*

산보한 사람   *the person who took a walk*

Notice that 해요 as an auxiliary verb may be either descriptive or processive, depending on the other words it is used with. When used with verbal nouns, 해요 takes whatever modifier forms would be appropriate to the grammar of the verbal noun. That is, each verbal noun is either descriptive (*being . . .*) or processive (*doing . . .*), just like each verb.

19.3. Modifier Clauses

Modifier clauses are used, in general, in the same way we use relative clauses in English. The only complication is the order of things: in Korean, the modifying clause always comes *before* the noun expression it modifies. In English, modifying verbs usually come after the word and modifying adjectives before; though in the case of adjectives we have a choice.

<u>English Order</u>

green **TREES**

TREES that are green

a nice, large **ROOM**

A **ROOM** that is nice and large

THE RICE I'm eating

THE MAN who is eating rice

<u>Korean Order</u>

green **TREES**

large-and-nice **ROOM**

I'm-eating-it **RICE**

is-eating-rice **MAN**

Any Korean sentence can be made into a modifier by using one of the modifier endings, and then placing a noun after it. You start with a complete sentence (long or short), put a modifier ending on the verb, and add a noun; **the new result is a noun expression**—no longer a sentence. The newly made noun expression then becomes a subject, or object, or whatever, just like any other noun expression.

> He
> Mr. Kim
> That nice lady
> The boy wearing the blue shirt
> The man who is sitting between Mr. Kim and Mrs. Pak

} is my friend.

Descriptive verbs are easy because for the most part they are just like English.

작은 집	*a small house*	←	집이 작아요
추운 날씨	*cold weather*	←	날씨가 추워요

The exceptions here are 있어요 and 없어요.

연필이 있는 사람	*the person **who has a pencil***
책이 없는 사람	*the person **who has no book***

Processive verbs are more complicated, because *(a)* they can be either present or past, *(b)* in Korean they come *before* the noun instead of in the usual English order *after* the noun; and *(c)* they can include direct objects. The noun modified may come from either the subject or the object of the modifying verb, but it is usually clear from the context which function is intended.

With modified noun as original subject:

밥을 먹는 사람   *the person who is eating*

밥을 먹은 사람   *the person who ate*

With modified noun as original object:

수진 씨가 닫는 문   *the door that Sujin is closing*

수진 씨가 닫은 문   *the door that Sujin closed*

Particles, of course, will make the meaning unambiguous.

김 선생님을 본 사람   *the person who saw Mr. Kim*

김 선생님이 본 사람   *the person Mr. Kim saw*

Now, here is an example of a normal sentence turned into a modifier twice: in the first switch, the modified noun is the subject of the modifier clause; in the second, it is the object.

1. 그 사람이 도서관에서 책을 빌렸어요.
  That person borrowed a book from the library.

2. 도서관에서 책을 빌린 (그) 사람이 누구였어요?
  *Who was the **person who borrowed** a book from the library?*

3. 그 사람이 도서관에서 빌린 책이 무슨 책이었어요?
  *What was **the book** that person **borrowed** from the library?*

Instead of coming from the subject or object of the underlying sentence, the noun modified may be the place at/from/to which the action applies, or the time, or some other ingredient of the situation.

4. 그 사람이 책을 빌린 도서관은 무슨 도서관이었어요?
  *Which **library** was it **that he borrowed** the book **from**?*

5. 그 사람이 도서관에서 책을 빌린 날은 수요일이었어요.
  ***The day that he borrowed** the book from the library was Wednesday.*

Here are some more sentences illustrating the use of modifiers. The English part of the sentence that becomes a modifier phrase when translated into Korean has been put in bold face for you to recognize it easily.

6. 흐린 날은 해가 나지 않아요.
    The sun doesn't come out on **cloudy days**.

7. 그 사람은 저의 친한 친구에요.
    He is my **close friend**.

8. 비싼 물건도 팔고 싼 물건도 팔아요.
    They sell both **expensive things** *and* **cheap things**.

9. 진호 씨의 집은 크고 좋은 집이에요.
    Chinho's house is **a nice large house**.

10. 비싸지 않은 것만 샀어요.
    I bought only **things that weren't expensive**.

11. 진호 씨가 본 사람을 나도 봤어요.
    I, too, saw **the man Chinho saw**.

12. 맥주 마시고 싶은 사람 있어요?
    Is there **anybody** *here [= a person]* **who wants to drink beer**?

13. 그 예쁜 치마를 입은 아이가 누구에요?
    Who is **that child who is wearing a pretty skirt?**

19.4. Postmodifier Patterns

Once you have mastered producing modifier forms of different types, you are well on your way to learning a major chunk of Korean structure—postmodifier patterns. By taking various special nouns and placing them after different types of modifier, Korean creates a variety of sentence patterns. Usually, if you know the meaning of the special noun after the modifier (called a postmodifier because it is specially privileged to appear after certain modifiers and render a new grammatical pattern), you can guess at the meaning of the new pattern. We show you two such patterns below.

19.4.1. Postmodifier Clauses with 길: *on the way to . . .*

The word 길 means *road, way, street.*

14. 길에서 놀지 말아요!
    Don't play in the street!

Following the processive modifier –는 form of verbs of motion like 가– *go* or 오– *come*, or other combinations based on these verbs, 길 renders a new pattern meaning *on the way*.

15. A. 어디에 가세요?
         Where are you going?

     B. 은행에 가는 길이에요.
         I'm on my way to the bank.

16. 학교에서 돌아오는 길에 장 선생님을 만났어요.
     On my way back from school I met Mr. Chang.

17. 기차역에 가는 길에 이 편지를 좀 부쳐 주실래요?
     Would you mind posting this letter for me on your way to the train station?

19.4.2. Postmodifier Clauses for *Ever, Never, Sometimes*

The nouns 일 and 적 both mean *event, act, experience*. The phrases 일이 있어요 and 적이 있어요 mean *the event* or *experience exists*. The phrases 일이 없어요 and 적이 없어요 mean *the event* or *experience does not exist*.

With modifiers from processive verbs, there are four uses to which you can put these expressions.

19.4.2.1. Postmodifier Clauses Using –(으)ㄴ for Past Tense

In combination with –(으)ㄴ, one gets a pattern that denotes *has had the experience, has (ever) done something*. This pattern is particularly compatible with the Exploratory Pattern in –어 보–, and almost always occurs in combination with it: –어 본 일(이) 있–/–없–, –어 본 적(이) 있–/–없.

A.
> -(으)ㄴ 일이 있어요, -(으)ㄴ 적이 있어요
> *has ever done*

18. 한국에 가 본 적이 있어요?

     Have you ever gone/been to Korea?
     [Literally: Does having-gone-to-Korea exist? or
      Is there such a thing as (your) having gone to Korea? or
      Has it ever happened that you went to Korea?]

Note that in this pattern it is usual to use the auxiliary 봐요, so the idea of having done something for the experience—in order to try it or check it out—is incorporated.

19. 네, 한국에 가 본 적이 있어요.
    Yes, I've been to Korea.

B.
┌───┐
│ -(으)ㄴ 일이 없어요, -(으)ㄴ 적이 없어요 │
│   │
│   *has never done*   │
└───┘

20. 한국에 가 본 일이 없어요?

    Haven't you ever been to Korea?
    [Literally: Does having-gone-to-Korea not exist? or
    Isn't there such a thing as (your) having gone to Korea? or
    Hasn't it ever happened that you went to Korea?]

21. 한국에 가 본 일이 없어요.
    I've never been to Korea.

19.4.2.2. Postmodifier Clauses using –는 for Non-Past Tense

In combination with –는, one gets a pattern that denotes *sometimes ("ever") has the experience, sometimes/occasionally ("ever") does something*: -는 일(이) 있-/-없-, -는 적(이) 있-/-없.

C.
┌───┐
│   -는 일이 있어요, -는 적이 있어요   │
│   │
│   *ever does; sometimes does*   │
└───┘

22. 혼자서 극장에 가는 일이 있어요?
    Do you ever go to the theater by yourself?
    [Literally: Do events of going by yourself exist? Does it ever happen that you go to the theater by yourself?]

23. 혼자서 극장에 가는 일이 있어요.
    I sometimes go to the theater by myself.
    [Literally: Events of going to the theater by myself exist. It (sometimes) happens that I go to the theater by myself.]

D.

> ### -는 일이 없어요, -는 적이 없어요
> *never does*

24. 혼자서 극장에 가는 일이 없어요?
     Don't you ever go to the theater by yourself?
     [Literally: Does going-to-the-theater by yourself not exist? Does it never happen that you go to the theater by yourself?]

25. 혼자서 극장에 가는 일이 없어요.
     I never go to the theater by myself.
     [Literally: Going-to-the-theater by myself does not exist. It never happens that I go to the theater by myself.]

Notice that 있어요 and 없어요 are kept constant through these expressions, letting the time be expressed in the modifiers. But you can change the tense of the final verb and get expressions like these.

26. 본 일이 있었어요   *had (once) seen*

27. 본 일이 없었어요   *had never seen*

28. 보는 일이 있었어요   *would occasionally see,*
                               had been seeing (at times)

29. 보는 일이 없었어요   *never used to see, hadn't been seeing (ever)*

And you can use the future-presumptive form in -겠-, especially with tentative meaning.

30. 그런 것을 본 일이 없겠지요.
     I don't suppose you've ever seen such a thing.

If you want to make the expression honorific, you can make either or both verbs honorific.

31. a.   편지를 쓰시는 일이 있어요?   or
     b.   편지를 쓰는 일이 있으세요?   or
     c.   편지를 쓰시는 일이 있으세요?
          Do you ever write letters?

However, most speakers nowadays seem to prefer to keep just the final auxiliary honorific, i.e., option (b).

32. 중국 음식을 먹어 본 적이 없어요?
     Haven't you ever eaten Chinese food?

33. 그 대학에서 공부한 일이 있어요.
     I've studied at that college.

34. 한국 노래를 들어 본 적이 있어요?
     Have you ever heard/listened to a Korean song?

35. 소주를 마셔 본 적이 있어요?
     Have you ever tried [drinking] soju?

36. 우리 남편은 한번도 병이 난 일이 없어요.
     My husband has never once been ill.

37. 편지도 써 본 일이 없어서 작가가 못 되겠어요.
     As I've never even tried writing letters, I'll never be a writer.

38. 그런 곳에 가 본 일이 있어요?
     Have you been to such a place?

19.5. The Retrospective Modifier -던

The retrospective modifier is made by attaching the one-shape ending –던 to simple bases. Verbs with this ending usually have the following basic meaning: . . . *that has been [doing so-and-so]*, or, in the past, . . . *that had been [doing so-and-so]*. That is to say, the retrospective modifier –던 is the modifier equivalent to the pattern –고 있었어요 *was VERBing*. The following two sentences show the contrast between these two constructions.

39. 그 사람이 여기서 신문을 읽고 있었어요.
     He was reading the newspaper here.

40. 여기서 신문을 읽던 사람
     The person who was reading or *had been reading the newspaper here.*

It is also possible, with little or no change in meaning, to attach –던 to a past base.

41. 여기서 신문을 읽었던 사람
     The person who was reading or *had been reading the newspaper here.*

For those speakers who report a difference in nuance between plain base + –던 and past base + –던, the difference is usually that the latter case is perceived as implying more remoteness in the past. And a growing number of speakers appear to be using –었던 as an equivalent to just past modifier – (으) ㄴ.

Here are some more examples of the retrospective modifier.

42. 오랫동안 만나고 싶던 사람이 오늘 왔어요.
    Someone I've been wanting to see for a long time has come (or is here) today.

43. 그 사람이 바로 제가 말씀 드렸던 사람이에요.
    He is precisely the person I was telling you about.

44. 김 선생님은 우리 학교에서 한국말을 가르치시던 분이에요.
    Mr. Kim is the one who used to teach Korean in our school.

45. 친구들하고 같이 놀던 시절이 지금도 생각나요.
    I can still remember the time I used to play with my friends.

46. 어제 하던 일을 아직까지 마치지 못 했어요.
    I still haven't been able to finish the work I was doing yesterday.

47. 어제 마시던 술이 좀 남았어요.
    There is some of the booze left which we were drinking yesterday.

주의!

Some Koreans say –든 for –던, and you may also see this spelling.

19.6. The Particle 보다

Observe the following example.

48. 이것보다 더 비싼 옷
    clothes more expensive than these

The particle 보다 means *more than* or *rather than*. Most often, 보다 is not translated next to the noun it follows but instead shows up as the modifier of an adjective elsewhere in the sentence—either the suffix *-er*, or the word *more*.

49. 이것은 그것보다 커요.
    This is bigger than that.
    *[= This thing, **more than** that thing, is big.]*

50. 여름이 겨울보다 좋아요.
    Summer is nicer than winter.
    *[= Summer, **more** or **rather than** winter, is nice.]*

51.　오늘은 어제보다 시간이 많이 있어요.
    *I have **more** time today **than** yesterday.*
    *[= Today, **more than** yesterday, I have lots of time.]*

52.　미국에는 영국보다 자동차가 훨씬 많아요.
    *There are many **more** cars in America **than** in England.*
    *[= **More than** in England, there are many cars in America.]*

53.　이 상점은 저 상점보다 값이 싸요.
    *Things are **less** expensive in this store **than** in that one.*
    *[= In this store **more than** that one, prices are low.]*

54.　오늘은 어제보다 바람이 더 불고 추워요.
    *It's **colder** and **windier** today than it was yesterday.*
    *[= Today **more than** yesterday is cold and windy.]*

Sometimes 보다 is followed by the particle 도 for emphasis.

55.　홍차보다도 커피가 먹고 싶어요.
    I'd rather have coffee (even more) than tea.

56.　산보다도 높고 바다보다도 깊어요.
    It is taller than the mountains and deeper than the sea.

And sometimes 보다 is followed by the particle 은 ~ 는 for extra contrast.

57.　수진 씨보다는 내가 바쁘지요.
    I'm certainly busier than you, Sujin.

Finally, the adverb 훨씬 is used to express that something is *way more . . . than, . . .er than by far, much . . .er than*, etc.

58.　밴쿠버는 런던보다 훨씬 아름답지요.
    Of course, Vancouver is far more beautiful than London.

19.7. Words for *Young* and *Old*

To say someone is *old* you use the expression 나이가 드셨어요 or 연세가 많으세요. Their modifier forms are 나이 드신 and 연세가 많으신. All these expressions are more polite and respectful than the more blunt equivalents 늙었어요, 늙은 and the related expression 늙은이 or 늙은 사람 for *an old person, an oldster.*

To say *someone is (still) young, though an adult*, you use the expression 젊어요; the modifier form is 젊은, and 젊은이 or 젊은 사람 *a young person, a young adult*. To refer to a child as being young you use a different expression 어려요 (어리-). The modifier form is 어린, so 어린이 or 어린아이 means *a young one, a child*.

But when you want to say someone *is older* or *younger than* someone else, you do not ordinarily use these expressions, they are, as it were, absolute—not relative. When you want to speak of relative age, you use the word for age (나이).

59.　나이가 위에요 (많아요)　　　　*the age is above (= higher)*,

60.　나이가 아래에요 (적어요)　　　　*the age is below (= lower)*.

So one can ask:

61.　누가 〔나이가〕 위에요? (누가 나이가 더 많아요?)
　　Who is the older (or oldest)?

To say *He is older or younger **than** me* you have to use the particle 보다 *than*.

62.　그 사람이 나보다 〔나이가〕 아래에요.
　　That person is younger than me.

There are several ways to say *How old are you?*

63.　a.　몇 살이에요?
　　　　lit.: *How many age-years is it?*

　　b.　몇 살 먹었어요?
　　　　lit.: *How many age-years have you eaten up?*

　　c.　몇 살 됐어요?
　　　　lit.: *How many age-years have you become?*

　　d.　연세(가) 어떻게 되세요?
　　　　lit.: *How is your esteemed age becoming?*

The word *old* has two meanings in English; we have been talking about the meaning that is the opposite of *young* and has to do with people. But *old* is also the opposite of *new* and can have to do with things as well as people. In that case, the Korean word is 낡아요; the modifier form is 낡은, so that 낡은 것 means *old things, things that have been around for a long time*. But instead of 낡은 you often find 헌 *that is worn (out) with age*, the modifier form from 헐어요 *gets worn (out), suffers from age and use*.

64.	헌 것	old (used) things
65.	헌 자동차	an old car
66.	헌 책	used book

The opposite of 헌 is 새 *new*.

67.	새 것	new things
68.	새 자동차	a new car
69.	새 옷	new clothes

But 새, like 이 *this*, functions as a pre-noun; to say *it is new* you have to use a special form 새로워요 (from 새로w-, dictionary form 새롭다); or you can say 새 것이에요 *it is a new one*.

19.8. Modifiers with 것 : *the fact of . . .ing; . . .ing*

A processive modifier in –는 plus 것 usually means *the act of doing so-and-so* or *the fact that one does so-and-so*.

70. 비가 오는 것
the fact that it's raining

71. 신문을 읽는 것
the fact that he's reading the newspaper

The plain modifier –(으)ㄴ plus 것 similarly means *the fact that one did* (processive) or *that it is* (descriptive).

72. 비가 온 것
the fact that it rained

73. 돈이 많은 것
the fact that one has lots of money

These expressions are used in sentences just like other noun expressions. In particular, you will find them as the object of 봐요 *sees (that)*, 알아요 *knows that*, 들어요 *hears/understands that*, and similar verbs. As the subject of 쉬워요, 어려워요, 좋아요, 싫어요 and the like, modifier plus 것 is sometimes the equivalent of the nominalizer ending in –기.

74. 피아노 치는 것이 좋아요. = 피아노 치기(가) 좋아요.
I like to play the piano.

75. 한국말로 말하는 것이 쉬워요.   =   한국말로 말하기(가) 쉬워요.
It is easy to speak in Korean.

And, in addition to the various special meanings shown in this section, 것 can have its usual meaning *one*, *thing* after modifiers, so that 보는 것 has not only the meanings *fact of seeing*, *fact that one sees*, etc., but also *the one who sees* and *the thing [one] sees*, etc.

> 주의!
>
> In all its meanings, 것 can always be abbreviated to 거.

Here are some more examples.

76. 김 선생님이 공원에서 신문을 읽는 것을 봤어요.
I saw Mr. Kim reading a newspaper in the park.

77. 비가 오는 것을 보고 있어요.
He's watching it rain.

78. 선생님이 저 아저씨하고 한국말로 이야기하는 것을 들었어요.
I heard you talking to that man over there in Korean.

79. 애기가 자는 것을 몰랐지요.
Of course, I had no idea that the child was sleeping.

80. 나는 그 작가가 부인이랑 헤어진 것도 알았지요.
I found out that writer has split up with his wife, you see.

81. 이 책값은 어머니가 옷을 하나 사는 것의 반밖에 안 돼요.
This book costs no more than half what it costs mother to buy one piece of clothing.

82. 우리 애들이 그 집에서 노는 것이 싫어요.
I don't like my children playing at that house.

83. 아버님은 우리가 운동하는 것을 보셨어요.
Father saw us playing (at our sports).

Exercises

Exercise 1: Modifying Subjects

Here are ten two-sentence groups. Each group of two has the same subject. You are to combine the sentences into one in such a way that the first is incorporated into the second as a modifier. For example, the first pair mean: *The person is reading a magazine in the next room. When did that person get here?* Your job is to combine these so that they mean: *When did the person who is reading a magazine in the next room get here?* Your sentence should be: 옆 방에서 잡지를 보는 사람이 언제 왔어요?

1. 그 사람이 옆방에서 잡지를 봐요. 그 사람은 언제 왔어요?
2. 그분이 여기서 영어를 가르쳐요. 그분은 영국사람이 아니에요.
3. 그 친구가 날마다 술집에 가요. 그 친구는 공부를 못 해요.
4. 그 자동차가 커요. 그 자동차는 진호 씨 것이에요?
5. 그 집이 크고 좋아요. 그 집은 수진 씨 집이지요?
6. 그 아이들이 라디오를 들어요. 그 아이들은 우리 조카에요.
7. 그 애기가 어려요. 그 애기는 우유만 먹어요.
8. 그 학교가 멀어요. 그 학교는 좋지 않아요.
9. 그 사람이 담배를 피우고 있어요. 그 사람은 우리 영미 씨에요.
10. 그 사람들이 한국에 살아요. 그 사람들은 친절해요.
11. 아까 열차가 도착했어요. 그 열차는 급행열차였어요.
12. 지금 노래를 듣고 있어요. 그 노래는 10년 전에 유행했어요.

Exercise 2: Modifying Objects

Here again are some two-sentence groups. Combine each group into one sentence in such a way that the first sentence becomes the modifier of the direct object of the second. Your first sentence, for example, should be: 제가 그 일을 한 사람을 만났어요. *I saw the man who did that work.*

1. 그 사람이 그 일을 했어요. 제가 그 사람을 만났어요.
2. 아이가 노래를 불렀어요. 제가 그 아이를 찾고 있어요.
3. 넥타이가 책상 위에 있어요. 제가 그 넥타이를 매고 싶어요.
4. 모자가 책상 위에 있었어요. 제가 그 모자를 썼어요.
5. 그 고양이가 예뻐요. 제가 그 고양이가 보고 싶어요.

6. 그 영국 사람이 한국말을 배워요. 제가 그 영국 사람을 만났어요.
7. 그 음식이 맛 없어요. 우리가 그 음식을 먹은 적이 있어요.
8. 그 노래가 재미있어요. 친구가 그 노래를 불렀어요.
9. 그 가수가 유명해요. 그 가수를 한번 만나고 싶어요.
10. 어머니가 요즘 이 책을 보세요. 나도 그 책을 봤어요.
11. 제가 문을 닫았어요. 그 문을 열어 주시겠어요?
12. 제가 컴퓨터를 샀어요. 그 컴퓨터를 쓰실래요?
13. 이모가 그 영화를 좋아해요. 이모부도 그 영화를 좋아해요.
14. 선생님이 그 사람을 만나셨어요. 그 사람을 제가 잘 알아요.
15. 형님이 넥타이를 매고 있어요. 그 넥타이를 나도 한번 매 봤어요.
16. 아버지가 저한테 선물을 주셨어요. 그 선물을 보셨어요?
17. 우리가 그 음식을 먹지 않아요. 그 음식을 개한테 줘도 좋아요?
18. 제가 노래를 불렀어요. 그 노래를 선생님도 아세요?
19. 아들이 돈을 썼어요. 그 돈을 누구한테 받았지요?
20. 우리가 한국에서 매일 그 음악을 들었어요. 그 음악을 기억하세요?

Exercise 3: More Practice with Modifiers

Now combine the two sentences so that the first becomes the modifier of the same noun in the second. Number 1, for example, has the subject *theater*; make it into a modifier for 극장 (in the phrase 극장에) of the second. Your completed sentence should be: 가까운 극장에 가고 싶어요. *I want to go to the theater nearby.*

1. 그 극장이 가까워요. 그 극장에 가고 싶어요.
2. 그 영화가 슬퍼요. 그 영화를 보고 싶지 않아요.
3. 도서관이 학교 옆에 있어요. 저는 그 도서관에서 주말마다 잡지를
   읽어요.
4. 그 학생이 한국에서 왔어요. 우리가 그 학생과 같이 차를 1잔 마셨어요!
5. 그 사람이 은행에서 일을 해요. 저는 그 사람의 집에서 살아요.
6. 학생이 어제 저한테 책을 줬어요. 저는 그 학생하고 같이 이야기하고
   있었어요.
7. 김 교수님이 우리 집에서 살고 계세요. 저는 김 교수님한테 생나는 선물을
   드리겠어요.
8. 어린이가 더러운 옷을 입고 있어요. 그 어린이한테 돈을 주고 싶었어요.
9. 그 수영장은 물이 너무 깊어요. 그 수영장에서는 수영하고 싶지 않아요.
10. 애인은 아주 멋져요. 저도 애인을 만나고 싶어요.

11. 술집이 너무 시끄러웠어요. 우리가 그 술집에서 나왔어요.
12. 저 아주머니가 책을 봐요. 그 책은 한국말 책일거에요.
13. 제가 자동차를 샀어요. 그 자동차는 크고 좋아요.
14. 제가 책을 샀어요. 그 책은 재미 있어서 좋아요.
15. 우리 아이가 옷을 벗었어요. 그 옷은 어디 있어요?
16. 우리 아들이 새 신을 신었어요. 그 신은 참 예쁘지요?
17. 제가 아까 그것을 마셨어요. 그것은 물이 아니었지요!
18. 가수가 돈을 벌어요. 그 돈은 많지요?
19. 수업에 들어가기 전에 제가 책을 읽었어요. 그 책은 한국말 책이었어요.
20. 제가 자동차를 사고 싶어요. 그 자동차는 값이 너무 비싸서, 사지
    못 하겠어요.
21. 제가 날마다 지하철을 타요. 그 지하철은 2호선이에요.

Exercise 4: Yet More Modifiers

These sentences, like the preceding ones, have a noun in common. Combine the sentences in such a way that the first sentence modifies the shared noun of the second. The first one will be: 제가 잡지를 보는 도서관은 가까워요. *The library where [at which] I read magazines is nearby.*

1. 제가 매일 도서관에서 잡지를 봐요. 그 도서관은 가까워요.
2. 장 선생님이 그 과를 가르쳤어요. 그 과부터 시작합시다!
3. 제가 어젯밤에 은행원을 만났어요. 그 은행원 집에서 학생 1명이 살고
   있어요.
4. 오빠가 오늘 아침에 학교를 지나갔어요. 그 학교에 제가 다녀요.
5. 제가 그 가수를 좋아해요. 그 가수한테 편지를 써 봤어요.
6. 제가 날마다 학교에 가요. 그 학교는 멀어요.
7. 우리가 그 집에 살아요. 그 집은 작아요.
8. 사장님이 그 사람한테 전화를 걸었어요. 그 사람은 누구였지요?
9. 우리가 교회에서 결혼을 했어요. 그 교회를 한 선생님이 구경하시겠어요?
10. 수진 씨가 그 집에 살아요. 나는 그 집을 잘 알아요.
11. 제가 일요일마다 성당에 나가요. 그 성당을 서 선생님이 못 찾으셨어요?
12. 제가 수진 씨를 음악회에서 만났어요. 그 음악회는 서울에서 열렸어요.
13. 제가 그 대학에서 공부를 해요. 그 대학을 구경하시겠어요?

Exercise 5: Retrospective Modifiers

Each of the following items contains two sentences. Make the first into a retrospective modifier and combine the sentence; then translate. For example, the first will be: 어제 왔던 사람이 또 왔어요. *The person who was here yesterday has come again.*

1. 어제 사람이 왔어요. 그 사람이 또 왔어요.
2. 1시간 수진 씨가 공원에서 신문을 읽고 있었어요. 그 사람이 아직도 신문을 읽고 있어요.
3. 어제 일을 했어요. 그 일을 아직까지 마치지 못 했어요.
4. 날마다 어떤 사람이 우리 집 앞으로 지나가요. 그 사람이 오늘은 안 지나가요.
5. 지난 주에 김 선생님이 이 교실에서 강의하셨어요. 그 김 선생님이 오늘은 안 나타나셨어요.
6. 친구가 오랫동안 보고 싶었어요. 그 친구를 오늘 드디어 만났어요.
7. 어제 저녁에 밥을 먹었어요. 그 밥이 아직도 남아 있어요.
8. 대학 시절 때 그 여자하고 친했어요. 아직도 그 여자를 가끔 만나고 있어요.
9. 그 오페라는 100년 전에 인기가 있었어요. 그 오페라는 오늘까지도 인기가 있어요.

Exercise 6: English to Korean Translation

Translate the following sentences into Korean.

1. Have you ever been to Korea?
2. I once got sick in Japan.
3. Haven't you ever argued with your boyfriend?
4. Have you ever tried sending a letter to Libya?
5. I've never had a tooth pulled.
6. Sometimes I attend church.
7. Sometimes I fight with my girlfriend.
8. Let's post this letter.
9. We needn't sell those old books, but we should buy some new ones.
10. I hate brushing my teeth and combing my hair.

Exercise 7: Korean to English Translation

Translate the following sentences into English.

1. 머리를 맥주로 감아 본 적이 있으세요?
2. 지난 달에 유럽 여행을 떠난 조카는 병이 났지만,
    곧 나아질겁니다.
3. 그런 비싸고 시끄러운 술집에는 가고 싶지 않아요.
4. 그 노래를 부르는 가수는 키가 크고 멋있는 여자에요.
5. 저기 앉아 있는 남자는 옛날에 인기가 있었던 영화배우입니다.
6. 내 친구하고 결혼한 여자는 상당히 귀여워요.
7. 나는 그 친구하고 상당히 친해도 가끔 싸우는 적이 있지요.
8. 올해에는 돈을 좀 빌려야겠습니다.
9. 그 책을 쓴 사람한테 편지를 써봤어요.
10. 서울에서 구경하셨던 대학들은 유명하고 좋은 학교들이었습니까?
11. 20년 전에 유행했던 옷을 입고 있는 저 여자를 보세요. 이상하지요?
12. 한국에는 여름에 바람이 많이 붑니까?

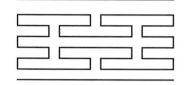 # Lesson 20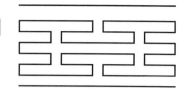

REVIEW 3

Summary of Lesson Notes

20.1. Pattern Review

20.1.1. The -고 Form

SIMPLE BASE + -고

    A. *VERBs and . . .*
    B. *having VERBed, then . . .*

1.   You've just arrived at a friend's house:

    친구의 어머니: 먹을 거 줄까?

    대답: 아니오, 밥 먹고 왔습니다.

2.   오늘은 바람도 불고 해도 났어요.

PAST BASE + -고

    VERBed and . . .

3.   그 사람은 영국에서 2년 살았고 독일에서도 살아 본 적이 있어요.

will VERB and . . .

4.   나는 독일에 가 봐야 되겠고, 지영 씨는 프랑스에 가 봐야 되겠어요.

20.1.2. Infinitive -어/-아 + 서

A. CAUSE and EFFECT

5.   연 선생님은 노래를 잘 부르셔서 여자들이 좋아해요.

B. SEQUENCE, usually with VERB of MOTION

6.   이번 주말에 백화점에 가서 치마하고 다른 선물을 삽시다.

20.1.3. Infinitive -어/-아 + 해요: Descriptive → Processive

1st and 2nd person

좋아요, 싫어요, 싶어요, 더워요, 부러워요

3rd/any person

좋아해요, 싫어해요, 싶어해요, 더워해요, 부러워해요

7.   나는 한국 술이 좋아요.
      나는 한국 술을 좋아해요.

8.   나는 가고 싶지 않아요.
      어머니는 가고 싶어하세요.

20.1.4. Infinitive -어/-아 in Compound Verbs

With verbs of motion				
올라요	ascends	→	올라가요	goes up
내려요	descends	→	내려와요	comes down
걸어요	walks	→	걸어가요	goes on foot

With 있어요 for resultant states				
앉아요	sits (bum in motion!) vs.		앉아 있어요	is seated
누워요	reclines	vs.	누워 있어요	is prone
서요	stands	vs.	서 있어요	is standing

20.1.5. Exploratory Pattern in -어/-아 + 봐요

묻다, 물어요	asks	→	물어 봐요
			asks [and sees what kind of response one gets]
먹어요	eats	→	먹어 봐요
			tries it to see what it tastes like
해요	does it	→	한번 해 보세요
			Give it a try once.

20.1.6. Infinitive -어/-아 + 줘요: *does the favor of VERBing*

9.	와요	→	와 주셔서 감사합니다.
10.	내가 할게요	→	내가 해 줄게요.

20.1.7. Unfinished Sentences and Afterthoughts with -서요 and -고요

11. 석준 씨랑 석범 씨는 왔어요. 석헌 씨도 오고요.

12. A. 어제 동창회에 왜 안 왔어요?
    B. 시간이 없어서요.

20.1.8. *So . . . I could die* with -어서 죽겠어요

13. 요즘 날씨가 무더워서 죽겠어요.

14. 눈이 아파서 죽겠어요.

15. 친구가 약속을 잘 어겨서 죽겠어요.

20.1.9. *Concerning . . .* with -에 대해서 / -에 관해서

16. 컴퓨터에 대해서는 잘 모릅니다.

17. 교수님이 한국경제에 관해서 설명해 주셨습니다.

20.1.10. . . . , *you see?* with -거든요

18. A. 술을 왜 그렇게 많이 사 왔어요?
    B. 대학교 선배들이 놀러 오거든요.

19. A. 왜 그렇게 피곤해 보여요?
    B. 어제 하루종일 아르바이트를 했거든요.

20.1.11. Any Base + -기 때문에 *Because*

| SIMPLE BASE | + -기 때문에 | *because does/is* |

20. 그 다방이 가깝기 때문에 거기서 친구들을 자주 만나요.

| PAST BASE | + -기 때문에 | *because did/was* |

21. 내가 오늘 아침에 청소했기 때문에 부엌이 깨끗하지요.

| FUTURE BASE | + -기 때문에 | *because will do/will be* |
(theoretically possible, but not often used)

20.1.12. Plain Base + -기 전에 *Before*

22. 숙박부에 기입하시기 전에 이 서류도 좀 보십시오.

23. 식사를 하기 전에 손을 먼저 씻고 와요.

24. 아침을 먹기 전에 꼭 세수를 합니다.

20.1.13. Plain Base + -기 시작하- *Begin to . . .*

25. 바람이 많이 불기 시작했어요. 비도 좀 오고요.

26. 요즘 우리 큰 아들은 면도를 하기 시작했어요.

27. 보통 오전 8시부터 길이 막히기 시작해요.

20.1.14. Infinitive -어/-아 + 야 *only if*

28. 해야 해요, 해야 돼요

29. 가 봐야 알지요.

30. 잠깐만 기다리세요. 옷을 갈아 입어야겠어요.

31. 물이 깨끗해야 빨래를 잘 할 수 있지요.

20.1.15. Infinitive -어/-아 + 도 *even though*

PLAIN INFINITIVE + 도 *even though does/is*

32. 돈을 5년동안 모아도 그 집을 못 살 거에요.

33. 공원이 가까워도 자주 안 가요.

34. 운동을 아무리 많이 해도 아직 뚱뚱해요.

PAST INFINITIVE + 도 *even though did/was*

35. 김 선생님 연구실에 매일 갔어도 못 만나 뵈었어요.

36. 시험 문제들이 대단히 쉬웠어도 다 못 풀었어요.

37. 방을 3번이나 청소했어도 방이 너무 더러워서 소용 없었어요.

Granting Permission

해도 좋아요(?), 해도 돼요(?), 해도 괜찮아요(?)

안 해도　　　좋아요(?) or 괜찮아요(?) or 돼요(?)

하지 않아도　좋아요(?) or 괜찮아요(?) or 돼요(?)

38. A.　이 매운 음식을 안 먹어도 돼요?
　　 B.　네, 먹지 않아도 돼요.

39. A.　내일까지 숙제를 끝내도 괜찮아요?
　　 B.　네, 괜찮아요.

Special Max-Min Expressions

40. 늦어도 3시까지 갈게요.

41. 적어도 3만 원은 주셔야 돼요.

42. 일러도 아침 7시가 돼야 올 수 있을 거에요.

20.1.16. Infinitive -어/-아 + 져요(지-) *gets ADJ . . . ,* *becomes ADJ . . .*

DESCRIPTIVE BASE + -어/-아 + 져요

더워요 → 더워져요

하고 싶어요 → 하고 싶어져요

43. 시끄러운 음악을 들으면 피곤해져요.

44. 여름에는 6월부터 날씨가 점점 더워져요.

45. 한국에 가서 한국말을 배우고 싶어졌어요.

20.1.17. BASE + -(으)ㄹ 수(가) 있어요/없어요 *can do/cannot do*

46. 다음 달까지 해 주실 수 있겠어요?

47. 주말에 가야 김 선생님을 만날 수 있을 거에요.

48. 그런 책은 한국에서 살 수 없지요.

20.1.18. ANY BASE + -(으)며 *and [at the same time]*

49. 공부를 잘 하는 학생들은 못하는 학생들을 도와주며 가르쳐야 됩니다.

50. 어제는 따뜻했으며 바람도 안 불었습니다.

51. 내일은 흐리겠으며 비도 오겠습니다.

52. 이 도시는 운동장도 많으며 공원도 많습니다.

20.1. 19. *Decides/agrees to do* with -기로 하-

53.　새해에는 좀 더 즐겁게 살기로 했습니다.

54.　앞으로 담배도 술도 안 하기로 했습니다.

55.　부모님한테 잘 해 드리기로 했습니다.

20.1. 20. *Through (the agency of)* with 통해(서)

56.　우리 회사는 머피 사장님을 통해서 그 무역회사하고 연결이 됐습니다.

57.　수지 씨의 도착시간을 누구를 통해서 알았어요?

58.　오페라표도 호텔을 통해서 예약할 수가 있어요?

20.1.21. Modifiers: The Modifier -(으) ㄴ

DESCRIPTIVE BASE	+ -(으) ㄴ	= *that is ADJ*

PROCESSIVE BASE	+ -(으) ㄴ	= *that did*

59.　이 책은 유명한 작가가 쓴 것이에요.

60.　매운 음식을 잘 못 먹어요.

61.　그 귀여운 아기는 브라운 선생님 아들이지요?

62.　네, 그리고 그 아름다운 여자는 사모님이고요.

63.　어제 밤에 보신 영화는 재미 있었어요?

64.　아침에 찾아오신 분은 이상한 넥타이를 매고 있었어요.

65.　나는 키가 큰 남자가 좋아요.

20.1.22. Modifiers: The Processive Modifier -는

| PROCESSIVE BASE | + -는 | = *that is doing* |

| BASES 있- + 없- | + -는 | = *that is staying/exists; that is lacking* |

66. 저기서 운동하는 사람들이 학생들이지요?

67. 공부를 늘 하는 학생은 시험을 잘 봐요.

68. 바람이 많이 부는 날은 아기하고 같이 나가지 않아요.

69. 병이 자주 나는 사람은 일찍 죽어요.

70. 있는 사람들은 없는 사람들을 도와줘야 돼요.

71. 나는 돈이 없어도 재미있는 남자가 좋아요.

20.1.23. Post-modifier Clauses

1 | VERB OF MOTION + -는 + 길에 *on the way* |

72. 교회에 가는 길에 고등학교 동창을 만났습니다.

73. 집에 들어가는 길에 차에 기름을 넣어야 합니다.

74. 공항에 나가는 길에 차 사고가 났습니다.

75. 집으로 돌아오는 길에 이발을 할게요.

76. 약국에 갔다 오는 길에 대학 후배집에 들릅시다.

2 | -(으)ㄴ 적 or 일(이) 있어요/없어요 *ever did/never* |

and

| -는 적 or 일(이) 있어요/없어요 *sometimes does/not* |

77. 외국에서 이발을 해 본 적이 있어요?

78. 그런 자동차를 운전해 본 일이 있어요?

79.   가끔 미국에 편지를 보내는 일이 있어요.

80.   한국에서 여행을 해 본 적이 없어요.

20.1.24. Comparisons with 보다

81.   그 아이는 누구보다도 더 귀여워요.

82.   한국 휘발유 값은 미국보다 더 비싸요.

83.   저는 기타를 치는 것보다 피아노를 치는 것을 좋아 해요.

20.1.25. Retrospective Modifier - 던

PLAIN BASE	+ -던	= *that was/used to be VERBing*

PAST BASE	+ -던	= *that once VERBed, had VERBed in remote past*

84.   그 잡지는 내가 어제 읽던 거 아니에요?

85.   You were eating an apple, then put it on the table for a moment to pop into the kitchen. You come back to find your friend eating your apple, and say:

       내가 먹던 거 왜 먹어요?!

86.   지난 주말에 찾아왔던 사람이 어제 또 왔어요.

87.   내 여자친구하고 헤어지던 날은 내 생일이었습니다.

20.1.26. Modifier Clauses + 것 *the fact of . . .ing/the fact of having done*

88.   A.   지금 뭐 하는 거에요?
       B.   단어를 외우고 있어요.

89. A. 제 아내를 못 보셨어요?
     B. 아까 호텔 로비에서 기다리시는 것을 봤어요.

90. 뉴욕 같은 큰 도시에서는 밤에 혼자서 돌아다니는 것은 위험해요.

91. 고등학교 선생들이 돈을 그렇게 조금 버는 것을 몰랐지요.

92. 한자를 쓰는 것을 어디서 배우셨어요?

English to Korean Translation

Translate the following sentences into Korean. Remember that you frequently do not have to translate literally. Always be on the lookout to utilize the new patterns you have learned in the last four Lessons.

1.   A.   Which Mr. Lee did you meet this evening?
     B.   The one who works at the bank.
2.   I became ill because of the apple I ate.
3.   The park my dog plays in is nearby [close].
4.   Have you ever heard that song before?
5.   My nephew is older than I am.
6.   Have you seen any good, cheap shoes at that market?
7.   My wife sang a beautiful song at the party last night.
8.   The day he went to Germany was Friday.
9.   Have you ever ridden an airplane?
10. I'm much busier than you [don't you know]!
11. I particularly like the teacher who lent me that money.
12. At the latest I have to go home by 10 PM.
13. I can neither swim nor play tennis.
14. Even though that man is awfully poor, he's always happy.
15. It doesn't matter whether you come home tonight or not.
16. I'll have to do it tomorrow.
17. It will probably already be warm in March.
18. I have to see the doctor before my wife gets back.
19. Although the store is near I'm thinking of going downtown.
20. Although the problem was easy, it still took two hours [don't you know]!
21. It isn't good to do nothing but fool around ["play"].
22. I cleaned up my room, so mother was pleased.

23. I don't like practicing on the weekend.

24. My brother collects stamps, but he hasn't got many yet.

25. A. Please tell me the answer to this question.

 B. I'm too busy, so I can't.

26. I hate studying.

27. She put on her makeup and then she went out.

28. A. Excuse me, but where is the bathroom?

 B. I don't know. Why don't you ask that old man ["grandfather"]?

29. The train was late so my friend and I missed the plane.

30. A. Wouldn't you like to try some *kimchee*?

 B. No, I'm not hungry and it's too spicy.

31. Mr. Oh is not standing. He's sitting down over there.

32. I couldn't go to Seoul because it rained so much.

33. That old man is a famous author. You didn't know, did you?

Korean to English Translation

1. 배가 고파도 고기는 못 먹지요.

2. 개를 때려도 돼요?

3. 늦어도 공항에 3시까지 가고 싶어요.

4. 오늘 저녁에는 집에 좀 늦게 들어와도 괜찮아요?

5. 지난 해 가을 우리 집에서 4주동안 살았던 일본학생한테 편지가 왔어요.

6. 그런 거 한번도 못 보셨을거에요.

7. 선생님 댁은 저희 집보다 훨씬 큽니다.

8. 내가 먹던 빵을 만호 씨가 왜 먹고 있어요?

9. 아까 이 선생님 부인하고 싸우던 그 남자는 누구였지요?

10. 그 크고 좋은 집을 우리가 살 겁니다.

11. 빵이랑 고기를 사러 가게에 나갔어요.

12. 우체국 맞은 편에 큰 시계가 있어요.

13. 날씨가 좋아서 걸어왔어요.

14. 만화를 보지 말고 야구를 좀 합시다.

15. 김 교수님은 선생님보다 아마 젊을 겁니다.

16. 19과는 집에서 혼자 배울 수 있을까요?

17. 이 모자도 써 봤어요?

18. 아침을 준비하러 부엌 안으로 들어갔어요.

19. 한국말 잘 하기가 참 어려워요.

20. 텔레비젼을 많이 보는 사람들은 눈이 점점 나빠 져요.

21. 저 사람은 나랑 많이 싸우던 사람이라서 싫지요.

22. 택시가 없어서 걸어 가야겠어요.

23. 우리 고모는 6개월 전에 딸을 낳으셔서 기뻐하세요.

24. 석준 씨가 한국에 돌아가서 혼자 계시던 아버님이 좋아하실 거에요.

25. A.   오늘 저녁에 애기를 좀 봐 주시겠어요?

    B.   왜요?

    A.   좀 나가고 싶어서요.

26. 공부만 하지 말고 운동도 좀 해야 되잖아요!

27. A.   누가 나이가 제일 많아요?

    B.   제가 1살 위에요.

28. 숙제를 다 했기 때문에 오늘은 좀 쉬어도 괜찮아요.

29. 내가 어제 부친 편지는 아마 아직 안 갔을거에요.

30. 그 우산을 선물로 사 주시겠어요?

31. A.   8시에 좀 깨워 주실래요?

    B.   왜요?

    A.   약속이 있거든요?

32. 아버지의 자동차를 운전해 본 일이 있어요?

33. 점심에 냉면을 먹을 수 있어서 좋아요.

34. 내가 아까 받은 편지가 없어졌어요!

35. 일을 다 마쳤어도 피곤하지 않아요.

36. 어제 밤에 술을 너무 많이 마셔서 늦게 잤어요.

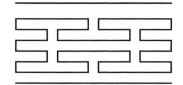 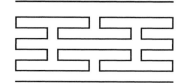

Lesson 21

금요일에 찾으러 오면 어떨까요?

In this lesson we observe Eric discussing plans for a long weekend with his friend Yŏngch'ŏl. Then we watch Chris Murphy having a pair of shoes made. This lesson introduces the conditional ending in -(으)면, an ending useful for *if* or *when(ever)* but also for expressing hopes and wishes, polite requests, obligation, and denial of permission. The lesson also introduces the intentive ending in -(으)려고, used to express intentions, the ending -(으)려면, which combines the meaning of the conditional and the intentive, and first realizations in -(는)군요, a kind of surprise form.

Korean Dialogues

Dialogue 1

Eric wants to go somewhere over the long weekend, and makes a suggestion to his friend Yŏngch'ŏl.

에릭	이번 연휴에 날씨가 좋으면, 바다에 수영하러 가려고 해요. 같이 갈래요?
영철	글쎄요. 바다는 좀 춥지 않을까요? 나는 산에 가면 좋겠어요.
에릭	어느 산에 가면 좋을까요?
영철	설악산이 경치가 좋아요.
에릭	설악산에 가려면 아침에 일찍 일어나지 않으면 안 되잖아요?
영철	게으름뱅이군요! 그러면 아침에 일찍 깨워 줄게요. 그렇게 하면 되잖아요!
에릭	네, 그렇게 합시다. 비만 오지 않으면 좋겠군요.

Dialogue 2

Chris Murphy has decided to have a new pair of dress shoes made.

크리스   구두 1켤레 맞추려고 하는데요.

아저씨   네. 사이즈가 어떻게 되시지요?

크리스   글쎄요. 나라마다 사이즈가 다 다르니까, 한번 재 주시지요.

(The salesman measures Chris's feet.)

아저씨   색깔과 모양은 어떤 것을 원하십니까?

크리스   지금 입고 있는 양복에 어울리는 구두가 필요하거든요.

         (pointing) 이런 모양에, 갈색으로 됩니까?

아저씨   물론 됩니다. 그런데, 좀 더 짙은 색깔이 낫지 않을까요?

         이건 어떻습니까?

크리스   네, 좋습니다. 그 걸로 하지요, 뭐.

아저씨   언제까지 필요하십니까?

크리스   금요일에 찾으러 오면 어떨까요?

아저씨   직접 찾으러 오시지 않아도 되고요, 저희가 댁으로 직접 배달해

         드리겠습니다.

크리스   와, 서비스가 상당히 좋군요.

Dialogue Notes

맞추려고 하는데요. *I'd like to have [a pair of shoes] made . . . [do you think you can oblige?].* You will learn more about the Imminent Elaboration ending −는데요 in a later lesson.

Reading Passage

행복

사람이 행복해지려면 무엇이 제일 중요합니까?

돈이 많으면 여러분은 행복할까요?

맛있는 음식을 많이 먹으면 행복할까요?

아니면 유명한 사람이 되면 행복하겠습니까?

그렇지만 아무리 돈이 많으며 맛있는 음식을 많이 먹으며 유명한 사람이 되어도,

　　　마음이 즐겁지 않으면 행복하지 못 합니다.

뭐니뭐니 해도 몸이 건강하지 않으면 아무 일도 할 수 없기 때문에,

건강이 무엇보다도 제일입니다.

Vocabulary

Adverbs

계속(해서)	continuously, still [at it], without interruption
계속하-	continues it/it continues
어제 비가 계속 왔어요.	It rained continuously yesterday.
곧	any moment now, right away, before long, at once
인제 곧 돌아올 거에요.	He'll be back right away.
글피	3 days from now
덜	less, little (opposite of 더)
오늘은 어제보다 덜 추워요.	Today is less cold than yesterday.
매우	very, exceedingly
뭐니뭐니 해도	say what you like
자꾸(만)	incessantly, constantly (often in an annoying way)
잘못	by mistake, wrongly, erroneously

제가 잘못 말했기 때문에 오해를 받았습니다.

Because I made a mistake in speaking, I created some misunderstanding.

직접	direct(ly); immediate(ly); personally, in person
학교에서 직접 왔습니다.	I came directly from school.
남 교수님한테 직접 들었습니다.	I heard it directly from Professor Nam.

Nouns

Health-Related

감기	a cold
몸살감기 or 감기몸살	a severe cold or flu brought on by exhaustion
감기에 걸렸어요.	I['ve] caught a cold.
몸살	general fatigue (from overwork)
몸살(이) 나-	suffer from general fatigue (from overwork)

People and Their Ways

게으름뱅이	lazybones, lazy person
거짓말	lie, fib
거짓말을 하지 마세요.	Please don't lie.
거짓말쟁이	liar
농담	joke, something said in jest
농담(을) 하-	joke, jest
멋쟁이	stylish person, sb who always dresses well
신사	gentleman
신사 숙녀 여러분	ladies and gentlemen
여러분	all of you; you all; y'all [without the down-home Southern feel]
잘못	a mistake, error, blunder
잘못(을) 했어요. 용서하십시오.	I did something wrong/I made a mistake. Please forgive me.
제 잘못이니까 사과드립니다.	It's my fault/mistake, so I apologize.
정치가	politician
진담	something said in all seriousness
농담이지요?	You're joking, aren't you?
아니오, 진담이에요.	No, I'm serious.

Natural Environment

경치	scenery
여기는 경치가 좋군요!	Say, the scenery here is nice!
공해	pollution
서울의 공해는 더 심해졌어요.	Pollution in Seoul has become even more severe.
등산	hiking
등산(을) 하-	engage in hiking
등산(을) 가-	go hiking
설악산에 등산하러 갑니다.	I'm going to Mt. Sŏrak to go hiking.
매연	exhaust fumes
서울에는 매연이 심해요.	The air pollution [from cars] in Seoul is severe.
설악산	Mount Sŏrak
연기	smoke
담배연기가 싫어요.	I don't like cigarette smoke.
부엌에서 연기가 나요.	There's smoke coming from the kitchen.

Other

과자	biscuit(s), cookie(s)
교과서	textbook
Note: can also be pronounced 〔교꽈서〕	
단추	button; snap
단추를 잠그-	do up a button
단추를 끼-	fasten a snap
매년	every year
매달	every month
매주	every week
모양	shape, appearance, style, design
불어	French language
사과	apology
사과(를) 합니다.	I apologize.
사과(를) 드립니다.	I apologize. (to sb esteemed)
사이즈	size
사탕	sweets, candy
연휴	a long weekend
오자 〔오짜〕	typo, misprint

Lesson Twenty-one / 122

-중	the middle; during, in the middle of
수업 중	in the middle of class, during class
수업 중에 떠들면 안 됩니다.	One shouldn't make noise in class.
사장님은 지금 회의 중이세요.	The boss is in a meeting now.
필요	need, necessity
필요하-	be necessary, needed
나는 돈이 필요해요.	I need money.
흠	flaw, defect
이 물건은 흠이 있어요.	This item has a defect.
저 사람은 약속을 자주 어기는 것이 흠이에요.	

One of her defects is that she often breaks her promises.

Weather-Related

개-	it clears up
날이 개면 좋겠어요.	I hope the weather clears up.
구름	cloud
끼-	(clouds/fog) form, gather
구름이 꼈어요.	It's cloudy.
선선하-	be cool, fresh
소나기	cloudburst, shower
소나기가 올 거예요.	There's going to be a shower.
안개	fog
안개가 꼈어요.	It's foggy.
옅은 안개	a thin fog
짙은 안개	a thick fog
태풍	typhoon
태풍이 불어요.	There's a typhoon blowing.

Color-Related

갈색	the color brown; brown . . .
갈색 구두	brown shoes
까만(색)	(the color) black; black . . .
남색	the color [navy] blue
노란(색)	(the color) yellow; yellow . . .
녹색	the color green; green . . .

밤색	the color chestnut brown; chestnut brown . . .
밤	chestnut
구운 밤	roasted chestnuts
보라색	the color purple; purple . . .
분홍색	the color pink; pink . . .
빨간(색)	(the color) red; red . . .
색깔, 색	color
오렌지색	the color orange; orange . . .
자주색	the color burgundy; burgundy . . .
주황색	the color orange; orange . . .
파란(색)	(the color) blue; blue . . . ; (the color) green; green . . .
파란 잔디	a green lawn
파란 하늘	blue sky
푸른(색)	(the color) blue; blue . . . ; (the color) green; green . . .
푸른 잎	a green leaf
푸른 하늘	blue sky
핑크색	the color pink; pink . . .
하늘색	the color light ["sky"] blue
하얀(색)	(the color) white . . .
회색	the color grey; grey . . .
흰(색)	(the color) white . . .

Verbs

Verbs That Take Objects

가지고 있-	have, have in one's possession
당기-	pull it
당기시오.	Pull. [on doors]
맞추-	order (to specifications), have (clothes) made to order
미-르-	push it
미시오.	Push. [on doors]

배달(을) 하-	deliver
배달부	delivery man
배달이 왔어요.	The delivery came/We got a delivery.
잠그-	fasten (buttons, snaps); lock (door, window)
잡-	catch, grasp, take hold of
장(을) 보-	go shopping (for food)
장 보러 갔어요.	He went shopping.
재-	take measurements of, measure

Descriptive and/or Sensory Verbs

고단하-	be tired, fatigued, weary
심하-	be severe, intense, extreme
심한 감기	a severe cold
옅-	be light (color)
졸리-	be sleepy; feel sleepy
졸려서 죽겠어요.	I'm incredibly sleepy.
중요하-	be important
짙-	be deep, rich, dark (color)
행복하-	be happy [in life]
행복	happiness

Intransitive Verbs (Processive Verbs That Cannot Take Objects)

결석(을) 하-	be absent (from school)
마음에 드-ㄹ-	be to one's liking ("enters one's mind")
[...에] 어울리-	fit, go well with, match with
저한테 빨간 색이 어울려요.	The color red suits me.
이 옷에 까만 구두가 어울려요.	Black shoes go well with these clothes.
조-ㄹ-	doze

<u>Other</u>

그러-, 그래요	do so, do like that
그러지요.	(Sure,) Let's do that.
점심을 같이 먹을까요?	Shall we have lunch together?
그러지요.	Sure [let's do it].
그렇-, 그래요	be so, be like that, be that way
그렇지요.	That's true isn't it?; Yes, that's right.
술은 건강에 아주 안 좋지요?	Alcohol is really bad for you, right?
네, 그렇지요.	Yes, that's right.

Lesson Notes

21.1. Verbs: Conditional Form in -(으)면

Verbs with the ending -(으)면 are in the CONDITIONAL form. The conditional ending is a two-shape ending; it attaches to consonant bases as -으면 and to vowel bases as -면. L-extending vowel bases attach -면 to the extended base with ㄹ: 사-ㄹ- → 살면 *if/when one lives*. Honorific conditionals are made by attaching the ending to the honorific base: -(으)시면.

Vowel-Base Verbs			
Base	**Gloss**	**Conditional**	**Honorific Conditional**
가-	*go*	가면	가시면
예쁘-	*be pretty*	예쁘면	예쁘시면
주-	*give*	주면	주시면
서-	*stand up*	서면	서시면
부르-	*call*	부르면	부르시면
파-ㄹ-	*sell*	팔면	파시면

Base	Gloss	Conditional	Honorific Conditional
입-	*wear*	입으면	입으시면
싶-	*want to*	싶으면	싶으시면
없-	*be lacking*	없으면	없으시면
받-	*get*	받으면	받으시면
있-	*have*	있으면	있으시면
찾-	*looks for; finds*	찾으면	찾으시면
벗-	*take off*	벗으면	벗으시면
들-	*listen, hear*	들으면	들으시면
젊-	*be young*	젊으면	젊으시면
앉-	*sit down*	앉으면	앉으시면
좋-	*be good*	좋으면	좋으시면
구w-	*broil*	구우면	구우시면

There is also a past conditional, formed by adding -으면 to the -ㅆ- of the past base to produce -었으면, and so on.

21.2. Uses of - (으) 면 (1): *If . . . ; When(ever) . . .*

The basic meaning of the conditional ending is *if [so-and-so happens]* or *when(ever) [so-and-so happens]*. This meaning is illustrated particularly well in the first of the following sentences. The others give further examples.

1. 너무 많이 걸으면 피곤해져요.
   If I walk too much, I get tired. or *When(ever) I walk too much, I get tired.*

2. 소나기가 오면 빨리 들어가야겠어요.
   If there's a shower, we'll have to hurry inside.

3. 오늘 오후에 날씨가 좋으면, 등산을 가려고 해요.
   If the weather is nice this afternoon, I'm thinking of going hiking.

4. 구름이 끼면 집에 있을래요.
   If it clouds over, I'd rather stay home.

5.   이 까만 것이 마음에 들면 사 줄게요.
     If you like this black one, I'll buy it for you.

6.   나 같으면 이 곳에서 일을 하고 싶지 않겠어요.
     [If it be like me =] If it were me, I wouldn't want to work in this place.

Most of these sentences—if the context called for it—could go into English in a slightly different tense form:

  a.   I wouldn't be able to go if it *rained.*
  b.   If it were nice this afternoon, I *would go* to the store.
  c.   If it rained, we *would stay* home.

There are a couple of special uses for the conditional that lead to English translations quite different from word-for-word versions of the Korean. These are discussed below.

21.3. Uses of - (으) 면 (2): Hopes and Wishes

A.   -(으)면 좋겠어요

A conditional sentence ending with 좋겠어요 *would/will be good* or *nice* may correspond to an English sentence expressing a **hope** or a **wish**:

7.   봄이 가지 않으면 좋겠습니다.
     I wish it would stay spring. [= *If spring didn't go, it would be good.*]

8.   한국말을 잘 하면 좋겠어요.
     I hope I speak Korean well. or *I wish I spoke Korean well.*
     [= *If I speak/spoke Korean well, it will/would be good.*]

9.   어서 방학이 되면 좋겠어요.
     I hope/wish vacation will/would get here soon.

10.   어느 상점에 가면 좋겠습니까?
      *Which store **shall we** go to?* [= *If we went to which store, would it be good?*]

These sentences shade into expressions of MILD OBLIGATION, as follows:

11.   한국에 가면 좋겠어요?
      Shall [or Should] we go to Korea? [= *Would it be good if we went to Korea?*]

12. 공부를 좀 더 하면 좋겠어요.
     You should study a little more.
     [= *It would be good if you'd study a little more.*]

13. a. 저는 산에 가면 좋겠어요.
         I wish we could go to the mountains. or *It would be nice if . . .*

     b. 저는 산에 갔으면 좋겠어요.
         I wish we could go to the mountains [but I know this is highly unlikely].

B. | -(었)으면 얼마나 좋겠어요? |

You can use this same pattern on a present (or past, for more hypothetical flavor) base in a rhetorical pattern to mean something like *How wonderful it would be if . . . !*

14. 시간이 더 있었으면 얼마나 좋겠습니까?
     How wonderful it would be if we had more time!

15. 까만색이 아니었으면 얼마나 좋을까요?
     How wonderful it would be if it weren't black!

16. 빨리 도착했으면 얼마나 좋겠어요!
     How wonderful it would be if we arrived quickly!

17. a. 그 분을 만나면 얼마나 좋겠습니까?
         How wonderful it would be to meet him!

     b. 그 분을 만났으면 얼마나 좋겠습니까?
         How wonderful it would be to meet him! [but I know it is highly unlikely]

21.4. Uses of -(으)면 (3): Polite Requests

A. | -(으)면 고맙겠어요: *I would be grateful if . . .* |

A conditional verb in -(으)면 followed by the future form 고맙겠어요 means literally *if you do so-and-so, I will be grateful.* This is a polite and somewhat oblique way of saying *please do so-and-so.*

18.   이 꽃을 주시면 고맙겠어요.
       I'd like you to give me these flowers. or *May I ask you to give me these flowers?*

Of course, there is nothing in the Korean to convey the abruptness of the most nearly literal English corresponding to this construction (*I'll thank you to leave me alone*); on the contrary, its indirectness gives it a flavor of greater courtesy in Korean. Here are some more examples:

19.   일찍 좀 오시면 고맙겠어요.
       I'd appreciate it if you'd come a little early.
       [= *If you'd come a little early, I'd be thankful.*]

20.   내일까지 배달해 주시면 고맙겠어요.
       I would be grateful if you could deliver it by tomorrow.

21.   미안하지만, 나가 주시면 고맙겠어요.
       I'm sorry, but I'd appreciate it if you left/went out.

The foregoing discussion may leave you feeling that the meaning of the Korean conditional is somewhat vague and difficult to pin down, and you are quite right. In terms of their real meaning—what they actually convey—Korean conditional sentences are likely to have English equivalents quite far afield from the word-for-word renditions. As a tag translation of the forms, *if* or *when* will do.

B.   해 주셨으면 합니다: *I should be grateful if . . .*

You have already seen in 21.3 that when you put the conditional on a past base it makes the *if*-clause more hypothetical. The flavor is much like when one uses a subjunctive in a language like French or Spanish, or like English *would that I could . . . ,* etc.

And just as one might use a subjunctive to make a polite request in a European language (German *ich möchte gern . . . ,* French *je voudrais . . . ,* English *I would like to . . . ,* etc.), you can use a past conditional in Korean to express a polite request. The dialogue for this lesson contains the following sentence.

22.   아침에 일찍 좀 깨워 주시면 고맙겠어요.
       I'd be grateful if you would wake me early in the morning.

By putting the favor requested in the past tense, and replacing 고맙겠어요 with 합니다 or 해요, you get the following:

23.   아침에 일찍 좀 깨워 주셨으면 합니다.
      I should be grateful if you would wake me early in the morning.

As we have tried to imply with our translation, this pattern, by virtue of its more remote past base and its honorific marker, is a somewhat stiff and formal request. Here are some more examples:

24.   일을 좀 더 열심히 해 주셨으면 합니다.
      I should be grateful if you would work a bit harder.

25.   다시 한 번 써 주셨으면 해요.
      I should be grateful if you would write it one more time.

21.5. Other Uses of the Conditional

Two more useful constructions with -(으)면 involve the verb 돼요, which in this case means something like *is permitted* or *allowed*; in the negative, *it won't do; it isn't allowed* or *permitted*. Notice that 안 됐어요 is the usual way to say *That's too bad; that's a shame* [= *I'm sorry to hear that*]; *that's no good*; 됐어요 is an idiomatic expression for *It's OK; That's all right.*

A. | -지 않으면 안 돼요 / 안 하면 안 돼요: **Obligation** |

A double negative expression consisting of the negative conditional followed by the negative form 안 돼요 results in an affirmative indication of **obligation**:

26.   새 양복을 맞추지 않으면 안 돼요.
      I ought to get a new suit made. [= *If I don't get a new suit made, it won't do.*]

The obligation this construction expresses is milder than the rather stern meaning conveyed by -어야 해요 *has to . . .* or *must . . .* , yet stronger than -으면 좋겠어요 meaning literally *it would be good if . . .* , that is, *I'd better . . .* etc.

B. ┌─ -(으)면 안 돼요: **Denial of Permission** ─┐

If the only negative verb is 안 돼요 (and notice that Koreans tend not to use the long negative in 되지 않아요 here, because the whole construction starts to get too tedious), then the sentence **denies permission**: it means *you may not . . .* or *you must not.*

27. 수업 중에 졸면 안 돼요.
     [*If you doze in class, it won't do. =*] *You may* [or *must*] *not doze in class.*

28. 거짓말을 하면 안 돼요.
     [*If you tell lies, it isn't permissible. =*]
     You mustn't or *may not* or *shouldn't*] *tell lies.*

Here are more examples of these two constructions.

29. 결석을 하면 안 돼요.
     You shouldn't be absent from class.

30. 선생님의 말씀을 안 들으면 안 돼요.
     You must do as the teacher says. [*If you don't listen to the teacher's words, it won't do.*]

31. 오늘 아침에 장을 안 보면 안 돼요.
     I've got to go shopping this morning. [*If I don't go shopping this morning, it will not do.*]

32. 고기를 너무 많이 먹으면 안 돼요.
     You mustn't eat too much meat. [*If you eat too much meat, it won't do.*]

33. 너무 게으르면 안 돼요.
     You shouldn't be too lazy.

34. 그 문 앞에 서 계시면 안 돼요.
     You mustn't stand in front of that door.

35. 먼저 가세요 – 윤 선생님 부인을 기다리지 않으면 안 되거든요.
     You go ahead—I ought to stay here and wait for Mrs. Yun.

36. 하루종일 방 안에만 계시면 안 돼요.
     You shouldn't stay in your room all day long.

SUMMARY: PATTERNS WITH -(으)면	
Form	**Meaning**
-(으)면 -었으면	*If/When(ever)* . . . *If/When(ever)* . . . (but more tentative, or contrary to fact)
-(으)면 좋겠어요 -었으면 좋겠어요 -(으)면 얼마나 좋겠어요? -었으면 얼마나 좋겠어요?	*I hope/wish* . . . *I hope/wish* . . . (but you reckon the possibility is unlikely) *How nice it would be if* . . . *How nice it would be if* . . . (but when the chances are more remote)
-(으)면 고맙겠어요 -어 주셨으면 합니다	*I would be grateful if* . . . *I should be obliged if you would* . . .
-지 않으면 안 돼요 안 하면 안 돼요 -(으)면 안 돼요	*must* . . . , *have to* . . . , *ought to* . . . *must* . . . , *have to* . . . , *ought to* . . . *cannot* . . . , *must not* . . . , *ought not* . . .

21.6. The Intentive -(으)려(고): *intending to* . . .

Observe the following sentences.

37. 택시를 잡으려고 백화점 앞에 있었어요.
    I was in front of the department store so as to catch a taxi (intending to catch . . .).

38. 내년에도 한국어 공부를 계속하려고 합니다.
    I intend to continue my Korean language studies next year, too.

The intentive verb ending -(으)려(고) is a two-shape ending pronounced -으려(고) after consonants, -려(고) after vowels and the extended base of L-extending verbs.

Base	Gloss	Intentive	Meaning
먹-	*eats*	먹으려(고)	*intending* or *desiring to eat*
앉-	*sits*	앉으려(고)	*with the intention* or *desire to sit, ready (willing) to sit*
가-	*goes*	가려(고)	*intending* or *desiring* or *ready* or *willing to go*
사-ㄹ-	*lives*	살려(고)	*with the intention* or *desire* or *willingness to live*

This form, usually followed by the quotation particle 고 (about which more in Lesson Twenty-seven), is used in sentences with some form of 하- or 그러- (그래요, 그럽니다) *do/think* after it, to mean such things as: *intends to [do], plans* or *wants to [do], is going* or *intending to [do], is ready* or *willing to [do], tries to [do], sets about [do]ing*, etc. The possible patterns are:

Polite Style
-(으)려고 해요
-(으)려고 그래요

Formal Style
-(으)려고 합니다
-(으)려고 그럽니다

The expression -(으)려고 하- is a kind of expanded form; the simple form is -(으)려 하-, and there is a contracted form with the 하- dropped.

Expanded	Simple	Contracted	
가려고 합니다	가려 합니다	가렵니다	*intends to go*
하려고 합니다	하려 합니다	하렵니다	*intends to do*
살려고 합니다	살려 합니다	살렵니다	*intends to live*

Note that in colloquial Korean, speakers often pronounce this form with double ㄹㄹ instead of single ㄹ, making 할려고 from 하려고. The *wanna/feel like . . .ing* pattern in -(으)ㄹ래(요) which you learned in Section 12.6., is in origin a contraction from this doubled 할려(고) 해요.

Instead of 하-, you may find just -려(고) ending a phrase, with the main verb later in the sentence, as in the first example sentence above.

You have also learned the purposive form -(으)러, which looks like an abbreviation of -(으)려; it is used only in phrases that involve *going or coming for the purpose of.* For example, 장 보러 가요 *goes to do the shopping* and 찾으러 갔어요 *went looking for (somebody)*. 찾으러 와요 is also used with the same meaning as 찾아와요 *comes visiting*, and 찾으러 가요 can mean the same thing as 찾아가요 *goes visiting*.

Here are more examples of -(으)려(고).

39. 한 석 달 더 있으려고 해요.
     I intend [or am prepared] to stay another three months.

40. 그림을 보여 드리려고 그래요.
     I'm going to show you some pictures.

41. 내일 그 책을 사려고 해요.
     I intend to buy that book tomorrow.

42. 저녁을 먹으려고 그랬지만 시간이 없어서 못 먹었어요.
     I was about to eat my dinner, but I couldn't because there was no time.

43. 오려고 그랬어요.
     I intended to come.

44. 언제 도착하렵니까?
     When do you intend to arrive?

45. 6시에 일어나려고 일찍 잤지만, 고단해서 8시까지 잤어요.
     I went to bed early intending to get up at 6, but I was so tired that I slept till 8.

46. 내가 바로 그 이야기를 하려고 그랬어요.
     I was just going to talk about that.

47. 저는 한국에 가려고 요즘 한국말을 공부하고 있어요.
     I'm learning Korean lately, with the intention of going to Korea.

48. 과장님을 좀 뵈려고 왔어요.
     I've come to see the head of department.

주의

Intentive -(으)려(고) and purposive -(으)러 forms are
made only on processive verb bases; there are no
-(으)려 or -(으)러 forms for descriptive verbs, nor for the copula.

21.7. -(으)려면: *If one intends to . . .*

49.   설악산에 가려면, 일찍 일어나지 않으면 안 돼요.
      If you want to (intend to) go to Mount Sŏrak, you have to get up early.

This complex ending is a combination of the intentive ending -(으)려 plus the conditional -
(으)면, and translates as *if one intends to do, if one is fixing to do, if one wants to do,*
and so on. It can only be used with processive simple bases. In highly colloquial Korean, -
(으)려면 is pronounced -(으)ㄹ래면, as if infected by the *wanna* form in -(으)ㄹ래요,
which you learned in Section 12.6. Here are more examples.

50.   기타를 잘 치려면 열심히 해야 돼요.
      If you want to play guitar well, you have to work hard.

51.   불어를 배우려면 프랑스에 가야 돼요.
      If you want to learn French, you have to go to France.

52.   등산할래면 설악산이 제일 아름다워요.
      If it's hiking you're interested in, Mount Sŏrak is the most beautiful.

53.   박 선생님께 보여 드리려면 빨리 하세요 – 내일 떠나시거든요.
      If you intend to show it to Mr. Pak, do it quickly—he's leaving tomorrow.

54.   멋있는 옷을 사려면 돈이 많아야 돼요.
      If you want to buy stylish clothes, you need lots of money.

55.   내일 떠나실래면 준비를 빨리 하셔야겠어요.
      If you want to leave tomorrow, you'll have to prepare quickly.

21.8. The Adverb 좀

The adverb 좀 has two meanings. In some sentences, it may mean *[do so-and-so] a little
bit.*

56.   밥을 좀 더 주십시오.
      Please give me a little more rice.

57.   한국말을 좀 합니다.
      I speak a little Korean.

In other sentences, it means *just* or *only*, limiting the action of the verb in much the same way the particle 만 limits the scope of a noun. Sometimes, the meanings *a little* and *please* overlap. Practically, 좀 softens a suggestion or command.

58. 좀 기다리시지요.
    [Why don't you] Wait just a bit.

59. 연필을 좀 주십시오.
    (Just) give me a pencil, please.

60. 좀 쉬어도 좋지요?
    Can we rest a bit?

61. 〔택시 안에서〕
    좀 천천히 가시지요.
    Go a bit slower, will you please?

21.9. First Realizations with -(는)군요!

The following sentences appeared in this lessons's dialogues.

62. 게으름뱅이군요!
    So, you're a lazy bones, I see!

63. 비만 오지 않으면 좋겠군요!
    Well, then, I guess we just have to hope it won't rain!

64. 와, 서비스가 상당히 좋군요!
    Wow, what great service! [I hadn't realized before . . .]

The two-shape ending -(는)군요! adds a surprised note to the sentences where it occurs and has the basic meaning of first realization: *Now (suddenly, finally,* or *for the first time) I see/realize that . . . !* Other English equivalents are *Well, I'll be ...!* or *Well, what do you know . . . ! Oh, [now] I see!, Now I realize . . .* or simply *Why!* (as an exclamation). Processive bases attach the shape in -는군요 (the -는 is in origin the processive modifier), and descriptive bases; past and future bases; as well as the two special verbs, 있- and 없-, attach the shape in -군요.

Processive Bases

하는군요!   *Why, he's [doing something]!*

Other Bases

있군요!   *Why, there's . . . !*

없군요!   *Well — there isn't . . . !*

했군요!   *Why, he did . . . !*

하겠군요!   *Well! He's going to . . . !*

Here are some more examples.

65. 오늘 밤 별이 참 많군요!
    My, what a lot of stars are out tonight.

66. 댁이 좋군요!
    Nice house you've got.

67. 아이구, 한국말을 잘 하시는군요!
    Oh! Your Korean is really good [I had no idea . . .].

68. 소나기가 곧 쏟아지겠군요!
    [Uh-oh, I suddenly realized . . .] it's going to pour any moment now.

69. 감기에 걸리셨군요!
    I see you've caught a cold!

Exercises

Exercise 1: Conditionals in -(으)면

Connect each of the two sentences with a conditional -(으)면 form and then translate the result into English.

1. 방학이 돼요. 집에 갈 거에요.
2. 감기에 걸려요. 물을 많이 마셔야 해요.
3. 비가 계속 와요. 등산을 못 가겠어요.
4. 마음에 들어요. 많이 사겠어요.
5. 날씨가 개요. 밖에 나갈 거에요.
6. 위험해요. 하지 마세요.
7. 애기가 울어요. 저를 불러 주세요.
8. 흠이 있어요. 사지 마세요.
9. 글피에 도착해요. 더 좋아요.

10.   해가 나요. 더워질 거에요.
11.   서울에 오래 있어요. 몸살이 나요.

Exercise 2: Expressing Wishes with - (으) 면

Each of the following sentences means *someone **does/is** something*. Make each mean *I **hope** someone **does/is** something*; then translate the sentence. For example, the first will be: 그 사람이 우리 친구가 되면 좋겠어요. *I wish he would become our friend; I hope he will become our friend.*

1.   그 사람이 우리 친구가 돼요.
2.   나는 돈을 많이 벌어요.
3.   그 친구가 나한테 전화를 걸어요.
4.   태풍이 불지 않아요.
5.   그 상점의 물건이 싸요.
6.   아이들이 말을 잘 들어요.
7.   어머니가 동생을 낳아요.
8.   이번 주말이 연휴에요.
9.   멋쟁이 남자친구가 있어요.
10.   학교에 걸어 갈 수 있어요.
11.   날씨가 선선해요.
12.   감기에 자주 걸리지 않아요.

In the following sentences, put the conditional ending on a past base.

13.   이 교과서에 오자가 많지 않아요.
14.   여자친구가 내일 도착해요.
15.   불어를 잘 해요.
16.   위험하지 않아요.
17.   매일 등산해요.
18.   우리 애기가 자꾸만 울지 말고 더 웃어요.
19.   정치가들이 자꾸만 거짓말을 하지 않아요.
20.   매주 시험을 보지 않아요.

Exercise 3: Denial of Permission with - (으) 면

Each of the following sentences means *someone **may** do something*. Change each so that it means *someone **may** **not*** or ***must** **not** **do*** something; then translate the sentence. For example the first will be: 아이들이 개와 같이 놀면 안 돼요. *The children mustn't play with the dog.*

1. 아이들이 개와 같이 놀아도 좋아요.
2. 우리 아들이 그 여자와 결혼해도 좋아요.
3. 나는 새 옷을 또 사도 좋아요.
4. 애기에게 사탕을 줘도 괜찮아요.
5. 성당에서 춤을 춰도 괜찮아요.
6. 수업 시간에 졸아도 좋아요.
7. 도서관에 가서 음악을 들어도 좋아요.
8. 여기서 신발을 벗어도 좋아요.
9. 선생님한테 농담해도 괜찮아요.
10. 그 핑크색 바지를 입고 나가도 돼요.
11. 정치가는 거짓말을 해도 좋아요.

Exercise 4: Obligation with - (으) 면

Each of the following sentences means *someone **does** something*. Make each mean *someone **ought to do** something*, then translate the sentence. For example, the first will be: 선생님은 이 책을 보시지 않으면 안 돼요 *You ought to read this book. You should read this book.*

1. 선생님은 이 책을 보세요.
2. 물을 많이 마셔요.
3. 우리는 십분쯤 쉬어요.
4. 학교에 자동차를 타고 가요.
5. 선생님은 그 사람을 만나세요.
6. 우리는 서울에 살아요.
7. 오늘 저녁에 넥타이를 매고 가요.
8. 우리는 그 영화를 구경해요.
9. 오늘 저녁에 우리는 라디오를 들어요.
10. 새 구두를 맞춰요.
11. 이 편지를 한시까지 배달해 드려요.
12. 이 책을 봐요.
13. 문을 잠그고 가세요.

Exercise 5: Polite Requests

Each of the following sentences means *you do something*. Make each mean ***I wish you would*** *do something for me,* ***I'd like you to*** *do something for me*; then translate the sentence. For example, the first will be: 내일 와 주시면 고맙겠어요. *I'd like you to come tomorrow.*

1.   내일 오세요.
2.   점심을 사세요.
3.   우리 아들을 찾으세요.
4.   한국말을 가르쳐 주세요.
5.   저한테 편지를 쓰세요.
6.   이 서류를 읽으세요.
7.   이 쪽으로 나가세요.
8.   노래를 부르세요.
9.   양복 단추를 잠그세요.
10.   수업 시간에 졸지 마세요.
11.   이 책은 흠이 있으니까, 다른 것으로 바꿔 주세요.

Exercise 6: Practice with - (으) 려고

A. Combine each of the two sentences below into a single sentence with -(으)려고 and translate into English.

1.   한국말을 배워요. 고려대학교에 다닙니다.
2.   새 양복을 맞춰요. 백화점에 가는 길입니다.
3.   등산해요. 설악산에 갑니다.
4.   음식을 좀 만들어요. 이것 저것 샀어요.
5.   청소를 해요. 문을 잠시 열었어요.
6.   돈을 찾아요. 은행에 가요.

B. Answer the following questions with a sentence using -(으)려고.

7.   그 책을 왜 샀어요?
8.   그 꽃을 왜 가지고 오셨어요?
9.   어제 왜 전화했어요?
10.   오늘 저녁에 뭐 하실 거에요?
11.   왜 벌써 집에 가요?
12.   왜 새 양복을 맞췄어요?

Exercise 7: Practice with - (으) 려면

Complete each of the following sentences in Korean, and translate into English.

1. 러시아말 배우려면 . . .
2. 우산을 사려면 . . .
3. 등산하려면 . . .
4. 오래 살려면 . . .
5. 시험을 잘 보려면 . . .
6. 목욕하려면 . . .
7. 여행하려면 . . .
8. 시험 준비를 하려면 . . .
9. 이걸 미국에 보내려면 . . .
10. 머리를 감으려면 . . .
11. 신발을 벗으려면 . . .
12. 걸어 가려면 . . .
13. 같이 기타를 연습하려면 . . .
14. 양복을 맞추려면 . . .

Exercise 8: Practice with - (는) 군요

Convert the following sentences into first realizations with - (는) 군요.

1. 피아노를 잘 치세요.
2. 눈이 많이 와요.
3. 바람이 많이 불어요.
4. 이 하얀 꽃이 참 예뻐요.
5. 피곤해요.
6. 몸살이 났어요.
7. 집이 가까워요.
8. 내일 춥겠어요.
9. 애인이랑 싸우셨어요.
10. 맥주 1잔 하니까, 시원해요.
11. 머리를 깎으니까, 기분이 좋아요.
12. 요즘 좀 선선해졌어요.
13. 그 남자가 마음에 들어요.
14. 빨간 색을 싫어 해요.

Exercise 9: English to Korean Translation

Translate the following sentences into Korean:

1.   If you have some money, please lend me some.
2.   You shouldn't joke with the teacher.
3.   If you like it, buy it.
4.   If the sun comes out, let's go out to the park.
5.   If it gets cloudy, let's go in.
6.   It won't do if you arrive 3 days from now.
7.   If you go hiking alone, it's dangerous.
8.   One mustn't doze during class.
9.   I have to help that politician.
10. If you intend to play outside, don't play until late.
11. If you intend to speak Korean well, you must eat lots of *kimchee*.

Exercise 10: Korean to English Translation

Translate the following sentences into English.

1.   때리면 울거에요.
2.   위험하면 안 갈래요.
3.   해가 나면 좋겠어요.
4.   5시까지 테니스를 계속 치려고 그래요.
5.   은행원이 되려면, 시험을 봐야 돼요.
6.   교과서를 읽어 주시면 고맙겠어요.
7.   어제는 바람이 많이 불었고, 오늘은 아마 태풍이 불거에요.
8.   친구가 오면, 성당에 같이 가려고 해요.
9.   애기가 하루종일 울지 않았으면 얼마나 좋겠어요!
10. 좀 더 있으려면, 옆 방에서 기다려야겠어요.
11. 거기 살기가 좋으면, 살러 갈까요?
12. 날씨가 안 좋으면, 등산을 못 가겠어요.
13. 고단해서 죽겠으니까, 농담하지 말아요!
14. 내 여자친구가 멋쟁이였으면 좋겠어요.
15. 글피에는 바다에 수영하러 가려고 해요.
16. 만호 씨는 기분이 좋으면 농담을 잘 합니다.
17. 나는 짙은 보라색보다도 옅은 보라색을 더 좋아해요.

18. 하루종일 피자를 배달하려면 고단하겠어요.
19. 어제 잠을 못 잤기 때문에 졸려서 죽겠어요.
20. 지금은 날씨가 선선하지만 점점 쌀쌀해질거에요.
21. 연휴에 심한 몸살감기 때문에 쉬지 않으면 안 됐어요.
22. 저 식탁의 모양과 사이즈가 마음에 꼭 들어요.
23. 만호 씨한테 직접 그 말을 들었어요.
24. 한국말을 잘 하려면 매일 공부하는 것이 매우 중요합니다.

 # Lesson 22

요즘 너무 무리하시는 것 같군요.

In this lesson, Dialogue 1 shows Chris Murphy joking with Miss Lee, his secretary, before formally receiving a business colleague in his office. In Dialogue 2, Sandy and a Japanese friend decide to go out for a change of scene. New patterns covered include *while* in -(으)면서, mild exclamations in -네요, abbreviated (or ㅎ-dropping) verbs of manner and color, *as long as you're at it* with -는 김에, and the *seems* pattern in modifier + 것 같아요. The lesson also reviews the auxiliary verb 마-ㄹ- (말다) before introducing a new usage of 말고, and introduces a new usage for particle (이)나.

Korean Dialogues

Dialogue 1

어제 밤에 머피 사장은 늦게까지 술을 마셨기 때문에 늦잠을 잤습니다. 커피를 1잔 빨리 마시고, 서둘러서 출근했어도, 40분이나 늦었습니다. 미스 리는 머피 사장이 나오기를 기다리고 있습니다.

미스 리   사장님! 웬일이세요? 걱정하고 있었습니다.

머피 사장   사장이 이렇게 늦으면, 못 쓰지요? 어제 밤에 혼 났거든요.

미스 리   그러셨어요? 요즘 너무 무리하시는 것 같군요.

              아침 식사도 못 하셨겠네요.

머피 사장   속이 나빠서 어차피 못 먹어요. 〔수첩을 보면서〕

              아니 – 오늘은 한국섬유의 강 사장이 오는 날 아니에요?

미스 리   벌써 와 계신데요. 접대실에서 커피를 드시고 계십니다.

머피 사장   큰일 났군요.

머피 사장은 서류를 잠깐 보고, 접대실 안으로 들어 갑니다.
강 사장은 커피를 마시면서 서류를 읽고 있습니다.

머피 사장	강 사장님! 미안합니다. 오래 기다리셨지요?

머피 사장　강 사장님! 미안합니다. 오래 기다리셨지요?

　　　　　미안해서 어떻게 하지요?

강　　　　별 말씀 다 하시네요. 이 보고서를 아직 못 읽었으니까, 오히려

　　　　　잘 된 것 같습니다. 인제 다 봤으니깐요.

머피 사장　그렇습니까? 사실, 저는 아직 읽지 못 했습니다.

강　　　　그런데, 머피 사장님, 안색이 안 좋으시네요. 좀 쉬었다가 이야기

　　　　　할까요?

Dialogue Notes

웬일이세요?	*What's the matter? What's up? What's all this about?*
벌써 와 계신데요.	*He's already here waiting* [honorific Resultant State in -어 계시-] *(and I can elaborate if you like).* You will learn more about the Imminent Elaboration ending -(으)ㄴ/는데요 in a later lesson.
별 말씀 다 하시네요.	Lit.: *You are saying all kinds of special things,* i.e., *Not at all,* in response to a compliment or an apology that one interprets humbly as being excessive or unnecessary.

Dialogue 2

Sandy is talking with her Japanese friend, Yuko, in Yuko's dormitory room at Korea University.

유꼬　　　나는 밤이면 고향 생각이 나요.

　　　　　고향 생각이 나면, 음악을 들으면서 술을 마셔요.

샌디　　　나도 가끔 고향에 있는 친구들이 보고 싶어요.

　　　　　친구들이 보고 싶어지면, 편지를 쓰지요.

　　　　　어제는 편지를 3통이나 썼어요.

유꼬　　　슬퍼지네요. 우리 이제 이런 얘기 하지 말고, 기분전환으로

　　　　　나가서 차나 마실까요?

샌디　　　네, 그러지요, 뭐. 우체국에 들렀다가 내가 아는 다방으로 갑시다.

잠시 후, 다방에서

유꼬   차 말고 다른 거 안 마실래요?

샌디   글쎄요. 시내에 나온 김에 술이나 마시지요, 뭐.

Reading Passage

우리 가족은 일요일이면 가끔 시골에 가서 기분전환을 합니다.

우리 가족은 지난 일요일에 조용하고 공기가 맑은 교외로 놀러 갔습니다.

오래간만에 시골에 가서 맑은 공기도 마시고 맛있는 고기도 실컷 먹었습니다.

아버지는 고기를 구우시고 어머니는 아버지와 이야기를 나누시면서 생선

        찌개를 끓이셨습니다.

나는 동생들과 같이 재미있게 놀면서 즐거운 시간을 보냈습니다.

우리는 교외에 나간 김에 사진도 많이 찍었습니다.

가족들하고 그렇게 교외에 나가면, 기분이 너무 좋아서 딴 세상에 온 것

        같습니다.

다음 달에도 잊지 말고 가족들과 함께 교외로 놀러 가야 하겠습니다.

Vocabulary

Adverbs

가만히	quietly; still; cautiously
가만히 있어요!	Be still. or Keep quiet.
문을 가만히 열었어요!	I opened the door cautiously.
나중에	later, afterward
마음껏	to one's heart's content
마음껏 쉬었어요.	I had a thorough rest.
부지런히	diligently
실컷	to one's heart's content, to the point where one is sick of it
실컷 먹었어요.	I ate to my heart's content. or I've had plenty.
어떤 때는	sometimes
어쨌든	anyhow, in any case, at any rate
어차피	anyhow, in any case, at any rate

어차피 시작한 거니까 도중에서 그만둘 수 없어요.

Anyhow, it's something we've [already] started, so we can't quit in mid-course.

얼른	quickly, immediately, at once
얼른 가세요.	Go at once.
오히려	rather (than), sooner (than); actually; on the contrary, contrary to what one expects

오히려 약을 먹지 않으면 더 빨리 낫겠지요.

Actually, you'll get better quicker if you don't take any medicine.

하여튼	anyhow, in any case, at any rate

Nouns

Foods and Eating

간	the saltiness of a dish or food
간(을) 보-	check the saltiness of a dish or food
간장	soy sauce
계란	(chicken-)egg
고구마	sweet potato
고추	(red) pepper

Lesson Twenty-two / 148

국	soup
만두국 〔-꾹〕	dumpling soup
감자국 〔-꾹〕	potato soup
떡국	ricecake soup
껌	chewing gum
껌(을) 씹-	chew gum
달걀	(chicken-)egg
만두	dumplings
찐 만두	steamed dumplings
튀긴 만두	deep-fried dumplings
야끼 만두	pan-fried dumplings
물만두	boiled dumplings
물고기 〔-꼬기〕	fish [live, in its natural habitat]
생선	fish [destined for human consumption]
소금	salt
소금을 뿌리-	sprinkle salt on
숟가락	spoon
젓가락	chopstick(s)
젓가락(을) 잘 쓰는군요!	Say, you're pretty good with chopsticks!
찌개	stew
찌개를 끓이-	make ["boil"] a stew
김치찌개	*kimchee* stew
된장찌개	*toenjang* stew
포크	fork
후추	(black) pepper

Places

고향	hometown
대기실	waiting room
대합실	waiting room [in, e.g., a station or terminal]
세상	the world
세상에!	Oh, my! My goodness! You don't say! [used by women]
슈퍼	supermarket (abbreviated from 슈퍼마켓)

응접실	reception room [in a home]
접대실	reception room [in, e.g., an office]

Other

공기	air
교통	traffic
기분전환	change of mood
기분전환으로	for a change of mood
보고서	(written) report
보고(를) 하-	report
섬유	textiles
소풍	a [school] outing, [school] picnic
소풍(을) 가-	go on a [school] outing or picnic
수첩	small notebook; pocket memo-book
실수	a mistake, blunder
실수(를) 하-	make a mistake
안색	one's complexion
야유회	a [company] outing, picnic
야유회(를) 가-	go on a [company] outing, picnic
-통	counter for letters

Verbs

Verbs That Take Objects

끄-	turn off, switch off (e.g., a light); extinguish
끓이-	boil it; make [a stew]
낮잠(을) 자-	nap, take a nap
늦잠(을) 자-	sleep late, wake up late
무리(를) 하-	overdo it; work or play too hard
볶-	to cook in a skillet or frying pan
볶음밥	fried rice
빠-르-	wash (clothes), launder
뿌리-	sprinkle it
사진(을) 찍-	take photos

삶-	boil it
계란을 삶-	boil an egg
감자를 삶-	boil potatoes
삼키-	swallow it
생각(을) 하-	think
어떻게 생각하세요?	What ["how"] do you think?
씹-	chew it
껌(을) 씹-	chew gum
염려(를) 하-	worry
염려 마십시오.	Don't worry.
찌-	steam it
찐 만두	steamed dumplings
출근(을) 하-	go/come to work; report for work
켜-	turn on, switch on (e.g., a light)
퇴근(을) 하-	go/come home from work; leave the office
출퇴근(을) 하-	commute to work
출근시간	the time when one leaves home for work
퇴근시간	the time when one gets off work/goes home
튀기-	deep-fry it

Descriptive and/or Sensory Verbs

그저 그렇-	be so-so
그저 그랬어요.	It was so-so.
날씬하-	be thin, slim
넓-	be wide, broad; spacious
넓은 운동장	a spacious playing ground
독하-	be strong (of drinks, e.g. 커피, 술)
따-	be different
딴 것	something different
딴 사람들	others
딴 세상에 온 것 같아요.	I feel like I'm in a different world.

맑-	be clear
맑은 공기, 물, 날씨, 소리, 정신	clean air, clear water, weather, sound, spirits
매콤하-	be somewhat spicy-tasting
못 되-	be bad, bad-natured, evil, wicked, good-for-nothing
못 된 사람	bad person, good-for-nothing person
그 사람은 못 됐어요.	He's a bad guy.
못 쓰-	be no-good, worthless [lit.: be useless]
반가w-	be pleased to see/hear someone/something
부지런하-	be diligent
속(이) 나쁘-	have a sore stomach, feel sick in the stomach
싱거w-	be bland, not salted enough
진하-	be thick (of liquid or makeup)
커피가 너무 진해요.	The coffee is too strong.
짜-	be (too) salty

Intransitive Verbs (Processive Verbs That Cannot Take Objects)

넘어지-	fall down
놀러 가-	go on an outing, excursion or picnic; go [to someone's house] to visit
주말에 교외로 놀러 갈까요?	Shall we go on an excursion outside of town on the weekend?
밀리-	be backed up, congested (cars, traffic)
차가 많이 밀리네요.	My, traffic is quite backed up.
불(이) 나-	a fire breaks out
서두르-	hurry, hasten, make haste
큰일(이) 나-	something serious happens; get in big trouble
큰일 났군요! 어떡하지요?	Now we're in big trouble! What should we do?
혼(이) 나-	have a hard time of it, have an awful experience

<u>H-Dropping Descriptive Verbs (Color-related)</u>

까맣-, 까매요	be black, dark
새까맣-, 까매요	be jet-black
노랗-, 노래요	be yellow
새노랗-, 노래요	be vivid yellow
빨갛-, 빨개요	be red
새빨갛-, 빨개요	be bright red
파랗-, 파래요	be blue
새파랗-, 파래요	be vivid deep blue
하얗-, 하얘요	be white
새하얗-, 하얘요	be bright white

Lesson Notes

22.1. Expressing *While* with -(으)면서(도)

The ending -(으)면서 means *while VERBing*. But before you decide to use it, you must remember two essential rules. Whatever action is named in the clause following the *while* . . . phrase must be done (1) at the same time and (2) by the same person as the -(으)면서 action.

1. 나는 아침을 먹으면서 신문을 읽어요.
   *I read the paper **while I eat breakfast**.*

2. 음악을 들으면서 고향을 생각했어요.
   *I was thinking of home **while at the same time** I was listening to the music.*

3. 노래를 하면서 춤을 춰요.
   ***They dance while singing simultaneously**.*

If the particle 도 is added to this construction, it contributes its usual meaning *though* or *even*:

4. 오빠는 늘 놀면서도 공부를 잘 해요.
   [*My brother, even while always playing, studies a lot.* =]
   While it's true my brother is always having fun, he studies a lot, too.

But sometimes the meaning is *although* even without the particle 도; notice that English *while* can mean *although*, too.

주의!

These -(으)면서도 clauses differ from -어도 clauses (*even though . . .*) in this respect: -어도 clauses may have different subjects or topics for the two clauses, while -(으)면서도 sentences have the same subject or topic for both.

Here are some more examples of these constructions.

5. 어머니를 생각하면서 사진들을 보고 있었어요.
I was looking at the photos, thinking about Mother.

6. 오늘 아침에 기차를 타고 오면서 보고서를 읽었어요.
This morning I read the report while I was coming on the train.

7. 어제 저녁에는 라디오를 들으면서 서류를 준비했어요.
Last night, I prepared the documents while listening to the radio.

8. 돈이 없으면서도 잘 써요.
Though I haven't got any money, I spend a lot.

9. 그 기차는 빠르면서(도) 좋아요.
The train is fast and nice, too. That is, *While fast, it is also good.*

10. 어머니는 일하시면서(도) 애기를 보세요.
My mother looks after the baby (even) while she works.
(Here, the 도 adds the meaning of *even*—it is, after all, quite an achievement to do this!)

22.2. Contrasted Topics with -(이)면

The conditional copula after nouns can act as a substitute for the topic particle 은/는 in its contrast function.

11. 낮이면 더워지고 밤이면 추워져요.
It warms up in the daytime and cools off at night.
[lit.: If it be daytime it becomes warm, and if it be night it becomes cold.]

12. 새들은 매년 봄이면 찾아오고 가을이면 돌아가요.
   The birds come to visit us every spring and go back in the fall.

13. 신문이면 어머님께 드리고 잡지면 저에게 주세요.
   Give it to father if it is a newspaper, and give to me if it is a magazine.

22.3. Mild Exclamations in -네요

Dialogue 2 in this lesson contained the following line.

14. 슬퍼지네요. 우리 이제 이런 얘기 하지 말고 . . .
   Gee, that's [really] sad. Let's stop talking about such things now and . . .

The one-shape ending –네요 makes a mild exclamation translatable as *Gee, . . . !* or *My, . . . !* or the like. Like other Korean exclamations, this ending is basically used for talking to oneself but in such a way that others notice your surprise. As such, it is inappropriate as a reply to a question. It can attach to both processive and descriptive verbs and to all three major types of base—plain, past, and future-presumptive. L-extending bases attach this ending to the shape without the ㄹ.

15. 이 커피가 진하네요!
   My, this coffee sure is strong!

16. 아이구, 실수를 했네요!
   Oh dear, I've really committed a blunder.

17. 설탕을 사야 되겠네요!
   Oh dear, we'll have to buy some more sugar.

18. 한국말을 잘 하시네요!
   My, you sure speak Korean well!

19. 돈을 잘 버네요!
   My, he sure earns a lot of money!

22.4. Abbreviated Verbs of Manner and Color

You have learned a set of Korean place words corresponding to the basic set of words you learned back in Lesson Five.

이	*this*	여기	*here; this place*
그	*that [nearby; aforementioned]*	거기	*there; that place*
저	*that [remote]*	저기	*over there*
어느	*what (one)* / 어디 *where; what place* -----------		

There is also a corresponding set of verb expressions. As processive (action) verbs, they are vowel-base verbs ending in 어- but with irregular infinitives like that of 하- (해).

Base	Polite Style	
이러-,	이래요	*does [it] this way*
그러-,	그래요	*does [it] that [nearby or afore-mentioned] way*
저러-,	저래요	*does [it] that [remote] way*
어떠-,	어때요	*does it how (or why)?*

As descriptive verbs (adjectives), they are a special class of base we can call H-DROPPING. They have consonant bases ending in -어ㅎ before one-shape endings only but vowel bases ending in -어 before two-shape endings, and their infinitives are irregular like that of 하- (해).

Base	Polite Style	
이러(ㅎ)-,	이래요	*is like this*
그러(ㅎ)-,	그래요	*is like that*
저러(ㅎ)-,	저래요	*is like that [remote]*
어떠(ㅎ)-,	어때요	*is like what? is how?*

Besides abbreviated verbs of manner like those above, the other main class of verbs in the "H-dropping" class is color adjectives. The following page shows the forms for each of these verbs.

ㅎ-Dropping Verbs: Sample Forms

	Base	Present Polite	Past Base	Future Base	Hon. Base	고- Form	Sus- pective	Condi- tional	Modi- fier
do *like that* [contrast with 그렇다 below]	그러-	그래요	그랬-	그러겠-	그러시-	그러고	그러지	그러면	그런
be *like that*	그러(ㅎ)-	그래요	그랬-	그렇겠-	그러시-	그렇고	그렇지	그러면	그런
be black	까마(ㅎ)-	까매요	까맸-	까맣겠-	까마시-	까맣고	까맣지	까마면	까만
be how?	어떠(ㅎ)-	어때요	어땠-	어떻겠-	어떠시-	어떻고	어떻지	어떠면	어떤

The behavior of these ㅎ-dropping bases is irregular enough to warrant the following rules of thumb when combining them with verb endings.

(1) If the ending begins with -(으)ㄴ, -(으)ㅁ, -(으)ㅅ, or -(으)ㄹ, ignore the (으), drop the ㅎ and treat the base like a vowel base:

까맣-	+	-(으)ㄴ	→	까만
까맣-	+	-(으)면	→	까마면
까맣-	+	-(으)ㄹ까요?	→	까말까요?
까맣-	+	-(으)세요	→	까마세요

(2) In all other cases, treat these bases as regular consonant base:

까맣-	+	-지만	→	까맣지만
까맣-	+	-고	→	까맣고
까맣-	+	-거든요	→	까맣거든요
까맣-	+	-던	→	까맣던
까맣-	+	-네요	→	까맣네요

There are two corresponding sets of adverbs for the pointing words.

이렇게	*like this, in this way*	이리	*this way (hither)*
그렇게	*like that, in that way*	그리	*that way (thither)*
저렇게	*like that (there), in*	저리	*that way (over there)*
어떻게	*how? in what way?;* *how come? why?*		

Adverbs of the first set (with -게, the regular adverbative; see Lesson Twenty-four) usually refer to manner; the second set (with -이, derived adverbs) usually refer to direction and are often followed by the particle -로, but they are sometimes used with the same meaning as adverbs of the first set. Here are sentences to illustrate some of these words.

20. 이곳 겨울 날씨는 이래요. 한국 겨울 날씨는 어때요?
     The weather here in winter is like this. What's the winter weather like in Korea?

21. 동생은 늘 그래요.
My little brother is always doing that or *is always like that.*

22. 어떻게 그렇게 잘 하세요?
How come you do it so well?

23. 이리 오십시오.
Please come this way.

24. 저리(로) 가면, 바다를 볼 수 있어요.
If you go that way over there, you can see the sea.

25. 그리 많지 않아요.
I don't have so/that many.

26. 저리 가!
Go away!

All of these words except the question forms occur in variant diminutive shapes called light isotopes: 요러 *like this*, 고러 *like that*, 조러 *like that (there)*, 요리 *this way*, 고리 *that way*, 조리 *that way over there*. The latter are especially common in the directional meanings. Compare the place nouns (Lesson Six) 여기/요기 = 이/요곳 *here, this place*, 거기/고기 = 그/고 곳 *there, that place (just mentioned* or *near you)*, 저기/조기 = 저/조 곳 *there, that place (previously mentioned* or *over there)*.

22.5. Verbs: Transferentive -다(가)

Transferentive verb forms, with the ending -다 (optionally followed by 가), indicate a *shift* or *transfer* in action: either of the verb action itself, or of its direction, or of the recipient of its benefit.

Attached to a plain base, the ending makes the form mean *when so-and-so happens . . .* ; this is followed by another action that *interrupts*, *transfers*, or *shifts* the trend of the first, so it is discontinued in favor of the second. (It is not clear from the construction alone whether the interruption is later resumed.)

Attached to a past base, the past transferentive form –었다(가) conveys the meaning *when so-and-so had happened/come full circle, then . . .* and the following verb tells of something contradictory or unanticipated that happened right after the action of the past transferentive form.

27. 어디 갔다 오셨어요?
    Where have you been?

28. 뛰어가다가 넘어졌어요.
    He was running and then fell down.

29. 아이가 울다가 잤어요.
    The baby cried itself to sleep.

30. 애기는 자다가 깨서 기분이 안 좋은 것 같아요.
    The baby woke up from a [deep] sleep, so doesn't seem to be in a good mood.

31. 시장에 가다가 우체국에 들렀어요?
    Did you drop by the post office on the way to the market?

32. 시장에 갔다가 우체국에 들를까요?
    Shall we go to the market [first] and then drop by the post office?

33. 3개월 전에 새 컴퓨터를 샀다가 팔았습니다.
    Three months ago I bought a new computer but then sold it [again].

34. 준비를 하시다가 질문이 있으시면 언제든지 전화하십시오.
    If, in the course of preparing, you should [suddenly] have any questions, call me any time.

35. 사무실에서 다른 걸 찾다가 10,000원짜리를 하나 찾았어요.
    I was looking for something else in the office when I found a 10,000-wŏn note.

Another construction involving transferentive forms employs two such forms, of opposite or contrasting meaning—either present or, more commonly, past—rounded off by a form of 해요 or 그러-, 그래요. This construction means that the two actions keep interrupting each other. For example:

36. 저 할머니는 연세가 많으셔서 정신이 왔다 갔다 하세요.
    That lady is old, so sometimes she's with it, and others not.

37. 달은 매달 커지다가 작아지다가 해요.   or
     달은 매달 커졌다가 작아졌다가 해요.
The moon waxes and wanes each month —
The moon gets big and gets small each month.

38. 이 하나가 늘 아팠다 괜찮았다 해요.
One of my teeth aches off and on.

39. 불을 켰다가 껐다가 그러지 말아요!
Stop turning the lights on and off!

Try not to confuse the past-tense transferentive form 갔다(가) *went, and then* . . . with the abbreviation 갖다(가) ← 가져다(가) *carry/bring and then* (shift) as seen here:

40. 이 국을 할아버지께 갖다가 드려요.
Take this soup and give it to grandfather.

The form 갖다(가) conveys the meaning *take and shift* (the position of). Thus, 갖다 주십시오 means *Please bring it to me*, a useful expression when ordering food in a restaurant.

The transferentive form 있다(가) *stays and then* has the additional meaning *in a little while* or *later on*; in this meaning it is often spelled 이따(가).

Here are more examples of transferentive forms.

41. 대사관에 갔다 왔어요.
I've been to the embassy. (I went to the embassy and then came back.)

42. 어제는 수학 선생님의 강의를 듣다가 잤어요.
Yesterday I fell asleep listening to the math teacher's lecture.

43. 갔다가 바로 오세요.
Come right back!

44. 걸어가다가, 피곤해서 버스를 탔어요.
While I was walking along [the street], I got tired and got on a bus.

45. 사람들이 들어 왔다 나갔다 하네요.
People keep coming in and going out.

46. 싼 것을 샀다가 비싼 것으로 바꿨어요.
   I bought a cheap one but I exchanged it for an expensive one.

47. 수저를 그렇게 들었다 놓았다 하지 말아요!
   Stop picking up and putting down your spoon and chopsticks like that!

48. 비가 오다 말다 하네요.
   It's raining off and on. (It keeps raining and then stopping.)

The last example shows that you use the auxiliary 마-ㄹ- *desist* (put after suspective -지) to make negative commands and suggestions when you want to use a negative instead of some completely different second verb. Another example:

49. 비가 오다 말았어요.
   It started to rain and then stopped.

22.6. More on the Auxiliary Verb 말아요

22.6.1. Review of 말아요

You have already learned that the suspective -지 followed by 말아요 is a way to make negative commands (section 12.2.) with a more literal translation of *avoid, refrain, desist from doing*. These expressions are largely limited to commands and suggestions.

50. 껌을 씹지 마세요.
   Please don't chew gum.

51. 무리를 하지 마세요.
   Please don't overdo it (Please don't strain yourself).

52. 잊어버리지 마세요.
   Don't forget it.

With verbal nouns and other expressions involving the auxiliary 해요 you get the expected form 하지 마-ㄹ- but sometimes the 하지 can be dropped, as in: 염려 마세요 *Don't worry* instead of the equally acceptable 염려하지 마세요.

An example that does not involve a verbal noun is 어려워(하지) 마세요 *Don't feel embarrassed*, with the emotional meaning of the adjective 어려워요 *It is difficult, I am embarrassed* (as in 어렵지만 *It is embarrassing (I am sorry to trouble you, but)* turned into a processive verbal phrase by using the infinitive -어 + 해요 (section 17.1).

Here are more examples of negative commands and suggestions with - 지 마-ㄹ- .

53. 내일 비가 오면, 등산을 가지 맙시다.
     If it rains tomorrow, let's not go hiking.

54. 내일은 일찍 일어나지 맙시다.
     Let's not get up early tomorrow.

55. 그 생선이 너무 비싸면, 사지 마세요.
     If that fish is too expensive, don't buy it.

56. 시간이 너무 늦었어요. 은행에 가지 마세요.
     It's too late. Don't go to the bank.

57. 오늘 저녁에 음식점에서 먹지 말아요.
     Don't eat at a restaurant tonight.

Within sentences containing a pair of opposite commands or suggestions, the first may be expressed by -지 말고 (*instead of . . . ing; without . . . ing*), as in the following sentence.

58. 숟가락으로 잡수시지 말고, 젓가락으로 잡수세요.
     Don't eat with a spoon—eat with chopsticks.

Here are more examples.

59. 음식점에서 만나지 말고, 호텔에서 만납시다.
     Let's not meet at the restaurant, let's meet at the hotel.

60. 버스로 가지 말고, 택시로 갑시다.
     Let's not take a bus, let's take a taxi.

61. 김치찌개를 시키지 말고, 만두국을 주문합시다.
     Let's not order kimchee stew—let's order dumpling soup.

From this use comes the handy phrase 잊지 말고 plus affirmative command *Don't forget to . . .* as in these sentences.

62. 잊지 말고 손을 씻으세요.
     Don't forget to wash your hands.

Lesson Twenty-two / 163

63. 잊지 말고 보고서를 준비하세요.
Don't forget to prepare the report.

64. 잊지 말고 어머니한테 그 이야기를 해 드리세요.
Don't forget to tell that to Mother.

65. 잊지 말고 구두를 닦으세요.
Don't forget to shine your shoes.

Recall that in statements and questions, *instead of* or *without VERBing* is expressed by -지 않고.

66. 음식점에서 만나지 않고, 호텔에서 만났어요.
We didn't meet at the restaurant; we met at the hotel.

67. 우리 애기는 저녁을 먹지 않고 잤어요.
Our baby went to sleep without eating supper.

22.6.2. Use of 말고 as a Pseudo-Particle

You will sometimes find 말고 used in the middle of a sentence directly after a noun or a noun + particle with the meaning *not being* . . . ; in this use we can say that the gerund is functioning as a pseudo-particle, and it does not call for a command or suggestion at the end of the sentence.

68. 차 말고 다른 거 안 마실래요?
Instead of tea, wouldn't you rather drink something else?

69. 이거 말고 저것을 사세요.
Buy that one and not this one.

70. 우리 아들 말고 다른 아이를 찾고 있어요.
They are looking for some other boy, not our son.

71. 이 까만 것 말고 갈색 가방이 없습니까?
Don't you have any brown suitcases instead of this black one?

22.7. *As long as you're at it . . .* with

-(으)ㄴ/-는 김에

Recall the following example from Dialogue Two.

72.　시내에 나온 김에 술이나 마시지요, 뭐.
　　　Seeing as we've [already] come downtown, what say we have a drink?

A processive verb followed by a past modifier in -(으)ㄴ or a processive modifier in -는 followed by 김에 means something like *incidental to VERBing, seeing as one is VERBing or has VERBed anyway, . . .* Quite often, such clauses are preceded by the adverb 이왕, which we can translate as *anyway, anyhow.* Here are some more examples.

73.　A. 제 전화번호 적어 드릴까요?
　　　　Shall I jot down my phone number for you?

　　　B. 이왕 쓰시는 김에 주소도 써 주세요.
　　　　As long as you're at it [writing], write your address, too.

74.　A. 슈퍼에 잠깐 갔다 올게요.
　　　　I'm just off to the supermarket briefly.

　　　B. 슈퍼에 가는 김에 과일 좀 사와요.
　　　　While you're at it, buy some fruit.

75.　A. 킹 선생님은 요새 어떻게 지내실까요?
　　　　How do you suppose Dr. King is getting along these days?

　　　B. 생각난 김에 전화해 보지요, 뭐.
　　　　Seeing as we've thought of it, what say we (try to) give him a call?

76.　A. 다음 주 파티 어떻게 할까요?
　　　　What shall we do about next week's party?

　　　B. 이왕 하는 김에 사람을 많이 초대하지요, 뭐.
　　　　As long as we're at it, we might as well invite lots of people, don't you think?

22.8. Modifiers with 것 같아요: *Seems* ...

77.　　사장님은 어떤 때는 무리하시는 것 같아요.
　　　　The boss seems to overdo it sometimes.

An expression meaning *seems* or *looks as if* is made by combining a modifier with the phrase 것 같아요, which means literally *is the same thing as* . . . or *is like the act/fact of* . . . The modifier may be processive, to show an action now in progress; or it may be past or future. With descriptive verbs, the plain modifier is used for non-past meanings.

This pattern has become extremely popular, especially with younger speakers. It is often used even in situations where there is absolutely no doubt or question of *seeming* or *appearing*, e.g.:

78.　　(coughing and sniffling)　　감기에 걸린 것 같아요.
　　　　　　　　　　　　　　　　　　I seem to have caught a cold.

Compare:

79.　　(내가/나는) 감기에 걸렸어요.
　　　　I caught a cold.

Here are more examples.

80.　　기차가 오는 것 같습니다.
　　　　The train seems to be coming.

81.　　피곤해 하는 것 같아요.
　　　　He seems to be getting tired.

82.　　그분이 바쁘신 것 같아서 나는 들어가지 않았어요.
　　　　He looked busy, so I didn't go in.

83.　　소금을 너무 많이 넣으신 것 같아요.
　　　　Seems you put in too much salt.

84.　　내 수첩을 잊어버린 것 같아요.
　　　　Seems I forgot my memo book.

The same phrase—것 같아요—has a more literal meaning when not preceded by modifiers: 내 것 같아요 (same as 내 것과 같아요) *It is like mine (my thing).*

Exercises

Exercise 1: Practice with -(으)면서

Each item below contains two sentences. Link the two together so that they mean *while someone does something, at the same time he does the other*, then translate the sentence. For example, the first will be: 사장님을 수첩을 보시면서 접대실 안으로 들어오셨습니다. *Looking at his diary, the company president entered the reception room.*

1. 사장님이 수첩을 보세요. 접대실 안으로 들어오셨습니다.
2. 나는 오늘 밤에 라디오를 듣겠어요. 공부하겠어요.
3. 우리는 공원에 가서 산보하겠어요. 꽃을 구경하겠어요.
4. 아버지는 신문을 읽으세요. 음악을 들으세요.
5. 나는 집 생각을 했어요. 어머니한테 편지를 썼어요.
6. 그 학생이 저녁을 먹어요. 테레비를 봐요.
7. 친구를 기다려요. 신문을 읽었어요.
8. 영화를 봐요. 울었어요.
9. 제임스는 껌을 씹어요. 담배를 피워요.
10. 어머니는 생선을 구우세요. 소금을 뿌리세요.

Exercise 2: Practice with -(으)면서도

Each item below contains two sentences. Link the two together so that they mean *while/even while someone does something, he does the other*, then translate the sentence.

1. 그 남자는 그 여자를 사랑합니다. 그 여자와 결혼을 하지 못 했습니다.
2. 그분은 웃습니다. 기뻐하지 않습니다.
3. 그 사람은 돈이 많습니다. 잘 쓰지 않습니다.
4. 젓가락을 잘 써요. 포크로 먹는 것을 더 좋아해요.

5.　일본 음식은 좀 싱겁습니다. 맛이 있습니다.
6.　저는 돈이 없습니다. 잘 씁니다.
7.　그 학생은 똑똑합니다. 실수를 많이 합니다.
8.　열심히 공부합니다. 어떤 때는 수업에 안 옵니다.
9.　그분은 부지런합니다. 어떤 때는 일을 안 합니다.
10.　값이 쌉니다. 물건이 좋습니다.

Exercise 3: Practice with -네요

Below are ten Korean sentences. Convert them into mild surprises and translate them into English.

1.　시험을 잘 봤어요.
2.　한국말 잘 하세요.
3.　일본말도 배워요.
4.　그분이 벌써 약속 시간을 결정했어요.
5.　이 커피가 진해요.
6.　길이 넓어요.
7.　오늘 날씨가 굉장히 더워요.
8.　아이구, 실수했어요.
9.　따님이 아주 예뻐요.
10.　약속을 잊어버렸어요.
11.　돈을 다 썼어요.
12.　내일 선생님이랑 얘기해야겠어요.
13.　대합실이 참 커요.
14.　매운 거 잘 먹어요.
15.　오히려 잘 된 것 같아요.

Exercise 4: Practice with -다가

Each item below contains two sentences. Link the two together with transferentive -다(가) so that they mean *someone does or did something, and then . . . [shift]*, then translate the sentence. For example, the first will be: 접대실에서 한 시간 기다렸다가 그냥 갔어요. *I waited for an hour in the reception room and then left.*

1. 접대실에서 한 시간 기다렸어요. 그냥 갔어요.
2. 수진 씨는 밥을 먹어요. 갑자기 안색이 이상해졌어요.
3. 젓가락을 써요. 포크로 바꿨어요.
4. 밤 늦게까지 보고서를 써요. 잤어요.
5. 버스에서 내려요. 넘어졌어요.
6. 생선만 며칠동안 먹어요. 병이 났어요.
7. 뉴스를 봐요. 너무 지루해서 테레비를 그냥 껐어요.
8. 집에 가요. 도서관에 들러야겠어요.
9. 학교에 와요. 영진 씨를 만났어요.
10. 비가 쏟아져요. 갑자기 개었어요.
11. 한국에서 회사에 다녀요. 캐나다에 왔습니다.
12. 야유회를 가요. 친구를 만났어요.
13. 사무실을 청소해요. 이 사진을 찾았어요.
14. 운동을 해요. 다리를 다쳤어요.
15. 음악을 들어요. 여자친구 생각이 났어요.

Exercise 5: Practice with -(으)ㄴ/-는 것 같아요

Convert each of the sentences below into a sentence in the *seems* pattern with -(으)ㄴ/-는 것 같아요, then translate the sentence. For example, the first will be: 수진 씨는 튀긴만두 말고 찐 만두를 좋아하는 것 같아요. *It seems Sujin likes steamed dumplings and not pan-fried ones.*

1. 수진 씨는 튀긴 만두 말고 찐 만두를 좋아해요.
2. 만호 씨는 부엌에서 계란을 삶아요.
3. 고추를 너무 많이 넣었어요.
4. 철호 씨는 안색이 갑자기 나빠졌어요.
5. 손님은 응접실에서 기다리고 계세요.
6. 오늘 차가 별로 밀리지 않아요.
7. 어머님이 찌개를 맛있게 끓이세요.
8. 사장님이 벌써 결정을 하셨어요.
9. 할아버지는 기분전환으로 밖에 나가셨어요.
10. 서울의 공기가 아주 안 좋아요.
11. 애들이 실컷 놀았어요.
12. 이 생선은 너무 짜요.
    그래요? 나한테는 오히려 너무 싱거워요.
13. 그 분은 매일 지하철로 출퇴근하세요.

14. 그렇지요?

네, 그래요.

15. 선생님은 요즘 너무 무리하세요.

Exercise 6: Practice with - (으) ㄴ / -는 김에

Each item below contains two sentences. Link the two together with the pattern in - (으) ㄴ / -는 김에 so that they mean *now that . . . ; seeing as . . . ; while one is at it . . .* , and so on, then translate the sentence. For example, the first will be: 시내에 나온 김에 백화점에 들러서 쇼핑이나 할까요? *Seeing as we're downtown, shall we drop in at a department store and do some shopping?*

1. 시내에 나왔어요. 백화점에 들러서 쇼핑이나 할까요?
2. 생각이 났어요. 그 사람한테 전화나 겁시다.
3. 이왕 준비를 해요. 보고서를 잘 씁시다.
4. 이왕 사요. 괜찮고 보기 좋은 것 을 삽시다.
5. 영국까지 가요. 프랑스 구경도 좀 하고 옵시다.
6. 도서관에 왔어요. 신문이나 보고 가야겠어요.
7. 우리 집에 오셨어요. 점심이나 드시고 가시지요.
8. 청소를 해요. 내 방도 좀 청소할래요?
9. 빨래를 해요. 이 바지도 좀 빨아 줄래요?
10. 한국말을 배워요. 한자도 좀 배워야겠어요.
11. 일어섰어요. 그 창문 좀 닫아 줄래요?
12. 말이 나왔어요. 이 문제에 대해서 좀 더 이야기합시다.
13. 친구의 생일 선물을 사요. 내 것도 하나 살까요?
14. 우체국에 가세요. 이 편지도 부쳐 주실래요?

Exercise 7: Korean to English Translation

Translate the following Korean sentences into English.

1. 잊지 말고 생선을 구우세요.
2. 그냥 서 있지 말고, 좀 도와주세요!
3. 새 자동차를 사셨네요!
4. 따님이 아주 귀엽네요! 그 사이에 많이 큰 것 같아요.
5. 아드님이 부지런하네요!

6. 돈을 많이 쓰면서도, 많이 벌지는 못합니다.

7. 그런 생각을 하지 마시고 편히 쉬십시오!

8. A. 영화는 어땠어요?

    B. 그저 그랬어요.

9. A. 돈을 그렇게 많이 벌면서 왜 그러세요?

    B. 내가 돈을 많이 버는 것 같아요?

10. A. 어떻게 알았어요?

    B. 어제 라디오에서도 듣고 신문에서도 봤습니다.

11. A. 오늘은 생선을 먹을까요?

    B. 그러지요.

12. A. 대사관에 들르면, 시간이 없겠지요?

    B. 그렇지요.

13. 〔손님에게〕 더 노시다가 가시지요.

14. 샤쓰를 입었다가 벗었어요.

15. 수미 씨는 계속 울었다 웃었다 하는 것 같아요. 웬일일까요?

16. A. 지금 안 가세요?

    B. 좀 쉬었다 갈게요.

17. 그렇게 왔다가 갔다가 하지 말고 가만히 앉아 있어요!

18. A. 어제 저녁에 뭐 했어요?

    B. 테레비를 보다가 잤어요.

19. 골프를 배우다가 너무 비싸서 그만뒀어요.

20. 값이 올랐다 내렸다 해요.

21. A. 요즘 날씨가 너무 좋아서 어디 좀 놀러 갔으면 좋겠어요.

    B. 말이 나온 김에 다음 주말에 부산에 놀러 갑시다.

Exercise 8: English to Korean Translation

Translate the following sentences into Korean.

1. I listen to music while reading that book.

2. In the daytime I feel happy, but at night I am sad.

3. Seeing as we've got to go to Korea, let's visit Japan, too.

4. My, this fish tastes bad!

5. You shouldn't be shy like that.

6. Oh dear, I've forgotten my friend's book again.

7. If you want to eat with chopsticks, you have to eat like this.

8. A. Please come this way.

B.   Go away!

9.   How did you earn so much money?

10.   My mother sometimes prepares food like that.

11.   If Mr. Kim visits us, let's not argue with each other.

12.   Please don't forget to boil this water.

13.   My sister is slim, but I am as fat as a pig.

14.   Let's sprinkle some salt on it.

15.   Don't forget to go to the shops. And while you're at it, post this letter.

16.   He is going to and fro [alternately].

17.   I went to Australia (and back).

18.   Sometimes my tooth hurts and my head hurts [alternately].

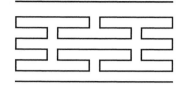 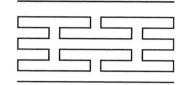

Lesson 23

영국에서 친구 한 명이 와 있는데, 그 친구를 데리고 가도 됩니까?

In this lesson, Dialogue One shows Chris Murphy accepting an invitation to a dinner party from his business acquaintance, Mr. Nam. In Dialogue Two, we see Eunice Murphy agonizing with Mrs. Kim as to what clothes to wear to the party. New patterns covered include the Imminent Elaboration pattern in -(으)ㄴ데(요)/-는데(요), *in spite of . . .ing* in -(으)ㄴ 데도/-는데도, prospective modifiers in -(으)ㄹ, the *when* pattern in -(으)ㄹ때, *seems like it will/might . . .* in -(으)ㄹ 것 같아요, and *was intending to, but . . .* in -(으)려다 (가).

Korean Dialogues

Dialogue 1

Mr. Nam, a recent business acquaintance of Chris Murphy, has called up Chris to invite him and Eunice to a dinner party.

남 사장   내일 밤에 조촐한 파티를 열려고 하는데요. 와 주셨으면 합니다.

머피 사장   아, 그러세요? 기꺼이 가겠습니다. 몇 시까지 갈까요?

남 사장   혼자서 오시려면 어려울 것 같아서, 제가 댁으로 모시러 갈게요.

머피 사장   아, 참 – 영국에서 친구 1명이 와 있는데, 그 친구를

              데리고 가도 됩니까?

남 사장   물론이지요. 내일 6시 반에 댁으로 갈게요.

Dialogue 2

남편이 파티에 초대를 받은 것을 말하자마자, 유니스는 걱정을 하기 시작합니다.
유니스는 초대를 받을 때마다, 언제나 새 옷을 사 입으려고 합니다.
그래서 김 선생님 부인하고 만났습니다.

유니스	내일 파티에 가야 하는데, 입을 옷이 없어서 어떻게 하지요?
미세스 김	지금 입고 있는 옷도 좋은데요, 뭐. 항상 새 옷을 입을 필요가 없잖아요?
유니스	그래도 이것보다 더 나은 옷을 입고 가고 싶어요. 싸고 좋은 옷을 파는 데를 아세요?
미세스 김	그럼요. 백화점에서 좋은 옷을 파는데 지금 가려면 시간이 너무 늦었을 거에요.
유니스	그럼, 내일 아침에 백화점에 갈 때 같이 안 가시겠어요?
미세스 김	같이 갔으면 좋겠는데, 언제쯤 가요?
유니스	점심 때 가려고 그러는데, 진영이네 집에서 만날까요?
미세스 김	네, 그러지요.

Notes

사 입으려고   lit.: *with the intention of buying and wearing*. This could be expanded as 사서 입으려고.

Reading Passage

수영이는 한국에서 태어난 재미교포 대학생입니다. 어렸을 때 부모님과 미국으로 이민 왔기 때문에, 말하자면, 수영이는 '일점오세'입니다.

재작년에 한국으로 여행하러 가려다가 돈이 모자라서 못 갔는데, 그래서 1년 동안 돈을 모아서 작년 여름 방학에 드디어 한국에 갔을 때 한국말을 잘 못해서 아주 불편했습니다. 한국에서 만난 한국 친구들을 만날 때마다, 친구들이 이렇게 물어 봤습니다.

"수영 씨는 한국 사람인데도, 왜 한국말을 못 합니까?"

처음에는 이런 질문을 받을 때마다 수영이는 기분이 나빠서 할 말이 없었지만, 나중에 이렇게 대답을 하기 시작했습니다:

"한국말 유전자가 따로 없잖아요. 미국에서 어렸을 때부터 자랐는데 한국말을 잘 못하는 것은 당연하지요."

택시를 탔을 때도 한국말을 더듬거려서 놀리는 택시 기사 아저씨들도 있었는데, 창피해서 혼났습니다.

수영이는 처음에 실망해서 한국말을 배울 것을 포기하려다가 다시 생각을 해서, 이제부터 한국말을 배우려고 대학교 한국어 코스에 등록했습니다. 그리고 수영이는 한국말을 유창하게 할 수 있을 때까지 한국말을 열심히 배우기로 마음 먹었습니다.

Vocabulary

Nouns

<u>Overseas Koreans</u>

교민	resident overseas Korean(s)
교포	overseas Korean(s)
캐나다교포	Korean Canadian
이민	immigration
이민자	immigrant
이민(을) 가-	emigrate
이민(을) 오-	immigrate
이세	second generation
일점오세	1.5 generation
재미	resident in the United States
재미교포	Korean American
재일	resident in Japan
재일교포	Korean Japanese

<u>University Life</u>

등록	registration
등록(을) 하-	register
몇 과목을 등록하셨어요?	How many courses did you register for?
문학	literature
한국문학	Korean literature
영문학	English literature
영문과 〔-꽈〕	English Literature Department
사은회 파티	party in honor of one's teacher
파티(를) 여-ㄹ-	have/host a party
성적	marks, grades
성적표	report card
종강 파티	end-of-term party
주인공	the "star"; the protagonist; person of honor at a party
코스	course

Sports

운동 선수	athlete
배구 선수	volleyball player
농구 선수	basketball player
축구 선수	soccer player
미식축구 선수	American football player
수구 선수	water polo player
아이스 하키 선수	ice hockey player

Health

수술	an operation (medical)
수술실	operating theatre
수술(을) 하-	perform an operation; have an operation
수술(을) 받-	have an operation
신경	nerve, nerves
신경(을) 쓰-	be nervous, worried
신경(이) 쓰이-	be nervous, worried
환자	patient; a sick person

Other

거실	living room
계절	season
사계절	the four seasons
한국은 사계절이 분명해요.	The four seasons are clearly distinguished in Korea.
국회의원	National Assemblyman, M.P.
기사 (아저씨)	driver, chauffeur
-네	-'s place (e.g., Pete's place)
동양화	Oriental painting
매월	every month
벨소리	"bell sound" = ringing
아무 NOUN (이)나	any NOUN at all, any NOUN whatsoever
아무 NOUN 도	no NOUN at all, no NOUN whatsoever
영수증	receipt
유전자	gene
팩스	fax
팩스번호	fax number
표현	[verbal] expression
표현(을) 하-	express

회의	conference
회의 중입니다.	She's in the middle of a conference.

Verbs

Descriptive and/or Sensory Verbs

공평하–	be fair
불공평하–	be unfair
나(ㅅ)–	be preferable, better [than = 보다]
분명하–	be clear, obvious
조촐하–	be small and neat
조촐한 파티	a "little party"
창피하–	be/feel embarrassed
통화중이에요	(phone) is busy; (someone) is on the phone
훌륭하–	be great, admirable

Verbs That Take Objects

놀리–	make fun of, tease
더듬거리–	stutter or speak haltingly
그 사람은 말을 더듬거려요.	He speaks haltingly.
데리–	take (person) along
데려가–	take (person) along
데려오–	bring (person) along
데리고 오–	bring (person) along
데리고 가–	take (person) along
마음(을) 먹–	make up one's mind to, resolve to (used with –기로)

사장님께 여쭤보기로 마음을 먹었습니다.

I resolved to ask the boss.

모시–	[HUMBLE] take a (person) along, accompany somebody
모셔가–	take (person) along
모셔오–	bring (person) along
모시고 오–	bring (person) along
모시고 가–	take (person) along
잘못 거–ㄹ–	dials a wrong number
잘못 거셨는데요.	I'm afraid you have the wrong number.
포기(를) 하–	give up, give up on

| 혼(을) 내- | give a person a hard time; teach someone a lesson, give a good scolding |
| 어머니가 아이를 혼 내셨어요. | The mother scolded the child. |

Intransitive Verbs (Processive Verbs That Cannot Take Objects)

나오-	[a subject] comes up
말이 나온 김에. . .	Seeing as the subject has come up . . .
들리-	stops by, drops in (same as 들르-)
언제 1번 우리 집에 들리세요.	Drop by the house some time.
실망(을) 하-	be disappointed, feel disappointed
우리 딸 때문에 실망했어요.	I'm very disappointed because of my daughter.
시험을 못 봐서 실망했습니다.	I'm disappointed because I did poorly on the exam.
여쭈-	asks sb esteemed
여쭤 보-	asks sb esteemed
한 가지 여쭤 봐도 됩니까?	May I ask you something?

Adverbs

기꺼이	with pleasure
기꺼이 해 드리지요.	I'd be happy to do it for you.
당연히	naturally, as a matter of course
당연하-	stand to reason, make perfect sense, be natural

게으름뱅이니까 성적표가 그렇게 나온 것은 당연하지요.

She's a lazy bum, so it stands to reason that her report card came out that way.

말하자면	as it were; so to speak
분명히	clearly, obviously
분명히 축구 선수일 거에요.	Obviously, he must be a soccer player.

Lesson Notes

23.1. Imminent Elaboration with Circumstantial -는데(요), -(으)ㄴ데(요)

Observe the following sentence.

1. 같이 갔으면 좋겠는데 . . .
   I'd like to go along, but . . .

Thus far, every verb ending you have encountered has been either a one-shape or a two-shape ending. This lesson introduces a special new kind of *three*-shape ending—composed of a modifier plus a restricted postmodifier. The gist of these as follows:

Base	Modifier	Post-Modifier
Descriptive Bases	-은/-ㄴ	데
All Other Bases, i.e.: Processive Bases All Past Bases All Future Bases 있- and 없-	-는	데

These are called restricted modifiers because their use in this configuration is restricted to just two postmodifiers: circumstantial 데 and 지 (which you will learn later). Probably the easiest way to learn these patterns is to simply memorize the two three-shape endings -는데, -은데, -ㄴ데, and -는지, -은지, -ㄴ지, keeping in mind the configuration above.

As shown above, descriptive verbs use the -(으)ㄴ modifier form, and processive verbs (together with all past bases, all future bases and the special verbs 있- and 없-) use the -는 modifier.

Descriptive	Processive	있 -	없 -
비싼데	가는데	있는데	없는데
비쌌는데	갔는데	있었는데	없었는데
비싸겠는데	가겠는데	있겠는데	없겠는데

The overall blanket meaning of patterns with -데 is circumstantial: *given the circumstance that . . .* or *in view of the circumstance that . . . .* The most practical English equivalents for the construction are usually *so* or *but* or an even vaguer *DOT-DOT-DOT* (" . . . ").

The patterns using circumstantial 데 have an additional important nuance, namely imminent elaboration. The -데 form signals:

1) *Don't jump in yet, I may well have something additional to say which is related to what I've just said.* Or
2) *Now that I've just told you this, perhaps you'd like to ask for clarification or elaboration?*

You can round off a -데 form with the polite style particle 요 and create a highly useful and lively sentence pattern.

Now let us go back and look at the sentences in this lesson's dialogue.

2. 내일 파티에 가야 하는데 . . .
    Tomorrow I have to go to a party . . .
    [and now let me elaborate to you why this circumstance is significant—namely, *I have no clothes to wear.*]

3. 지금 입고 있는 옷도 좋은데요, 뭐.
    (But) the clothes you're wearing now are fine . . .
    [and I could go on to elaborate on what a silly thing that is you've said . . . or, perhaps I could go on to say more about just *how* nice your clothes are, etc.]

4. 백화점에서 비싼 옷을 파는데 . . .
    They sell expensive clothes in the department store, but . . .
    [and now let me elaborate to you more on this circumstance—namely, *the time has got too late.*]

Sometimes, you can give a polite reply to a (often misguided) question with a -데 form.

5. A. 미국 분이세요?
       Are you American?

    B. 아닌데요. 영국 사람인데요.
       I'm afraid not—I'm English. [Why—are you looking for an American?]

6. A. 박 교수님 계세요?
       Is Professor Pak in?

    B. 지금 안 계시는데요.
       I'm afraid not [—would you like me to elaborate?]

Lesson Twenty-three / 181

Another extension of this Imminent Elaboration function of – 데 (요) is polite exclamations.

7.   재미있는 분들 같은데요!
They seem like such interesting people!
[and I could elaborate about just how interesting they look . . .]

When a modifier-plus-데 appears at the end of a sentence, with 요 in polite style and without
요 in the intimate style (see Lesson Twenty-six), it often has an exclamatory meaning: *how . .
. ! what a . . . ! my, such a . . . !* The Imminent Elaboration nuance is still present, because it
is as if you were saying . . . *and I could go on forever about how great/neat it is.* Here are
some more examples.

8.   비가 많이 왔는데 (요)!
What a lot it rained!
[looks like we'll have to cancel tennis . . . !]

9.   오늘은 날이 참 추운데요!
My, what a cold day it is!
[we'll have to take the baby back in . . . !]

10.   이 방은 너무 작은데요!
This room is too small!
[I refuse to stay here . . . !]

11.   이 환자는 곧 수술을 해야 하겠는데요!
We'll have to operate on this patient at once!
[. . . or else he'll croak!]

12.   이 동양화는 훌륭한데요!
How splendid this oriental picture is!
[. . . and you said you couldn't paint!]

13.   I'ㅍㄷ 표현을 들어 본 일이 없는데요!
I've never heard such an expression before!
[. . . are you sure you heard it right?]

14.   경치가 좋은데요!
My, what fine scenery!
[this country is full of surprises . . . !]

A special suspensive intonation, here marked by three dots (. . .), often accompanies this
pattern: the voice hesitates, with a slight dip. The function is as if to say *Don't jump in
yet—I've still got the floor.* Here are more examples.

15.   날이 이렇게 추운데 . . . 어디에 가세요?
Where are you going on such a cold day?

16. 이번 시험은 쉬웠는데 . . . 왜 이렇게 못 봤어요?
    This ["time's"] exam was easy; why have you done so poorly?

17. 오늘은 바람이 불고, 비가 오는데 . . . 일찍 집에 들어갑시다.
    The wind is blowing and it is raining today; (in view of this) let's go home early.

18. 오늘은 대단히 바쁜데요. (. . .)내일 만나도 괜찮을까요?
    I'm very busy today. Would it be all right to get together tomorrow?

19. 이번 봄에 한국으로 가는데요. (. . .) 거기 봄 날씨는 어떻습니까?
    I'll be going to Korea this ["time's"] spring, so what's the weather like there in spring?

20. 오늘 먼 길을 가야 하는데, 아침을 많이 먹읍시다.
    (In view of the circumstance that) we have a long way to go today, let's eat a big breakfast.

21. 아이들이 길에서 놀면 안 되는데, 왜 여기서 놀고 있지요?
    The children shouldn't play in the street; why are they playing here?

22. 파티 하는 날을 오는 토요일로 정했는데요. (. . .) 오시겠어요?
    We've decided on next Saturday as the day to have our party; will you come?

23.2. *In spite of . . .ing* with -는/-(으)ㄴ데도

You will sometimes find the circumstantial construction followed by the particle 도 meaning *but* or *even though*.

23. 비가 오는데도 와 주셔서 고맙습니다.
    Thank you for coming to see me in spite of the rain.

24. 영문과를 졸업했는데도 영어를 잘 못 해요.
    Even though/in spite of the fact he graduated from an English Department, he can't speak English well.

This usage can be taken as an abbreviation of . . . 데도 불구하고 *disregarding the circumstance that.*

25. 추운데도 (불구하고) 나가서 놀고 싶어요?
    You want to go out and play in spite of the cold?

23.3. Other Uses of 데

In addition to the circumstantial and exclamatory uses, 데 occurs as a quasi-free noun (that is, a noun that cannot begin a sentence but must always be modified by something in front of it) with the meaning *place, spot* or sometimes *circumstance, occasion*—from which the other uses are derived. When the meaning is *place* the noun 곳 can often be used instead. Here are some examples.

추운 데	*a cold spot*
경치가 좋은 데	*a place where the scenery is nice*
다른 데 (약속이 있어요)	*(has an engagement) somewhere else*
네가 옷을 산 데	*the place you bought the clothes*
아무 데나	*any place at all*

You will notice that the usual modifiers are used, not the restricted modifiers: 본 데 means only *the place I saw* (or *saw it*) and 봤는데 means only *(given the circumstance that) [one] saw it (so)* . . . . But 추운데 is ambiguously (1) *cold spot* and (2) *(given the circumstance that) it is cold, (so)* . . . since the restricted processive modifiers are limited to use with processive verbs or with pasts and futures. For usage (1), Korean usually separates the modifier from 데 with a space: 추운 데.

Some of the phrases with the quasi-free noun 데 come to have specialized meanings: 표 파는 데 *the place where they sell tickets = the ticket seller's, the ticket window,* 옷 벗는 데 *the place where one undresses = the (un)dressing room.*

23.4. The Postnoun -네 and Diminutive -이

23.4.1. The Postnoun -네

The postnoun -네 makes an explicit plural for nouns referring to people. It can be combined with 들, and has the following two main usages.

a. Plural Marker

우리,	우리네,	우리네들	*we (all)*
저희,	저희네,	저희네들	*we (all)* (humble)
당신네,	당신네들		*you all*
너희,	너희네,	너희네들 〔니네들〕	*you all* (intimate)
자기네,	자기네들		*they themselves*

b. (after a name)

a. . . . *and his/her relatives/family*   b. . . . *'s place*

26. 철수네 집에서 만날까요?
     Shall we meet at 철수's place?

철수네   철수 *and his family; chez* 철수
                                    철수*'s place*

만호네   만호 *and his family; chez* 만호
                                    만호*'s place*

23.4.2. The Diminutive -이

The diminutive suffix -이 attaches to personal names ending in a consonant to indicate affection or endearment. Normally it can only be used of close friends or children and if used with an adult's full name (surname + given name) or just given name, sounds sarcastic or disparaging.

수진이	*little Sujin; Sujin to whom I feel close*
민숙이	*little Minsuk; Minsuk to whom I feel close*
김영삼이	*Kim Young-sam (that weasel . . .)*
영삼이	*Young-sam (that weasel . . .)*

Note that, when attached to a personal name ending in a consonant, –네 usually attaches to this diminutive name form in 이 (nothing to do with the subject marker 이!). For example:

수진이네   *Sujin's place; Sujin and her family*
민숙이네   *Minsuk's place; Minsuk and her family*

23.5. Modifiers (2): Prospective Modifier –(으)ㄹ

Observe the following phrases.

27.   운동할 사람
       a person who will exercise

28.   테니스 칠 사람
       a person who will play tennis

The 할 and 칠 in these phrases are in the prospective modifier form of 해요 *does* and 쳐요 *strikes*. This form has the meaning *who* or *that is to [do so-and-so]* or *who* or *that is to [be so-and-so]*: 운동할 사람 is literally *a (who-is-going-) to-exercise person* and 테니스 칠 사람 is *a who-will-play-tennis person*.

The two-shape prospective modifier ending –을/–ㄹ is pronounced –을 after consonants and –ㄹ after vowels.

CONSONANT BASES

GLOSS	BASES	PROSP. MODIFIER	DICT. FORM
wear	입–	입을	입다
hear, listen	들–	들을	듣다
lack	없–	없을	없다
close it	닫–	닫을	닫다
take off	벗–	벗을	벗다
look for	찾–	찾을	찾다
eat	먹–	먹을	먹다
read	읽–	읽을	읽다
be young	젊–	젊을	젊다
wear (shoes)	신–	신을	신다
sit down	앉–	앉을	앉다

CONSONANT BASES (CONT.)

GLOSS	BASES	PROSP. MODIFIER	DICT. FORM
walk	걸-	걸을	걷다
be good	좋-	좋을	좋다
hot	더 w-	더울	덥다
get better	나(ㅅ)-	나을	낫다

VOWEL BASES

GLOSS	BASES	PROSP. MODIFIER	DICT. FORM
wait for	기다리-	기다릴	기다리다
do like that	그러-	그럴	그러다
become	되-	될	되다
write	쓰-	쓸	쓰다
buy	사-	살	사다
give	주-	줄	주다
look at	보-	볼	보다
live	사-ㄹ-	살	살다
be far	머-ㄹ-	멀	멀다
call	부르-	부를	부르다

ㅎ-DROPPING BASES

GLOSS	BASES	PROSP. MODIFIER	DICT. FORM
be like that	그렇-	그럴	그렇다
be red	빨갛-	빨갈	빨갛다

There is also a past prospective modifier, of more limited use, formed by adding the ending -을/-ㄹ to the past base: 어려요 *is young* → 어렸어요 *was young* → 어렸을 때 *when [one] was young.* Past prospective modifier forms of adjectives, as you see, have special uses, discussed below (section 23.5.)

주의!

When a word that begins with ㅂ, ㄷ, ㅈ, ㄱ, or ㅅ (but not ㅍ, ㅌ, ㅊ, ㅋ!) directly follows the prospective modifier with no intervening pause, the initial consonant is usually reinforced, i.e. pronounced double (ㅃ, ㄸ, ㅉ, ㄲ, ㅆ). This doubling is usually ignored in the Korean spelling:

그 사람이 있을 곳 *the place where he will be* (pronounced 꼳)
편지를 쓸 사람 *the person who will write the letter* (pronounced 싸람)

When a word beginning with *i* or *y* directly following the prospective modifier with no intervening pause, the modifier ‑ㄹ is pronounced double:

할 일 *things to do* (pronounced 할릴)
내일 만날 여자 *the woman I'm meeting tomorrow* (pronounced 만날 려자)

23.6. Prospective Modifier Clauses

Prospective modifier clauses—clauses ending with a prospective form—modify nouns in the same way as other modifier clauses, with one of these meaning relationships.

A. 할 A

an A which is to do something or else *an A to which something is to be done*

가르칠 사람	*a person who is to teach*
	a person whom someone is going to teach
	= who is going to be taught
만날 선생	*a teacher who is to meet [someone]*
	a teacher whom [someone] is going to meet

B. A 이/가 할 B

a B which A is to do (A is the subject of the modifying verb)

내가 심을 꽃	*the flowers that I'm going to plant*
만호 씨가 할 공부	*the studying which Manho is to do*

C. | B 을/를 할 A |

an A which is to do something to B (B is the object of the modifying verb)

꽃을 심을 사람
the person who is going to plant the flowers

D. | A 이/가 B 을/를 할 C |

a C where (when, etc.) A is to do B

내가 공부를 할 학교
the school I'm going to study at

졸업할 날
the day we'll graduate

Here are some more examples of the different types of prospective modifier.

29. 이 일을 할 사람이 있어요?
Is there anyone here who'll do this work?

30. 만나실 선생님이 한국 분이세요?
Is the teacher you're going to see Korean?

31. 먹을 것이 없어요.
We haven't got anything to eat.

32. 내일 아침에 서울로 갈 사람이 있어요?
Is there anyone here who's going to Seoul tomorrow morning?

33. 이 코스를 가르칠 선생님의 성함은 어떻게 돼요?
What's the name of the teacher who is to teach in this course?

34. 내가 오늘 밤에 꼭 해야 할 공부를 다 마치지 못 했어요.
I wasn't able to finish all the studying I was supposed to do this evening.

23.7. Plain/Past Base + -(으) ㄹ 때 : *When* ...

The noun 때 means *time* and is used with other nouns as follows.

그 _____	*that ____*	그 때	*at that time, then*
점심	*lunch*	점심때	*lunchtime*
방학	*vacation*	방학 때	*vacation time*
크리스마스	*Christmas*	크리스마스 때	*Christmas time*
5살	*five years old*	5살 때	*when I was five*

With a prospective modifier form before it, 때 means *when*, as in: 갈 때 *when you go* (or *went*). The modifier is always in the prospective form in this construction—regardless of the time meaning of the corresponding English verb. Thus, the following type of construction is impossible.

*간 때 *when I went.*

Another meaning of this construction is *time to do something*.

35. 시작할 때가 됐어요.
     It's [has become] time to begin.

Past prospective modifiers of descriptive verbs and the copula are used before 때 to indicate specifically past conditions that are now over, as here:

36. 어렸을 때
     when [someone] was young [she isn't young anymore]

37. 선수였을 때
     when [he] was an athlete [he isn't an athlete anymore]

Occasionally, though, if the speaker wishes to emphasize the pastness of the event, he or she can use a past base with even a processive verb: 한국에 갔을 때 *when [he] went to Korea.*

38. 내가 밥을 먹고 있을 때 누가 왔어요?
     Who came when I was eating?

39. 비가 올 때 우산이 있어야 돼요.
     You need to have an umbrella when it rains.

40. 그 사람이 갈 때는, 나도 갈 거에요.
     When he goes, I'm going too.

41. 박 선생님이 학교에 가실 때, 저도 같이 가도 괜찮아요?
     When you go to school, Mr. Pak, may I go with you?

42. 한국에 살 때, 한국말을 배우겠어요.
     When I live in Korea, I'll learn to speak Korean.

43. 복동이가 애기였을 때, 아주 귀여웠지요.
     When Poktong-i was a baby, you see, he was very cute.

44. 돈이 없었을 때, 이렇게 좋은 음식을 먹지 못 했지요.
     When I had no money I couldn't eat food like this, you know.

23.8. More on - (으) ㄹ 때 *Time When . . .*

23.8.1. - (으) ㄹ 때마다 *Every time . . . ; Whenever . . .*

The particle 마다 means *each; every,* and you have learned it already. Here are some examples which go over the usage you have already learned, and also take things a little bit further.

계절마다   *every season*
토요일마다   *every Saturday*
사람마다   *every person, everybody*

For certain expressions, you have a choice between equivalent pure Korean and Sino-Korean.

날마다   or   매일   *everyday*
해마다   or   매년   *every year*

You can also attach 마다 to the pattern with - (으) ㄹ 때 introduced in section 23.7 above.

45. 시내에 나갈 때마다, 비가 와요.
    Every time I go downtown, it rains.

46. 전화를 걸 때마다, 통화중이에요.
    Every time I call, the line is engaged.

47. 시험을 볼 때마다, 신경이 많이 쓰여요.
    Every time I take an exam, I get really nervous ["lots of nerves get used"].

23.8.2. - (으) ㄹ 때부터 *Ever since . . .*

You have learned the particle 부터 meaning *starting from*, as in:

48. 수업은 1시부터 2시까지 합니다.
    We have class from 1 o'clock until 2 o'clock.

Analogous to the case with - (으) ㄹ 때마다 above, you can add 부터 to - (으) ㄹ 때 to derive a new pattern meaning *ever since the time when.*

49. 오늘 아침에 일어날 때부터 피곤했습니다.
    I've been tired from the moment I got up this morning.

50. 서울에 도착할 때부터 계속 바빴습니다.
I've been continuously busy from the time I arrived in Korea.

51. 남자친구가 떠날 때부터 울기 시작했어요.
I started crying from the moment my boyfriend left.

23.8.3. -(으)ㄹ 때까지 *Until* . . .

Finally, another useful pattern with -(으)ㄹ 때 involves the particle 까지 *until.*

52. 제가 선생님께 여쭤 볼 때까지 기다리세요.
Please wait until I ask the teacher.

53. 해가 날 때까지 기다립시다.
Let's wait until the sun comes out.

54. 그분이 일어나실 때까지 기다려야겠어요.
We'll have to wait until he gets up.

23.9. *Seems like it will* . . . with -(으)ㄹ 것 같아요

Analogously to what you learned in section 19.8 about -는 + 것 and -(으)ㄴ + 것, the prospective modifier -(으)ㄹ + 것 can have the meaning *the fact that one/it will do/be.*

55. 비가 올 것
the fact that it will rain

56. 재미 있을 것
the fact that it will be interesting/fun

And analogously to what you learned in section 22.8 about -는것 같아요 and -(으)ㄴ 것 같아요, the pattern -(으)ㄹ 것 같아요 has the meaning *seems* or *looks as if it will/might do/be.*

55ₐ. 오후에 비가 올 것 같은데요.
Looks like it's going to rain in the afternoon.

56ₐ. 그 영화는 재미 있을 것 같아요?
Do you think ["does it seem"] that movie will be interesting?

57. 이 번 학기에 성적이 잘 나올 것 같습니다.
Looks like I'll get good grades this semester.

58. 내년에 우리 장인어른이 미국으로 이민을 가실 것 같습니다.
Looks like my father-in-law will emigrate to the States next year.

23.10. *was going to . . . , but* with -(으)려다가

You have already learned the intentional pattern in -(으)려고 해요 (often pronounced -(으)ㄹ려고 해요), the source for the "wanna" pattern in -(으)ㄹ래요. You can combine this pattern with the transferentive -다(가) pattern learned in section 22.5 to render a pattern that means *I was going to [do something], but [then—SHIFT—I changed my mind, or something else happened, etc.]*: -(으)려다가 from -(으)려[고 하-]다가. In colloquial Korean, this combined pattern is often built on the "wanna" form, so you will often hear -(으)ㄹ래다가 alongside -(으)려다가. Here are some examples.

59. 처음에는 혼자만 가려다가, 친구도 1명 초대했지요.
     At first, I was just going to go alone, but then I invited a friend, too.

60. 팩스로 보내 드릴래다가, 비쌀 것 같아서 그냥 편지로 보냈어요.
     I was going to send it to you by fax, but since it seemed it would be expensive, I just sent it as a letter.

61. 양주를 마실래다가 너무 비싸서 소주를 시켰어요.
     We were going to drink whiskey, but it was so expensive we ordered soju.

62. 때리려다가 나보다 훨씬 큰 것 같아서 말았지요.
     I was going to hit him, but he seemed so much bigger than me that I thought better of it.

63. 뉴스를 볼래다가 졸려서 그냥 잤지요.
     I was going to watch a bit of the news but was sleepy, so just went to bed.

64. 한국말로 하려다가 준비할 시간이 없어서 영어로 해야겠습니다.
     I was going to do it in Korean, but I had no time to prepare, so I'll have to do it in English.

65. 일본학을 전공하려다가 한국학이 훨씬 재미 있을 것 같아서 한국학으로 바꿨어요.
     I was going to major in Japanese Studies, but Korean Studies seemed so much more interesting that I changed to Korean Studies.

Exercises

Exercise 1: Practice with -(으)ㄴ/-는데

Each of the following items contains two sentences. Combine the sentences with the Imminent Elaboration pattern and then translate the resulting sentence into English. For instance, the first will be: 그 학생은 공부하는데, 수진이는 왜 공부하지 않아요?

1. 그 학생은 공부해요. 수진이는 왜 공부하지 않아요?
2. 나는 시계가 없어요. 하나 살까요?
3. 그분을 만나야겠어요. 그분이 어디 가셨지요?
4. 그게 좋아요. 사지 못 하겠어요.
5. 그분이 집에 돌아갔어요. 왜 오셨지요?
6. 그분이 자주 나오세요. 한번 만나 보세요.
7. 눈이 와요. 가시겠어요?
8. 바람은 많이 불어요. 별로 춥지 않아요.
9. 저는 학교에 가요. 그분은 가지 않으세요.
10. 샌디 씨는 한국에서 태어났어요. 한국말을 잘 못 해요.

Exercise 2: More Practice with -(으)ㄴ/-는데

Fill in the blanks with the appropriate form of the Imminent Elaboration pattern and then translate the resulting sentence.

1. A. 배가 고파요.
    B. 나도 배가 ____ 밥 먹을까요?
2. A. 커피 한잔 주세요.
    B. 커피는 ____ 홍차 안 마실래요?
3. A. 누구를 기다려요?
    B. 영진 씨를 ____ 아직 안 와요.
4. A. 버스를 ____ 늦었어요.
    B. 다음에는 지하철을 타고 오세요.
5. A. 어제 갈비를 ____ 굉장히 맛있었어요.
    B. 어디에서 먹었는데요?
6. A. 어제 시험을 ____ 아주 어려웠어요.
    B. 열심히 공부해야지요.

Exercise 3: Practice with -(으)ㄹ

Each of the following items contains two sentences. Combine the sentences with a prospective modifier; then translate the combined sentence. For example, the first will be: 우리가 살 집은 시골에 있어요. *The house where we're going to live is in the country.*

1. 우리가 그 집에서 살 거에요. 그 집은 시골에 있어요.
2. 내가 편지를 쓰겠어요. 그 편지가 많아요.
3. 김 선생님이 내년부터 학교에서 가르칠거에요. 그 학교를 아세요?
4. 오늘 저녁에 우리가 음식을 먹을 거에요. 그 음식은 한국 음식이겠지요?
5. 우리 아들이 친구한테 전화를 걸거에요. 그 친구는 박 사장님 아들이지요.
6. 의사가 내일 환자를 수술해요. 그 환자는 운동선수에요.
7. 그 사람이 내일 아침 장 선생을 만날거에요. 그 사람은 미국에서 온 선교사지요?
8. 오늘 밤에 그 유명한 가수가 노래를 부를거에요. 그 노래는 무슨 노랠까요? 〔무슨 노랠 = 무슨 노래일〕
9. 내일 손님이 오실거에요. 그 손님은 할아버지 친구분이시지요.
10. 내가 도서관에서 책을 빌리겠어요. 그 도서관은 우리 집에서 가까워요.
11. 형님이 내일부터 회사에 나갈거에요. 그 회사는 보험회사에요.
12. 이번 주말에 우리가 손님들을 초대하겠어요. 그 손님들은 국회의원들이에요.

Exercise 4: Practice with Modifiers

Fill in the blanks below with the appropriate modifier form and then translate the resulting sentence.

1. 우리는 내일 영화를 보러 갑니다.

   내일 ＿＿＿ 영화는 "드라큐라"에요.
2. 일요일에 친구를 만날겁니다.

   일요일에 ＿＿＿ 친구는 대학생입니다.
3. 오늘은 아주 바쁩니다.

   ＿＿＿ 일이 그렇게 많으세요?
4. 누가 노래를 부르겠습니까?

   노래를 ＿＿＿ 사람은 손을 드시지요.
5. 커피랑 홍차가 있는데, 커피 ＿＿＿ 분은 손을 드십시오.
6. 내일 사진을 찍으러 갑시다.

사진 ＿＿ 데는 덕수궁입니다.
7. 다음 주일에 파티가 있어요.

그런데, 파티에 갈 때 ＿＿ 옷이 하나도 없어요.

Exercise 5: Practice with -(으)ㄹ 때

Each of the following items contains two sentences, the second of which begins with 그 때 *at that time*. Link the two sentences with -(으)ㄹ 때 so that the meaning of the combined sentence is *When . . .* Then translate the resulting sentence.

1. 우리가 노래를 불렀어요. 그때 친구가 왔어요.
2. 우리가 미국에서 살았어요. 그 때 한국 음식을 먹을 수 없었어요.
3. 내가 친구 집에 전화를 걸었어요. 그 때 통화중이었어요.
4. 내가 심 선생님을 찾았어요. 그 때 심 선생님이 집에 안 계셨어요.
5. 부모님이 젊으셨어요. 그 때 음악회에 자주 가셨어요.
6. 한국에 살았어요. 그 때 친구들과 술을 많이 마셨어요.
7. 우리가 돈이 많았어요. 그 때 일을 너무 안 했어요.
8. 작년에 한국에 갔어요. 그 때 좋은 친구를 많이 만났어요.
9. 우리가 그 한국 노래를 불렀어요. 그 때 아이들이 참 좋아 했어요.
10. 내가 대학교를 졸업했어요. 그 때 우리 집은 가난했어요.
11. 날씨가 좋아요. 그 때 갑시다.
12. 시간이 있어요. 그 때 여행을 많이 하세요.
13. 물건 값이 싸요. 그 때 많이 사겠어요.

Exercise 6: Exclamatory -(으)ㄴ/-는데요

Make each of the following sentences mean *My, but it's . . . !* or *How . . . it is!* For example, the first will be: 밖이 추운데요! *My, but it's cold outside!*

1. 밖이 추워요.
2. 그 여자가 예뻐요.
3. 한국 경치가 좋아요.
4. 우리가 만난 선생님은 무서워요.
5. 이 길이 나빠요.
6. 이 소설은 재미있어요.
7. 도서관이 가까워요.
8. 김 선생님 댁이 커요.

9. 비가 많이 왔어요.

10. 이 책은 어려워요.

Exercise 7: Practice with -(으)려다가

Below are a number of exchanges. Fill in the blanks with the appropriate form in -(으)려다가 and then translate the exchange into English.

1. A. 어제 등산을 가셨습니까?

    B. 아니오, _____ 너무 피곤해서 포기했어요.

2. A. 사장님께 전화를 했습니까?

    B. 아니오, 오늘 아침에 _____ 손님이 찾아와서 못했습니다.

3. A. 넥타이를 매고 가야 되는 모임인데, 넥타이는 왜 안 맸어요?

    B. 넥타이를 _____ 너무 더울 것 같아서 그만뒀어요.

4. A. 그 영화를 봤어요?

    B. 아니오, 극장에서 _____ 시간이 없어서 놓쳤어요. 비디오가 나올 때까지 기다려야겠어요.

5. A. 버스를 타고 왔어요?

    B. 아니오, 버스를 _____ 늦을 것 같아서 택시를 타고 왔지요.

6. A. 이번 학기에 심 선생님 코스를 택할 거에요?

    B. 아니오, _____ 너무 어려울 것 같아서 다른 과목으로 바꿨어요.

7. A. 친척들이 다 미국에 계십니까?

    B. 네, 캐나다로 이민을 _____ 미국이 더 나을 것 같아서 다들 뉴욕으로 갔어요.

8. A. 동생은 왜 안 데리고 왔어요?

    B. _____ 동생이 재미 없어 할 것 같아서 혼자 왔어요.

9. A. 모임 날을 정했어요?

    B. 네, 다음 주일 일요일로 _____ 수진 씨한테는 불편할 것 같아서, 토요일로 바꿨어요.

10. A. 다음 달 멕시코 갈 때 어머님도 모시고 갈 거에요?

    B. 아니오, _____ 요즘 좀 편찮으셔서 안 모시고 가는 게 좋을 것 같아요.

Exercise 8: Korean to English Translation

Translate the following sentences into English.

1. 김 선생님한테 전화를 걸려고 그랬는데 계속 통화중이었어요.
2. 비행기를 놓쳤는데도 시애틀까지 갈 수 있었어요.
3. 박 선생님을 오래간만에 찾아 뵌 김에 사진도
    찍었습니다.
4. 어제 저녁에 에릭 씨네 집에 갔다왔어요.
5. 내일 칠 시험은 어려울 것 같습니다.
6. 수술을 받아야 할 때는 신경이 많이 쓰이지요.
7. 그 산이 상당히 높은데요!
8. 그 책을 사시면 저에게 꼭 빌려 주세요.
9. 거기서 싸고 멋있는 옷을 파는데 잠깐 들렀다가 갈까요?
10. 말을 안 하려고 했는데 말이 나온 김에 할 이야기를 해야겠네요.

Exercise 9: English to Korean Translation

Translate the following sentences into Korean.

1. When I was at university I did a lot of sports.
2. Please wait until the teacher comes.
3. It is necessary to study Korean if you intend to go to Korea.
4. Did you buy a briefcase?
    I was going to, but there was nothing I liked, so I didn't buy one.
5. Did you eat lunch?
    I was going to, but my stomach hurts a bit, so I didn't eat.
6. I was going to write a letter, but I faxed.
7. I had a headache when I was writing that letter.
8. You've never been to Russia . . . so why don't you go?
9. Every time I wear that suit my mother is pleased.
10. At first I was going to go alone, but my friend went, too.

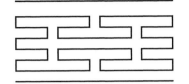 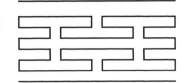

Lesson 24

경찰서에 갔다올 동안에
집 좀 봐 주시겠어요?

In this lesson, Dialogue One shows Eunice discussing a burglary with the 할머니 next door. Dialogue Two is a somewhat formal-sounding TV interview caught by Eric and Sandy on the news. This lesson introduces a number of new postmodifier patterns built on the -(으)ㄴ / -는/-(으)ㄹ modifiers learned in recent lessons, e.g., *after . . .ing* in -(으)ㄴ 후에, new ways to say *while . . .ing, because of . . .ing* in -(으)ㄴ/-는 바람에, *it would be best to* in -는 게 좋겠어요, new ways to express intentions, and *as soon as; in accordance with* in -(으)ㄴ/-는 대로. Other patterns covered include adverbative -게, and the two related patterns of causatives in -게 해요 and *gets so that, turns out so that* in -게 되-.

Korean Dialogues

Dialogue 1

Eunice is experiencing a bit of an emergency at home at the apartment, and has just called out 할머니 from the neighboring apartment.

유니스	경찰서에 갔다 올 동안에 집 좀 봐 주시겠어요?
할머니	왜요? 무슨 일이 있었어요?
유니스	제가 아까 샤워를 하는 사이에 도둑이 들어와서 우리 테레비를 훔쳐갔어요.
할머니	그래요? 아무도 못 봤는데요. 경찰서에 직접 가지 말고 전화를 하는 게 낫지 않아요?
유니스	아, 전화를 하는 게 좋겠네요.
	너무 놀란 바람에 지금 제 정신이 아니에요.
할머니	경찰서에 전화 한 후에 잊지 말고 보험회사에도 알리세요.
	다행이네요, 테레비만 훔쳐 갔으니깐. 다음부터는 조심해야지요.
유니스	네, 그래야겠어요, 할머니. 고맙습니다.

Dialogue Notes

제 정신이 아니에요   *I'm not in my right mind; I'm not myself.*

Dialogue 2

Eric and Sandy are watching the Korean television news before going to bed and catch this snippet from an interview with a Korean diplomat about to leave for an assignment in the United States.

기자	미국에는 언제 떠나실 예정입니까?
외교관	준비가 되는 대로 곧 떠날 생각입니다.
기자	무슨 직책으로 미국에 가시게 됩니까?
외교관	주미 한국 대사관 서기로 갑니다.
기자	무슨 일을 중심적으로 추진하시겠습니까?
외교관	한미간의 문화 교류를 촉진시키고 싶습니다.
기자	그러면 구체적으로 어떤 계획이 있으십니까?
외교관	우선 미국에 한국 문화를 적극적으로 소개할 예정입니다.

Reading Passage

수영이는 대학을 졸업한 후에 한국의 큰 보험회사에서 일을 하려고 합니다.

수영이는 요즘 한국말을 아주 열심히 공부하고 있습니다.

밥을 먹는 동안에도 한국 신문을 읽고, 목욕을 하는 동안에도 단어를 외웁니다.

여름 방학에도 아무데도 놀러 가지 않고 공부만 했습니다.

요즘에는 집에서도 부모님한테 한국말로 이야기하려고 노력을 하고 있습니다.

어제는 밤 늦도록 공부하는 바람에 아침에 코피가 났습니다.

지난 달에는 파티에서 한국유학생을 1명 사귀었습니다.

한국 남자친구는 수영이한테 한국말을 가르쳐 주고 언제나 수영이한테

　　　한국말로 이야기하게 합니다.

수영이는 물론 그 친구한테 영어를 가끔 가르쳐 줍니다.

결국 2사람은 서로 사랑하게 됐습니다.

남자친구는 한국말을 할 때 수영이가 알아들을 수 있게 천천히 말합니다.

내년에 2사람은 한국에 가서 결혼할 계획입니다.

그래서 수영이는 미국에서 자랐는데도 결국 한국에서 살게 됐습니다.

Vocabulary

Nouns

<u>International Exchange</u>

교류	interchange
국제교류	international [human] exchange
국제–	international . . .
국제관계	international relations
문화	culture
발전 〔–쩐〕	development
경제발전	economic development
발전(을) 하–	it develops
발전(을) 시키–	develop it
방문	a visit
방문(을) 하–	visit, make a visit
방문학자	visiting scholar
여권 〔–kkwɔn〕	passport
외무부	Ministry of Foreign Affairs
유학	study abroad
유학(을) 시키–	send somebody to study abroad
유학생	international student, student studying abroad
주–	residing in, resident/staying (in)
주한 미국 대사관	U.S. embassy in Korea
주미 대한민국 대사관	ROK embassy in the United States
한미 (← 한국 + 미국)	Korea-United States
한미간	between Korea and the United States
한미간의	pertaining to [the relationship] between Korea and the United States
한미간의 문화 교류	cultural exchange between Korea and the United States

<u>Church</u>

권사	(church) Elder [female]
기도	prayer
기도(를) 하–	pray

반주	accompaniment
반주자	accompanist
반주(를) 하-	accompany (musically)
설교	sermon
설교(를) 하-	give a sermon
성가대	(church) choir
성가대원	member of (church) choir
성경	Bible
성경 공부	Bible Study
성서	Bible
예배	church service
예배(를) 드리-	attend a church service; worship
장로	(church) Elder [male]
지휘자	conductor, director [of a musical group]
집사	(church) deacon

Cops and Robbers

경찰	policeman
경찰서	police station
-놈	[usually abusive] "guy," S.O.B.
도둑놈	thief, burglar
나쁜 놈	S. O. B. [term of abuse]
고약한 놈	S. O. B. [term of abuse]
도둑	thief, burglar
도둑(을) 맞-	be burgled, robbed

Studying

과학	science
복습	review, revision
복습(을) 하-	review, revise
수학	mathematics, math
시간표	time table, schedule
역사	history
예습	preparation (of lessons), preview
예습(을) 하-	prepare (lessons), preview

장학금	scholarship
전문	specialty
전문가	specialist, expert
전문지식	specialized knowledge, expertise

Other

계획	plan
그릇	bowl, dish, vessel, plate
노력	efforts, hard work
노력(을) 하-	makes efforts
눈물	tears
눈물(을) 흘리-	cry, shed tears
다행	luck, fortunate
다행이네요.	How fortunate!
다행히(도)	fortunately, as [good] luck would have it
바닷가	the seashore, seaside; beach
바둑	game of "Go," "paduk"
바둑(을) 두-	play *paduk*
볼륨	volume
봉급	salary, wages
불행	unhappiness, misfortune
불행하-	be unfortunate, unhappy
불행히(도)	unfortunately, as [bad] luck would have it
불행하게(도)	unfortunately, as [bad] luck would have it
사랑	love
사랑에 빠지-	fall in love
첫눈에	at first sight
서기	secretary, clerk
아무것도	nothing at all
엉망	a mess, a wreck
연봉	annual salary
월급	monthly salary
예정	plan, prearrangement, schedule
온몸	one's entire body
온 세상	the whole world

입맛	one's appetite, one's desire to eat
입장	position, standpoint, stand (on an issue)
자연	nature
대자연	the Great Outdoors, Mother Nature
장기	Korean chess
장기(를) 두-	plays *changgi*
전쟁	war
제안	a suggestion, proposal
중심	center, core, crux
서울을 중심으로	with Seoul as the center; centering on/emphasizing Seoul
중심적으로	primarily, with something as one's main focus
직책	duties, responsibilities of office
코피	nosebleed
코피(가) 나-	get a nosebleed

Adverbs

결국	ultimately, as a result, in the end, in the final analysis
구체적으로	concretely, specifically
끝으로	finally, lastly
둘째로	secondly, second of all
밤 늦도록	until late in the night
소극적으로	passively, in a feeble or unaggressive way
싹	entirely, completely
싹 없어졌어요.	It disappeared entirely.
우선	first, firstly; as a matter of priority
우연히	by chance, by coincidence

길을 가다가 수미 씨를 우연히 만났어요.

I was walking down the street and happened to meet Sumi.

적극적으로	positively, actively, in an outgoing way
첫째로	firstly, first of all

Verbs

<u>Verbs That Take Objects</u>

가지-	possess, hold, take
가져가-/가져오-	take/bring (thing) along
갖고 있-	have s.th. with one, have
가지고 가-	take (thing) along
가지고 오-	bring (thing) along
거절(을) 하-	refuse somebody/something
초대를 받았는데 거절했어요.	I was invited, but I refused.
고치-	fix it, repair it
사귀-	make friends with, get to know
친구를 사귀어요.	Makes a friend.
나쁜 사람들과 사귀어요.	Keeps company with bad sorts.
선택(을) 하-	select, choose
택하-	select, choose
이 번 학기에 몇 과목을 택해요?	How many courses are you taking this term?
수입(을) 하-	import something
수출(을) 하-	export something
알리-	let somebody know; inform
내일까지 약속 시간을 저한테 알려 주세요.	

Please let me know the appointment time by tomorrow.

잃어버리-	lose something
조심하-	be careful about
말씀을 조심하세요.	Be careful what you say.
촉진(을) 시키-	expedite, promote, facilitate
추진(을) 하-/시키-	promote something, propel something forward
취소(를) 하-	cancel it
취소(가) 되-	it gets cancelled
훔치-	steal it, swipe it
흘리-	spill it; shed (tears)
커피를 흘렸어요.	I spilled my coffee.

Descriptive and/or Sensory Verbs

고약하–	be ugly, wicked, nasty, hard to deal with
고약한 냄새	a horrible smell
어두w–	be dark

Intransitive Verbs (Processive Verbs That Cannot Take Objects)

그치–	[rain/snow] stops
기침(을) 하–	cough
냄새(가) 나–	it smells
맛있는 냄새가 나네요.	Something smells good!
놀라–	be surprised
깜짝 놀랐지요.	I was so surprised!
못 생겼–	ugly ("didn't turn out")
배(가) 나오–	get a big belly
배탈(이) 나–	get an upset stomach, get sick to one's stomach
사고(가) 나–	an accident happens/occurs
상하–	[food/one's mood] spoils, goes off, goes bad

친구가 약속을 어겨서 기분이 상했어요.

I've lost my good mood because my friend didn't keep our appointment.

샤워(를) 하–	take a shower
일어서–	stand up
입원(을) 하–	be/get hospitalized, go into hospital
자라–	it grows
지난 번보다 많이 자랐네요.	She's grown a lot since last time!
출발(을) 하–	set off, depart
어제 부산으로 출발했습니다.	They set off for Pusan yesterday.
출장(을) 가–	go away on business, make a business-related journey
일본으로 출장을 가셨습니다.	She has gone to Japan on business.
터지–	it bursts
전쟁이 터졌어요.	War broke out.
배가 터질 것 같아요.	I think my stomach will burst.
퇴원(을) 하–	get out of/be discharged from hospital

Lesson Notes

24.1. Modifier Clauses: -(으)ㄴ 후에
After . . .ing

You have already learned the expression 후에 for *later, afterward*, as in the following example.

1. 1시간 후에 다시 오세요.
    Come again in ["after"] an hour.

An expression made up of a modifier clause plus 후에 *after*, 뒤에 *in back of, behind*, or 다음에 *next (after)* means *after (something) happens* or *happened* or *has happened*. The modifiers in these expressions are from processive verbs and have the regular ending -(으)ㄴ.

> ### 주의!
> You do *not* use a similar construction with 전에 *before*; instead you use an entirely
> different verb form (-기 전에), which you learned in Lesson 17.9.

Here are some more examples of the *after* construction.

2. 집에 돌아온 후에 공부를 했어요.
    After I got home, I studied.

3. 영화가 끝난 후에 술 마시러 술집에 갔어요.
    After the movie finished, we went to a bar to drink.

4. 우리가 음악을 들은 뒤에 다방에 가서 차를 1잔 마셨어요.
    After listening to the music, we went to a tabang and drank a cup of tea.

5. 큰 다음에는 더 좋은 옷을 사서 주겠어요.
    Once you're big[ger], I'll buy (and give you) better clothes.

In the last example, 커요 (usually a descriptive verb *is big*) is used as a processive verb *gets big(ger), grows*. You have had several bases that function either as descriptive (*is*) or processive (*becomes*): 늦어요 *is/becomes late*, 나아요 (base 나(ㅅ)-) *is/gets better*, 흐려요 (base 흐리-) *is/gets cloudy*. But you must not assume that every descriptive verb can be converted in this way: usually you have to use the infinitive plus auxiliary expression -어져요 as shown by 작아져요 *it gets small(er)*. You can, of course, use this expression with descriptive verbs that are also used as processives: 커져요 can mean 커요 *gets big(ger)*.

Lesson Twenty-four / 208

24.2. Modifier Clauses: *While . . .ing*

To say *while (something) is happening* you use a processive modifier $(-는)$ on a simple base (processive) followed by 도중 *middle, midst* or 동안 or 사이 *interval*. This may or may not have the particle 에 after it.

공부 하는 } 도중 동안 사이 } (에) *while studying, in the middle of studying*

If you want to say *i s (in the middle of) doing*, a form of the copula follows the noun. Note that this is only possible with 중:

6. 공부 하는 중이에요 (*도중이에요,*동안이에요, *사이에요).
    [He] is in the midst of studying.

You may recall the expression for *The line is engaged*: 통화 중이에요. Here are some more analogous NOUN plus 중이에요 expressions.

7. 수업 중이에요
    is in class

8. 회의 중이에요
    is in conference

9. 일본을 방문 중이에요
    is visiting Japan

10. 시험 중이에요
    is in [the middle of] an exam

Occasionally you will find a processive verb in the simple modifier form $(-(으)ㄴ)$ before 동안 or 사이 (but not before 중).

11. 학교에 간 사이에 or 간 동안에
    (in the interval) while we were (in the state resulting from having gone) away at school

12. 집에 들어온 사이에 or 들어온 동안에
    while (in the state resulting from having come) inside the house

And there are a few descriptive verbs that occur with $-(으)ㄴ$ 중.

13. 바쁘신 중에 (이렇게 시간을 내 주셔서 감사합니다.)
     (Thanks for finding time for me) in the midst of your being busy.

Here are some more examples of this construction.

14. 김 선생님이 점심을 잡수시는 동안에 나는 신문을 봤어요.
     While Mr. Kim ate lunch, I read the newspaper.

15. 어제 시내에 가는 도중에 교통사고가 났습니다.
     Yesterday on the way downtown a traffic accident happened.

16. 아버지가 목욕하시는 사이에 손님이 집에 오셨어요.
     While you were taking a bath, Father, we had a caller.

17. 일하는 동안에 다른 사람과 이야기하면 안 돼요.
     You mustn't talk to other people while they're working!

18. 한국에서는 식사하는 도중에 말을 많이 하면 안 됩니다.
     In Korea one shouldn't talk a lot in the middle of [eating] a meal.

19. 선생님이 이야기를 하시고 있는 동안에 저는 피곤해서 잤어요.
     I was so tired I fell asleep while the teacher was talking.

20. 사장님이 나가신 사이에 우리는 아무것도 안 했지요.
     While the boss was out, we didn't do anything, you know.

24.3. -(으)ㄴ/-는 바람에: *Because of . . .ing*

A processive modifier (-는) or descriptive modifier (-(으)ㄴ) plus 바람 *reason, cause* + a particle 에 means *because of doing~being* or *by reason of the fact that (someone) is/was doing* or *is/was, (in) conjunction (with) doing~being; (as a) consequence (of) doing~being; (as a) result (of) doing~being.* The consequence in a sentence with this pattern is typically adverse or negative.

21. 공부를 못 하는 바람에 (대학에 못 갔습니다.)
     Because [he] of not being good at studying (something unpleasant or less-than-satisfactory happened—I wasn't able to go to university).

22. 눈이 오는 바람에 (30분이나 늦었습니다.)
     Because [he] it is/was snowing (something unpleasant or less-than-satisfactory happened—we were over 30 minutes late).

23. 날씨가 너무 추운 바람에 (감기에 걸렸어요).
Because the weather is so cold (something unpleasant or less-than-satisfactory happened—I caught a cold).

24. 날씨가 너무 더운 바람에 (땀을 많이 흘렸어요.)
Because the weather was so hot (something unpleasant or less-than-satisfactory happened, i.e., we sweated a lot.)

This pattern is similar in meaning to -기 때문에 (17.7), but unlike 때문, it cannot be followed by a form of the copula instead of by a particle, meaning *It's because*.

25. 공부를 열심히 하기 때문이에요.
It's because I'm studying so hard.

*추운 바람이었어요.
It was because it was cold.

The other important difference is that the pattern with 바람에 tends to imply that the speaker is somehow displeased with or inconvenienced by the event in the 바람에 clause. Here are some more examples.

26. 비가 너무 많이 오는 바람에 산보를 가지 못 하겠네요.
We won't be able to go walking because it's raining too much.

27. 전쟁이 나는 바람에 대학교에 가지 못 했어요.
I was not able to go to university on account of the war breaking out.

24.4. Verbs: Adverbative Form -게

So far you have seen several adverbs formed with the adverbative -게: 쉽게 *easily*, 늦게 *late*, 재미 있게 *in a fun way~interestingly*, 어떻게 *how? in what way?*, 이렇게, 그렇게, 저렇게 *like this, in this way*, etc. Here are some examples of these.

28. 어떻게 생각하십니까?
What (how) do you think?

29. 쉽게 말하면, 이렇습니다.
To put it simply (easily), it's like this.

Verbs have an adverbative form made by attaching the ending -게 to the base. The adverbative ending is used only with simple bases, plain or honorific—and not with past or future bases.

The -게 forms may tell *how* something is done, or *how* the subject of the action is.

30.   늦게 왔어요.
      She came late.

31.   A. 어떻게 하는 것입니까?
         How does one do it?

      B. 이렇게 하는 겁니다.
         You do it like this.

Or it may tell *how* something changes *so that it is* (something new)—referring either to the subject of an intransitive verb or to the object of a transitive verb.

32.   얼굴이 빨갛게 됐어요.
      He turned red in the face. [= His face became red/got so that it was red]

33.   라디오 볼륨을 크게 했어요.
      I turned up the radio. [Lit.: *I made the radio volume bigger.*]

Here are some further examples.

34.   좀 더 크게 말씀 해 주십시오.
      Please speak a little louder.

35.   그 상점에서 물건을 싸게 팔아요?
      Do they sell things cheap(ly) at that store?

36.   이 책을 재미있게 읽었어요.
      [I read this book with pleasure =] I had a good time reading this book.

37.   지난 번의 강의를 재미있게 들었어요.
      [I heard the last [time's] lecture with pleasure =] I enjoyed hearing the last lecture.

38.   이것을 다르게 할까요?
      Shall we make this one different?

39.   지난 밤에 춥게 주무셨지요?
      You must have been cold [= slept cold] last night, right?

Both processive and descriptive verbs make adverbatives, but there is no form for the copula. Where you might expect such a form (*-이게 *so that it is*) you find instead the adverbative form of the processive verb 돼요 *becomes* (되-): 되게 *so that it becomes*.

24.5. Causatives in -게 해요

Adverbative forms in -게 combine into phrases with 해요 to mean *causes [him/it] to do something* or *causes [him/it] to be some way*. For example:

40.   신문을 읽게 해요
      causes [someone] to read the newspaper; makes [someone] read the newspaper

41.   맥주를 차게 해요
      causes the beer to be cold; makes the beer cold; chills the beer

If the -게 form is a processive verb, it might be translated by *make* or *let* or *have*.

42.   먹게 해요
      makes [someone] eat or *lets [someone] eat* or *has [someone] eat*

The Korean expresses simple causation, emphasizing neither coercion (like *make*) nor permission (like *let*). With descriptive verbs, the translation *make* is more common.

Notice the particles used in this construction. Assume that B performs an action—either one that takes a direct object (transitive: e.g., *reads a book*) or one that does not take a direct object (intransitive: e.g., *goes to bed*).

Transitive Pattern:	B 가 C 를 해요.
Example:	아이가 책을 읽어요. *The child reads the book.*

Intransitive Pattern:	B 가 해요.
Example:	아이가 쉬어요. *The child rests.*

When these patterns are transformed into the causative -게 해요 construction, the following patterns result.

Transitive Pattern:	A가 B 에게 C 를 하게 해요.
Example:	어머니가 아이에게 책을 읽게 해요.
	The mother makes/has/lets the child read the book.

Intransitive Pattern:	A가 B 를 하게 해요.
Example:	어머니가 아이를 쉬게 해요.
	The mother makes/has/lets the child rest.

Here are more examples of this causative construction in –게 해요.

43. 남편이 부인한테 교회에 못 나가게 했습니다.
The husband wouldn't let his wife go to church.

44. 아이를 밖에 못 나가게 했습니다.
They wouldn't let the child go out.

45. 동생한테 그 책을 사게 했어요.
I let my brother buy that book.

46. 아이들을 길에서 못 놀게 해야 해요.
You have to see to it that children don't play in the streets.
[= You have to make children not play . . .]

47. 남편은 집에 있게 해야겠어요.
I'll have to make/have/let my husband stay home.

48. 기다리시게 해서 미안합니다.
I'm sorry to have kept you waiting.

49. 아이들을 일찍 자게 했습니다.
I made the children go to bed early.

50. 선생님이 학생들에게 숙제를 하게 하셨습니다.
The teacher made the students do their homework.

51. 나는 동생한테 밥을 먹게 했어요.
I made/had/let my little brother eat his food.

52. 라디오를 좀 작게 하세요!
Turn the radio down a little.

In addition to this sort of periphrastic (or round-about) causative, some verbs have special derived causative forms; these are discussed in a later volume. Some verbal nouns are often made causative by using 시켜요 [시키-] in place of 하게 한다, as in this example from Dialogue Two.

53.   한미간의 문화 교류를 촉진시키고 싶습니다.
       I want to promote cultural exchange between Korea and the United States.

54.   우선 한국 학생을 미국에 많이 유학시킬 생각입니다.
       First of all, I am planning to send many Korean students to the United States to study.

24.6. -게 돼요: *gets so that . . . , turns out so that . . .*

An adverbative –게 form followed by 돼요 *becomes, is* means *gets to be so that . . . ,* expressing the gradual inception of an externally controlled condition.

55.   교회에 오시면 차차 아시게 됩니다.
       If you come to church, you'll gradually come to understand.

This construction is similar in meaning to two others: the infinitive of a descriptive verb followed by 져요 *becomes, begins to be,* and the construction –기(를) 시작해요 *begins to [do]* with verbs.

56.   더워 져요.
       It's getting hot.

57.   웃기(를) 시작했어요.
       She began to laugh.

Here are some more examples of the construction in –게 돼요.

58.   재미있게 됐습니다.
       It turned out to be interesting.

59.   그 다음에는 어떻게 됐어요?
       What happened after that?

60.   못 가게 됐습니다.
       It's turned out that I can't go.

61. 내일부터 도서관에서 일하게 됐어요.
   (It has developed that) I'm to begin working at the library tomorrow.

62. 거기서 저녁을 먹게 됐습니다.
   It worked out/turned out that I ate dinner there.

63. 언제 미국에 가시게 됩니까?
   When are you scheduled to go the United States?

64. 그분을 우연히 만나게 됐지요.
   I came to meet him quite by chance.

65. 시간이 지나면 많은 것을 잊어버리게 됩니다.
   One comes to forget many things with the passing of time.

66. 공원에서 산보를 하다가 장 선생님을 만나게 됐지요.
   While taking a walk in the park, I happened to run into Mr. Chang.

As the last example shows, sometimes the best translation is *happens to*, *gets to*, *manages to*, *has the good fortune to*.

24.7. -는 게 좋겠어요: *It would be best to . . .*

Observe the following examples.

67. 아, 전화를 하는 게 좋겠네요.
   Oh, you'd best make a phone call, then.

68. 경찰이 올 때까지 좀 쉬는 게 좋겠어요.
   It would be best if you rested a bit until the police come.

A processive plain base followed by –게 (abbreviated from 것이 *thing; fact*) and 좋겠어요 (lit.: *the fact of VERBing will/would be good*) means *it would be best if one VERBed; you'd best VERB; VERBing would be the best option*, and so on. Here are some more examples.

69. 내일 시험이 있으면 일찍 일어나는 게 좋겠어요.
   If you have an exam tomorrow, you'd best get up early.

70. 길을 잘 모르시면 조심해서 운전하시는 게 좋겠어요.
     If you don't know the way ["well"], you'd best drive carefully.

71. 벌써 10시네요! 빨리 떠나는 게 좋겠어요.
     It's already 10! We'd best leave quickly.

72. A.   오늘 비가 올 거에요.
          It's going to rain today.

     B.   그러면, 우산을 가져가는 게 좋겠네요.
          Then we'd better take an umbrella.

73. 내일 일찍 일어나야 되기 때문에, 일찍 자는 게 좋겠어요.
     Because you have to get up early tomorrow, you'd best go to bed early.

24.8. Expressing Intentions

One way to express an intention in Korean is by using a future-tense verb: 하겠어요 *I will do it*. Another option is to use the Intentional pattern in -(으)려고 합니다. But there are a number of other more specific ways to specify that you *intend* to do something. For instance, with verbs of going and coming, you can use the purposive form -(으)러 (가요/와요).

Yet another strategy involves the use of the prospective modifier -(으)ㄹ followed by a NOUN plus COPULA phrase. The Reading Passage of this lesson contained the following sentence.

74. 내년에 2사람이 한국에 가서 결혼할 계획입니다.
     The two of them are planning to go to Korea next year to get married.

The noun 계획 means *plan*. Preceded by the prospective modifier -(으)ㄹ and followed by a form of the copula -이에요, it gives a pattern meaning *It is the plan to VERB, [one] plans to VERB*. Other similar words are 예정 *prearrangement, plan*, 생각 *thought, idea, plan*, and 작정 *intention, plan, project*, all of which go into the following patterns.

. . . -(으)ㄹ 계획이다
     [it is the plan or intention=] plans, intends

. . . -(으)ㄹ 예정이다
     [it is the plan or intention=] plans, intends

. . . -(으)ㄹ 생각이다
[it is the thought or idea=] is thinking of . . .ing

. . . -(으)ㄹ 작정이다
[it is the decision or project=] decides, plans

Here are some examples of these patterns.

75.   A. 언제쯤 떠날 예정입니까?
      When do you plan to leave?

      B. 내일모레쯤 떠날 생각입니다.
      I'm thinking of leaving the day after tomorrow or so.

76.   적극적으로 배울 작정입니다.
      I plan to study with a positive attitude.

77.   여행을 많이 할 생각입니다.
      I think I'll travel a lot.

78.   졸업한 후에 동양에서 일할 계획입니다.
      I plan to work in East Asia after graduating.

79.   수업이 끝난 후에 영식이네 집에 들릴 계획입니다.
      After class is over, I plan to stop in at Yŏngshik's place.

80.   10월에 대사님이 우리 학교를 방문할 계획이십니다.
      The ambassador is planning to visit our school in October.

81.   내년에 일본에 갈 때, 가족을 데리고 갈 계획입니다.
      Next year when I go to Japan, I intend to take my family.

24.9. -(으)ㄴ/-는 대로: *as soon as . . . ; in accordance with . . .*

The postmodifier 대 is used with 로 after it in two kinds of constructions.

1. -는 대로: *As soon as . . .*

With a processive modifier (-는 대로), it means *as soon as [so-and-so] happens.*

82. 김 사장님이 나오시는 대로 알려 주세요.
     Please let me know as soon as Company President Kim comes out.

Recall there is another way to say *as soon as*: -자(마자).

2. -(으)ㄴ/-는 대로: *According to; in accordance with . . .*

With modifiers of any appropriate tense, 대로 means *according to, in accordance with, as, with [something] still as it was.* Here are some examples.

83. 하고 싶은 대로 하세요.
     [Do according to what you will do =] Do as you like.

84. 들은 대로 말해 보세요.
     [Speak according to what you heard =] Tell what you heard!

85. 선생님이 말씀하시는 대로 하세요.
     Do as the teacher says.

The expression 될 수 있는 대로 means *as much as possible [= according to what is possible, in line with what can be done], insofar as it is possible*:

86. 될 수 있는 대로 빨리 가십시오.
     [As much as possible, go quickly =] Go as quickly as possible.

87. 운동을 될 수 있는 대로 매일 하십시오.
     Please do your best to exercise every day.

The expression 대로 is also used after a few nouns, with similar meaning.

마음대로	*[following one's mind=] as [one] wants, wishes, likes*
뜻대로	*[in line with the intention or meaning=] as [one] expected*
선생님 말씀대로	*[in accordance with your words=] as you say*

Here are more examples of 대로 in sentences.

88. 사실대로 말하십시오.
[Speak according to=] Stick to the facts.

89. 내가 하는 대로 해요.
Do as/like I do.

90. 들어오시는 대로 제가 전화해 드리지요.
I'll call you as soon as he comes in.

91. 될 수 있는 대로 빨리 돌아가야겠어요.
I'll have to get back home just as soon as possible.

92. 생각대로 하십시오. Or: 좋으신대로 하십시오.
Do as you think best. Or: Do as you like.

93. 그대로 두세요.
Leave it as it is.

94. 김 선생님이 말씀하신 대로, 한국에 좋은 데가 많아요.
As Mr. Kim said, there are many nice places in Korea.

Exercises

Exercise 1: Practice with -(으) ㄴ· 후에~다음에

In each of the following pairs, the second sentence starts with 그 후/다음에 . . . *After that . . . .* Combine the two sentences into one. For example, the first will be: 저녁을 잘 먹은 후에 산보를 했어요 *After eating a good dinner, I took a walk.*

1.   저녁을 잘 먹었어요. 그후에 산보를 했어요.
2.   도서관에 가서 책을 1권 빌렸어요. 그 다음에 집에 돌아가서 읽었어요.
3.   선생님은 다방에서 차 1잔 마셨어요. 그후에 어디로 가셨어요?
4.   아버지가 은행에서 돈을 많이 찾으셨어요. 그 다음에 멋 있는 자동차를 사셨어요.
5.   음악회가 끝났어요. 그후에 우리는 공원에 가서 친구들을 만날까요?
6.   할아버지가 신문을 보셨어요. 그후에 학교에 전화를 거셨어요 .
7.   복동이가 머리를 빗었어요. 그후에 모자를 쓰고 나갔어요.
8.   아주머니가 그릇을 씻었어요. 그 다음에 애기를 데리고 가게에 가서 뭘 샀어요.
9.   영화가 끝났어요. 그후에 술을 마시러 술집에 갈래요?
10. 할머니가 병이 나셨어요. 그후에 바닷가로 가서 쉬셨어요.
11. 전화를 걸었어요. 그 다음에 이야기하지요, 뭐.
12. 고쳤어요. 그 다음에 고장이 1번도 안 났습니다.
13. 복습하세요. 그 다음에 좀 쉬세요.

Exercise 2: Practice with -는 동안~사이에

In each of the following pairs, the second sentence starts with 그 동안/사이(에) *During that . . .* and the first ends with a verb. Combine the two sentences into one. For example, the first will be: 저는 이를 닦는 동안 동생의 이야기를 듣지 못 했어요. *While I was brushing my teeth I couldn't hear what my little brother was saying.*

1.   저는 이를 닦았어요. 그 동안에 동생의 이야기를 듣지 못 했어요.
2.   한국말을 공부해요. 그 동안에 영어로 말하면 안 되지요.
3.   재미있는 책을 보고 있었어요. 그 동안에 도둑이 들어왔어요.
4.   교수님이 예쁜 여자하고 이야기를 하고 계셨지요. 그 사이에 부인이 왔다 갔어요!

5. 도둑이 집에 들어왔어요. 그 동안에 우리 개가 잠을 잤어요.

6. 아버지가 외국에 가셨어요. 그 동안에 어머니가 동생을 낳으셨어요.

7. 내가 편지를 쓰고 있었어요. 그 동안에 동생은 우표를 사러 나갔어요.

8. 우리가 영화를 보고 있었어요. 그 동안에 밖에 눈이 많이 왔어요.

9. 형님이 미국에서 공부하고 계셨어요. 그 동안에 나는 결혼했어요.

10. 한국에서 전쟁이 일어났어요. 그 동안에 일본은 많이 발전했어요.

11. 한국에 살았어요. 그 동안에 재미있는 사람을 많이 만나봤어요.

12. 우리가 재미 있게 놀았어요. 그 동안에 만호 씨는 혼자서 일을 했어요.

Exercise 3: Practice with - 는 중이에요

The next exercises are designed to give you some more practice on the modifiers you learned in Lesson 19. Each of the following sentences means *someone **is doing** . . .* Change it to mean *someone **is in the midst of doing** . . . .* For example, the first will be: 나는 한국말 공부를 하는 중이었어요. I was in the midst of doing my Korean lesson. [Of course, it would be possible to say . . . 하고 있는 중 instead of . . . 하는 중; but the meaning is clear without the -고 있- because of the force of 중.]

1. 나는 한국말 공부를 하고 있었어요.

2. 아이들이 음악을 듣고 있어요.

3. 그 사람이 소설을 읽고 있어요?

4. 저 두 사람이 장기를 두고 있었어요.

5. 아들이 복습을 하고 있었어요.

6. 아내가 물건을 사고 있어요.

7. 동생이 피아노를 치고 있었어요.

8. 저녁을 먹고 있었어요.

9. 두 사람은 싸우고 있었어요.

10. 선생님은 외국 여행을 하고 계셨어요.

Exercise 4: Practice with -는 중에

Each of the following items contains two sentences. The first means *someone is doing [this]*; the second, beginning with 그러는 중에, means *In the midst of that happening*. Combine the two sentences into a single one meaning *in the midst of someone's doing [this], [that] happens*. For example, the first one will be: 내가 공부하는 중에 손님이 오셨어요. *While I was in the middle of studying, guests dropped in.*

1.   내가 공부하고 있었어요. 그러는 중에 손님이 오셨어요.
2.   선생이 편지를 쓰고 있었어요. 그러는 중에 전화가 왔어요.
3.   아내가 전화를 걸고 있었어요. 그러는 중에 애기가 문을 열고 방에서 나갔어요.
4.   내가 어제 밤에 신문을 보고 있었어요. 그러는 중에 이상한 소리를 들었어요.
5.   우리가 그 영화를 보고 있었어요. 그러는 중에 도둑이 들어왔어요.
6.   제가 설거지를 하고 있었어요. 전기가 나갔어요.
7.   바둑을 두고 있었어요. 그러는 중에 날이 어두워졌어요.
8.   도둑하고 싸웠어요. 그러는 중에 코피가 터졌어요.
9.   저는 예습을 하고 있었어요. 그러는 중에 불이 났어요.
10.   한국을 방문했어요. 그러는 중에 학생들이 데모하는 것을 봤어요.
11.   한동안 운동을 못했어요. 그러는 중에 배가 나왔어요.
12.   오랫동안 외국생활을 했어요. 그러는 중에 한국 경제가 많이 발전했어요.

Exercise 5: Intentions

Each of the following items contains two sentences. The first means *someone is going to do [something]*; the second is an Intention pattern built on 그러-. Combine the two sentences into a single one meaning *intends~plans to do [something]*. For example, the first one will be: 친구들과 같이 등산을 갈 예정입니다. *I'm planning to go hiking with my friends.*

1.   친구들과 같이 등산을 가겠습니다. 그럴 예정입니다.
2.   내일은 그 대학교를 방문하겠습니다. 그럴 예정입니다.
3.   조금 이따가 회의를 하겠습니다. 그럴 예정입니다.
4.   약혼식은 서울에서 하겠습니다. 그럴 생각입니다.
5.   그리고 결혼식은 캐나다에서 하겠습니다. 그럴 계획입니다.
6.   입원하겠습니다. 그럴 생각입니다.
7.   한국에 나와 있는 동안에 장기를 배우겠습니다. 그럴 생각입니다.

8. 성경 공부를 좀 하겠습니다. 그럴 작정입니다.
9. 그분의 제안을 거절하겠습니다. 그럴 작정입니다.
10. 앞으로는 예배를 한국말로 드리겠습니다. 그럴 생각입니다.
11. 여러 가지 물건을 수출하겠습니다. 그럴 계획입니다.

Exercise 6: Practice with -게 되-

Each of the following items contains two sentences. The first means *something or someone is a certain way*; the second reads 그렇게 됐습니다 *it turned out that way*. Combine the two sentences into a single one meaning *it became~turned out a certain way*. For example, the first one will be: 그분 얼굴이 빨갛게 됐습니다. *His face turned red.*

1. 그분 얼굴이 빨개요. 그렇게 됐습니다.
2. 만호 씨는 장학금을 받아요. 그렇게 됐습니다.
3. 팔을 다쳐서 농구를 못합니다. 그렇게 됐습니다.
4. 교통이 복잡합니다. 그렇게 됐습니다.
5. 한국신문을 읽을 수 있습니다. 그렇게 됐습니다.
6. 그것이 하얗습니다. 그렇게 됐습니다.
7. 내일의 회의는 취소했습니다. 그렇게 됐습니다.
8. 이번 일요일에 교회에서 반주를 합니다. 그렇게 됐습니다.
9. 내년에 런던대학에 방문학자로 갑니다. 그렇게 됐습니다.
10. 내년부터는 외무부에서 근무합니다. 그렇게 됐습니다.
11. 언니는 내년부터 유학을 갑니다. 그렇게 됐습니다.
12. 내일 종강 파티에 못 갑니다. 그렇게 됐습니다.
13. 회사 일로 한국에 왔습니다. 그렇게 됐습니다.
14. 그분의 입장을 이해합니다. 그렇게 됐습니다.
15. 전에는 고생을 많이 했지만 이제는 잘 살아요. 그렇게 됐습니다.

Exercise 7: Practice with Causatives in -게 하-

Each of the sentences below means *somebody does something* or *somebody is a certain way*. Rewrite them to mean *Sumi has/had* or *makes/made somebody do something* or *become a certain way* using the pattern in -게 해요, then translate. For example, the first one will be: 수미 씨는 할머니한테 경찰서에 전화를 거시게 했습니다. *Sumi had* 할머니 *call the police station.*

1. 할머니는 경찰서에 전화를 거셨어요.

2.	박 선생님은 대사관에 들리셨어요.
3.	아들이 바둑을 못 둡니다.
4.	딸이 하루종일 복습을 합니다.
5.	애들이 밤늦도록 예습을 합니다.
6.	아들이 수학숙제를 끝까지 했어요.
7.	만호 씨가 내일의 성경 공부에 못 가요.
8.	애들이 날마다 자기 전에 기도를 해요.
9.	자기 딸이 반주를 해 줬어요.
10.	만호 씨가 성가대원이 됐어요.
11.	방문교수가 한 학기 동안 강의를 했어요.
12.	딸이 유학을 못 갔어요.
13.	아들이 좀 더 적극적으로 공부를 했어요.
14.	애들이 제대로 앉아요.
15.	아들이 자동차를 고쳤어요.
16.	만호 씨가 커피를 흘렸어요.
17.	수진 씨가 약속을 취소했어요.
18.	남편이 출장을 못 갔어요.
19.	아이들이 일찍 자요.
20.	남편이 술을 못 마셔요.
21.	아이들이 껌을 못 씹어요.
22.	거기는 위험하니까, 아이들이 거기서 못 놀아요.
23.	어머니가 기뻐하세요.
24.	방이 좀 더 따뜻해요.
25.	그 사람이 화가 났어요.
26.	유학생들이 일찍 등록했어요.

Exercise 8: Practice with -(으)ㄴ/-는 대로

Each of the following items contains two sentences. Combine them so that the first sentence becomes a clause in -(으)ㄴ/-는 대로. For example, the first one will be: 선생님이 시키시는 대로 하세요. *Do as the teacher says.*

1.	선생님이 시키세요. 하세요.
2.	일을 끝내요. 갈거에요.
3.	생각이 나요. 말을 했어요.
4.	아버지가 한국에서 도착하세요. 바로 이사갈 예정입니다.
5.	가르쳐 주셨어요. 그렇게 집을 찾았어요.
6.	제가 불러요. 한번 써보세요.

7. 회의가 끝나요. 얼른 집에 와요.
8. 내일 수업이 끝나요. 점심을 먹으러 갑시다.
9. 소식이 들어와요. 알려 드릴게요.
10. 고향에 도착합니다. 편지를 쓰겠습니다.
11. 준비가 다 됩니다. 떠납시다.
12. 눈이 그쳐요. 출발할까요?

Exercise 9: Practice with 바람에

Each of the following items contains two sentences. Combine them so that the first sentence becomes a clause in -(으)ㄴ/-는 바람에. For example, the first one will be: 안경을 잃어 버리는 바람에 영화를 제대로 못 봤지요. *On account of losing my glasses I couldn't see the film properly.*

1. 안경을 잃어버렸어요. 그러는 바람에 영화를 제대로 못 봤지요.
2. 버스가 늦게 왔어요. 그러는 바람에 저도 늦었지요.
3. 애기가 자꾸 기침을 했어요. 그러는 바람에 잠을 제대로 못 잤어요.
4. 남편이 갑자기 출장을 갔어요. 그러는 바람에 파티를 취소했습니다.
5. 옆 집에서 이상한 소리가 났어요. 그러는 바람에 밤중에 깼어요.
6. 부엌에서 이상한 냄새가 났어요. 그러는 바람에 입맛이 싹 없어졌어요.
7. 갑자기 비가 쏟아졌어요. 그러는 바람에 온몸이 젖었어요.
8. 시내에서 사고가 났어요. 그러는 바람에 차가 많이 밀렸어요.
9. 깜짝 놀랐어요. 그러는 바람에 넘어졌어요.
10. 상한 음식을 먹었어요. 그러는 바람에 배탈이 났어요.
11. 애기가 정신없이 놀았어요. 온 집안이 엉망이에요.

Exercise 10: Practice with -는 게 좋겠어요

Change the final verb form in the following sentences to a gentler suggestion with -는 게 좋겠어요.

1. 오늘은 집에서 쉬세요.
2. 나는 배탈이 나서, 밥을 먹지 말아야겠어요.
3. 저는 할 일이 많거든요? 혼자 가세요.
4. 매운 것을 잘 못 드시니까, 냉면을 드시지 마세요.
5. 저는 많이 마시지는 않았지만, 만호 씨가 운전을 하세요.
6. 머리가 아프시면 일찍 주무세요.

7. 목사님, 설교를 영어로 하세요.
8. 그런 것은 장로님께 여쭈어보세요.
9. 집사님께서 기도를 하세요.
10. 코피가 났으면 좀 누워 계세요.

Vocabulary Drill

Each word in the left-hand column has a matching word in the right-hand column of somewhat **opposite meaning**. Call off the pairs one at a time, and translate them.

지난 봄	웃어요
어려워요	같아요
일해요	도시
게을러요	낮아요
높아요	놀아요
비싸요	내년 봄
시골	부지런해요
울어요	싸요
달라요	쉬워요
이야기를 해요	이야기를 들어요

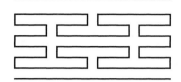

Lesson 25

REVIEW 4

Summary of Lesson Notes

25.1. Pattern Review

25.1.1. Conditional -(으)면

A) -(으)면 좋겠어요

1. 나도 한번 첫눈에 사랑에 빠졌으면 좋겠어요.

2. 바둑을 잘 둘 수 있으면 좋겠어요.

3. 한국말을 배우는 김에 한국역사에 대해서도 좀 배우면 좋겠어요.

B) -(었)으면 얼마나 좋겠어요?

4. 한국말로 예배를 드릴 수 있었으면 얼마나 좋겠어요?

5. 한국의 경제가 이렇게 계속 발전했으면 얼마나 좋겠어요?

6. 외무부에서 여권이 빨리 나왔으면 얼마나 좋겠어요?

C) -(으)면 고맙겠어요

7. 예정대로 내일까지 끝내 주시면 고맙겠어요.

8. 이 서류를 팩스로 정치학과에 보내 주시면 고맙겠어요.

9. 제 입장을 이해해 주시면 고맙겠습니다.

D)　해 주셨으면 합니다

10.　강의를 하실 때 한국경제를 중심으로 해 주셨으면 합니다.

11.　좀 더 구체적으로 설명해 주셨으면 합니다.

12.　좀 더 적극적으로 노력해 주셨으면 합니다.

E)　–지 않으면 안 돼요 / 안 하면 안 돼요

13.　어제 밤 늦도록 일을 하지 않으면 안 됐어요.

14.　지난 주에 난 사고 때문에 자동차를 고치지 않으면 안 됩니다.

15.　중요한 일이니까 과장님께 알려 드리지 않으면 안 되겠어요.

F)　–(으)면 안 돼요

16.　상한 냄새가 나니까 먹으면 안 돼요.

17.　기침을 많이 하는 걸 보니까 오늘 학교에 가면 안 되겠어요.

18.　배가 너무 불러서 더 먹으면 안 되겠어요.

25.1.2. Intentive -(으)려(고)

19.　내일도 안 아프면 퇴원을 하려고 합니다.

20.　이번 학기에 어떤 과목들을 택하려고 합니까?

21.　저희 회사는 다음 달부터 캐나다에서 맥주를 수입하려고 추진하고
　　있습니다.

25.1.3. -(으)려면

22. 무리를 하지 않으려면 이번 주말에 집에서 그냥 쉬는 게 좋겠어요.

23. 내일 출발하시려면 준비를 빨리 하셔야겠네요.

24. 주말까지 그 일을 끝마치려면 부산으로 출장 가는 것을 취소해야겠네요.

25.1.4. -(는)군요!

25. 화가 났어요? 안색이 안 좋군요!

26. 샤워를 하는 사이에 도둑을 맞으셨군요!

27. 장기를 잘 두시는군요!

28. 국제관계를 전공하는군요!

25.1.5. -(으)면서(도)

29. 그 학생은 농구선수이면서도 성적은 언제나 좋습니다.

30. 수진 씨는 재미교포 이세이면서도 한국말을 잘 합니다.

25.1.6. Mild Exclamations in -네요

31. 이 환자는 다시 수술을 해야겠네요.

32. 재미있는 표현이네요.

33. 그렇게 하시면 좀 불공평하네요.

34. 어머님이 많이 실망하셨겠네요.

25.1.7. ㅎ- Dropping Verbs of Manner and Color

35.　택시 기사 아저씨는 하얀 장갑을 끼고 있었어요.

36.　나는 술을 조금만 마셔도 얼굴이 새빨개져요.

37.　이 노란 사탕은 더 맛이 있는 것 같아요. 어떻습니까?

25.1.8. Transferentive -다(가)

38.　영문학을 전공하다가 재미가 없어서 한국학으로 바꿨어요.

39.　고려대학교 쪽으로 가는 김에 수진이네 집에 들렀다 가야겠어요.

40.　잠을 자다가 깨서 아직 제 정신이 아니에요.

41.　대학교 정문을 지나가다가 수미 씨를 우연히 만났어요.

25.1.9. More on Auxiliary 말아요

42.　실망하지 말고 더 적극적으로 노력해 보세요.

43.　잊지 말고 과장님께 여쭤 보세요.

44.　미식축구 말고 그냥 축구도 좋아하세요?

25.1.10. -는/-(으)ㄴ 김에

45.　부산에 출장을 가는 김에 거기서 사는 사촌형을 만날까 해요.

46.　여기 오신 김에 며칠 더 놀다가 가시지요.

47.　말이 나온 김에 이번 주말의 계획을 좀 더 구체적으로 이야기해
　　　볼까요?

25.1.11. -(으)ㄴ/-는 것 같아요

48. 벨소리가 나는 것 같지 않아요?

49. 실례지만 이 영수증은 제 것이 아닌 것 같아요.

50. 요즘 아버지는 일 때문에 신경을 많이 쓰시는 것 같아요.

51. 어제의 교통사고로 수진 씨는 많이 다친 것 같았어요.

25.1.12. Imminent Elaboration: -는데/-(으)ㄴ데(요)

52. 야유회에 부모님을 모시고 와도 좋은데요.

53. 기침을 많이 하는 걸 보니까 오늘 학교에 가면 안 되겠는데요.

54. 거기는 전쟁이 곧 터질 것 같아서 가지 않는 게 좋겠는데요.

25.1.13. -는/-(으)ㄴ데도

55. 저 환자는 수술을 2번이나 받았는데도 또 수술을 받아야 해요.

56. 오늘 하루종일 아무것도 안 먹었는데도 배가 안 고파요.

57. 바쁘신데도 와 주셔서 감사합니다.

58. 날씨가 추운데도 바닷가에 가려고 해요?

25.1.14. Prospective Modifier -(으)ㄹ

59. 내일 사진 찍을 데는 어디에요?

60. 걱정마세요. 염려할 것 없습니다.

25.1.15. -(으)ㄹ 때

61. 생선 찌개를 끓일 때 뭘 넣으세요?

62. 야유회를 가실 때 주로 어디로 가십니까?

63. 어렸을 때 어떤 음식을 좋아했어요?

64. 속이 나쁠 때 어떤 약을 먹는 게 좋아요?

25.1.16. Building on -(으)ㄹ 때

-(으)ㄹ 때마다

65. 나는 버스에서 내릴 때마다 잘 넘어져요.

66. 나는 서두를 때마다 실수를 합니다.

-(으)ㄹ 때부터

67. 배구를 어렸을 때부터 잘 했어요.

68. 섬유회사에서 일을 시작할 때부터 계속 바빴습니다.

-(으)ㄹ 때까지

69. 기차가 도착할 때까지 여기 대합실에서 기다려야겠네요.

70. 내가 이 보고서를 다 읽을 때까지 좀 기다려 줘요.

25.1.17. -(으)ㄹ 것 같아요

71. 튀긴 만두가 맛이 있을 것 같아요? 아니면 물만두가 맛이 있을 것
    같아요?

72.　A:　이 만두국의 간을 좀 볼래요?
　　B:　네, . . . 소금을 조금만 더 뿌리면 딱 좋을 것 같은데요.

73.　언제 결정하실 것 같습니까?

25.1.18. -(으)려다가

74.　지난 주말에 소풍을 가려다가 비가 와서 못 갔어요.

75.　서울 시내에서 죠깅을 하려다가 공해가 너무 심해서 그만뒀어요.

76.　아까 계란을 삶아서 먹으려다가 계란이 없어서 빵을 먹었어요.

25.1.19. -(으)ㄴ 후에

77.　사장님께 사과를 드린 후에 출장을 떠났습니다.

78.　등산을 갔다온 후에 너무 피곤해서 12시간이나 잤어요.

79.　신발을 여러 가지 본 다음에 짙은 밤색 구두 1켤레를 샀습니다.

25.1.20. -는 도중/동안/사이(에)

80.　내가 다방에서 조는 사이에 사무실에 팩스가 3장이나 왔어요.

81.　바쁘신 중에 시간을 내 주셔서 감사합니다.

82.　우리가 즐겁게 이야기하는 동안에 비행기가 벌써 밴쿠버에 거의 다 왔습니다.

83.　중국집 배달부가 지금 배달하는 중이에요.

84.　제가 일하는 도중에 불이 꺼졌습니다.

25.1.21. -는 바람에

85.   아까 소나기가 오는 바람에 늦었습니다.

86.   주말에 몸살이 나는 바람에 일을 하나도 못했습니다.

87.   연휴에 출장을 가는 바람에 하나도 쉬지 못했습니다.

25.1.22. Adverbative -게

88.   이번 연휴를 즐겁게 보내셨습니까?

89.   저 영화를 아주 재미있게 봤어요.

90.   지난 번 한국에 갔을 때 감기에 아주 심하게 걸렸어요.

91.   2사람은 오래오래 행복하게 살았습니다.

92.   이 대학에 어렵게 들어왔어요.

25.1.23. -게 해요

93.   너무 고단하면 수진 씨한테 장을 보게 하지요, 뭐.

94.   만호 씨한테 수업 도중에 졸지 못 하게 해야겠어요.

95.   화장을 더 짙게 할까요? 더 옅게 할까요?

96.   치마를 더 길게 할까요? 더 짧게 할까요?

25.1.24. -게 돼요

97.   A: 회사를 그만 두실 거에요?
      B: 아니오, 계속 다니게 됐어요.

98. A: 그걸 어떻게 알았어요?
     B: 친구한테서 간접적으로 알게 됐어요.

99. 요즘 보라색을 좋아하게 됐어요.

25.1.25. -는 게 좋겠어요

100. 이 파란색 말고 저 녹색을 사는 게 좋겠어요.

101. 신발을 맞추기 전에 먼저 발을 재는 게 낫지 않을까요?

102. 요즘 도둑들이 많이 돌아다니니까 창문들을 잠그고 가는 게 좋겠어요.

25.1.26. -(으)ㄹ 예정/생각/작정/계획이다

103. A: 언제 출발하세요?
     B: 인제 곧 떠날 예정입니다.

104. 시간이 좀 나면 새 양복을 맞출 생각입니다.

105. 다음 주말에 설악산에 등산 갈 작정입니다.

106. 어떤 색깔을 선택할 계획이십니까?

25.1.27. -(으)ㄴ/-는 대로

107. 성적표를 받는 대로 나에게 직접 연락해 줘요.

108. 그 쪽 날씨가 개는 대로 전화를 해 주세요.

109. 어린이들은 어른들이 하시는 대로 따라 해야 돼요.

110. 할아버지가 좋아하시는 대로 결정합시다.

111.	모든 일이 계획하신 대로 됐습니까?

112.	약속시간을 제 마음대로 정해도 돼요?

Review Exercises

Exercise 1: Korean to English Translation

Translate the following sentences into English.

1.	나는 여행을 너무 많이 하면 고단해집니다.
2.	내일까지 숙제를 하지 않으면 안 돼요.
3.	연필을 하나 빌려 줄래요?
4.	하루종일 바닷가에서 쉴 수 있으면 얼마나 좋겠어요?
5.	12시까지 출발하는 게 좋겠어요.
6.	미안하지만 될 수 있는 대로 빨리 좀 떠났으면 좋겠는데요.
7.	그 신발을 사려다가 흠이 있는 것 같아서 딴 걸 샀어요.
8.	그 분이 언제 도착할 예정입니까?
9.	다시 겨울이 됐으면 좋겠어요.
10.	추우시면 단추를 끼세요.
11.	그 시험을 다음 주 월요일까지 보지 않으면 안 돼요.
12.	잠을 자기 바로 전에 뭘 많이 먹으면 몸에 나쁜 것 같아요.
13.	아름다운 자연경치가 좋으시면 밴쿠버에서 등산을 한번 가 보세요.
	네, 그러지요.
14.	의사 선생님 뵈려고 지금 시내에 가는 길입니다.
15.	이 불고기는 싱겁네요!
16.	이 커피는 진하고 좋은데요!
17.	좀 이따가 대사관에 들러야 합니다.
18.	여기서 불이 나면 위험하겠는데요.
19.	수업 중에 껌을 씹으면 안 돼요. 선생님한테 혼 나요.
20.	걱정만 하지 말고 언제 한번 마음껏 놀아 보세요.
21.	죄송하지만 오늘의 회의는 다음에 해도 될까요?
22.	차문을 잊지 않고 잠갔어요?
23.	런던까지 오신 김에, 저희 집에서 며칠 더 놀다 가시지요.
24.	선생님이 화를 내셔도 껌을 계속 씹을 작정입니다.
25.	요즘 한국말 공부가 어때요?
	그저 그래요.

Lesson Twenty-five / 237

26. 술 1잔 하고 차로 가지 말고 택시를 타고 갑시다.
27. 아드님이 대학을 졸업해서 얼마나 기쁘시겠습니까?
28. 어려워하지 말고 직접 교수님한테 가서 여쭤 봐요.
29. 해가 나면 기분전환으로 어디 산보나 하러 나가려고 합니다.

Exercise 2: English to Korean Translation

Translate the following sentences into Korean.

1. I tried calling Professor Hong, but I dialed the wrong number.

2. Even though he graduated last year, he isn't bright at all.

3. Mr. Nam's place is very big, but I don't like it.

4. I have a conference tomorrow, so I'm worried.

5. Have you met the person who will sing for us tonight?

6. There aren't any cheap things to buy at that shop.

7. When you buy an oriental painting, you have to be careful.

8. When you're worried, you ought to have a strong drink, you know.

9. Every time I called, the line was busy.

10. Wait until James goes to Korea.

11. When you meet that diplomat, I'll take a picture for you.

12. When I played tennis last year, I got so that I wanted to be an athlete.

13. When I had my operation, I didn't have to go to work for one month.

14. It's getting cloudy; let's go home.

15. I'm planning to go to Japan this autumn; what sorts of presents should I buy?

Lesson 26

저 안내소에 가서 물어 보자.

In this lesson, Dialogue One shows two of Chin-yŏng's friends on a train on their way into Seoul Station. In Dialogue Two, we observe a conversation between Chin-sŏp (Chin-yŏng's brother), and his father. Both dialogues are meant to exemplify the main points of this lesson—the Plain and Intimate Styles. Thus, in Dialogue One we see a group of close friends giving and receiving a mixture of Plain and Intimate Style forms to and from each other. In Dialogue Two, we witness another typical situation—an adult or superior gives Plain and Intimate Style forms to a child or inferior, and receives Polite and/or Formal Style forms in return. In addition to these two new speech styles, this lesson introduces the *because of . . . -ing* pattern in -느라(고) and yet one more usage for transferentive -다(가).

Korean Dialogues

Dialogue 1

Po-hŭi and Kyŏng-suk, two of Chin-yŏng's high school friends from Inch'ŏn, are coming into Seoul by train to see Chin-yŏng at Ehwa University. They had called Chin-yŏng earlier to say they would be in town, but Chin-yŏng doesn't know exactly when to expect them.

기차 안에서:

보희	〔창밖을 내다 보면서〕 여기가 무슨 정거장이냐?
경숙	글쎄, 역곡역이야.
보희	서울은 얼마나 더 가면 될까?
경숙	역곡 다음 정거장이 바로 온수역이니까, 서울 거의 다 왔어.
보희	그럼, 시내까지 몇 분이나 더 걸리니?
경숙	글쎄, 한 30분 더 걸리겠지. 우리 시내서 뭘 할까?
보희	난 창경궁에도 가보고, 덕수궁에도 가보고, 롯데 백화점에 가서 쇼핑도 할래.

경숙	그것도 좋지만 이대에 가서 진영이부터 만나야지.
보희	그렇게 시간이 많을까? 그럼 우선 진영이부터 찾아 가지, 뭐.
경숙	기차가 선다! 시청역이야! 빨리 내려라!

시청역 안에서:

보희	가만히 있어 보자 – 이대는 신촌에 있거든. 여기서 지하철 타고 갈 수 있는데, 어떻게 가면 좋지? 저 안내소에 가서 물어 보자.

안내소에서:

보희	여보세요. 지하철 지도를 구할 수 있습니까? 있으면, 2장만 주십시오.

진영이 기숙사 방에서:

진영	참 잘 왔다. 떠나기 전에 전화나 미리 하고 오지 . . .
경숙	전화를 하려고 그랬는데, 지하철역 안에서 헤매느라고 못 했지. 그렇지만, 니가 이렇게 있어서 다행이다.

Dialogue 2

It is supper time at the Kim household. Mr. Kim pops his head into Chin-sŏp's room.

아버지	방 안에서 뭘 하냐?
진섭	공부하고 있어요.
아버지	이제 그만하고 밥 먹자.
진섭	네, 곧 갈게요.

A few moments later, at the dinner table

어머니	꼭꼭 씹어 먹어라!
진섭	네, 잘 먹겠습니다.
어머니	저녁 먹은 후에 시간 좀 있니?
진섭	왜요? 잠깐 나갔다 와야 하는데요.
어머니	그럼 일찍 좀 들어와라, 응? 나하고 이야기 좀 하자.

Dialogue Note

꼭꼭	*well, thoroughly, firmly*

Reading Passage

경숙이는 며칠째 열이 나고 기운이 없으며 먹으면 금방 토해서 집 근처에 있는 대학병원에 진찰을 받으러 갔다. 아픈 사람이 많아서 꽤 오래 기다려야 했다. 진찰실에서 우선 간호원이 경숙이의 맥박과 체온과 혈압을 쟀다. 그 다음에 한 시간쯤 다시 기다렸다가 의사가 진찰실로 들어와서 친절하게 이야기하면서 진찰을 해 줬다. 결국 의사 선생님으로부터 받은 진단은 감기몸살이라서 경숙이는 주사를 맞고 다시 집으로 돌아갔다.

경숙이는 이미 주사를 맞았기 때문에 염려를 할 필요가 없었지만, 그래도 그 이튿날 건강이 걱정이 돼서 아무것도 생각하지 않고 집에서 그냥 쉬었다. 그런데 이상하게 집에서 며칠간 푹 쉬었는데도 계속 토하고 소화도 안 되고 온몸이 아파서 다시 병원으로 돌아가는 수밖에 없었다.

지난 번처럼 같은 간호원이 이번에는 피검사까지 하고 같은 의사가 진찰을 했는데, 이번에 나온 진단은 '독감'이었다. 그래서 경숙이는 또 다시 주사를 맞고 집에 돌아오는 길에 마음 속으로 이렇게 생각했다:

"그 병원과 의사는 엉터리다. 다음에는 딴 병원으로 가 봐야겠다."

다행히도 며칠 더 쉰 후에 경숙이는 다 나았다.

Reading Passage Note

며칠간   *for a ["period of a"] few days*

Vocabulary

Verbs

Verbs That Take Objects

구하–	look for [work, a job]; buy, get, obtain
그 책은 구하기 힘들어요.	That book is hard to buy/come by.
끄–ㄹ–	drag; pull, draw
내다 보–	look out (at)
거리를 내다 봐요.	Looks out onto the street.
내려다 보–	look down at/upon
드려다 보–	look in (through), peep in (through)
비키–	get out of the way
길을 비켜 주세요.	Please clear the way. or Please get out of the way.
처다 보–	look up at; stare at
추방(을) 하–	expel, drive out, banish
토하–	vomit, throw up
아침에 먹은 것을 토했다.	I threw up what I ate for breakfast.

Descriptive and/or Sensory Verbs

급하–	be urgent
급히	hastily, in a rush
기운(이) 없–	have no energy
다–ㄹ–	be sweet
시–	be sour
쓰–	be bitter
착실하–	be steadfast, thorough
친절하–	be kind
불친절하–	be unkind
편리하–	be convenient
흔하–	be common
흔히	often, commonly

Intransitive Verbs (Processive Verbs That Cannot Take Objects)

문병(을) 가–	to visit (a sick person)
할아버지한테 문병을 갈까요?	Shall we pay a sick visit to granddad?
문병(을) 하–	to visit (a sick person)
애(를) 쓰–	make efforts, try hard

애를 썼어.	Well done (i.e., thanks for your efforts).
회복(을) 하–	recover (e.g., from illness)
회복(이) 되–	recover (e.g., from illness)

Nouns

<u>Health and Hospitals</u>

간호사	nurse
검사	inspection, test
검사(를) 하–	inspect, test, examine
피검사	blood-test
–도	degrees (with Sino-Korean numbers)
독감	flu
맥; 맥박	pulse
맥(을) 짚–	take someone's pulse
맥박(을) 재–	take someone's pulse
변비	constipation
소화	digestion
소화(가) 안 되–	has indigestion
소화제	digestive tablet(s); medicine to help digestion
열	a fever (high temperature)
열(이) 있–	have a fever (high temperature)
열(이) 높–	have a high temperature, run a high fever
응급치료	first-aid treatment
응급차	ambulance
의과 대학 [–≤]	medical school
인턴	intern
전염병 〔–뼝〕	contagious disease/illness
주사	a shot, an injection
주사(를) 맞–	get a shot, have an injection
주사(를) 놓–	give a shot, administer an injection

간호원이 환자한테 주사를 놓아 줬다.

   The nurse gave the patient an injection.

진단	diagnosis
진찰	a check-up, medical examination
진찰(을) 받–	have a check-up; consult a doctor
진찰실	(medical) consultation room
체온	body temperature
체온(을) 재–	takes a person's temperature
치료	medical treatment

치료(를) 받-	receive/undergo medical treatment
피	blood
혈압	blood pressure
혈압(을) 재-	take somebody's blood pressure

Branches of Medicine

내과 〔-꽈〕	internal medicine
산부인과 〔-꽈〕	obstetrics & gynecology
소아과 〔-꽈〕	pediatrics
외과 〔-꽈〕	surgery
외과 의사 〔-꽈〕	surgeon
이비인후과 〔-꽈〕	ear/nose/throat specialist
치과 〔-꽈〕	dentistry
치과 의사	dentist

Weather

-도	degrees (with Sino-Korean numbers)
섭씨	Celsius
예보	forecast, prediction
일기예보	weather forecast
온도	atmospheric temperature
일기	the weather
화씨	Fahrenheit

People

가정의	family doctor
개인	individual person
개인적으로는 모릅니다.	I don't know her personally.
그	he, that person [male]
독신	[still, as yet] unmarried person
저 사람은 아직 독신이에요.	He's still single.
독신자	unmarried person (by choice)
저 사람은 독신자예요.	He's a bachelor.
말썽꾸러기	troublemaker (child), rascal
장난꾸러기	mischief-maker, little monkey (child)
총각	unmarried young man
파출부	maid

<u>Other</u>

가루	powder
고추가루 〔-까루〕	red pepper powder
후추가루 〔-까루〕	black pepper powder
거리	distance
장거리	long-distance
단거리	short-distance
교통사고	traffic accident
문장	sentence
미군	American army
미8군	U.S Eighth Army
방해	a disturbance, obstruction
방해(가) 되-	get in the way
방해(를) 하-	disturb someone
시장	mayor
시합	a match, contest, game (sport)
용돈 (-똔)	pocket money
인형	doll
줄	line (of text); line (that you stand in)
줄(을) 서-	stand in line
위로부터 둘째 줄을 읽어 주세요.	Please read the second line from the top.
지갑	wallet; purse
지도	map
허락	permission
허락(을) 받-	get permission
허락(을) 하-	permit, allow
현관	entrance vestibule

Adverbs

미리	in advance, ahead of time
푹	(sleep) deeply; (rest) soundly

Lesson Notes

26.1. The Plain Style

Most of the sentences of this lesson are in the Plain Style, the characteristic endings of which are:

-ㄴ다, -는다, -다	Statements
-느냐	Questions (Type 1)
-니	Questions (Type 2)
-(으)라	Commands (Type 1)
-어라/-아라	Commands (Type 2)
-자	Suggestions ("Let's . . .")

The Plain Style has a number of functions. It occurs often in writing, e.g., in newspapers, textbooks or in written announcements, as a matter-of-fact and neutral style. In spoken language, it can be used between intimates, or from a person higher in status to somebody lower in status (like the father to his son in this lesson's Dialogue 2). But you are advised to avoid using Type 1 Plain commands (in -(으)라) in speech. One often overhears little Korean children, or even adults sometimes, using Plain style indicatives with a special nuance something like a boast.

The Plain Style is also a fundamental building block for reported speech in Korean, about which you will learn more in the next lesson.

26.1.1. Plain Style Statements

Statements in the Plain Style end with Plain Style verb forms. These forms, unlike statement forms in the other styles, have different endings depending on whether the verb is processive or descriptive.

26.1.2. Descriptive and Processive Verbs

Descriptive verbs form Plain Style statements by attaching the ending -다 to the base; for L-extending vowel bases the ending is attached to the **extended** base (i.e., the base keeps the ㄹ). If the base ends in a consonant, there are the usual sound changes to make:

MEANING	BASE	STATEMENT	PRONUNCIATION
high, tall	높-	높다	놉따
easy	쉬 w-	쉽다	쉽따
better	나[ㅅ]-	낫다	나따
late	늦-	늦다	느따
small	작-	작다	작따
young	젊-	젊다	점따
good	좋-	좋다	조타
disliked	싫-	싫다	실타
much/many	많-	많다	만타
cheap	싸-	싸다	same
cloudy	흐리-	흐리다	same
bad	나쁘-	나쁘다	same
blue/green	푸르-	푸르다	same
far	머-르-	멀다	same
long	기-ㄹ-	길다	same

Processive verbs are made into Plain Style statements by an ending which has the shape
-ㄴ다 when attached to vowel bases (including the *unextended* shape of L-extending bases)
and -는다 when attached to consonant bases. If the base ends in a consonant, there are the
usual sound changes to make.

MEANING	BASE	STATEMENT	PRONUNCIATION
wear	입-	입는다	임는다
broil	구w-	굽는다	굼는다
close it	닫-	닫는다	단는다
comb	빗-	빗는다	빈는다
seek; find	찾-	찾는다	찬는다
put	놓-	놓는다	논는다
sit down	앉-	앉는다	안는다
not do (. . . -지)	않-	않는다	안는다
listen; hear	들- (듣다)	듣는다	든는다
eat	먹-	먹는다	멍는다
read	읽-	읽는다	잉는다
wait	기다리-	기다린다	same
tie	매-	맨다	same
write	쓰-	쓴다	same
not know	모르-	모른다	same
become	되-	된다	same

MEANING	BASE	STATEMENT	PRONUNCIATION
buy	사-	산다	same
live	사-ㄹ-	산다	same
hang it	거-ㄹ-	건다	same

Honorific bases, of course, are treated like other bases that end in 시: 젊으시다 (somebody esteemed) *is young*, 들으신다 (somebody esteemed) *listens*, 노신다 (somebody esteemed) *plays*. Choice of -다 or -ㄴ다 depends on whether the underlying base is descriptive or processive.

26.1.3. Bases That Can Be Either Processive or Descriptive

There are some verbs that straddle the fence and belong in both the processive and the descriptive categories. The verb 해요, for example, takes the ending -다 with descriptive verbal nouns and the ending -ㄴ다 with processive verbal nouns.

PROCESSIVE		DESCRIPTIVE	
입원(을) 한다	*enter (hospital)*	심하다	*be serious*
방문(을) 한다	*visit*	흔하다	*be common*
퇴원(을) 한다	*be discharged (from hospital)*	깨끗하다	*be clean*
운전(을) 한다	*drive*	친절하다	*be kind*
염려(를) 한다	*worry*	불친절하다	*be unkind*
준비(를) 한다	*prepare*	피곤하다	*be tired*

Similar is the negative auxiliary 않아요, which takes either -다 or -는다, depending on what kind of verb it is making negative.

NEGATIVE PROCESSIVE VERB		NEGATIVE DESCRIPTIVE VERB	
앉지 않는다	*doesn't sit*	좋지 않다	*isn't good*
먹지 않는다	*doesn't eat*	가깝지 않다	*isn't near*
눕지 않는다	*doesn't lie down*	멀지 않다	*isn't far*
살지 않는다	*doesn't live*	나쁘지 않다	*isn't bad*
준비하지 않는다	*doesn't prepare*	깨끗하지 않다	*isn't clean*
공부하지 않는다	*doesn't study*	피곤하지 않다	*isn't tired*

Notice what happens with 이러다 ~ 이렇다 *does/is this way*, 그러다 ~ 그렇다 *does/is that way*, and 저러다 ~ 저렇다 *does/is that way over there*.

Processive Plain		Polite	Descriptive Plain	
이런다	*does this way*	이래요	이렇다	*is this way*
그런다	*does that way*	그래요	그렇다	*is that way*
저런다	*does that way*	저래요	저렇다	*is that way*

Two other bases you have had that can be either processive or descriptive are:

Processive			Polite		Descriptive	
낫는다	*gets better*	←	나아요	→	낫다	*is better*
큰다	*gets big(ger)*	←	커요	→	크다	*is big*

26.1.4. Plain Style: The Bases 있-, 없-, and 계시-

The base 있- is particularly tricky; you will recall it has three meanings.

1. *stays*
2. *exists*
3. *has* (with the object possessed taking the subject particle 이/가)

In the first meaning (*stays*) 있- is processive, hence 안 있는다 ~ 있지 않는다 *doesn't stay*, 못 있는다 ~ 있지 못 한다 *can't stay*, and 있는다 *stays*.

In the other two meanings (*exists*; *has*), 있- is descriptive, and takes just -다 rather than -는다.

The honorific base 계시- has two meanings: *stays* and *exists*. In both meanings, Koreans treat it as either processive or descriptive, with no apparent difference in meaning. Thus, for *Grandfather is not at home* both 할아버지가 안 계시다 and 할아버지가 안 계신다 are possible.

The base 없- *does not exist* is always descriptive, hence we find only 없다.

The auxiliary 있- in (1) -고 있- *is doing*, and (2) resultant states in -어 있- behaves like *exists*, i.e., it is descriptive.

1.   (안) 타고 있어요   *is (not) riding*
   - →   안 타고 있다;   타고 있지 않아요   *isn't riding*
   - →   타고 있지 않다;   못 타고 있어요   *can't be riding*
   - →   못 타고 있다

2.　(안) 앉아 있어요　　　　　　　　　　　　　　*is (not) seated*
　　→　　안 앉아 있다;　　앉아 있지 않아요　　*is not seated*
　　→　　앉아 있지 않다;　못 앉아 있어요　　　*can't be seated*
　　→　　못 앉아 있다

26.1.5. Plain Style: Past and Future Forms

Past and future bases of *all* verbs (whether descriptive or processive) attach -다: -었다 and -겠다. Here are some examples.

PROCESSIVE VERBS

앉-	sit	앉았다	*sat*
		앉겠다	*will sit*
먹-	eat	먹었다	*ate*
		먹겠다	*will eat*
사-ㄹ-	live	살았다	*lived*
		살겠다	*will live*
부르-	call	불렀다	*called*
		부르겠다	*will call*
공부하-	study	공부했다	*studied*
		공부하겠다	*will study*

DESCRIPTIVE VERBS

비싸-	be expensive	비쌌다	*was expensive*
		비싸겠다	*will be expensive*
좋-	be good	좋았다	*was good*
		좋겠다	*will be good*
머-ㄹ-	be far	멀었다	*was far*
		멀겠다	*will be far*
빠르-	be fast	빨랐다	*was fast*
		빠르겠다	*will be fast*
피곤하-	be tired	피곤했다	*was tired*
		피곤하겠다	*will be tired*

26.2. Plain Style Questions
26.2.1. Type 1 Questions: -(으)냐, -느냐

Questions in the Plain Style consist of modifier forms (-(으)ㄴ, -는) plus the postmodifier 야. Processive verbs and 있- and 없- use the processive modifier form (-는 + 야, spelled -느냐).

하-	do	하느냐	does [he] do?
가-	go	가느냐	does [he] go?
먹-	eat	먹느냐	does [he] eat?
사-ㄹ-	live	사느냐	does [he] live?
부르-	call	부르느냐	does [he] call?
있-	stay, be, have	있느냐	does [he] stay?
			is [he]? does [he] have?
없-	lack	없느냐	does [he] lack?

In colloquial Korean, the processive Plain Style question form in -느냐 is usually used in its abbreviated form, -냐 (← -(느)냐), thus making it indistinguishable from the descriptive form.

1. 어디 갔다왔냐? (from 어디 갔다왔느냐?)
    Where have you been?

Descriptive verbs (which of course lack processive modifier forms) use the simple modifier form (-ㄴ + 야 and -은 + 야, spelled -냐 and -으냐).

비싸-	be expensive	비싸냐	is [it] expensive?
좋-	be good	좋으냐	is [it] good?
머-ㄹ-	be far	머냐	is [it] far?
빠르-	be fast	빠르냐	is [it] fast?
가까w-	be close	가까우냐	is [it] close?
싶-	feel like/want	싶으냐	does one feel like/want?
어떻-	is how?	어떠냐	is how? is like what?

Notice that ㄹ-extending bases attach this ending to the unextended base (without the ㄹ) and that ㅎ- dropping verbs drop their ㅎ. In the case of ㅂ-w verbs, in colloquial Korean you will also hear, instead of the correct 가까우냐, forms like 가깝냐 *is it close?* which treat the base as ending in ㅂ-.

Lesson Twenty-six /251

For past and future, the processive modifier ending –는 (+ 야 → –느냐) is attached to the past and future bases of *all* verbs.

갔느냐	*did he go?*	가겠느냐	*will he go?*
먹었느냐	*did he eat?*	먹겠느냐	*will he eat?*
살았느냐	*did he live?*	살겠느냐	*will he live?*
불렀느냐	*did he call?*	부르겠느냐	*will he call?*
비쌌느냐	*was it expensive?*	비싸겠느냐	*will it be expensive?*
좋았느냐	*was it good?*	좋겠느냐	*will it be good?*
가까웠느냐	*was it close?*	가깝겠느냐	*will it be close?*
싶었느냐	*did one feel like/want?*	싶겠느냐	*will one feel like/want?*
어땠느냐	*was how?*	어떻겠느냐	*will be how?*

26.2.2. Type 2 Questions: –니

The second type of Plain Style questions has the one-shape ending –니. This ending can attach to any base and is widely used (reciprocally) among intimates or by elders to children.

먹–	*eat*	먹니	*does [he] eat?*
비싸–	*be expensive*	비싸니	*is [it] expensive?*
좋–	*be good*	좋니	*is [it] good?*
머–ㄹ–	*be far*	머니	*is [it] far?*
빠르–	*be fast*	빠르니	*is [it] fast?*
가까w–	*be close*	가깝니	*is [it] close?*
싶–	*feel like/want*	싶니	*does one feel like/want?*
어떻–	*be how?*	어떠니	*is how?*
갔니	*did he go?*	가겠니	*will he go?*

Notice that ㄹ-extending bases attach this ending to the unextended base (without ㄹ).

The Plain Style question ending –니 differs from the sequential ending –(으)니(까)
in that it is a one-shape ending:

    1. it is always pronounced –니;

    2. the sequential ending is pronounced –니 only after vowels, and –으니
       after consonants.

Thus, the sequential form and the Type 2 Plain Style question forms are pronounced alike
for vowel verbs (including the ㄹ-extending ones, which appear unextended) but
differently for all consonant bases—including *any* past or future base. For example:

BASE		TYPE 2 QUESTION –니?		SEQUENTIAL –(으)니(까)	
가-	*go*	가니	*does [he] go?*	가니	*goes, so . . .*
아-ㄹ-	*know*	아니	*does [he] know?*	아니	*knows, so . . .*
부르-	*call*	부르니	*does [he] call?*	부르니	*calls, so . . .*
먹-	*eat*	먹니	*does [he] eat?*	먹으니	*eats, so . . .*
했-	*did*	했니	*did [he] do?*	했으니	*did, so . . .*
하겠-	*will do*	하겠니	*will [he] do?*	하겠으니	*will do, so . . .*

In greeting a child, instead of using the expression 안녕하십니까? (or 안녕하세요?) *Are
you well?* you may say 잘 있었니? (Plain Style), 잘 있었어? (Intimate Style). For
good-bye, instead of 안녕히 가십시오! and 안녕히 계십시오! (or 안녕히 가세요! and
안녕히 계세요!), you say 잘 가거라! or 잘 가라 and 잘 있어라! or just 잘 가! and
잘 있어!

26.3. Plain Style: Suggestions in -자

Corresponding to the Formal Style ending -(으)ㅂ시다 *Let's . . .* is the one-shape Plain Style suggestion ending -자. It is quite common in colloquial speech.

BASE			PLAIN SUGGESTION	
사–	*buy*	→	사자	*let's buy it*
먹–	*eat*	→	먹자	*let's eat*
사–ㄹ–	*live*	→	살자	*let's live*
부르–	*call*	→	부르자	*let's call*
들–	*listen*	→	듣자	*let's listen*

Only processive verbs occur in suggestions. The ending -자 attaches to bases just like the suspective -지, with the usual sound changes required for bases ending in consonants. Both endings are attached to the extended shape of L-extending verbs (hence 놀지, 놀자 *play*).

26.4. Plain Style Commands

26.4.1. Plain Style Commands Type 1: -(으)라

The first type of Plain Style commands has the ending -으라 (attached to consonant bases) or -라 (attached to vowel bases) to make forms that correspond in meaning to the Formal Style ending -(으)ㅂ시오, -(으)십시오. This ending -라 is added to the extended form of L-extending bases (e.g., 걸라 *hang it!* ← 거–ㄹ–, 놀라 *play!* ← 노–ㄹ–, etc.). For example:

BASE		PLAIN COMMAND (1)	
가–	*go*	가라	*go!*
먹–	*eat*	먹으라	*eat!*
사–ㄹ–	*live*	살라	*live!*
부르–	*call*	부르라	*call!*

> **주의!**
> Only processive verbs have command forms.

Type 1 Plain command forms are hardly ever used in colloquial Korean on their own, and this is why the conversation at the beginning of this lesson has 먹어라 *eat!* (Plain Style, Type 2). You are most likely to encounter Type 1 Plain command forms (usually of the verb 하- *do*) in, say, a textbook, where the exercises might tell you:

2.   다음 문장들을 영어로 번역하라.
      Translate the following sentences into English.

Or on a poster at a student rally, as in:

3.   미군을 추방하라!
      Throw out the American Army!

The Type 1 Plain style negative commands are made with 말라 (often pronounced 마라).

> 가지 말라   *don't go*
> 먹지 말라   *don't eat*

You may be wondering why we are introducing a form like this which is hardly ever used in spoken Korean. This is because the Type 1 Commands (along with the Type 1 questions) are a crucial building block in Reported Speech/Quotations, the subject of the next lesson.

26.4.2. Plain Style Commands Type 2: -어라, -아라, -여라

Whereas Plain Style commands in -(으)라 (Type 1) are hardly ever used in spoken Korean, Type 2 commands are used all the time, either reciprocally among intimates or from elders to children.

Type 2 Plain Style commands are formed by adding the particle 라 to the infinitive.

BASE		PLAIN COMMAND (2)	
가-	*go*	가라	*go!*
먹-	*eat*	먹어라	*eat!*
사-ㄹ-	*live*	살아라	*live!*
부르-	*call*	불러라	*call!*
쓰-	*write*	써라	*write!*
구ｗ-	*broil*	구워라	*broil!*

In the case of most vowel-base verbs ending in -아, -에, and -애 the bases and infinitives are the same; thus, the two types of Plain Style imperatives are pronounced alike.

BASE		QUOTED (TYPE 1) IMPERATIVE		TYPE 2 IMPERATIVE	
사-	*buys*	사라	*[tells him] to buy*	사라	*buy!*
매-	*ties*	매라	*[tells him] to tie*	매라	*tie!*
베-	*cuts*	베라	*[tells someone] to cut*	베라	*cut!*

The special base 하- *do* behaves as follows (recall that the colloquial infinitive 해 is derived by contraction from the more bookish 하여).

BASE		QUOTED (TYPE 1)		TYPE 2		BOOKISH TYPE 2
하-	*buys*	하라	*[tells him] to buy*	해라	*buy!*	하여라 *buy!*

A few common verbs have an irregular infinitive form before the imperative particle 라 (though some people use the regular infinitive—for some or all of the verbs):

BASE		IMPERATIVE MADE WITH IRREGULAR INFINITIVES		IMPERATIVE MADE WITH REGULAR INFINITIVES
가-	*go*	가거라	*go!*	가라
자-	*sleep*	자거라	*go to sleep!*	자라
되-	*become*	되거라	*become!*	되라 (or 되어라)
있-	*be, stay*	있거라	*stay!*	있어라
앉-	*sit*	앉거라	*sit!*	앉아라
들- (듣다)	*listen*	듣거라	*listen!*	들어라
오-	*come*	오너라	*come!*	와라

For all except the last (오- → 오너라), the irregular infinitive ends in -거. Negative commands are regularly made by following the -지 form of the verb with 말아라, but this is often abbreviated to 마라:

보지 말아라!   or   보지 마라!
Don't look!

26.5. Plain Style: The Copula.

The Plain Style statement form of the copula is -이다 (base 이- plus descriptive verb ending
-다). Other statement forms of the copula behave just like those of descriptive verbs. The past
form is -이었다 and the future -이겠다. Questions are also like descriptive-verb questions:
-이냐. (The copula, again like descriptive verbs, lacks suggestions and command forms).
The only negative possible for the copula is 아니, since there is no long form; thus, the plain
form is 아니다. Here are some examples.

4.   만호 씨는 총각이 아니다.
      Manho is not a bachelor.

5.   박 선생님의 아들은 장난꾸러기냐?
      Is Mr. Pak's son a troublemaker?

6.   수미 씨의 할아버지는 외과 의사셨다.
      Sumi's grandfather was a surgeon.

7.   한국에서는 소아과 의사들은 다 부자다.
      Pediatricians in Korea are all rich.

26.6. Intimate Style

The Intimate Style is used among intimates, for example, among close friends, or when
children talk to each other, and is also used by adults speaking to children. In colloquial
Korean as spoken between intimates, Plain Style forms (especially statements and suggestions)
are often mixed together with Intimate Style forms.

The rule for forming the Intimate Style is simple: take any Polite Style ending and remove the
polite particle 요. In just a few cases (marked in shadow below), the Intimate Style is
slightly different from the Polite Style-minus-요. Here are the Polite Style endings you have
learned so far with corresponding Intimate forms.

	POLITE STYLE	INTIMATE STYLE
Present	해요	해
Past	했어요	했어
Future	하겠어요	하겠어

	POLITE STYLE	INTIMATE STYLE
Honorific Polite	하세요	하셔
Copula	-이에요	-이야
Probably Future	할 거에요	할 거야
Casual Polite	하지요	하지
	했지요	했지
	하겠지요	하겠지
Suggestions/ Tentative Questions	할까요?	할까?
Wanna	할래요	할래
Rhetorical Retorts	하잖아요	하잖아
	했잖아요	했잖아
	하겠잖아요	하겠잖아
Immediate Futures	할게요	할게
Mild Surprises	하네요	하네
You See	하거든요	하거든
Sudden Realization	하군요	하군 or 하구나
	하는군요	하는군 or 하는구나

A few special points about the intimate style should be mentioned.

1. The verb 같아요 *is (a)like, is the same* in the Intimate Style is often pronounced 같애 rather than 같아.

2. The copula is usually pronounced 이야 after consonants (corresponding to polite-style 이에요) and 야 after vowels (corresponding to 에요).

책이에요	(Polite)	but	책이야	(Intimate)	*It's a book.*
홍차에요	(Polite)	but	홍차야	(Intimate)	*It's black tea.*

However, recall that when NOT sentence-final, the copula is usually 이어 (after consonants), and 여 (after vowels).

책이어도	*though it's a book . . .*
책이어서	*it's a book, so . . .*
홍차여도	*though it's English tea . . .*
홍차여서	*it's English tea, so . . .*

Lesson Twenty-six / 258

3. The copula is sometimes dropped altogether in the intimate style. At other times it may be reduced to "y" and pronounced as part of the preceding vowel. Compare these probable-future forms, all meaning *will probably come*.

POLITE STYLE	INTIMATE STYLE
-(으)ㄹ 것이에요	-(으)ㄹ 것이야
-(으)ㄹ 거에요	-(으)ㄹ 거야

4. Negative commands are regularly made by following the -지 form of a verb with 마라, but this is often abbreviated to 마.

> 보지 마라! or 보지 마!
> *Don't look!*

26.7. *Because of . . . ing* with -느라(고)

Processive verbs have an ADJUNCTIVE form: the one-shape ending -느라(고). This ending typically has the meaning *what with . . .ing, on account of the process of . . . ing, as a result of . . . ing* or *because of . . . ing*: The subject of the two clauses is always the same. Here are some representative verb bases with this ending.

BASE	GLOSS	PROCESSIVE ADJUNCTIVE	PRONUNCIATION
하-	*do*	하느라(고)	same
기다리-	*wait*	기다리느라(고)	same
노-ㄹ-	*play*	노느라(고)	same
들- (듣다)	*listen*	들느라(고)	든느라(고)
걸- (걷다)	*walk*	걸느라(고)	건느라(고)
받-	*receive*	받느라(고)	반느라(고)
빗-	*comb*	빗느라(고)	빈느라(고)
찾-	*look for*	찾느라(고)	찬느라(고)
있-	*stay*	있느라(고)	인느라(고)
입-	*wear*	입느라(고)	임느라(고)
놓-	*put*	놓느라(고)	논느라(고)
지(ㅅ)-	*make*	짓느라(고)	진느라(고)
구w-	*broil*	굽느라(고)	굼느라(고)

Sometimes you will hear this ending without the 고:

8.　공부하느라, 편지를 쓰느라, 참 바쁘다.
　　What with studying and writing letters, I'm very busy.

But usually it is followed by 고, with no change in meaning.

9.　할머니를 문병 가느라고, 밤 늦게 잤다.
　　What with visiting my sick grandmother (and all), I went to bed late.

10.　점심 먹느라고 늦었어.
　　What with eating lunch and all I was late = Lunch made me late.

11.　대학교에 다닐 때, 연애하느라고 공부를 못 했어.
　　I was so busy dating when I attended university that I didn't [couldn't] study.

12.　편지를 쓰느라고 뉴스를 놓쳤다.
　　I missed the news trying to get a letter written.

13.　자동차를 고치느라고 애를 썼다.
　　I've made efforts to repair the automobile. = I tried to get the car fixed. = I had a rough time [in the process of] getting the car fixed

14.　A.　내가 부탁한 것 가지고 왔니?
　　　　Did you bring the thing I asked [you to do a favor for me] for?

　　　B.　미안해, 급히 오느라고 잊어버렸어.
　　　　I was in such a rush coming that I forgot.

15.　A.　애기가 어디 있냐?
　　　　Where's the baby?

　　　B.　저기서 노느라고 정신이 없지.
　　　　He's absorbed in playing over there.

16.　A.　어제 텔레비젼에서 축구시합을 봤냐?
　　　　Did you see the soccer on TV yesterday?

　　　B.　아니, 자느라고 못 봤어.
　　　　No, I missed it because I was sleeping.

17. A. 들고 오느라고 힘들었지?
       It must have been difficult to carry here.

    B. 안 무거우니까, 괜찮았어.
       It isn't heavy, so it was no problem.

18. 어머니: 뭐 하느라고 벌써 용돈을 다 썼니?
       What have you been doing to spend all your pocket money already?

    아들: 술 마시느라고 그랬어요.
       I spent it all on booze.

19. 이렇게 추운데 오시느라고 수고하셨어요.
       It's so cold—thank you for taking the trouble to come.

20. 회의하느라고 그 분을 만나지 못 했다.
       I wasn't able to meet him because I was in a conference.

21. 늦잠 자느라고 이도 닦지 못 하고 왔어.
       I overslept, so I came without even brushing my teeth.

22. 전화를 기다리느라고 나가지도 못 했지.
       Because I was waiting for a phone call, I couldn't even go out.

26.8. The Copula Transferentive: Special Uses

26.8.1. Infinitive + 다 (-어/-아다)

There is a special use of the transferentive copula -이다 (always pronounced 다 here because it follows infinitives, which end in vowels). It is inserted into verb phrases, between the infinitive and its following verb, where the last verb is 줘요 (드려요) *does for someone*, 봐요 *looks* (in some direction), or the like.

The 다 (optionally followed by 가) shows that there is a shift in the direction of the action (as looking toward something) or in the recipient of the benefit (as in favors). In phrases with 줘요 or 드려요 *does for someone*, the 다(가) indicates that the favor is done either in a different place from where the recipient is or else after the elapse of a considerable length of time: there is thus a shift in either space or time, often both.

These are typical -어 ~ -아다 phrases.

23.   책을 사다 줘요/드려요
buys a book for someone

24.   가져다 줘요 → 갖다 줘요 (= 가져와요)
brings it to someone

25.   의자를 끌어다 놓아요
pulls up a chair (to sit on)

26.   밥을 해다 놓아요
gets dinner ready (so we can eat)

27.   표를 사다 놓을게요
I'll buy the tickets in advance

Notice also the following compound verbs built on this pattern:

드려다 봐요	내다 봐요	쳐다 봐요
looks in	*looks out*	*stares at*

26.8.2. Errand-Type Requests with -어 ~ -아다 주-

One special use of the -어 ~ -아다 pattern involves favors. You have already learned how to combine infinitives in -어 ~ -아 with the verb 주- *give* to express favor giving. However, if the infinitive vowel in this pattern is embellished with the transferentive -다, emphasis is given to the fact that the favor in question involves a shift in space—a sort of errand. Observe the following examples.

28.   만호 씨, 우유 좀 사 주세요.   vs.
       만호 씨, 집에 돌아 오는 길에 우유 좀 사다 주세요.
       Manho, please buy some milk [on your way home].

29. 어머니, 잡지 좀 빌려 주세요.　vs.

    어머니, 돌아오시는 길에 도서관에서 잡지 좀 빌려다 주세요.
    Mother, please borrow a magazine [from the library on your way home].

30. 수미 씨, 이 컵 좀 씻어 주세요. vs.
    수미 씨, 부엌에 가서 이 컵 좀 씻어다 주세요.
    Sumi, please [go to the kitchen and] wash this cup.

26.8.3. Directional Particle 에 + 다 (에다, 에다가)

The copula transferentive is also used after the particle 에 to emphasize a shift of location or purpose.

31. 상 위에다 놓으세요.
    Please put it on the table.

32. 종이 위에다 쓰세요.
    Please write on the paper.

33. 무엇에다 쓰는 겁니까?
    What do you use it for?

A special contraction is 어디(에)다 → 어따 *where to?* The particle 에, as you have seen, often drops after front vowels (이, 에, 애). You can see these forms below.

34. 이것을 어디다 놓을까요? or
    이것을 어따 놓을까요?
    Where shall I put this?

35. 김치 옆에(다) 놓으세요.
    Put it beside the kimchee.

In all these uses the copula transferentive is optional; that is, you can freely leave the 다 out and the meaning will be much the same but without the emphasis on *shift*.

Exercises

Exercise 1: Plain Style Statements

Change each of the following statements to the Plain Style, translating each one as you go. For example, the first will be: 김 사장님 사모님도 오신다. *Mr. Kim's wife is coming too.*

1. 김 사장님 사모님도 오세요.
2. 시장의 장모가 유명한 정치가에요.
3. 독감에 걸려서 대학병원에서 치료를 받아야겠어요.
4. 몸살이 나서 온 몸이 아프고 기운이 없어요.
5. 그 사람의 딸은 아직도 어려요.
6. 일기예보가 잘 안 맞아요.
7. 박 선생님이 우리 아버지한테 전화를 거실 거에요.
8. 선생님께서 그 사람한테 재미있는 편지를 쓰셨어요.
9. 그 사람의 아이들이 다니는 학교가 집에서 멀지 않아요.
10. 뉴스를 봐야 하는데 우리 장난꾸러기가 자꾸 방해를 해요.
11. 귀가 아프면 이비인후과에서 진찰을 받아야 해요.
12. 그 강은 짧고 얕아요.
13. 운동한 후에 맥주를 마시면 시원해요.
14. 아이들은 일찍 자고 싶어하지 않아요.
15. 그 부인이 밥을 할 때 남편도 도와요.
16. 그 생선은 한국에 흔해요.

Exercise 2: Plain Style Questions

Change each of the following questions to Plain Style questions and translate them. For example, the first will be: 우리 아버지가 병이 나셨느냐? *Is our father ill?* After you have finished converting the endings, practice producing the resultant Plain Style questions in their more colloquial guise without -느-. In other words, the first sentence in more colloquial Korean would be rendered as: 우리 아버지가 병이 나셨냐?

1. 우리 아버지가 병이 나셨어요?
2. 그 우체국은 가까워요?
3. 학생들이 점심을 어디서 먹어요?
4. 그분의 부인은 열이 높아요?

5. 간호사가 불친절했어요?
6. 그 산부인과 의사는 착실해요?
7. 의사 선생님이 어디서 사세요?
8. 누구를 불렀어요?
9. 밖이 춥지 않아요?
10. 내일 무엇을 하고 싶어요?
11. 친구가 퇴원하기 전에 문병을 갔어요?
12. 왜 그렇게 기운이 없어요?
13. 간호사가 체온을 재는 것을 잃어버렸어요?
14. 그 전염병에 걸리면 토하고 열이 심하게 나요?
15. 그 말썽꾸러기가 홍역에 걸렸어요?
16. 교통사고가 나서 길이 복잡하지 않아요?
17. 운전할 때 응급차가 오면 길 어느 쪽으로 비켜야 돼요?
18. 오늘은 몇 도인데 이렇게 시원해요?
19. 섭씨 영(0)도는 화씨 몇 도예요?

Exercise 3: Plain Style Suggestions

Change each of the following suggestions to the Plain Style, and then translate them. For example, the first will be: 일찍 일어나서 산보하자 *Let's get up early and take a walk.*

1. 일찍 일어나서 산보합시다.
2. 선생님한테 곧 허락을 받읍시다.
3. 수지 씨가 떠나지 못하게 방해를 합시다.
4. 좀 쉴까요?
5. 고춧가루를 그만 칩시다.
6. 인턴한테 주사를 맞읍시다.
7. 이 연필을 깎읍시다.
8. 체온을 먼저 재고 맥박을 잽시다.
9. 꽃을 좀 사 가지고 갑시다.
10. 문을 좀 열지요.
11. 회사에 전화를 겁시다.
12. 소화가 잘 안 되면 곧 검사를 해 봅시다.

Exercise 4: Plain Style Commands

Change each of the following commands to the Plain Style and translate them. The first will be: 여기 앉아라 *Sit here!*

1. 여기 앉으십시오.
2. 그 책을 학교에 가지고 오세요.
3. 새 구두를 신어요!
4. 옷을 벗으십시오!
5. 댁에 계세요.
6. 그 책을 읽으세요.
7. 오늘 밤에 넥타이를 매십시오.
8. 의사한테 전화를 거세요.
9. 돈을 많이 쓰지 말아요!
10. 영어를 하지 마십시오.
11. 그렇게 큰 소리로 부르지 마세요.

Exercise 5: English to Korean (Plain Style)

Put the following short English sentences into Korean using the Plain Style. Do each one three times, once into the present, once into the past, and once into the future. Warning: this exercise is designed to catch you out. Think carefully!

1. I help the teacher.
2. I drive to work.
3. In the evening I'm tired.
4. He is always like that.
5. I listen to music.
6. London is clean.
7. Grandfather is not at home.
8. I visit my brother.
9. I have two dogs and a cat.
10. He stays with my friend (honorific).
11. Manho is taller than Sujin.
12. There are no papers under your desk.
13. This film is really bad.
14. I don't study very often.

Exercise 6: Practice with -느라고

Use an appropriate verb in the -느라고   form to complete the sentences below.

1. A. 어제 왜 안 왔어요?

   B._____.

2. A. 요즘 상당히 바쁘신 것 같아요.

   B._____.

3. A. 졸려요?

   B._____.

4. A. 벌써 용돈을 다 썼어요?

   B._____.

5. A. 어제 왜 전화도 안 했어요?

   B._____.

6. A. 아이들이 굉장히 배가 고팠던 것 같네요.

   B._____.

7. A. 어제 병원에 가서 주사를 맞았어요?

   B._____.

8.   _____느라고 신문도 읽지 못 했어요.

9.   _____느라고 이렇게 늦었습니다.

10.   _____느라고 그렇게 바빴습니다.

11. _____느라고 샤워도 못 하고 그냥 나왔어요.

12. _____느라고 일을 마치지 못 했습니다.

13. _____느라고 여행 준비도 못 했습니다.

Exercise 7: More English to Korean (Plain Style)

Here are more sentences like those in Exercise 5. Follow the same instructions.

1. That dog is very big.
2. I do it like this.
3. I don't stay here alone.
4. I give my mother a book.
5. He calls his girlfriend every day.
6. There is a doll on that chair.
7. My house is not far from here.
8. I stay in my room in the evenings.
9. I don't sit in that chair.
10. I don't have that book.
11. That food is not very good.
12. I wear different shoes every day.
13. My sister plays with the dog.
14. It's too cold.

Exercise 8: Practice with -어다/-아다

In each of the sentences below, either (a) embellish the verb with -어다/-아다 or (b) fill in the blank with an appropriate -어다/-아다 form to emphasize a shift in location. Be sure to insert a phrase that spells out the shift in space.

1. 엄마, 빵 좀 사 주세요.
2. 수진 씨, 이 젓가락 좀 씻어 주세요.
3. 만호 씨, 비디오를 하나 좀 빌려 줘요.
4. 에릭 씨, 이 가방 좀 들어 줄래요?
5. 샌디 씨, 저것 좀 받아 줘요.
6. 수영 씨, 은행에 가서 돈 좀 _____.
7. 너무 늦었으니까 내가 데려 줄께요.
8. 커피 1잔 타 드릴까요?
9. 손님을 지하철역까지 모셔 드렸어요.
10. 들어 드릴까요?
   네, _____.

Exercise 9: Yet More English to Korean (Plain Style)

Translate the following short sentences into Korean using the Plain Style:

1. Is it good?
2. Does he go to university on Tuesday?
3. Let's sell our house!
4. Was it cold?
5. Call the police at once!
6. Did he ever live in the States?
7. Are these books easy to come by ("common")?
8. Go and get a shave!
9. Let's eat together this evening.
10. Will he eat that bread?

Exercise 10: Korean to English Translation

Translate the following sentences into English.

1. 점심을 먹을 때 방해를 받고 싶지가 않다.
2. 나갈 때 잊지 말고 문을 잠가라!
3. 이 김치는 고추가루를 너무 많이 넣은 거 아니니? 매워서 죽겠어.
4. 1달 전에 입원을 했는데도 낫지 않는 것 같다.
5. 별로 똑똑하지 못하지만 착실은 하지.
6. 얼른 이 집에서 나가거라!
7. 어제 오래간만에 대학교 동기동창을 만났다.
8. 이 지하철역이 집에서 가까워서 참 편리해.
9. 그 인형을 어디서 샀냐? 비쌌니?
10. 사업을 잘 하셔서 그렇게 부자가 됐지.
11. 어제 내 가방을 또 잃어버렸다.
12. 그 사람은 어느 의과대학을 나왔니?
13. 오늘은 바람이 시원하게 분다.
14. 계속 독신으로 살거냐? 결혼할 생각이 있냐?
15. 주말에 백화점들에 손님들이 많았다.
16. 그 학생은 준비를 하나도 안 한다.
17. 할머니 생신이시니까 저녁이나 사 드리자.
18. 올 9월 연휴에 도꾜에 같이 가고 싶니?
19. 내가 할아버지 문병을 간 사이에 도둑놈이 들어 와서 파출부의
    지갑을 훔쳐갔어.

Vocabulary Drill

Translate the following sentences into Korean in each of the ways indicated.

1. Sujin's husband _____.
    has a cold
    has a headache
    had a checkup last week

2. Manho's son _____.
    graduated from medical school last year
    is studying pediatrics
    is an intern at the hospital

3. My friend and I _____.
    paid a visit to Mr. Pak [who was sick]
    gave flowers to the teacher
    drive, even though the streets are crowded

4. A _____ examined me.
    medical student
    an intern
    an ear-nose-throat doctor

5. Is Yongho _____?
    completely recovered now
    's fever still high
    out of the hospital now

6. The nurse just _____.
    came out of the operating room
    went into the examining room
    gave the patient a shot

7. Shall I tell you about _____ ?
    my operation
    the first-aid treatment I had
    my blood test

8. Does the child _____?
    have a contagious disease
    have a fever
    study literature in school

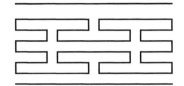 **Lesson 27**

주말에 선약이 있다고 들었어.

The lesson begins with two conversations, one about travel plans, and the other about relationships. The reading passage concerns a failed hiking expedition. Both the dialogues and the reading passage are meant to exemplify reported speech, an important area of Korean grammar that is based upon the Plain Style forms learned in the last lesson. Besides introducing the various patterns for direct and indirect quotations, this lesson also introduces the *according to* pattern in -에 의하면, and some new meanings for and a review of the particle (으)로.

Korean Dialogues

Dialogue 1

다음 주에 제주도에서 회의가 있기 때문에 남 사장은 식구들과 비서 미스 김을 데리고 이번 주말에 제주도에 가서 짧은 휴가를 갖으려고 합니다.

부인	애들한테 내일 제주도에 같이 가겠느냐고 물어 봤어요?
남주형	응. 간다고 했어.
부인	애들은 오늘 몇 시까지 들어 오라고 했어요?
남주형	6시까지 들어오라고 했는데 큰 애는 좀 늦겠다고 했어.
부인	미스 김은 생각해 보겠다고 했는데, 뭐라고 해요?
남주형	생각해 보고 오늘 저녁에 전화해 달라고 했어.
부인	내가 미스 김한테 될 수 있으면 같이 가자고 했어요.
남주형	가고 싶은데 주말에 선약이 있다고 들었어. 전화하겠지, 뭐.

Notes

응.	Plain or Intimate equivalent of 네 or 그래요 *yes.*
될 수 있으면	*if at all possible.*

Dialogue 2

어제 진영이는 밤 늦게 샌디한테 전화를 해서, 만나서 이야기 하고 싶은 것이 있다고 그랬습니다. 그래서 학교 근처의 식당에서 아침을 같이 먹고 있습니다.

진영	밤 늦게 갑자기 전화를 걸어서, 미안!
샌디	아니야, 괜찮아. 그런데 뭐가 이렇게 급하니?
진영	〔얼굴을 약간 붉히면서〕 사실, 내가 철수 씨하고 결혼할 것 같애. 만난 적 있지?
샌디	와, 정말이야? 축하해!
진영	그런데, 철수 씨가 결혼하면, 학교를 그만두래.
샌디	그래? 그래서, 진짜 학교를 그만두고 시집 갈 거니?
진영	철수 씨한테는 그냥 생각해 보겠다고 그랬지. 근데, 난 공부를 더 하고 싶거든.
샌디	더 해야지. 아니, 진영아, 그 남자 너무하다. 철수 씨한테 공부를 더 하고 싶다고 그랬어?
진영	응, 했지.
샌디	그런데, 뭐래?
진영	농담하지 말래. 마이동풍이야. 결혼한 여자가 계속 공부를 더 해서 뭘 하겠느냬.
샌디	부모님들은 뭐라셔?
진영	부모님한테는 아직 얘기 안 했어.
샌디	너 큰일 났구나. 빨리 정신을 차리고, 딴 남자를 찾아 봐라.

Notes

근데	Colloquial for 그런데.
같애	Colloquial for 같아.
아니	In origin, a truncation of 아니오, but here it functions as a kind of exclamation: *Hang on — ! Wait a minute — !*
마이동풍	This is a Sino-Korean proverb, the characters for which read 馬 *horse*, 耳 *ear*, 東 *east*, and 風 *wind*, i.e., "the east wind in a horse's ear." The meaning is *utter indifference to what somebody says*, or *turning a deaf ear*.
너 큰일 났구나.	*You're in big trouble!* The ending in -구나 is the Plain Style equivalent of the First Realization ending in -군(요) learned in section 21.9.

Reading Passage

나는 오늘 친구들과 같이 산에 가기로 했다. 그런데 어제 일기예보에 의하면 오늘
비가 온다고 했기 때문에 조금 걱정이 됐다. 오늘 아침에 일어나자마자 나는 동생
한테 비가 오느냐고 물어봤다. 동생은 날씨가 좋다고 대답하면서 오늘 테니스를
같이 치자고 했다. 내가 친구들과 등산할 약속이 있어서 같이 테니스를 칠 수 없
다고 말했지만 동생은 계속 등산을 가지 말고 자기하고 테니스를 치자고 졸랐다.
할 수 없이 동생한테 등산을 같이 가자고 했다. 약속 장소에는 벌써 친구들이
모두 나와서 나를 기다리고 있었다. 우리를 보고 빨리 오라고 하면서 친구들이
동생한테 산꼭대기까지 올라가려면 힘들지 않겠느냐고 물어 봤다. 동생은 전에도
자주 산에 가 봤으니까 걱정하지 말고 빨리 떠나자고 했다. 그렇지만 결국 우리는
동생 때문에 산꼭대기까지 올라갈 수 없었다. 집에 돌아와서 나는 동생한테 바보
라고 계속 놀렸다.

Notes
할 수 없이   *without having any choice in the matter.*

Vocabulary

Nouns
<u>People</u>

단골	regular (customer/place)
단골손님	regular customer
대통령	president (of country)
바보	fool; idiot; dummy
뺨	cheek(s)
살	flesh
살(이) 찌-	get fat, gain weight
살(이) 빠지-	lose weight
피부	skin
학자	scholar

Things
돌   stone, rock
벌레   bug, insect
    바퀴벌레   cockroach
    공부벌레 〔-뻘래〕   nerd; somebody who does nothing but study
벽   wall
불꽃놀이   fireworks
산꼭대기   mountain top, peak
천장   ceiling

Words and Texts
논문   (academic) paper; thesis
뜻   meaning
    무슨 뜻이에요?   What does it mean?
명령   order, command
    명령(을)하-   order, command
    사장님은 이 보고서를 빨리 마치라고 명령하셨어요.

    The boss ordered us to hurry up and finish this report.
발표   announcement; public presentation
    발표(를)하-   announce; make a presentation; present (a paper)
    대사님은 이 행사에 대해서 발표를 하실겁니다.

    The ambassador is going to make an announcement about this function.
선언   pronouncement, declaration
    선언(을) 하-   pronounce, declare
추측   conjecture, guess, inference
    추측(을) 하-   surmise, guess, infer

Other
NOUN 건너 (에)   across from NOUN
소리   noise, sound
    목소리   voice
    소리(를) 지르-   shout, cry out
소위 NOUN   a so-called NOUN
약간   some, a little, a few; somewhat
    아까 복동이의 체온을 재 보니까 열이 약간 있는 것 같아요.

    I took Poktong's temperature just a little while ago and it seems he has a slight fever.
자기   I (myself), he (himself), she (herself), etc.
    동생은 공부하지 말고 자기하고 놀자고 졸랐다.

    My little brother bugged me to play with him instead of studying.
    자기 일은 자기가 해야 한다.   People should take care of their own problems.
    상호는 자기가 하겠다고 말했다.   Sangho said he would do it himself.
    상호는 자기 집으로 돌아갔다.   Sangho went back to his (own) house.

장소	place, venue
시간과 장소를 정했니?	Have you decided on the time and place?
정부	government
제목	title (of book/work)
직장	job, work, workplace
직장(을) 구하-	look for work, look for a job
해결	solution (to a problem)
해결(을) 하-	resolve (a problem)
해결(이) 되-	be/get resolved
행사	happening, formal event, function

Adverbs

새로	newly, anew
새로 지은 집	a newly built house
원래	originally; actually

Verbs

Verbs That Take Objects

그러-	say (so); think (so)
그 사람이 뭐라고 그랬어요?	What did she say?
기르-	breed, raise, grow
끊-	break it off; hang up (the telephone)
떨어지-	fall; run out of something
설탕이 떨어졌네.	We're all out of sugar.
믿-	believe (also in the religious sense)
예수님을 믿으십니까?	Do you believe in Jesus?

그 회사가 곧 파산이 될 거라고 믿고 있습니다.

I believe that company will soon go bankrupt.

여기-	consider
앞으로는 나를 오빠로 여겨라.	In future, think of me as your big brother.
우물쭈물하-	waffle, prevaricate, beat around the bush

(말을) 우물쭈물하지 말고, 똑바로 이야기 하세요.

Stop waffling, and give me the straight story.

제출(을) 하-	turn in, submit, hand in
조르-	pester for, keep after for

애기는 아빠한테 사탕을 사 달라고 졸라요.

The baby pesters his daddy to buy him candy.

만호는 어머니한테 돈을 달라고 졸라요.

Manho pesters his mother to give him money.

Lesson Twenty-seven / 275

차리-	prepare, make ready; collect, concentrate
음식(을) 차리-	prepare food
정신(을) 차리-	collect one's senses, keep one's presence of mind

축하(를) 하-	congratulate
생일을 축하합니다.	Congratulations on your birthday = Happy Birthday.
축하 드립니다.	Congratulations.

Descriptive~Causative Pairs

| 밝- | be bright, light, clear |
| 밝히- | make bright or clear; clarify, explain |

대통령이 정부가 이 문제를 적극적으로 해결하겠다고 밝혔습니다.

The president explained that the government would resolve this problem in a positive manner.

붉-	be red; crimson
붉은 빰	red cheeks
붉히-	make it red, redden it
얼굴(을) 붉히-	turn red (in the face)

Intransitive Verbs (Processive Verbs That Cannot Take Objects)

몸조리(를) 하-	take care of one's health; recuperate
장가(를) 가-	get married (of a man)
장가(를) 보내-	marry, marry off (man)
시집(을) 가-	(woman) get married
시집(을) 보내-	marry, marry off (woman)
부자한테 시집 갔어요.	She married a rich man.
오래 가-	go/last a long time
[-으로] 변하-	change; turn/metamorphose into
파산(이) 되-	go bankrupt
화(가) 나-	get angry (w/ 한테)
화(를) 내-	get angry (w/ 한테)

<u>Descriptive and/or Sensory Verbs</u>

점잖–   be well-behaved, decent, respectable

얌전하–   be of good upbringing; be well-behaved and
                                            quiet

Lesson Notes

27.1. Quotations: Direct and Indirect

There are two ways to report what someone has said, asked, commanded, or suggested: a direct quotation, which gives the exact words spoken, and an indirect quotation, which gives only the gist. Both kinds of quotations are used in Korean, as in English, but Korean uses the direct quotation less frequently.

27.1.1. Direct Quotations

In the direct quotation, often introduced by 말하기를 . . . *what is said is* . . . or 묻기를 . . . *what is asked is* . . . , the references such as *me* and *you* and the endings of the verbs (Polite, Formal, Honorific, and so forth) can be left as originally spoken. In other words, the direct quotation reproduces somebody's words *verbatim*.

The direct or verbatim quotation is followed by -(이)라고, or 하고 *quote*, usually added right on as a particle, and is followed by a quoting verb—such as 말해요 *says*, 물어요 *asks*, 물어봐요 *inquires*, etc. (If you introduce a question with 묻기를 . . . , you usually end with just 말해요 rather than with 물어요.) For example:

1.   선생님이 (말하기를) "내일모레까지 숙제를 제출하세요" 라고(하고)
      말씀하셨어요.
      The teacher said "Hand in your homework by tomorrow."

2.   신문 기자가 "영국에 다시 오실 생각이 있습니까?" 라고(하고) 물었어요.
      The newspaper reporter asked: "Do you have any plans to return to England?"

3.   "한국말을 잘 하시네요" 라고 말했어요.
      She said, "My, you speak Korean well!"

4.   "얼른 나가십시오!" 하고 소리를 질렀어요.
      He shouted: "Get out immediately!"

Note that in Korean 생각(을) 하- *think* and other similar verbs (믿- *believe*, 여기- *consider*) count as verbs of quoting, and that thoughts are reported with the same quotation patterns you are learning here.

If you choose to replace the quoting verb with either 해요 *says* or 그래요 *says (like that)*, *says so*, you **cannot** use 하고 as the quotation particle. Instead, you must use the quotation particle in -(이)라고. That is, Korean does not allow patterns of the following shape:

> *"QUOTATION" 하고 했어요.
> *"QUOTATION" 하고 그랬어요.

Instead, Korean only allows:

> "QUOTATION"(이)라고 했어요 (as below).
> "QUOTATION"(이)라고 그랬어요 (as below).

5.   단골손님이 "다시 안 오겠습니다!" 라고 했어요.
     The regular customer said: "I'm never coming again!"

6.   "곧 갈게요" 라고 그랬어요.
     She said: "I'll be right there."

27.1.2. Indirect Quotations

Indirect quotations are less frequently introduced by 말하기를 . . . or 묻기를 . . . . In indirect quotations, you have to:

(a) change references to persons (so that *He said "I will see you and him"* may become *He said that he would see me and you*);

(b) you must be careful not to retain honorifics that would not be appropriate to the "changed" persons; and

(c) you must put the verb form into a single neutral style that is used mainly in quotations—the Plain Style (Type 1) that you learned in the last lesson.

The Plain Style was explained in the preceding lesson. After the indirect quotation, which is always quoted in Plain Style, you add the quotation particle 고 *(saying) that* . . . , but 고 can freely drop, just as *that* does in English. When the particle is present (as in 간다고 해요 *says that he will go*) we call it an expanded quotation; when the particle drops (as in 간다 해요 *says he will go*) we call it a simple quotation. Simple quotations are more common in written Korean than in spoken Korean.

The simple quotation is sometimes abbreviated further, by dropping the base 하- of the verb *say* altogether, leaving forms like 간대요 *says he'll go* (← 간다[고 해]요). These we call contracted quotations. Along with expanded quotations, contracted quotations are very common in spoken Korean.

Observe the following quoted statements, given in several forms.

What was said: 갑니다. or 가요, etc. *I'm going.*

	S/he said . . .	S/he says . . .
Direct quote-1:	(말하기를) "갑니다" 라고 했어요. *He said, "I am going."*	. . . 라고 해요.
Direct quote-2:	"갑니다" 하고 말했어요. *He said, (saying) "I am going. "*	. . . 하고 말해요.
Indirect, expanded:	간다고 했어요. *He said that he was going.*	간다고 해요.
Indirect, simple:	간다 했어요. *He said he was going.*	간다 해요.
Indirect, contracted:	간댔어요. *He said he was going.*	간대요.

If you want to mention the person who did the saying, the usual place is at the beginning.

7. 김 선생님이 가자고 말씀하셨어요.
    Mr. Kim suggested that we go.

But if the quotation is very long, it is common to put the subject next to the final quoting verb.

8. 오늘 날이 좋아서 산보나 가자고 김 선생님이 말씀하셨어요.
    Mr. Kim suggested we go for walk or something since the weather's so nice today.

Of course, if you start with 말하기를, you will want to put the subject in front of that (김 선생님이 말씀하시기를).

Here are more examples of how Plain Style statements are used to make indirect quotations.

9. 돈이 없다고 해요.
    He says he has no money.

Lesson Twenty-seven / 279

10. 일찍 자야 한대요.
    He says he has to go to bed early.

11. 공원에서 산보 하고 싶다고 했어요.
    He said he'd like to take a walk in the park.

12. 일을 하겠다고 그랬어요.
    He said he'd do the job.

13. 여관에 편지가 왔다고 했어요.
    He told me a letter had come for me at the inn.

14. 전화 하시겠다고 그랬습니까?
    Did you say you were going to make a telephone call?

15. 한국말 공부를 잘 한다고 이야기를 들었어요.
    I hear he's studying Korean well.

16. 참 바쁘다고 해요.
    He says he's very busy.

27.2. More on Quoted Questions

Observe the following examples.

What was said:	가십니까? or 가세요? or 가요? etc. *Are you going?*	
	S/he said/asked . . .	**S/he says/asks . . .**
Direct quote - 1:	(묻기를) "가십니까?" 라고 했어요.	. . . 라고 해요.
	He said, "Are you going?"	
Direct quote - 2:	"가십니까?" 하고 물었어요.	. . . 하고 물어요.
	He asked (saying), "Are you going?"	
Indirect, expanded:	가느냐고 물었어요.	가느냐고 물어요.
	He asked whether I was going.	
Indirect, simple:	가느냐 물었어요.	가느냐 물어요.
	He asked if I was going.	
Indirect, contracted:	가느ㄴㅐ 쓰어요 (rare)	가느ㄴㅐ요
	He asked if I was going.	

Recall that in colloquial Korean the processive -느냐 is sometimes abbreviated to -냐 (있냐 from 있느냐, 먹냐 from 먹느냐). After vowels (가냐 from 가느냐) this sounds like the descriptive -(으)냐 (비싸냐 from 비싸- *be expensive*, 머냐 from 머-ㄹ- *be far*). Here are more examples of quoted questions.

17. 무엇을 하(느)냐고 물어 봤어요.
    I asked them what they were doing.

18. 어디 가(느)냬요.
    He asks where I'm going.

19. 내 책을 어디다 두었(느)냐고 물었어요.
    I asked her where she had put my book.

20. 아버지가 나한테 돈이 없(느)냐고 물으셨어요.
    Father asked me if I was out of money.

21. 선생님에게 시간이 있으시냐고 여쭤 봅시다.
    Let's find out if the teacher has some time.

22. 부산이 머냐고 물어 보세요.
    Ask if Pusan is far.

23. 의사한테 병이 오래 가겠(느)냐고 물어 보십시오.
    Ask the doctor if the illness will last long.

24. 왜 그랬(느)냬요.
    She asks why they did that.

Quoted negative questions are usually made on the long negative, as the following examples demonstrate.

25. 가지 않(느)냐고 물었어요.
    I asked if he was not going.

26. 먹지 않았(느)냐고 물었어요.
    I asked if he had not eaten.

27. 좀 쉬지 않겠(느)냐고 물었어요.
    I asked if we weren't going to take a break (rest).

28. 거기가 춥지 않으냐고 물어 보세요.
    Find out if it isn't cold there.

29. 길이 나쁘지 않으냬요.
    She's asking if the road isn't bad.

30. 길이 나쁘지 않았(느)냬요.
    She's asking if the road wasn't bad.

27.3. More on Quoted Suggestions

Observe the following examples.

What was said: 가십시다! or 가요! or 가자! *Let's go!*

	S/he said . . .	S/he says . . .
Direct quote-1:	(말하기를)"가십시다" 라고 했어요.	. . . 라고 해요.
	He said, "Let's go!"	
Direct quote-2:	"가십시다" 하고 말했어요.	. . . 하고 말해요.
	He said, (saying) "Let's go!"	
Indirect, expanded:	가자고 했어요.	가자고 해요.
	He suggested that we go.	
Indirect, simple:	가자 했어요.	가자 해요.
	He suggested we go.	
Indirect, contracted:	가쟀어요.	가쟤요.
	He suggested we go.	

Suggestions, like statements, appear as expanded quotations in –자고 해요, simple quotations in –자 해요, and contracted quotations in –쟤요. Here are more examples of quoted suggestions.

31. 오늘 저녁에 어머니한테 같이 공부하자고 그랬어요.
    We suggested to mother that we study together this evening.

32. 복순이가 밖에 가서 놀쟀어요.
    Poksun-i suggested we go outside and play.

33.　내 친구가 여기 있지 말자고 했어요.
　　　My friend suggested we don't stay here.

34.　영어로 하지 말고, 한국말로 하재요.
　　　He suggests that we speak in Korean instead of English.

35.　불꽃놀이가 보고 싶으면 시내 가까운 곳에 있자고 했어요.
　　　He suggested we stay near downtown if we wanted to see the fireworks.

27.4. More on Quoted Commands

Observe the following examples.

What was said:　　　　　　　　　　　가십시오! *Go!*

	S/he said . . .	S/he says . . .
Direct quote-1:	(말하기를) "가십시오" 라고 했어요.	. . . 라고 해요.
	He said, "Go!"	
Direct quote-2:	"가십시오" 하고 명령했어요.	. . . 하고 명령해요.
	He ordered (saying): "Go!"	
Indirect, expanded:	가라고 했어요.	가라고 해요.
	He told me to go.	
Indirect, simple:	가라 했어요.	가라 해요.
	He told me to go.	
Indirect, contracted:	가랬어요.	가래요.
	He told me to go.	

Commands, like statements, appear as expanded quotations in -(으)라고 해요, simple quotations in -(으)라 해요, and contracted quotations in -(으)래요. Note that quoted commands use only the Plain Style Type 1 form in -(으)라고 and not the Type 2 form -어라/-아라.

In commands, the person *to* whom the command is directed is marked with the particle 한테 (or 에게) meaning *to*. This particle is not translated in English when the command verb is *tell*: *He told* [Literally: to] *the child to come home early*. Here are some more examples of quoted commands.

36. 내가 그 사람한테 오라고 했어요.
I told him to come.

37. 애들한테 공부하라고 그럴까요?
Shall I tell the kids to study?

38. 아들한테 텔레비젼을 보지 말라고 했어요.
I told my son not to watch TV.

39. 가지 말래요.
She says I shouldn't go.

40. 오빠가 나한테 오늘 아침 일찍 일어나랬어요.
My older brother told me to get up early this morning.

41. 누나가 나한테 그런 이야기를 듣지 말랬어요.
My older sister told me not to listen to such stories.

42. 영어로 하지 말고, 한국말로 하랬습니다.
He told us to speak in Korean instead of English.

43. 어머니가 나한테 집에 있으라고 그러셨어요.
Mother told me to stay at home.

27.5. The Copula in Quotations

In the preceding lesson, you learned that the Plain Style statement form of the copula is -이다 (base 이- plus descriptive verb ending -다). But this form is not used in quotations; instead, it is replaced by the special form -이라. Since it has no long form, the only negative possible for the copula is 아니; thus, the plain form 아니다 becomes 아니라 in quotations. Here are some examples of the copula in quotations.

44. 누구냐고 물어보세요.
Find out who it is.

45. 김 선생님이시냐고 물어보세요.
Ask if it's Mr. Kim.

46. 김 선생님이 아니시냐고 했어요.
I asked if it isn't Mr. Kim.

47. 우리 아들이었대요.
He says it was my son.

48. 음악회가 토요일이라고 들었어요.
I heard the concert is [on] Saturday.

49. 재미 있는 책이래요.
She says it's an interesting book.

50. 친구들이 뭐래요?
What do your friends say?

51. 복동이한테 그게 내 것이라고 그래요.
You tell Poktong-i that that is mine.

27.6. Special Uses of the Quoted Copula

When the copula is quoted in present statement form, it is pronounced 이라. Translation of the quoted copula sometimes involves unexpected expressions like *says it to be = calls it.* Here are a few more examples of quoted copula statements.

52.   이것은 무엇이라고 해요?
  or   이건 뭐라고 해요?
  or   이건 뭐라 해요?
  or   이건 뭐래요?
            What do you call this thing?

53. 녹음기라고 해요.
It's called a cassette recorder.

54. 이것은 한국말로 뭐라고 해요?
What do you call this in Korean?

55. 누구라고 그랬어요?
Who did you say it was?

56. 어디랬어요?
Where did you say it was?

57. 누구시라고 그럴까요?
    [on the telephone] *Who shall I say is calling?*

A special quoting construction involving this form of the copula translates the English phrase *an A called X* (as in *a fish called Wanda*). The expanded form of this construction is:

X 이라고 하는 A   (완다라고 하는 물고기)

As you can see, this is simply the regular quoting pattern (X 이라고 해요) made into modifier for another noun expression. The simple, unexpanded form is:

X 이라 하는 A   (완다라 하는 물고기)

But ordinarily the abbreviated form is used.

X 이라는 A   (완다라는 물고기)

And often you will hear it further reduced to:

X 이란 A   (완다란 물고기)

When you hear this reduced form it sounds just like X 이란 A, the reduction of X 이라 (고) 한 A, *an A that has been called X*, and the meaning is so close that it often wouldn't matter which way you interpreted what you hear. Compare this meaning of *an A called X* with the use of simple modifiers in equational constructions:

X 인 A
an A that is [=] X

X 이 된 A
an A that is [has become] X

58. 선생인 내 형님 or 선생이 된 내 형님
    my older brother who is [has become] a teacher

59. 의사인 김복남 or 의사가 된 김복남
    Pongnam Kim, who is [has become] a doctor

Here are more examples of the modifying quoted copula.

60. 라디오라는 말은 영어에요, 한국말이에요?
    Is the word 라디오 *English or Korean?*

61. 부산이라는 도시는 어디에 있어요? or 부산이란 도시는 어디에 있어요?
    Where is the city [called=] of Pusan?

62. 신체란 말은 무슨 뜻이에요?
    What does the word 신체 *mean?*

63. 어제 김복동이라는 사람이 찾아왔어요.
    Somebody named Poktong Kim came to visit yesterday.

27.7. -에 의하면 . . . *According to . . .*

The expression -에 의하면 following a noun means *according to [the noun]*, and is often
followed by a quotation construction. Here are some typical examples.

64. 신문에 의하면, 북한은 곧 파산이 될 거랍니다.
    According to the newspaper, North Korea will go bankrupt any day now.

65. 일기예보에 의하면 내일 비가 올 거래요.
    According to the weather forecast, it will rain tomorrow.

66. 의사 선생님에 의하면 그 여자는 암에 걸렸답니다.
    According to the doctor, she has caught cancer.

67. 뉴스에 의하면 루시디라는 유명한 작가가 아직 숨어 있답니다.
    According to the news, the famous writer Rushdie is still hiding.

27.8. Using 달라(고) 하- to Quote 주세요 *Give me*

When the original utterance to be quoted used the verb 주- *give* in the sense of *Give m e* or *Do m e the favor of . . .ing* (as opposed to *Give [it] to somebody else*), you have to quote it with a completely separate verb: 달라(고) 하-. Note that this can abbreviate to 달래요. For example:

68. A. 그 책 좀 주세요.
         Please give me that book.

     B. 네?
         Excuse me?

     A. 그 책 좀 달라고 그랬어요.
         I asked you to give me that book.

69. A. 에릭이 샌디한테 만호한테 책을 주라고 했습니다.
         Eric told Sandy to give the book to Manho.

     B. 에릭이 샌디한테 할머니한테 책을 드리라고 했습니다.
         Eric told Sandy to give the book to grandmother.

     C. 에릭이 샌디한테 (자기한테) 책을 달라고 했습니다.
         Eric told Sandy to give the book to him(self).

70. A. 내일까지 전화해 주세요.
         Please call me by tomorrow.

     B. 내일까지 전화해 달라고 했어요.
         He said for you to call him by tomorrow.

71. 뭐 달래요?
     What does she want? (i.e., She says "give me what?")

72. A. 애기 때 사진 좀 보여 주십시오.
         Please show me some of your childhood pictures.

     B. 뭐라고요?
         What's that?

A. 애기 때 사진 좀 보여 달라고요.
I say, please show me some of your baby photos.

73. 수미 씨는 잘 생긴 남자를 좀 소개해 달래요.
Sumi wants me to introduce her to a good-looking guy.

27.9. The Particle (으)로: More Meanings

The sentences below show the particle (으)로 in a new meaning, as a stylistic variant of the copula gerund -이고, meaning *is* [such-and-such a noun] *and*.

74. 그 사람은 유명한 학자로, 서울대 영문과 교수시지요.
He's a famous scholar and is a professor in the Department of English at Seoul National University.

75. 그 병은 부인에게 흔히 있는 병으로, 오래 가지 않아요.
It is a common illness for women and does not last long.

This meaning of -(으)로 blends in with another translation that is often useful for it: *as* or *for* (= *in the capacity/function of*), as follows.

76. 이 방을 교실로 씁니다.
They use this room as (for) a classroom.

77. 대학 교수로 계세요.
He teaches at the university. [= He is at the university as a professor.]

However, the equivalent for English *for a foreigner* as in sentence 78 below calls for a different pattern: NOUN 치고는.

78. 외국사람 치고는, 한국말을 잘 하지요?
He speaks Korean well for a foreigner, doesn't he?

In the meaning in sentence 79, the particle (으)로 is sometimes followed by the particle 서 to strengthen its meaning:

79. 선생으로서, 그렇게 하면 안 되지요.
As a teacher, you ought not to do that sort of thing.

Below is a summary of some of the more common uses of this particle.

EXCHANGE:

80.　비싼 것을 싼 것으로 바꿨어요.
　　　I exchanged an expensive one for a cheap one.

DIRECTION:

81.　왼쪽으로 가세요.
　　　Go to the left.

82.　나한테로 오세요.
　　　Come to me.

TIME:

83.　앞으로 또 만납시다.
　　　See you again in the days ahead/in future.

MANNER:

84.　정열적으로 노래를 해요.
　　　He sings passionately.

CHANGE OF STATE:

85.　큰 바퀴벌레로 변했어요 (= 큰 바퀴벌레가 됐어요).
　　　He turned into [became] a big cockroach.

MEANS:

86.　연필로 쓰세요.
　　　Write in [with a] pencil.

87.　비행기로 갑시다.
　　　Let's go by plane.

MATERIAL:

88.　나무로 (돌로) 지은 집입니다.
　　　It's a house made of wood (of stone).

CAUSE, REASON, PURPOSE:

89.　교통사고로 죽었어요.
　　　He died in ["because of"] a traffic accident.

Exercises

Exercise 1: Quoted Statements

누가 누구에게 뭐라고 했어요?

Quote each of the following statements below using the indirect quotation pattern introduced in this lesson, then translate the resulting Korean sentences into English. For example, the first sentence will be: 진희가 호철한테 다음 주에 미국에 간다고 했어요. *Chinhŭi told Hoch'ŏl she's going to the United States next week.*

1.   진희   → 호철 : 다음 주에 미국에 가요.

_____.

2.   진희   → 호철 : 그 술집은 우리 단골집입니다.

_____.

3.   진희   → 호철 : 내일 눈이 올겁니다.

_____.

4.   진희   → 호철 : 전쟁때 고생을 많이 한 것 같습니다.

_____.

5.   진희   → 호철 : 그런 영화는 보기 싫습니다.

_____.

6.   진희   → 호철 : 에릭 씨 아버님이 유명한 학자십니다.

_____.

7.   진희   → 호철 : 아버지가 수영하러 가고 싶어하십니다.

_____.

8.　진희　→　호철 : 밖에서 가방을 들고 있겠습니다.

_____.

9.　진희　→　호철 : 수철 씨는 교통사고로 죽었습니다.

_____.

10.　진희　→　호철 : 김치 없으면 못 삽니다.

_____.

11.　진희　→　호철 : 회사가 파산이 돼서 화가 났습니다.

_____.

12.　진희　→　호철 : 병이 나았지만 몸조리를 잘 못하고 있습니다.

_____.

13.　진희　→　호철 : 대통령을 모시러 갑니다.

_____.

14.　진희　→　호철 : 결국에는 오래 가지 못하고 파산을 선언했어요.

_____.

15.　진희　→　호철 : 친구가 장가를 갑니다.

_____.

16.　진희　→　호철 : 저 학생은 아주 얌전합니다.

_____.

17.　진희　→　호철 : 4월에 논문을 제출해야 합니다.

_____.

Exercise 2: Quoted Questions

누가 누구에게 뭐라고 했어요?

Quote each of the following questions below using the indirect quotation pattern introduced in this lesson; then translate the resulting Korean sentences into English. For example, the first sentence will be: 진호가 진주한테 왜 그러(시)냐고 했어요. *Chinho asked Chinju why she was doing that.*

1.　　진호　→　진주 : 왜 그러십니까?

_____.

2.　　진호　→　진주 : 서울에 언제 도착했습니까?

_____.

3.　　진호　→　진주 : 어디에 가고 싶습니까?

_____.

4.　　진호　→　진주 : 오늘 아침에 일찍 일어났습니까?

_____.

5.　　진호　→　진주 : 학생입니까?

_____.

6.　　진호　→　진주 : 같이 영화 보러 가지 않겠습니까?

_____.

7.　　진호　→　진주 : 생일날에 뭘 할 것입니까?

_____.

8.　　진호　→　진주 : 짐이 무겁습니까?

_____.

9.　　진호　→　진주 : 요즘 영국 날씨가 좋습니까?

_____.

10.   진호 → 진주 : 내일 오시겠습니까?

_____.

11.   진호 → 진주 : 나를 바보로 여기세요?

_____.

12.   진호 → 진주 : 왜 그렇게 살이 빠지셨습니까?

_____.

13.   진호 → 진주 : 소리를 지르려면 산꼭대기로 올라가야겠지요?

_____.

14.   진호 → 진주 : 그 소설 제목이 뭐에요?

_____.

15.   진호 → 진주 : 저 가게는 단골이 많습니까?

_____.

Exercise 3: Quoted Suggestions

뭐라고 했어요?

Quote each of the following suggestions below using the indirect quotation pattern introduced in this lesson; then translate the resulting Korean sentences into English. For example, the first sentence will be: 진희가 호철한테 시청 역에서 내리자고 했어요. *Chinhŭi suggested to Hoch'ŏl that they get off at City Hall station.*

1.   진희 → 호철 : 시청역에서 내립시다.

_____.

2.   진희 → 호철 : 돼지 한 마리 기릅시다.

_____.

3.   진희 → 호철 : 산꼭대기까지 올라 가지 맙시다.

_____.

4.　　진희　　→　호철 : 담배를 끊읍시다.

_____.

5.　　진희　　→　호철 : 고기를 구웁시다.

_____.

6.　　진희　　→　호철 : 다음 주에 떠나지 맙시다.

_____.

7.　　진희　　→　호철 : 선생님께 이야기합시다.

_____.

8.　　진희　　→　호철 : 창문을 좀 엽시다.

_____.

9.　　진희　　→　호철 : 박 선생님께 편지를 씁시다.

_____.

10.　　진희　　→　호철 : 시험 날짜를 발표합시다.

_____.

11.　　진희　　→　호철 : 벽과 천장은 흰색으로 합시다.

_____.

Exercise 4: Quoted Commands

뭐라고 했어요?

Quote each of the following commands below using the indirect quotation pattern introduced in this lesson; then translate the resulting Korean sentences into English. For example, the first sentence will be: 박 선생님이 장 선생님한테 예수님을 믿으시라고 했어요. *Mr. Pak told Mr. Chang to believe in Jesus.*

1.   박 선생님   →   장 선생님 : 예수님을 믿으십시오.

——.

2.   박 선생님   →   장 선생님 : 밖에서 잠깐만 기다리십시오.

——.

3.   박 선생님   →   장 선생님 : 이번 주일에는 오지 마십시오.

——.

4.   박 선생님   →   장 선생님 : 그 여자한테 장가 가지 마십시오.

——.

5.   박 선생님   →   장 선생님 : 좀 더 일찍 출근 하십시오.

——.

6.   박 선생님   →   장 선생님 : 이 책의 제목을 바꾸십시오.

——.

7.   박 선생님   →   장 선생님 : 저렇게 큰 소리로 떠들지 마십시오.

——.

8.   박 선생님   →   장 선생님 : 영어로 발표하지 마십시오.

——.

9. 박 선생님 → 장 선생님 : 빨리 앉으십시오.

_____.

10. 박 선생님 → 장 선생님 : 이를 닦으십시오.

_____.

11. 박 선생님 → 장 선생님 : 사실을 밝히십시오.

_____.

12. 박 선생님 → 장 선생님 : 명령하지 마십시오.

_____.

13. 박 선생님 → 장 선생님 : 추측하지 마십시오.

_____.

14. 박 선생님 → 장 선생님 : 바퀴벌레를 잡으십시오.

_____.

Exercise 5: Quoted Requests for Favors

누가 누구에게 뭐라고 했어요?

Quote each of the following requests for favors below using the indirect quotation pattern introduced in this lesson; then translate the resulting Korean sentences into English. For example, the first sentence will be: 홍빈이 호철한테 새로 산 양복을 보여 달라고 했어 요. *Hongbin asked Hoch'ŏl to show him the new suit he bought.*

1. 홍빈 → 호철 : 새로 산 양복을 보여 주세요.

_____.

2. 홍빈 → 호철 : 집 주소 좀 가르쳐 주십시오.

_____.

3.   홍빈 → 호철 : 시계를 잠깐만 빌려 주세요.

_____.

4.   홍빈 → 호철 : 내일 교수님께 연락을 해 주세요.

_____.

5.   홍빈 → 호철 : 내일 공항에 나와 주세요.

_____.

6.   홍빈 → 호철 : 후추를 주세요.

_____.

7.   홍빈 → 호철 ; 시간이 있으면, 오늘 좀 도와 주세요.

_____.

8.   홍빈 → 호철 ; 잠깐만 기다려 주세요.

_____.

9.   홍빈 → 호철 : 형이 있으면, 전화 좀 바꿔 주세요.

_____.

10.   홍빈 → 호철 : 만원만 주세요.

_____.

11.   홍빈 → 선생님 : 제가 쓴 논문을 한번 봐 주세요.

_____.

Exercise 6: Quotes, Direct and Indirect

Translate the following sentences into Korean, doing each one twice. The first time use a direct quotation form; the second time use an indirect quotation pattern.

1. My teacher asked if I'd done my homework.
2. Manho told me that I mustn't sleep so much.
3. My father says he's going out drinking tonight.
4. Chinho's asking what the weather is like.
5. Mother said I have to come home early.
6. Sujin says that I'm too fat.
7. Yongho asked me if we lived in Pusan.
8. My younger brother said that father was ill.
9. Mina'll probably tell me to find a different girlfriend.
10. Suji told me to give it to Reverend Park.

Exercise 7: Indirect Quotes, Three Ways

Translate the following sentences into Korean, again doing each one twice. Use a different form of indirect quotation for each. Make sure that during the course of the exercise you use the expanded, the simple, and the contracted forms of indirect quotes.

1. The student told me not to talk so quickly.
2. Manho considers the president to be a thief.
3. Sujin told Mr. Kim that that book is hers.
4. The doctor told me I should rest more.
5. Did you say Manho'd eaten all the apples?
6. Sangho believes that this year is worse than last.
7. Mother told me to go to Japan next year after I graduate.
8. Mia asked whether that is the building where Sangho used to work.
9. My mother thinks I eat too much, but I think I've lost weight.
10. I heard she's looking for a new job.

Exercise 8: Korean to English Translation

Translate the following sentences into English.

1. 동생이 내가 내일 입을 바지를 빌려도 괜찮(으)냐고 물었어요.
2. 내 여자친구가 딴 여자를 보지 말라고 그랬어요.
3. 저 할아버지께서는 모든 정치가들을 거짓말장이라고 생각하십니다.
4. 하숙집 아주머니한테 김치를 좀 덜 맵게 만들라고 해야겠어요.
5. "조르다"라는 말은 무슨 뜻이에요?
6. 그렇게 게으르던 학생이 일본말 교수가 됐다고요?
7. 박 선생님 부인을 잠깐 뵐 수 있게 일찍 가자고 했습니다.
8. 아버지가 나한테 너무 놀면 안 된다고 말씀 하셨습니다.
9. 그 아저씨는 회사원으로, 옆 집에 산다고 들었어요.
10. 김 선생님은 아침마다 일찍 출근하시고 저녁마다 늦게 들어오신다고
    부인이 불평을 하십니다.
11. 이 기차가 서울로 가는 기차냐고 한번 확인합시다.
12. 내가 약을 매일 먹지 않았는데도 곧 낫겠다고 의사 선생님이
    그러셨습니다.
13. 이 책의 제목이 무슨 뜻입니까? 영어로는 뭐라고 번역해야 됩니까?
14. 〔파티에서〕
    저, 이분이 서울대에서 오신 이현희 교수라고 하시는데
    인사하시지요.
15. 미국학생 치고는 그 학생은 참 열심히 합니다.
16. 오늘 저녁의 공연이 몇 시에 시작하(느)냐고 물어 볼까요?
17. A. 남 선생님 부부는 연애결혼을 했대요? 중매결혼을 했대요?
    B. 원래 소위 캠퍼스 커플이었다는데요.
18. 어머니가 나한테 너무 늦어 지면 만호네 집에서 자래요.
19. 형: 아버지가 뭐라셔?
    동생: 용돈이 더 필요하냐고.
    형: 그래서 뭐라고 대답했냐?
    동생: 더 필요하다고 그랬지– 필요 없다고 얘기를 했겠어?

Exercise 9: From Contracted to Expanded Quotations

The dialogue below contains a number of contracted quotation forms. Rewrite the dialogue replacing the contracted forms with expanded forms, and translate the dialogue.

강의실에 가는 길에 석만이는 에릭을 만났습니다.

석만	야, 에릭아, 어디 가냐?
에릭	수업이 끝나서 집에 간다. 참, 진영이가 전화 좀 해 달래. 저녁 9시쯤 하래.
석만	그래? 알았어. 영철이가 이번 주말에 뭐 하느냬? 영화 보러 가재.
에릭	무슨 영화를 보재?
석만	잘 모르겠는데 대한극장에서 한대.
에릭	그래? 주말에 특별히 할 일도 없는데 가지, 뭐. 근데 무슨 영화냐고 물어 봐.
석만	알았어. 그럼 5시에 대한극장 앞에서 만나자고 할께.
에릭	만나는 김에 저녁을 같이 먹고 영화를 보자고 하자.
석만	그래, 영철이한테 물어 보고 전화를 해 줄께.
에릭	영철이 만나면 나한테 전화 좀 해 달라고 해 줘.
석만	알았어, 나중에 보자.

 # Lesson 28

요즘도 서점에서 그 책을 팔던가요?

In this lesson, Dialogue One shows Chris Murphy discussing a best-selling novel with Mr. Kim. Dialogue Two presents a snippet of Eunice gossiping at a posh reception. One of the main points of this lesson is retrospective aspect, a series of forms that imply that the subject has some sort of evidence (usually sensory) for a past event. In addition, the lesson introduces a number of other patterns that incorporate retrospective morphemes in them, like the ending in -던데(요), conditionals in -더라면, and the popular colloquial ending -더라고(요). Besides these, the lesson introduces the *to the extent that* pattern in -(으)ㄹ 정도(로), a new way to say *after . . .ing* in -고 나서, and -기 위해(서) *for the sake of.*

Korean Dialogues

Dialogue 1

Chris Murphy is beginning to develop an interest in Korean literature and asks Mr. Kim, his Korean teacher, about a recent best-selling novel.

크리스	김 선생님, 요즘 새로 나온 "태백산맥" 이라는 소설 읽어 보셨어요?
김 선생	네, 아주 재미있던데요.
크리스	재미있다고 들었는데 아직 읽어 보지 못 했습니다.
김 선생	친구한테서 빌려서 읽었거든요. 책을 돌려주지 않았더라면 좋았겠어요. 근데, 크리스 씨가 읽기에 좀 어려울 거에요. 10권이나 되거든요.
크리스	요즘도 서점에서 그 책을 팔던가요?
김 선생	교보서점에는 그 책이 벌써 다 팔렸던데요.
크리스	10권짜리 대하소설이 서점에 없을 정도로 잘 팔린다면, 작가가 돈을 많이 벌었겠네요.
김 선생	역시 비지네스맨이군요. 그런데, 작가보다 출판사가 돈을 더 벌었겠던데요. 벌써 100만 부 정도가 팔렸더라고요.

Dialogue 2

어떤 상류 사회 모임에서

유니스	저 남자가 전에 파티에 가서 만났던 정치가가 아니에요?
미세스 김	글쎄요. 그런데 그때는 다른 여자하고 왔던데 . . .
유니스	맞아요. 가서 소개해 달라고 그럴까요?
미세스 김	이번 선거기간 중에 생긴 사건들 때문에 나는 정치가라면 무조건 싫어졌어요.
유니스	그래도 나라를 위해서 최선을 다하는 사람도 있잖아요? 와인 1잔 마시고 나서 가 봅시다.
미세스 김	그건 그래요. 원하신다면 그러지요.

Reading Passage

크리스 씨 일기장에서

지난 크리스마스와 설날 때에 우리 식구들은 한국의 시골로 여행을 좀 다녀왔다. 시골로 여행하는 동안 한국의 시골이 서울과 다른 점이 많다는 것을 깨달았다. 아이들의 이야기에 의하면 "시골에 가니까, 비로소 진짜 한국에 온 것 같더라"는 것이다.

서울은 외국 대도시와 별로 다른 점이 없는데, 지방에는 아직도 한국의 고유풍습이 그대로 남아 있는 것 같았다. 또한 서울의 가족제도는 점점 핵가족 제도로 변하고 있지만, 시골에서는 아직도 놀랄 정도로 대가족 제도를 지키고 있는 것 같았다. 이번 여행을 통해 배운 것들 중에서 제일 재미있게 생각한 예를 든다면, 다음과 같다.

우리는 어린애가 태어나서, 그 이튿날 2살 먹는 것을 봤다. 정월 초하루날 어떤 집에서 초대해서 갔는데, 그중에 한 사람이 자기 아들의 애기를 꺼냈다. 아내가 아이의 나이를 물었는데, 2살이라고 하면서, 그 전날 태어났다고 대답했다. 아내는 영문을 몰라서 설명을 해 달라고 그랬더니, 그분이 설명하기를 섣달 그믐에 태어났으니 1살을 먹고, 그 이튿날이 설날이니 1살을 더 먹어, 2살이 됐다고 했다.

그래서 우리는 다음과 같은 중요한 점을 배웠다. 즉, 한국에서는 생일로 나이를 치지 않고, 애기가 태어나는 대로 으례 1살을 먹고, 설날이 되면, 또 1살을 먹게 된다. 그러니 정월에 만났던 애는 태어난 지는 이틀밖에 안 됐지만 당연히 2살이 되는 것이다. 그 애는 하루만 늦게 태어났더라면 1살이 됐을 것이다.

Vocabulary

<u>Places</u>

금강산	Diamond Mountains, Kŭmgang Mountains (in North Korea)
대도시	big city, metropolis
보석상	jewelry shop
산맥	mountain range
태백산맥	the T'aebaek Mountains
록키산맥	the Rocky Mountains
세계	world, the world
소도시	small city

<u>School-Related</u>

고등학교	high school
중학교	middle school
초등학교	elementary school
점	point, dot, mark
지난 번 시험 점수 몇 점이었어요?	What did you get on the last test?
90점 받았습니다.	I got a 90. or I got 90 points/percent.
점수	grade mark
점수를 잘 받았습니다.	I got a good mark.
총장	president (of university)
학장	dean (at university)

<u>Politics</u>

공산주의	communism
민주주의	democracy
사건 〔사껀〕	scandal, notorious event
사회	society
사회학	sociology
사회학자	sociologist
사회주의	socialism
상류사회	high society, polite society
선거	election
스캔들	scandal (often sexual)
싸움	fight, struggle

야당	opposition party
여당	government party
중류사회	the middle classes, middle-class society
평화	peace
하류사회	the lower classes, lower-class society
후보	candidate
대통령 후보	candidate for president
국회의원 후보	candidate for member of the national assembly

Time-Related

기간	time period, interval
섣달	December
섣달 그믐	New Year's Eve
설날	New Year's Day
이튿날	second day, next day, day after
장마철	rainy season
전날	previous day
정월	January
초하루(날)	the first day

Other

관객	spectator, audience
고유 . . .	indigenous, inherent
골뱅이	snail; the "@" in email addresses

제 이메일 주소는 iamme'골뱅이'hanmail'점'net입니다.

My email address is iamme-@-hanmail-"dot"-net.

귀중품	valuables
대가족	large family
대가족 제도	extended family system
대부분	the most part, the greater part; for the most part
목적	goal, objective
무기	weapon(s), arm(s)
박수	applause
박수(를) 치-	applaud
배꼽	navel, belly button
배꼽(이) 빠지-	navel falls out (w/ laughter)
-부	copy (counter for books, etc.)
비지네스맨	businessman
성공	success

성공(을) 하-	be successful
소설	a work of fiction; novel
단편소설	short story
중편소설	novella
장편소설	full-length novel
대하소설	epic novel; multivolumed novel
엉덩이	rump, bottom, derriere
예	example
예를 드-ㄹ-	give an example
예를 들면	for example
예를 든다면	for example
예를 들자면	for example
왕	king
이메일	email
이메일(을) 띄우-/보내-	send an email
정도	extent, degree
제도	system, institution
가족제도	family system
지방	the country(side), the provinces
처자식	wife and children
출판사	publishing company
출판(을) 하-	publish it
풍습	custom(s), habit(s)
고유풍습	indigenous customs
하품	yawn
하품(을) 하-	yawn
핵	nucleus
핵가족	nuclear family
핵무기	nuclear weapons

Adverbs

그대로	intact, just as it is
꽤	rather, quite
무조건 〔-껀〕	unconditionally
비로소	for the first time
역시	sure enough
으레	customarily, usually, habitually
퍽(이나)	very, quite, rather

Verbs

<u>Verbs That Take Objects</u>

경험(을) 하-	experience it
경험	experience
구하-	save it, rescue it
깨달- (ㄹ ~ ㄷ)	realize, come to realize
꺼내-	bring up, broach (a subject); take out (e.g., from one's pocket)
돌려 주-	give back
바치-	offer up, sacrifice
웃기-	be (act) funny; make one laugh
이루-	achieve, bring about
목적(을) 이루-	achieve one's goal
꿈(을) 이루-	achieve/realize one's dream
치-	reckon, calculate
생일로 나이를 치지 않고 . . .	(in Korea) instead of calculating age on the basis of birthdate . . .

<u>Descriptive and/or Sensory Verbs</u>

거만하-	be arrogant
겸손하-	be modest
충분하-	be enough, plenty, sufficient
충분히	enough (adv.), sufficiently
흥미(가) 있-	be interesting, amusing
흥미(가) 없-	be uninteresting, dull, not at all amusing

<u>Intransitive Verbs (Processive Verbs or Idioms That Cannot Take Objects)</u>

고장(이) 나-	s.th. breaks, breaks down, gets out of order
보이-	be visible, "shows"
빠지-	fall (into); come out/fall off (hair, etc.)
생기-	comes about, happens
영문(을) 모르-	not understand what is going on, have no idea why

질문(을) 하-	ask a question
최선을 다 하-	do one's best
최선을 다 하겠습니다.	I'll do my best.
팔리-	be sold, get sold, "sell (well)"

Lesson Notes

28.1. Retrospective Aspect

28.1.1. Retrospective Sentences

Korean has a set of RETROSPECTIVE verb endings; those that occur at the end of statements may be translated *it has been observed that*, or *I have sensory evidence to the fact that [so-and-so happens]* rather than the matter-of-fact *[so-and-so happens]* of other statement endings. Retrospective questions mean *has it been observed* or *has [someone] noticed/ does someone have sensory evidence to the effect that [so-and-so] was happening]?* rather than simply *does* or *did [so-and-so happen]?*

Retrospective endings tend to go on plain bases, but you can also attach them to a past or future base if, at the time you are referring to in the past, the original statement would have used a past or future base.

This is a difficult matter for English speakers to grasp, since it does not directly translate anything we say; it involves a dimension of meaning that English lacks. The translation is sometimes *I saw . . .* or *I noticed . . .* , sometimes *I heard . . .* or *I understand . . .* , or *They say*, sometimes just *did* or *was* or *was doing* [when someone was observing]. Here are the retrospective endings for the various styles.

	STATEMENT	QUESTION	APPERCEPTIVE
FORMAL STYLE			
Plain Base	-습디다 [after cons.]	-습디까?	-더군요!
	-ㅂ디다 [after vowel]	-ㅂ디까?	
Past Base	-었습디다 [etc.]	-었습디까? [etc.]	-었더군요!
Future Base	-겠습디다	-겠습디까?	-겠더군요!

Lesson Twenty-eight / 308

	STATEMENT	QUESTION	APPERCEPTIVE
POLITE STYLE			
Plain Base	-데요 (-더라고요, -던데요)	-던가요?	-더군요!
Past	〔-었데요〕	-었던가요?	-었더군요!
Future	〔-겠데요〕	-겠던가요?	-겠더군요!
PLAIN STYLE			
Plain Base	-더라	-더냐?, -디?	-더군!
Past Base	〔-었더라〕	-었더냐?, -었디?	-었더군!
Future Base	〔-겠더라〕	-겠더냐?, -겠디?	-겠더군!

Here are some examples from the Formal, Polite, and Plain Styles.

1. 할아버지 1: 그 회사의 제품이 어떻습니까?
    How are that company's products (in your experience)?

   할아버지 2: 고장이 잘 납디다.
    As I recall, they break easily.

2. 수진: 만호 씨를 못 봤어요?
    Have you seen Manho?

   진희: 집에 가데요.
    He's on his way home [or was when I just saw him, anyway].

3. 복남이가 학교에 갔더라.
    Pongnam has/had gone to school [I noticed his bag was gone].

4. 복남이가 학교에 가더라.
    Pongnam was on his way to school [I saw him].

5. 할아버지 1: 만호는 어디 있습니까?
    Where's Manho?

   할아버지 2: 도서관에 갑디다.
    He was going to the library [I saw].

6. 그 사람이 1시간 전에 책을 읽고 있더라.
    I saw him reading a book about an hour ago.

As you can see from the table on the previous page, the retrospective form in the Polite Style is -데요. However, this rather colloquial form can sound the same as the contracted quotations in -대요. So what does one do when one wants to say something retrospectively in this style and avoid this possible ambiguity? The easiest thing is just to shift into one of the other styles. Another way is to rephrase the sentence to take advantage of the retrospective modifier -던 and say something like *it's a fact that it has been observed that it happened*: -던 것이에요 or -던 거에요 (Polite). A final strategy is to quote the plain style retrospective in -더라, i.e., -더라고, then round it off with the polite particle 요: -더라고요. See section 28.4.1 below.

Here are some more sentences ending with retrospective forms.

7.　　언제 가겠다고 하던가요?
　　　Did you hear him say when he's going? [According to your recollection, when did he say he would go?]

8.　　그런 사람이 많이 있던데요!
　　　I've been given to understand that there are many such people.

9.　　어머니가 고기를 사 오셨던가요?
　　　[Do you know] did Mother go buy the meat?

10.　　어제는 퍽 춥던데요.
　　　It was quite cold yesterday [I found].

11.　　금강산은 참 굉장한 산이더라고요!
　　　The Diamond Mountains are incredible mountains indeed (I was there)!

12.　　얼마나 크던가요?
　　　How big was it? How big do you remember it to be?

13. 그 환자가 꼭 죽겠더라고요!
     [*From what I observed of his condition*] *that patient is going to die for sure.*

14. 사흘만 있으면 꽃이 피겠던데요!
     In three days the flowers will be in bloom [from what I have seen of them].

28.1.2. Apperceptive Retrospective Sentences

As you have learned in section 21.9, apperceptive sentences, with such meanings as *why . . .*
! what do you know . . . ! . . . I see! are made for processive verbs by following the
processive modifier form –는 with the –군 or –구면; descriptive verbs, as well as all past
and future bases, attach the ending –군 or –구면 directly to the base.

If the apperceptive is followed by 요, it is in the Polite Style; without 요, it is compatible with
either the Intimate or Plain Style. The Intimate Style variants in –(는)구나 are especially
intimate or friendly.

The retrospective form of these apperceptive sentences is made as follows: a one-shape
ending –더군 or –더구면 is attached to any base.

Turn back to the list of examples in Section 28.1 and turn them all into apperceptive statements.
(Some may seem a bit strange, but you can probably think of a situation in which the *[as I
recall, I thought to myself] oh, I see . . . !* meaning is appropriate.)

28.2. More on Retrospective Modifiers in –던

You have already been introduced to the retrospective modifier –던 in section 19.5., where
you saw it in its function as the modifier equivalent to the progressive pattern in –고 있었어
요 *was doing*. In this latter function, –던 attaches only to simple bases. However, –던 can
also attach to past bases (–었–), in which case it implies that the action of the verb carried on
for a time in the past, then ceased. Retrospective –던 on a plain base does not imply that the
action actually came full circle (compare 가는 길에 with 갔던 길에 below).

The special phrase 갔던 길에 means *on the way back (from having gone somewhere)*. This
contrasts with a processive modifier phrase, 가는 길에, which means *on the way (going to
a place)*. Here are some more examples of –던 on past bases.

15. 어제 왔던 사람이 또 왔습니다.
   That person I saw come yesterday is here again.

16. 시장에 갔던 길에, 박 선생을 만났습니다.
   On the way back from the market, I met Mr. Pak.

17. 공항에 나가는 길에 미국 대통령이 도착하는 것을 봤어요.
   On the way out to the airport, I saw the U.S. president arriving.

18. 옛날에 유명했던 경기고등학교가 이 자리에 있었어요.
   Kyŏnggi High School, which used to be famous in prior days, used to be on this spot.

19. 학생이었던 시절을 생각하고 있었어요.
   I was thinking of the days when I was a student.

20. 그 사람이 전에 파티에 가서 만났던 사람 아니에요?
   Isn't that the person we met at that party one time?

28.3. -던데(요)

This pattern combines two forms you already know—the retrospective marker -더- and the imminent elaboration form in -ㄴ데(요). This combined pattern preserves the original meanings of both composite elements. Thus, verbs with this form in statements mean something like *[it has been observed that] so-and-so happened/is happening/will happen*, [and/but there is more I could tell you about it].

21. 선배: 수진 씨 집에 있냐?

   후배: 아까 없던데요.
   Senior: Is Sujin at home?
   Junior: She wasn't there just a moment ago [—would you like more info?]

22. 아침에 종로에서 좋은 구두를 팔던데, 한번 가볼까?
   They were selling some nice shoes on Chongno in the morning; shall we go and take a look?

23. A. 호철 씨도 가겠댔어요?

   B. 못 가겠던데요.
   A. Did Hoch'ŏl say he was going to go, too?
   B. [I'm afraid] it seemed he wouldn't be able to go [would you like more elaboration?]

28.4. Retrospective Conditionals in -더라면

28.4.1. *If . . .* Clauses in Conditionals

Observe the following examples.

24.　좀 더 열심히 배웠더라면 . . .
　　　If I had studied a little harder . . .

25.　계속해서 공부했었더라면 . . .
　　　If I had kept at it and studied . . .

26.　거만하지 않았더라면 . . .
　　　If she hadn't been arrogant . . .

Retrospective conditional forms are made by attaching the retrospective marker -더- to the past base of the verb, then putting on the conditional ending -라면.

　　　　　했더라면　　　*if [one] had done*

Another way to say the same thing is to add -다면 to the past base of the verb.

　　　　　했다면　　　*if [one] had done*

These expressions have a past conditional meaning *if so-and-so had happened*. Although there is a separate past conditional form, made by attaching -으면 to past bases (-었으면, see Lesson 21), the retrospective conditional—which has the same meaning—is the one most commonly used.

28.4.2. *Then . . .* Clauses in Conditionals: Review of Past-Past, Past-Future, and Past-Past Future.

27.　한국어를 더 열심히 했었더라면, 지금은 유창하게 말할 수 있을 거에요.
　　　If I had studied Korean more, by now I would have been able to speak fluently.

You learned about verb forms with two tense markers (past-past, past-future) in section 14.4. As you will recall, the past-past is used when the event is more remote, often with some later reversal or change implied: 왔어요 means *came = is here*, 왔었어요 means *came (and left) = was here*.

The future marker -겠- has two meanings, as you have seen. Sometimes it refers to a definite event in some future time: *will do/be* or *would do/be*. But other times it refers to a likely or probable present event: *probably does/is = evidently must do/be*. You can have both these meanings when the future marker is attached to the past marker (-었을 거에요), but you have to add the meaning of the past to your translation.

1. *will have done/been* or *would have done/been*
2. *probably has done/been = evidently must have done/been*

Here are some examples.

갔었을 거에요 [= 갔었겠지요]
1. *will/would have gone (and returned) = will/would be back from going*
2. *probably went (and returned) = evidently must be back from going*

왔었을 거에요 [= 왔었겠지요]
1. *will/would have come = will have been here*
2. *probably came (and left) = evidently must have been here*

[Note: In the first meaning, definite future, choice of *will* or *would* in the English translation depends on the tense of the other verbs in the English sentence.]

Here are some more examples. Notice that the first part of the sentence often ends with a retrospective conditional -(었)더(라)면.

28.　시간이 있었더라면, 걸어 갔겠지요 [= 갔을 거에요].
If we had had time, we would have walked (there).

29.　자동차를 타고 왔더라면, 시간이 좀 더 있었겠지요 [= 있었을 거에요].
If we had taken a cab (here), we would have had a little more time.

30.　오늘 아침에 날이 좋지 않았더라면, 공원에 가지 못 했었겠지요
　　[= 했었을 거에요].
If it hadn't been nice out this morning, we wouldn't have been able to go to the park.

31.　내 책을 집에 가지고 갔다면, 공부를 할 수 있었겠지요
　　[= 있었을 거에요].
If I had taken my book home, I would have been able to do my studying.

32.   박 선생이 오늘 왔다면, 서울 구경을 갔겠지요 [= 갔을 거에요].
      If Mr. Pak had come today, we would have gone [= be out] sight-seeing (around)
      Seoul.

33.   오늘 오후에 비가 왔더라면, 공원에 가지 말라고 했었겠지요
      [= 했었을 거에요].
      If it had rained this afternoon, I would have told them not to go to the park.

28.5. Additional Uses of the Quotation Pattern in -고

28.5.1. Converting Plain Style Retrospective -더라 to Polite Style: -더라고(요)

As you have learned, Korean verb endings can often add or subtract the Polite 요 to make Polite Style or Intimate Style endings, as the case may be. However, not every Korean verb ending allows you to attach 요, and the Plain Retrospective in -더라 is one such form (in fact, none of the Plain Style endings can attach 요).

However, Koreans still feel the need for a polite retrospective ending, and one strategy they have developed is to, as it were, quote the -더라 and then round this off with the Polite 요, much in the same way you learned to use 요 to round off unfinished sentences in -서 and -고.

34.   꽤 좋더라고요.
      . . . and it's quite good [I recall].

35.   친구들이 다 와 있더라고요.
      The friends were all there [I recall].

36.   선생님이 벌써 가셨더라고요.
      The teacher had already gone [I recall].

37.   야당후보가 대통령이 되겠더라고요.
      It seemed probable that the opposition party candidate would become president [I
      recall].

28.5.2. Quotation Repeats

Again, much in the same way you use 요 to round off unfinished sentences in –서 and –고, you can attach 요 to a quotation to round it off as a Polite sentence. The most common instances of this are when asking for and giving repeats. For example:

38.   A. 돈이 있어요?
     B. 네?
     A. 돈이 있(느)냐고요.
     A. *Do you have any money?*
     B. *What?*
     A. *(I said,) Do you have any money?*

39.   A. 가고 싶지 않아도, 가야 해요.
     B. 네?
     A. 가고 싶지 않아도, 가야 한다고요.
     A. *Even if you don't want to, you have to go.*
     B. *What?*
     A. *(I say,) even if you don't want to, you have to go.*

40.   A. 어제 밤에 일이 너무 많아서 한잠도 못 잤어요.
     B. 뭐라고요?
     A. 어제 밤에 하나도 못 잤다고요, 일이 하도 많아서요.
     A. *I didn't get any sleep at all last night, I had so much work.*
     B. *What's that?*
     A. *I say, I didn't get any sleep last night because I had **so** much work.*

28.6. Errand Reporting

Observe the following sentence.

41.   여보! 시계 찾아왔어요?
     Honey, did you go and get the watches?

Errands involve three things: you **go**, you **do** something, and you **come** back. In English we report an errand by mentioning the first two of these operations: *He went and bought me a newspaper*, etc. We seldom mention the final "coming back." (If the errand is reported from the other end, of course, the "going" and "coming" are reversed: you **come**, you **do** something, and you **go** back).

In Korean you sometimes mention only the last two operations when you report an errand, you say such things as *He bought me a newspaper and came*, etc. (If the "going" and "coming" are reversed, you get such sentences as the Korean *He got the watch and went =*

English *He came and got the watch*). This sort of sentence in Korean is usually limited to situations where, as a result of the errand, the object is taken away (or brought), so you can't use it with all verbs that you might consider errands. Here are some examples.

42. 술을 2병 더 사오면 고맙겠어요.
    I'd like you to go and buy a couple more bottles of wine.

43. 그 구두가 너무 작으면 큰 것으로 바꿔 가세요.
    If the shoes are too small come (to our store) and exchange them for larger ones.

44. 새 모자를 사 오세요.
    Go and buy a new hat.

45. 어제 신문을 찾아다 주세요.
    Go and get me yesterday's newspaper.

As you can see from the last example (as well as from the first one of this section) the verb 찾아요 *seeks (out), looks for, finds* is often translated *gets*. Another meaning you have learned is visits: 선생님 댁을 찾아갔어요 *I went to visit/call on my teacher.*

Not every case of -어 와요 or -어 가요 is an errand, as you can see from such expressions as 가져 와요 *brings* and 가져가요 *takes*, 걸어가요 *walks (away)* and 걸어와요 *walks (here)*, etc.

Although 가요 usually translates English *goes* and 와요 is usually equivalent to English *comes*, there are some situations in which the two are reversed from the English pattern. In Korean the reference is always to where the *speaker* is located when speaking. On the telephone from "our" house you might promise a little friend 내가 수진 씨 집에 갈게요 *I'll [go =] come over to your house, Sujin* rather than 내가 수진 씨 집에 올게요 *I'll come over (here) to your house, Sujin*, since that would imply you were already at "his" house when talking. In other words, 와요 means *comes **here*** and 가요 means *goes* or *comes **there***.

Another way to talk about errands that you already know (and which is more widely useful since it is not limited to situations where the object is taken away or brought) is to use the infinitive of the movement verb usually followed by the particle 서: 가/와서 . . . *goes/comes and . . . [does].*

46. 사장님은 공항에 나가셔서 손님을 만나셨어요.
    The company president went out to the airport and met the guest.

Lesson Twenty-eight / 317

28.7. -(으)ㄹ 정도(로): *To the extent that . . .*

The noun 정도 means *extent*.

47. 한국말은 어느 정도 압니까?
    To what extent to you know Korean?

48. 그 정도면 충분해요.
    That's plenty [lit. *if it be that extent, it is sufficient*].

Used as a postmodifier after the prospective modifier -(으)ㄹ, this word yields a pattern that means *is/does to the extent that VERB*. Here are some examples.

49. 내 동생은 엉덩이가 보일 정도로 짧은 치마를 입고 있었다.
    My younger sister was wearing a skirt so short that you could practically see her bottom.

50. 배꼽이 빠질 정도로 재미있게 웃었다.
    We laughed so much our belly buttons almost fell out.

51. 우리 사장님은 매일 아침 5시에 일어날 정도로 부지런하다.
    Our company president is so hard-working as to get up every morning at 5 o'clock.

주의!

We learned earlier that one of the functions of the Plain Style in 한다, 하다, etc. is for objective written prose of the sort one might find in the newspaper or in a report or academic paper. But note that in this context, it is considered inappropriate to use the honorific marker -(으)시-. Thus, one would not normally find the final verb in sentence (51) above rendered as *부지런하시다 (if it were in a written report or the like).

28.8. -고 나서 *after VERBing . . .*

A Plain base followed by -고 나서 means *after doing [it], . . .* This pattern is used only with processive verbs.

52.　연극이 끝나고 나서 관객들은 오랫동안 박수를 쳤다.
　　　After the play had finished, the spectators applauded for ten minutes.

53.　왕이 죽고 나서 나라가 발전했다.
　　　The nation developed after the king died.

54.　내가 영국에 오고 나서 내 동생이 결혼했다.
　　　My brother got married after I came to England.

28.9. NOUN (을/를) 위해(서) *for the sake of NOUN*

28.9.1. NOUN (을/를) 위해(서)

A noun followed by (을/를) 위해(서) means *for the sake of NOUN.*

55.　너를 위해서라면, 뭐든지 할 수 있다.
　　　If [you say] it's for you[r sake], I can do it.

56.　세계평화를 위해서 싸우겠다.
　　　I will fight for [the sake of] world peace.

57.　처자식을 위해서 열심히 돈을 벌었다.
　　　He diligently earned money for his wife and children.

58.　세계평화를 위한 싸움.
　　　The struggle for world peace.

28.9.2. VERB -기 (를) 위해 (서)

A summative verb form in -기 (which is a kind of noun, after all) followed by (를) 위해 (서) means *in order to VERB* (i.e., *for the sake of VERBing*).

59. 세계평화를 이루기 위해서 항상 기도를 해야 돼요.
     In order to achieve world peace, we must pray constantly.

60. 나라를 위해서 몸을 바친 사람들이 정말 훌륭해요.
     Those who offered their lives for the sake of the country are truly great.

61. 그 사람은 비서와 결혼하기 위해서 부인과 헤어졌어요.
     He separated from his wife in order to marry his secretary.

Exercises

Exercise 1: Practice with Retrospectives

The following sentences say *Someone does/did so-and-so* or ask *Does/did someone do so-and-so?* Change each to make it mean *Someone has been observed* (or *Has someone been observed?*) *to do so-and-so*, using various retrospective verb forms; then translate the sentence into normal English.

1.   김 선생은 하던 일을 빨리 마치고 갔어요.
2.   동생이 우체국에 혼자 가고 있었어요.
3.   학장이 총장한테 전보를 쳤어요.
4.   베이커 선생이 김 선생한테 한국말로 이야기했어요.
5.   한국에서는 고등학교 때는 열심히 공부하지만, 대학교에서는 주로 놀아요.
6.   관객들이 모두 서서 오랫동안 박수를 쳤어요.
7.   에릭은 학생시절에는 사회주의를 꽤 좋아했어요.
8.   그 교수의 강의는 굉장히 지루했어요.
9.   지난 번 소풍 갈 때 날씨가 굉장히 쌀쌀했어요.
10. 여당후보가 야당후보를 공산주의자라고 해요.
11. 집에 있는 모든 귀중품을 다 팔았어요.
12. 신부님의 자동차가 고장났어요 .

13. 그 사람이 처자식을 위해서 최선을 다하고 있어요.
14. 장마철에는 우산을 들고 나가도 소용이 없어요.
15. 보석상에 퍽 좋은 금시계가 있었어요.
16. 제 친구는 여자친구하고 벌써 헤어졌어요.
17. 어제 극장에는 빈 자리가 하나도 없었어요.
18. 대통령의 자동차가 참 크고 좋아요.
19. 그 비서가 꽤 거만해요.

Exercise 2: Korean to English Translation

Translate the following Korean sentences into English.

1. 우리 모두의 성공을 위해서 한 잔 듭시다.
2. 새 대통령이 "경제발전을 위해서 최선을 다 하겠습니다"라고 했어요.
3. 환자를 위해서 의사들이 열심히 일하고 있어요.
4. 훌륭한 사람이 되기 위해서 겸손해야 돼요.
5. 수술을 하기 위한 준비가 다 됐어요?
6. 돈을 벌기 위해서 아르바이트를 하고 싶어요.
7. 그 남자는 부인이랑 안 헤어지기 위해서 고생을 많이 했어요.
8. 가수가 관객들을 위해서 옛날 노래를 불렀어요.
9. 그 소설을 쓰기 위해서 연구를 많이 했어요.
10. 공산주의 사회에서는 예술을 위한 예술이 없어요.

Exercise 3: Practice with -고 나서

Each of the following items contains two clauses joined by -(으)ㄴ 후에 *after . . .ing*.
Replace this pattern with -고 나서 and translate the resulting sentences into English.

1. 자동차가 고장이 난 후에 걸어다니기 시작했어요.
2. 총장님이 학생들하고의 모임을 마친 후에 학장들하고 만났어요.
3. 선거가 끝난 후에 대통령이 테레비에 나왔어요.
4. 공산주의가 생긴 후에 세계 경제가 복잡해졌어요.
5. 신부님이 전보를 치신 후에 성당에 나가셨어요.
6. 공항에 갔다온 후에 또 공항에 가야 했어요.
7. 그 지루한 강의를 다 들은 후에 박수도 안 쳤어요.
8. 고등학교 친구들하고 술을 마신 후에 바로 집에 돌아갔어요.

9.   그 여자 친구하고 헤어진 후에 오랫동안 혼자 있었어요.
10.   어제 아르바이트를 한 후에 심심해서 영화를 보러 갔어요.
11.   그 회사가 파산이 된 후에 사장님이 갑자기 없어졌어요.
12.   장가를 간 후에 살이 쪘어요.
13.   대학을 졸업한 후에 그 사람이 유명한 학자가 됐어요.

Exercise 4: Korean to English Translation

Translate the following Korean sentences into English.

1.   요즘 우리 여자친구하고 문제가 생겼지만, 헤어질 정도는 아니에요.
2.   그 남자를 꽤 사랑하는데, 결혼하고 싶을 정도로 사랑하지는 않아요.
3.   이 김치는 입안이 아플 정도로 매워요.
4.   그 코메디안은 너무 웃겼습니다. 배가 아플 정도로 많이 웃었습니다.
5.   그 영화는 눈물이 나올 정도로 슬펐어요.
6.   그 친구의 병세가 심해요?
       수술을 해야 할 정도로 심하대요.
7.   여기서는 얼마나 멀어요?
       걸어갈 수 없을 정도로 멀어요.
8.   그 미국여자는 놀랄 정도로 일본말을 잘 하데요.
9.   길이 하나도 안 보일 정도로 안개가 많이 꼈어요.
10.   지하철에는 타지도 못 할 정도로 사람이 많았어요.
11.   사흘 동안 자리에서 못 일어날 정도로 허리가 아팠어요.
12.   그 가게는 문을 닫아야 될 정도로 물건이 안 팔린대요.
13.   요즘 정신이 없을 정도로 바빠졌어요.
14.   기분이 나쁠 정도로 농담을 많이 하고 있었어요.
15.   그 강의는 하품이 나올 정도로 지루했어요.

Exercise 5: Practice with -더라면

The following items are retrospective conditional clauses: unfinished *if* sentences. Make up a reasonable completion for each; say the whole sentence aloud, then translate.

1. 새 집을 지었더라면 . . .
2. 집 앞에는 꽃을 심었더라면 . . .
3. 어제 그 상점에 갔더라면 . . .
4. 어제 저녁에는 일찍 잤더라면 . . .
5. 오늘 아침 학교에 늦게 오지 않았더라면 . . .
6. 일 하기 전에 좀 쉬었더라면 . . .
7. 어제 날이 따뜻했더라면 . . .
8. 너무 비싸지 않은 물건을 샀더라면 . . .
9. 제 구두를 닦아 주었더라면 . . .
10. 이 모자를 사기 전에 써 봤더라면 . . .
11. 사모님이 오늘 오후에 상점에 가지 말자고 했더라면 . . .
12. 작지 않고, 컸더라면 . . .

Exercise 6: More Practice with -더라면

This exercise is the reverse of the preceding one. The completions for retrospective conditional sentences are given; you are to supply the condition and translate. For example, if the given portion were . . . 더 좋았겠지요 (좋았을 거에요), you might supply the clause 공부 했더라면 . . . or 공부 했다면 . . . *I wish I had studied* [= *If I had studied, it would have been better*].

1. . . . 자동차를 파셨겠지요.
2. . . . 저녁을 일찍 먹었겠지요.
3. . . . 상관 없었겠지요.
4. . . . 기차를 타고 왔을거에요.
5. . . . 구경을 갔을거에요.
6. . . . 좀 더 따뜻했겠지요.
7. . . . 지금은 한국말을 잘 하겠지요.
8. . . . 어머니한테 책을 사가지고 왔겠지요.
9. . . . 시골에 살았겠지요.
10. . . . 공원에서 산보를 했을거에요.
11. . . . 친구가 화를 내지 않았겠지요.

Lesson Twenty-eight / 323

Exercise 7: Manipulating Retrospectives

Below are a number of sentences in Korean. Convert the verbs in them into retrospective forms, using the speech style indicated, then translate the result.

The Formal Style
1. 질문을 많이 하는 학생들이 제일 똑똑해요.
2. 만호 씨는 동생하고 밖에서 야구를 해요.
3. 대부분의 한국 남자들은 양주를 좋아해요.
4. 러시아말로 쓴 책이었어요?
5. 집에 들어 왔을 때도 계속 머리가 아팠어요?

The Plain Style
6. 매주마다 그 여자한테서 선물을 받아요?
7. 아버지는 밭에서 일을 하셨어요?
8. 관객들이 박수를 오래 쳐 줬어요.
9. 그 사람의 집에 귀중품이 많았어요?
10. 은행에 언제 가신다고 그랬어요?

The Polite Style
11. 집 주위에는 꽃들이 다 피었어요.
12. 그 작가는 최근에 소설을 쓴댔어요?
13. 의사 선생님은 오늘 넥타이를 안 매고 계셨어요.
14. 책상 위에 성냥을 못 봤어요?
15. 저녁을 먹고 나서 싸움을 했어요?

Exercise 8: Practice with -(으)ㄹ 정도(로)

Below are ten questions in Korean. Answer them in full sentences, making use of the pattern in -(으)ㄹ 정도(로) and the hints provided in parentheses.

1. 어느 정도로 짧게 잘라 드릴까요? (귀가 나와요)
2. 지난 겨울에 눈이 많이 왔어요? (네, 밖에 못 나가요)
3. 어제 술을 많이 마셨어요? (네, 너무 취해서 걸을 수 없었어요)
4. 밖에 비가 많이 와요? (네, 우산이 있어도 소용이 없어요)
5. 김치 맛이 어때요? (눈물이 나와요 ~ 매워요)
6. 손이 아직도 아픕니까? (네, 잠을 못 자요)

7. 만호 씨한테 야단쳤어요? (네, 목이 아파요 ~ 소리 질렀어요)

8. 한국말을 어느 정도 할 수 있어요? (전화로 이야기를 주고 받아요)

9. 샌디 씨는 한국말이 많이 늘었지요? (네, 놀랐어요)

10. 수진 씨는 가끔 말을 더듬거리지요? (네, 어떨 때는 나도 못 알아들어요)

Exercise 9: English to Korean Translation

Translate the following sentences into Korean. Make sure to use a variety of different patterns, conversation styles, and honorifics.

1. On the way back from school I met my Russian teacher, who was very tired.

2. They say his lectures are really boring.

3. Could you repair this watch by Friday for me, please?

4. A. Is your house large?

    B. What?

    A. I said, is your house large?

5. On the way to school I saw a car accident.

6. A. If you don't want to go you don't have to.

    B. What?

    A. I said, if you don't want to go you don't have to.

7. I received a telegram while I was eating breakfast.

8. A. Where have you been?

    B. What?

    A. I asked where you had been.

    B. I'm sorry. To Pusan.

9. On the way back from Boston I told my wife that I much prefer London.

10. The friend I met yesterday suggested we go to the pub together this evening.

11. A. Do you like politics?

    B. What?

    A. I asked whether you like politics.

    B. Of course not!

12. It's best not to go for many picnics during the rainy season.

13. Do Koreans usually add black pepper to their food?

14. A. Don't fool around so much.

    B. What?

    B. I said, don't fool around so much.

 # Lesson 29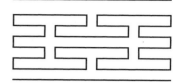

여보, 차키 어디 있는 지 아나?

In this lesson, Dialogue One follows the Murphys as they head off for a dinner at the Kims' house. Dialogue Two picks up Chris Murphy's growing literary interest again and summarizes the famous Korean folktale, the *Tale of Ch'unhyang*. This lesson introduces a number of new patterns built on the -기 form, including *decides/agrees to do* with -기로 해요. These patterns are followed by two major new constructions built on post-modifier 지: *[TIME] since* in -(으)ㄴ지, and oblique questions in -(으)ㄴ지, -는지, -(으)ㄹ지. Finally, the lesson introduces two new ways to make questions in -(으)ㄴ/-는가(요) and -나(요).

Korean Dialogues

Dialogue 1

오늘은 머피 선생 부부가 김 선생 부부를 저녁 식사에 초대했다. 그래서 저녁 7시까지 머피 선생 집으로 가기로 했다.

김 선생	여보, 차키 어디 있는 지 아나?
김 선생 부인	시간이 없으니까 택시를 타고 가요, 여보.
김 선생	당신이 화장하느라고 늦었지 – 여자들이 화장하면 왜 이렇게 시간이 걸리는지 모르겠네.

김 선생 부부는 7시 30분에 머피 선생 집에 도착했다.

김 선생	늦어서 정말 죄송합니다.
유니스	집 찾으시느라고 고생하셨나요?
김 선생	(와인 1병 건네 주면서) 아니오, 집은 쉽게 찾았는데, 길이 막혀서 좀 늦었지요.
유니스	그냥 오셔도 되는데 왜 이런 걸 사 가지고 오셨어요?
크리스	저녁이 벌써 다 준비됐으니까, 식당으로 들어가시지요.

식당에서

김 선생 부인	댁에서 주로 어떤 음식을 드시나요?
유니스	한국음식을 먹기도 하고 서양음식을 먹기도 해요.
	〔남편에게〕 중국음식도 자주 먹는 편이지요, 여보? 〔김 선생
	부인에게〕 중국요리는 저 사람이 하거든요.
김 선생 부인	한국음식은 만들기가 귀찮아서 잘 안 만들게 되지요?
	가끔 외식도 하세요?
크리스	가끔 외식을 하기는 하지만 너무 바빠서 외식을 같이 한
	지가 1달이 넘었어요.
유니스	근데 이 사람이 일 때문에 운동을 못해서 살이 너무 쪘어요.

Dialogue Notes

저 사람	*my spouse* (lit.: "that person"). This is a common and polite way to refer to one's husband or wife.
여보	*"dear"; "honey"*. Used as a term of address between spouses only.
이 사람	*my spouse* (lit.: "this person"). Same as note above.

Dialogue 2

Chris Murphy is pursuing his burgeoning interest in Korean literature and has another question for his Korean teacher, Mr. Kim.

크리스	선생님, 한국사람들의 제일 인기 있는 옛날 이야기가
	무엇인가요?
김 선생	우리 한국사람이 제일 좋아하는 옛날 이야기는 아마도
	춘향전일 거에요.
크리스	그것을 누가 썼나요?
김 선생	고전소설인데 원래 작가가 누구인지 알 수 없지요.
크리스	어떤 줄거리인가요?
김 선생	한 마디로 말하면, 사랑얘기지요. 낭만 소설을 좋아하시면,
	한번 읽어 보세요.

Dialogue Notes

| 춘향전 | *The Tale of Ch'unhyang*. Ch'unhyang (lit.: "spring fragrance") is the name of the heroine, –전 means "tale of; story of, biography of." |

Reading Passage

춘향전

옛날 옛날에 춘향이라는 기생의 딸이 있었는데, 마음도 좋고 아름답기도 했다.
감사의 아들 몽룡과 사랑을 하게 돼, 2사람은 결혼을 하기로 했다. 그러나, 천한
기생과 높은 양반의 자식이라는 신분의 차이로, 정당한 혼인을 하지 못하고,
숨어서 몇 달 살았다.

불행하게도, 몽룡의 아버지가 더 높은 벼슬을 얻는 바람에, 몽룡도 할 수 없이
그 아버지를 따라 서울로 돌아가게 됐다. 물론, 춘향이를 데리고 가려고 했지만,
부모의 반대로, 춘향이를 그냥 그곳에 두고, 3년 후에 다시 오겠다는 약속을
하고 갔다.

몽룡이가 떠난 지 얼마 안 돼서, 그 지방에 새 감사가 왔다. 그 새로 들어온 감사
인 변학도가 여러가지 수단을 써서 춘향이를 자기의 첩으로 삼으려고 했다.
그러나 춘향이는 결코 응하지 않았기 때문에 변학도는 춘향이를 죽이기로 했다.
변학도가 춘향이를 죽여 버리려는 그 순간에, 암행어사가 된 몽룡이 나타나서,
춘향이를 구했다. 결국 2사람은 아들도 낳고 딸도 낳고 오래오래 행복하게 잘 살
았다.

Reading Text Notes

몽룡	*Mongnyong.* Name of the good magistrate's son.
신분의 차이로	*because/on account of their difference in social status.*
아버지를 따라	*following his father; after his father.*
변학도	*Pyŏn Hakto.* Name of the evil magistrate.
죽여 버리려는	*intending to kill her once and for all . . .* The 버리 – adds a note of finality to the infinitive 죽여.
. . . 는 순간에	*just at the instant when he was going to [execute her].* The word 순간 here is functioning like a postmodifier.

Vocabulary

Nouns
Traditional Romances

감사	magistrate, auditor
고전	an old book; a classic
고전소설	Korean traditional novel
기생	a "kisaeng," Korean *geisha*
낭만	(being) romantic
낭만소설	a romance (i.e., novel in the romance genre)
와, 낭만적이다!	My, how romantic!
벼슬	a government post, official rank
부부	husband and wife couple
암행어사	secret inspector-general, undercover agent of the king
양반	yangban (traditional Korean gentry or nobility)
줄거리	plot
첩	concubine; mistress

     자기의 첩으로 삼으려고 했지만 . . .

     Tried to take [Ch'unhyang] as his concubine, but . . .

혼인	wedding, matrimony
혼인(을) 하–	get married, enter into matrimony

Sports

결승전	the finals
준결승전	semifinals
심판	umpire, referee
심판(을) 하–	umpire, referee
위반	transgression; foul
교통위반(을) 하–	commit a driving/traffic infraction
주차위반(을) 하–	commit a parking infraction
속도위반(을) 하–	commit a speeding violation; speed

Manuscripts, Words and Deadlines

–마디	counter for words
한 마디 할까요?	Shall I say a few words?
반말	Intimate Style
존댓말	Polite or Formal Style; respectful speech

Lesson Twenty-nine / 329

번역	translation
번역(을) 하-	translates it
번역가	translator
동시	same time; simultaneously
마감	deadline
마감일	deadline
원고	a manuscript, draft
원고료	manuscript fee
원고지	manuscript paper
통역	(simultaneous) interpreting
동시통역(을) 하-	do simultaneous interpreting
통역사	interpreter

Other

남	others, strangers
부분	portion, part, section
부분적으로	partially, in part(s)
서양사람	a Westerner
수단	a way or means; a measure; a trick
모든 수단을 다 쓰고 있지요.	I'm using every trick I know.
순간	moment, instant
시차	time difference; jet-lag

어제 서울에서 도착했는데, 시차 때문에 정신이 하나도 없어요.

I arrived from Seoul yesterday, and am completely out to lunch because of the jet lag.

신분	social status, station in life
신분증 〔-쯩〕	ID card
자식	child(ren), offspring
존경	respect
존경(을) 하-	respect someone
존경(을) 받-	be respected
주차	parking
주차장	parking lot
주차(를) 하-	park the car
차이	difference
폭풍우	a storm
피해	damage, harm
피해(를) 입-/받-	suffer damage, harm

Verbs

Verbs That Take Objects

건네-	hand over, turn over, transfer
교정(을) 하-	proofread it
기고(를) 하-	submit an article
두-	put, place; leave (behind)
반대(를) 하-	oppose
반대	opposition
밤(을) 새-	stay up all night
사형(을) 하-	execute
사형	capital punishment, the death penalty
삼-	make something of (a person or thing)
그를 사위로 삼을 작정인가?	Are you planning to make him your son-in-law?
얻-	get, obtain
이기-	win; beat
죽이-	kill

Intransitive Verbs (Processive Verbs That Cannot Take Objects)

고생(을) 하-	suffer hardship(s), suffer
넘-	exceed, be more than; pass beyond
1달이 넘었어요.	It has been more than a month.
외식(을) 하-	dine out, eat out
(-한테) 지-	lose (to)
지각(을) 하-	arrive late (for school or work)

Causative~Passive and/or Intransitive~Causative Pairs

깨-	break it
깨지-	get broken
숨-	hide, conceal oneself
어디에 숨어 있었냐?	Where were you hiding?
숨기-	hide it, conceal it
숨기지 않고 말을 했다.	He spoke openly (without hiding anything).

Descriptive and/or Sensory Verbs

미끄러w-	be slippery
정당하-	be legitimate, rightful
천하-	be of low birth; be lowly, ignoble
특별하-	be special, particular
특별히	especially, particularly

Adverbs

깜빡	(forgot) totally
깜빡 잊어버렸다.	I completely forgot.
서로	mutually, to each other
할 수 없이	unavoidably, without having any other recourse

Lesson Notes

29.1. More Summative Forms:
-기도 하-, -기는 하-, -기만 하-

You have already learned that the summative form -기 turns a verb base into a noun. Thus, you should not be surprised to learn that summative forms in -기, just like any other noun, can take certain particles after them. This section introduces three new patterns based on -기 plus common particles you already know.

29.1.1. -기도 하- (I): *really does/is*

A plain base -기 form with 도 해요 after it means *really does/is*, *sure does/is* or *does/is indeed*. This form usually goes with the mild exclamation pattern in -네요.

1.   무겁기도 하네요.
     It sure is heavy!

2.   많이 오기도 했네요.
     There sure are a lot of them (come) here!

3.   비싸기도 하네요.
     It is expensive indeed!

4.   부지런하기도 하네요.
     He's really hard working!

Note that the past and future elements, as usual, attach to the auxiliary verb 해요. The honorific, also, usually attaches to the final auxiliary.

5.   참 자주 가기도 하시네요.
     He really goes [there] frequently.

29.1.2. -기도 하- (II): *does/is **both** x **and** y*

If there are two instances of -기도 해요 right together (either descriptive or processive), the meaning is *does/is **both** x **and** y*. Here are some more examples.

6. 잘 치기도 하고, 못 치기도 해요.
   Some (exams) I get through, some I don't.

7. 좋기도 하고, 나쁘기도 해요.
   It's both good and bad. = It has its good points and its bad points.

8. 춥기도 하고, 덥기도 해요.
   It [e.g., a country] is both cold and hot. = There are cold parts and hot parts.

9. 춥기도 하고, 바람이 불기도 해요.
   It's both cold and windy.

Notice that this construction is used for comparing actions or descriptions that are expressed by *verbs*. For comparing actions expressed by *verbal nouns* (as well as other nouns), it is the nouns that have 도 after them, as below.

10. 운동도 하고, 산보도 가요.
    He both engages in sports and takes walks.

But it is somewhat more natural to use 하기(도 해요) after descriptive verbal nouns, as shown below.

11. 바쁘기도 하고, 피곤(하기)도 해요.
    We're both busy and tired.

You can have a verbal noun in one part of the construction and a verb in the other part, as in the following example.

12. 공부도 하고, 놀기도 해요.
    He both studies and plays around.

29.1.3. -기는 하지만: *does/is, to be sure, but . . .*

A plain base -기 form with 는 followed by either itself or 하- in the -지만 *but* form means *does/is, to be sure, but.*

13.　이 책을 읽기는 하지만 (~ 읽지만) 뜻을 몰라요.
　　　*I **am** reading this book, but I don't understand it.*

14.　공책에 그 단어를 쓰기는 했지만 (~ 썼지만) 잘 못 썼어요.
　　　*I **did** write the words in my notebook; but I didn't write them properly.*

15.　그것을 먹기는 먹었지만 (~ 했지만) 맛이 없었어요.
　　　*I **did** eat it, all right, but it had no flavor.*

Notice that the past or future markers attach only to the -지만 form in this construction—not to the -기 form—which remains constant.

29.1.4. -기만 하-: *does nothing but . . .*

The construction -기만 해요 means *does nothing but* or *only -es (does only).*

16.　자기만 해요.
　　　I do nothing but sleep.

17.　먹기만 해요.
　　　Only eats; does nothing but eat.

18.　놀기만 해요.
　　　Fools around all the time; does nothing but play.

Notice that, in theory, English *I read only books* and *I only read books* are different; similarly, in Korean 책만 읽어요 *Books are all I read* is theoretically different from 책을 읽기만 해요 *All I do is read books.* But in both languages, this distinction is often ignored.

With verbal nouns, you can omit 하기: 공부(하기)만 해요 *I do nothing but study.* Somewhat similar are cognate objects, as in 잠을 자요 *sleep (a sleep)*: you can say either 잠을 자기만 해요 or just 잠만 자요 for *does nothing but sleep (one's sleep).*

29.2. *Is on the . . .ing side; Is fairly ~ pretty . . .* with -(으)ㄴ/-는 편이-

Dialogue One contained the following example:

중국음식도 자주 먹는 편이지요, 여보?
We eat Chinese food pretty often, too, don't we honey?

The noun 편 literally means *side; direction*, but as a postmodifier following the modifiers -(으)ㄴ (for past tense and/or adjectives) and -는 (for present tense with processive verbs) and in conjunction with the copula -이-, it forms a pattern which literally means *is on the . . . side, is on the . . .ing side*. In other words, it yields a pattern that corresponds roughly to colloquial English *is pretty (adjective), is fairly (adjective)* or *does something in a fairly/pretty ADVERB matter*. The ADVERB here is important—sentences with the processive modifier in -는 typically have an adverb modifying the processive verb used. Here are some examples.

19. 머피 사장님은 한국말을 잘 하시는 편입니다.
    Director Murphy speaks Korean pretty well.

20. 우리 컴퓨터가 자주 고장나는 편이라서 다른 걸로 바꾸기로 했어요.
    Our computer breaks down rather frequently, so we decided to trade it in for another.

21. 2만 원이라면 비싼 편이 아니네요.
    If it's 20,000 wŏn, it's not so expensive!

22. 수진: 어제 만난 남자는 어땠어?
    How was the guy you met yesterday?

    진희: 약간 거만한 편이었어.
    He was a bit on the arrogant side.

23. 만호: 저 분이 겸손하신가요?
    Is she modest?

    진희: 네, 겸손한 편이라고 할 수 있지요.
    Yes, I guess you could say she's fairly modest.

24. 수진: 시험 잘 봤니?
    Did you do well on the test?

    진희: 이번에는 잘 못 본 편이야.
    This time I didn't do so well.

29.3. The Postmodifier 지: *[TIME] since*

A past modifier followed by 지 (i.e., base plus -(으)ㄴ 지) is used for expressions meaning *(TIME) since.* The 지 can be followed optionally by the particle 가, with no change in meaning. Here are some examples.

25.   나는 그 친구를 본 지(가) 벌써 4년이 돼요.
       It's been four years now since I've seen that friend.

26.   부산에 가 본 지가 참 오래 됐어요.
       It's a very long time since I've been to Pusan.

27.   중국말 해 본 지가 벌써 10년이 넘었어요.
       It's been more than ten years now since I've tried talking Chinese.

The pattern for these expressions is as follows:

As Subject: As Predicate:

PAST MODIFIER + 지(가)   TIME WORD +   –이에요   *it is*
                                          돼요   *becomes*
                                          넘어요   *exceeds*
                                          지났어요   *passed*

28.   술집에 간 지(가)   오래 됩니다.
       Time since I've gone to a bar   is long.
       It's a long time since I've gone to a bar.

29.   소설을 읽은 지(가)   석 달이 됐어요.
       Time since I've read a novel   is three months.
       It's been 3 months since I read a novel.

Here are some more examples of this construction.

30.   선생님을 만난 지(가) 오래 됩니다. (or 됐습니다)
       It's been a long time since we've seen you.

31.   편지를 받은 지(가) 3주가 됐어요.
       It's been three weeks since I got a letter.

32. 여기 온 지(가) 5년이 됐어요.
It's been five years since I came here.

33. 김 선생님을 만난 지(가) 얼마나 됩니까?
How long is it since you've seen Mr. Kim?

Notice that a negative modifier clause in this construction actually refers to the same situation as if the clause were affirmative; the situation is just viewed differently.

34. 김 선생님을 만난 지가 석 달이 돼요.
It's been three months since I met Mr. Kim [= I have known him for 3 months].

35. 김 선생님을 못 만난 지 석 달이 돼요.
It's been three months that I haven't seen Mr. Kim. [= I haven't seen Mr. Kim for three months.]

29.4. The Postmodifier 지: Oblique Questions in 지

An oblique question is used as part of a larger sentence that contains an information verb like these:

알아요	*knows, realizes*	몰라요	*doesn't know*
기억(을) 해요	*remembers*	생각(이) 나요	*remembers, recalls*
잊어(버려)요	*forgets*	가르쳐요	*tells [= teaches]*
궁금해요	*wonders*		

Oblique questions can also be used as part of a larger sentence that contains verbs of asking and saying like these:

물어봐요	*asks*	말해요	*says*

In English, the actual question is a relative clause introduced by a question word: *whether, where, who, which*, etc. In Korean, the actual question is stated as a modifier plus 지.

29.4.1. Mechanics of Oblique Questions in 지

As you might expect from the term "postmodifier," oblique questions in 지 are built on modifiers, and take the shapes -(으)ㄴ지, -는지, -(으)ㄹ지, (and -(으)ㄹ는지 with the same meaning). Thus, these endings attach to bases and behave in much the same way as the modifier endings in -(으)ㄴ, -는, and -(으)ㄹ.

Mechanics of Oblique Questions in 지	
Descriptive Bases	-(으)ㄴ지
Processive Bases (plus 있-/없-)	-는지
All Past Bases	Past Base + -는지 (-았는지, 었는지, etc.)
Future	-(으)ㄹ지 or -(으)ㄹ는지 Or: Plain Base + -(으)ㄹ 것인지

29.4.2. Oblique Questions in 지 with 알아요 and 몰라요

An oblique question in 지 with the verbs 알아요 and 몰라요 is usually paired with its negative counterpart to produce an equivalent to English *(not) know whether (or not)* . . . :

36. 수진이가 공부하는지 안 하는지 압니까?
    *Do you know **whether** Sujin's studying (or not)?*

37. 수진이가 공부했는지 안 했는지 모르겠습니다.
    *I don't know **whether** Sujin studied (or not).*

38a. 수진이가 공부할 것인지 안 할 것인지 압니까?
    *Do you know **whether** Sujin's going to study (or not)?*

    or

38b. 수진이가 공부할지 안 할지 압니까?
    *Do you know **whether** Sujin's going to study (or not)?*

When the oblique question contains a question word in it (*who, what, where, when, why,* etc.), there is no need to pair it with a negative counterpart:

39. 그 사람이 누군지 (← 누구인지) 알아요?
    Do you know who he is?

40. 영미 씨가 생일파티에 왜 안 왔는지 모르겠어요.
   I have no idea why Yŏngmi didn't come to the birthday party.

41. 주말에 내가 무엇을 했는지 알아요?
   Do you know what I did on the weekend?

42. 만호 씨가 어디에 갔는지 모르세요?
   Don't you know where Manho went?

43. 수진 씨가 언제 올 것인지 혹시 아세요?
   Do you happen to know when Sujin will arrive?

Note also that sentences without a negative counterpart sound much better when there is a time or manner adverb present (an emphatic intonation also makes these sentences better):

44. 수진 씨가 공부를 잘 하는지 아세요?
   Do you know whether Sujin is a good student?

45. 수진 씨가 요즘 공부를 하는지 아세요?
   Do you know whether Sujin is studying lately?

Thus, oblique questions combine two expressions: a question clause in 지 and a verb. The chief difference is that in English the question part comes *after* the verb; in Korean, it comes *before*. If the Korean oblique question contains a question word, it is the translation of this word that introduces the corresponding relative clause in English.

46. 어디에 가는지 알아요?
   *Do you know **where** he's going?*

47. 언제 먹을지 알아요?
   *Do you know **when** he's going to eat?*

48. 무엇을 했는지 알아요?
   *Do you know **what** he did?*

If there is no question word in Korean, English supplies *whether* or *if* to introduce the clause.

49. 미국에 가는지 안 가는지 알아요?
   *Do you know **whether (if)** he's going to the United States?*

50. 저녁을 집에서 먹을지 안 먹을지 알아요?
   *Do you know **whether (if)** he's going to eat supper at home?*

51. 이발을 했는지 안 했는지 알아요?
   *Do you know **whether (if)** he got a haircut?*

Here are some more examples with oblique questions in 지 plus 알아요/몰라요:

52. 저 사람이 어떤 사람인지 알아요?
   Do you know what kind of a person she is?

53. 여기서 먼지 안 먼지 알아요?
   Do you know whether it's far from here?

54. 어떤 것이 좋을지 모르겠어요.
   I don't know what would be good.

29.4.3. Oblique Questions in 지 with Information Verbs

Oblique questions in 지 with information verbs have none of the restrictions seen in the section above with 알아요 and 몰라요:

DESCRIPTIVE

55. 그 책이 비싼지 물어보세요.
   Ask whether that book is expensive.

56. 그분이 왜 그렇게 거만하신지 이야기 좀 해 줄래요?
   Would you mind telling me why he's so arrogant?

PROCESSIVE (PRESENT)

57. 이 책을 왜 읽는지 물어보세요.
   Ask her why she's reading this book.

58. 상호 씨가 지금 어디에 살고 있는지 생각이 안 나요.
   I can't remember where Sangho is living now.

59. 이 선생님이 PC를 쓰시는지 기억이 안 납니다.
   I can't remember whether Mrs. Lee is using a PC or not.

All oblique questions in the past require the use of Past Base plus –는지.

DESCRIPTIVE

60. 서울이 추웠는지 물어보세요.
Ask whether Seoul was cold.

61. 내 친구 생일이 어제였는지 그저께였는지 기억이 안 나요.
I can't remember whether my friend's birthday was yesterday or the day before yesterday.

PROCESSIVE

62. 번역을 다 했는지 물어보셨어요?
Did you ask her whether she had finished the translation?

63. 결승전에서 졌는지 이겼는지 기억이 안 납니다.
I can't remember whether they won or lost in the finals.

64. 아이들과 같이 있었는지 없었는지 생각이 안 나요.
I can't remember whether they had their children with them or not.

Oblique questions in the future require the use of Plain Base plus -(으)ㄹ지 or -(으)ㄹ 것 인지 (or its abbreviate form -(으)ㄹ 건지) for *all* verbs. You will occasionally encounter forms in -겠는지 but these are marginal and should be avoided in your own speech.

FUTURE

DESCRIPTIVE

65. 번역을 내일까지 할 수 있을지 물어보세요.
Ask him whether he'll be able to finish the translation by tomorrow.

66. 결승전에서 질 건지 이길 건지 두고 봐야지요.
We'll just have to wait and see whether they win or lose in the finals.

67. 아이들과 같이 올지 궁금해요.
I'm curious as to whether their children will be coming with them.

Note that when an oblique question is given with the information verb 물어요 *asks*, the sentence means the same thing as a Plain Style question quoted:

68. 밥을 먹(느)냐고 물었어요.　　or　　밥을 먹는지 물었어요.
I asked whether he was eating.

69. 언제 공부하(느)냐고 물어봅시다. or 언제 공부하는지 물어봅시다.
Let's ask him when he does his studying.

Here are more examples of oblique questions.

70. 여기서 우체국이 얼마나 먼지 아세요?
   Do you know how far it is from here to the post office?

71. 이 책을 읽어야 할지 저 책을 읽어야 할지 모르겠어요.
   I don't know whether I've got to read this book or that book.

72. 뭐가 뭔지 모르겠습니다.
   I don't know what is what.

Oblique questions are sometimes used as a complete sentence, followed by the polite particle 요, with the meaning *I wonder . . .* ; 누구신지요 *I wonder who you are.* 다 왔는지요 *I wonder if everyone is here/we are almost there.* 비가 오겠는지요 *I wonder if it will rain.* This kind of question, used with honorifics, is a favorite of television reporters conducting interviews, e.g.:

73. 부인과 결혼하시겠다는 결심을 언제 하셨는지요?
   When did you resolve to marry your wife?

Structures like these can be analyzed as reductions from or abbreviations of the more explicit: 결심을 언제 하셨는지 〔말씀해 주세〕요.

29.5. Polite Questions with . . . 가요 and . . . 나요

29.5.1. Plain Base + - ㄴ / - 은, -는 ＋ 가요

Observe the following examples.

74. 이것이 김치인가요?
   Is this kimchee?

75. 누구의 것인가요?
   Whose are they?

One special way of asking questions in the polite style is to use 가 preceded by a modifier, instead of the regular form used at the end of sentences. This is more commonly done with descriptive verbs and the copula.

76. 좋은가요?
     Is it nice?

77. 먼가요?
     Is it far? (base 머-ㄹ-)

78. 책인가요?
     Is it a book?

However, you will occasionally hear a processive verb used the same way.

79. 공부하는가요?
     Is he studying?

Theoretically, for the future, you should be able to use -(으)ㄹ까요: 공부할까요? *Is he going to study?* But, as you have already learned, for first persons (*I/we*) this more commonly has the meaning *shall we/I . . . ?* or *how about . . .ing?* and, in the case of third persons (*he, she, it, they*) with anything other than plain processive bases, *Do you suppose that . . .?* (section 12.4).

There are special future processive and past processive modifiers –겠는 and –었는 that are restricted to positions before certain postmodifiers only: 가, 야 (section 26.2), 지 (section 29.5), and 데 (section 21.5). Theoretically, to say *Have you eaten?* you should be able to say 먹은가요?, but in real life 먹었는가요? is more common, and still more common is 먹었나요? (explained below). Similarly, to say *Will you eat?* one could (theoretically) say 먹을까요?, but 먹겠는가요? is more common (for that meaning), and still more common is 먹겠나요?

80. 그 자동차가 빠른가요?
     Is that car fast?

81. 저녁에 먹을 게 많은가요?
     Is there plenty to eat for supper?

82. 방학 동안에도 학교에 학생이 많이 있는가요?
     Are there many students in the school during the vacation, too?

83. 이 방이 말씀하신 교실인가요?
   Is this room the classroom you have spoken about?

84. 선생님(의) 아버님은 연세가 몇이신가요?
   How old is your father?

29.5.2. Any Base + -나요

Observe the following examples.

85. 오늘 저녁에 손님이 몇 분 오시나요?
   How many guests are coming tonight?

86. 손님이 오시면, 얼마나 오래 계시나요?
   When the guests come, how long will they stay?

Polite questions of this second type are more common with processive than with descriptive verbs. This second type uses the ending -나(요), which is attached to bases of processive verbs and of 있- *(there) is* and 없- *(there) isn't*, as well as to any past or future base.

A convenient rule to follow with both types of complex questions is the following: use the -가요-type questions described above with present descriptive verbs only and the -나요-type described here with everything else (processive bases, and with any past or future base). Here are some more examples of complex questions with -나요.

87. 그 사람이 매일 밤 오나요?
   Does he come here (= Is he here) every night ?

88. 집에서는 보통 한국음식을 드시나요?
   Do you usually eat Korean food at home?

89. 제가 선생님 자리에 앉아 있나요?
   Am I sitting in your seat?

90. 그 도시에는 고등학교가 없나요?
   Isn't there any high school in that city?

91. 그 음악가가 연주하는 것을 몇 번이나 봤나요?
   How many times have you seen that musician play?

92.　8시 반이면 늦지 않겠나요?
　　　Won't 8:30 be (too) late?

93.　누가 이 그릇을 깼나요?
　　　Who broke these dishes?

Exercises

Exercise 1: Practice with -기만 해요

Each of the following sentences means *(someone) does (this)*. Change it to mean *(someone) does only (this)—does nothing but [this]*. For example, the first will be: 우리 개가 늘 짖기만 해요 *My dog just barks all the time.*

1.　우리 개가 늘 짖어요.
2.　어머니가 라디오를 들어요.
3.　아들이 밖에 나가지 않고, 집에 있어요.
4.　할아버지가 날마다 신문을 보셨어요.
5.　우리 남편이 담배를 피워요.
6.　우리 친구가 말하지 않고, 앉아 있어요.
7.　애기가 먹어요.
8.　너는 왜 늘 쉬니?
9.　너는 왜 항상 노니?

Exercise 2: Practice with -기도 해요

Each of the following sentences means *someone does* or *is*. Change it to mean *someone really does* or *really is*. For example, the first will be: 그 꽃이 좋기도 하네요 *Those flowers certainly are nice!*

1.　그 꽃이 좋네요.
2.　나는 영화 구경을 가고 싶네요.
3.　그 사람은 돈이 많네요.
4.　아들이 돈을 잘 쓰네요.
5.　학교가 집에서 가깝네요.
6.　우체국이 교회에서 머네요.
7.　그 사람은 편지 쓰기를 좋아하네요.

8.   그 애기가 어리네요.
9.   우리 사장님이 젊으시네요.
     [Most common to make just 해요 honorific.]
10. 애기가 밤에 잘 자데요.
11. 날이 춥네요.
12. 이 편지가 무겁네요.
13. 그 여자가 통역을 잘 하네요.
14. 통역가의 태도가 이상하네요.

Exercise 3: Practice with -기는 . . . 지만

Each of the following sentences is joined by the *but* pattern in -지만. Join them using the pattern in -기는 . . .-지만 and translate the resulting sentence in to English.

1.   원고료는 받았지만, 원고는 아직 못 쓰고 있어요.
2.   그 회의에는 가겠지만, 가기 싫어요.
3.   그 사람도 초대했지만, 안 오면 좋겠어요.
4.   컴퓨터를 샀지만, 잘 안 써요.
5.   폭풍우가 있었지만, 큰 피해는 없었어요.
6.   졸리지만, 끝까지 봐야지요.
7.   지각을 했지만, 온 김에 일이나 해야지요.
8.   귀찮지만, 처자식을 위해서 하는 거니까 해야지요.
9.   맛이 없지만, 많이 잡수세요.
10. 번역가가 번역을 했지만, 엉터리였어요.

Exercise 4: Practice with -(으)ㄴ/-는 편이다

Make up sentences with the following phrases using the pattern in -(으)ㄴ/-는 편이다.

1.   금년의 독감은 작년 것보다
2.   할아버지는 소화가 잘 안 되시-
3.   우리 아들은 남을 적극적으로 도와주-
4.   잘 생기-
5.   수진이는 친구를 쉽게 사귀-
6.   질문을 많이 하-
7.   최선을 다 하-
8.   잘 팔리-

9. 점잖-
10. 친절하게

Exercise 5: Practice with -(으)ㄴ/-는가요 and -나요

Change each of the following questions into a new question in either -가요 or -나요, whichever is more appropriate, and translate the result into English.

1. 다음 달에 한국에 가세요?
2. 요즘 무엇을 하세요?
3. 마감이 언제에요?
4. 원고료가 얼마였어요?
5. 가방이 가벼워요?
6. 그렇게 하면 좀 귀찮지 않아요?
7. 교정을 다 보셨어요?
8. 누가 이 그릇을 깼어요?
9. 이 번역은 잘 됐어요?
10. 호철 씨 약혼자가 예뻐요?
11. 그분이 사장님이세요?
12. 김치가 너무 매워요?

Exercise 6: More Practice with -(으)ㄴ/-는가요

Translate the following sentences into Korean using the -(으)ㄴ/-는가요 questions you have learned in this lesson.

1. Is it far?
2. Do you think I will be able to play with him tomorrow?
3. Is the room too hot?
4. Is that building higher than our house?
5. Is that text book the one written by Professor Pak?
6. Is the scenery beautiful in Korea?
7. Is that thing a pencil?
8. Is his car stylish?
9. Is the air fresh in the center of Seoul?
10. Is the phone busy (engaged) again?

Exercise 7: More Practice with -나요

Translate the following questions into Korean using the -나요 forms.

1. Was that the car you wanted to buy?
2. Has he just come back from a foreign country?
3. Did you take any exams last year?
4. Is he going to be angry when he sees what you've done?
5. Did he smile when you gave him that present.
6. Is this going to be the place where he'll live.
7. Have you eaten breakfast?
8. Will you want to come out with me after you've been to town?
9. Did he buy a new hat in Toronto?
10. When do you graduate?

Exercise 8: Korean to English Translation

1. 내일부터 일찍 일어나기로 했어요.
2. 그 여자랑 결혼하기로 했습니다.
3. 오후 3시 비행기로 떠나기로 합시다.
4. 그 친구한테 내가 쓰던 컴퓨터를 주기로 약속했어요.
5. 이제부터 술을 끊기로 했어요.
6. 오늘부터 서로 반말로 하기로 하자, 응?
7. 어머니한테 술을 안 마시기로 약속했어요.
8. 이 책을 교재로 쓰기로 결정했어요.
9. 어디서 만나기로 했어요?
10. 이 부분을 번역하지 않기로 결정했어요.
11. 요즘 뭐 하느라고 그렇게 바빠요?
12. 요즘 애기를 보느라고 정신이 하나도 없지요.
13. 자동차를 고치느라고 밤을 샜어요.
14. 오시느라고 수고하셨어요.
15. 시험 준비를 하느라고 바빠요.
16. 보고서를 쓰느라고 그 사람을 만날 시간이 없었어요.
17. 늦잠을 자느라고 버스를 놓쳤어요.
18. 무엇을 하시느라고 요새 학교에도 안 나오세요?
19. 무엇을 하시느라고 이렇게 매일 지각하세요?
20. 원고를 교정하느라고 다른 일은 못 마쳤어요.

Exercise 9: English to Korean Translation

1. I hope the lesson is easy.
2. I've decided not to eat the fish.
3. We've decided to stay up all night.
4. I've promised the company president to do the proofreading by next week.
5. The students are both hard-working and lazy.
6. This computer is both annoying and expensive.
7. All he ever does is read books.
8. My dog does nothing but sleep.
9. Is it OK if I submit this manuscript a little late (–나요)?
10. I see from reading the report that we shall have to write it again!
11. When I arrived home, the windows were all open.

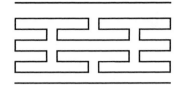 **Lesson 30**

REVIEW 5

Review of Lesson Notes

30.1. Pattern Review

30.1.1. Plain Style Statements

1. 어제 응급실에서 치료해 준 인턴은 아주 젊다.

2. 그 치과의사를 개인적으로 모른다.

3. 주사를 맞았기 때문에 염려할 필요가 없었다.

4. 어제 공부를 하느라고 잠을 못 잤으면 피곤하겠다.

5. 일기예보를 들었는데 내일은 날씨가 좋지 않다고 한다.

6. 내 동생은 친한 친구가 입원을 했어도 문병을 가지 않는다.

7. 우리 옆집 장난꾸러기는 날마다 큰다.

8. 의사가 먹으라는 소화제는 너무 크다.

9. 서울의 겨울날씨는 주로 이렇다.

10. 내 친구는 수업 중에 음악을 듣는다. 야단을 맞아도 항상 그런다.

30.1.2. Plain Style Questions

Type 1 Questions: -(으)냐, -느냐

11. 운전할 때 응급차가 오면 어떻게 해야 하(느)냐?

12. 어제 너를 진찰하던 내과 의사는 총각이냐?

13. 매일 애인한테 장거리 전화를 거(느)냐?

14. 교통사고가 난 곳이 여기에서 머냐?

15. 대학교를 다닐 때 어떤 사람하고 연애를 했(느)냐?

16. 꽃을 사 가지고 할아버지한테 문병을 가면 어떠냐?

17. 우선 졸업을 하고 결혼을 하면 어떻겠(느)냐?

Type 2 Questions: -니

18. 내일 가려고 하는 병원이 집에서 머니?

19. 우선 의사한테 진찰을 받아 보는 것이 어떠니?

20. 약속장소가 시청에서 가깝니?

21. 한국 여름은 무척 무덥다고 들었는데 얼마나 더웠니?

22. 그 회사는 정말 다음 달에 파산이 되겠니?

30.1.3. Plain Style Suggestions

23. 요즘 감기가 유행하니까 조심하자.

24. 시끄러운 음악말고 조용한 음악을 듣자.

25. 이번 사은회파티에는 총장도 부르자.

30.1.4. Plain Style Commands

<u>Type 1: -(으)라</u>

26.   길거리에 쓰레기를 버리지 말라.

27.   서두르지 말고 천천히 운전하라.

28.   거짓말을 하는 정치가는 추방하라.

<u>Type 2: -어/아/여라</u>

29.   한국말을 배우는 김에 한국 역사에 대해서도 좀 배워라.

30.   안색이 안 좋으니 유럽으로 출장 가는 것을 취소해라.

31.   요즘 유행하는 전염병을 조심해라.

32.   다음부터 응급차를 보면 오른쪽으로 비켜라.

30.1.5. Intimate Style

33.   한국은 교통이 너무 복잡해서 큰일이야.

34.   탁 교수님은 너무 착실하고 부지런하셔.

35.   병원에 가면 우선 맥박과 체온을 재고 피검사를 할 거야.

36.   둘이 동갑이니까 서로 반말을 하잖아.

37.   매주 수요예배가 끝나고 성경공부 안 할래?

38.   한국에서는 새 학기가 3월에 시작하거든.

30.1.6. *Because of . . . ing* with -느라(고)

39. 호주에서 친구가 와서 같이 노느라고 시험 공부를 못 했습니다.

40. 음악을 듣느라고 아버지가 부르시는 소리를 못 들었습니다.

41. 지금 동생이 개를 찾느라고 동네를 헤매고 다닙니다.

42. 병원에 가느라고 친구하고 만날 약속을 취소했습니다.

30.1.7. The Copula Transferentive: -어/-아다

43. 아버지한테 샌드위치를 싸다 드렸습니다.

44. 친구한테 문병을 갈 때 꽃을 사다 줬습니다.

45. 친구한테 도서관에서 책을 2권 빌려다 줬습니다.

46. 수미한테 이 서류를 영어로 번역을 해다 줘야 합니다.

30.1.8. Quoted Statements

47. 수미 씨가 경제학을 전공하는데 정치학으로 바꿔야 하겠다고 했습니다.

48. 친구가 대학 정문을 지나다가 유명한 영화배우를 우연히 만났다고 했습니다.

49. 엄마가 우리한테 요즘 아버지가 사업 때문에 신경을 너무 쓰신다고
     하셨습니다.

30.1.9. Quoted Questions

50. 대학원생이 교수한테 논문을 언제까지 제출하면 되(느)냐고 했습니다.

51. 목사님이 저한테 성경을 매일 읽고 기도를 하(느)냐고 물으셨습니다.

52. 나는 친구한테 오늘 저녁에 좀 만날 수 있(느)냐고 물었습니다.

30.1.10. Quoted Suggestions

53. 사촌이 기분전환으로 노래방에 가서 노래를 실컷 부르자고 했습니다.

54. 친구가 건강이 무엇보다도 중요하니까 운동을 시작하자고 했습니다.

55. 동생이 시내에 나온 김에 영화도 보고 헌책방에도 가자고 했습니다.

30.1.11. Quoted Commands

56. 엄마가 요즘 교통사고가 많이 나니까 조심해서 운전하라고 하셨습니다.

57. 아버지가 젊었을 때 여행을 많이 하고 좋은 친구를 많이 사귀라고 하셨습니다.

58. 저희 선생님이 언제나 최선을 다하라고 하셨습니다.

59. 친구가 한국으로 유학을 가려던 계획을 취소하라고 했습니다.

30.1.12. Special Uses of the Quoted Copula

60. 어제 길에서 만났던 분은 누구시라고 했습니까?

61. '엉터리 의사'를 영어로 뭐라고 합니까?

62. 저 사람은 자기가 유명한 배우라고 하는데 배우 같지 않습니다.

63. '편지'라는 한국 영화를 봤는데 무척 슬펐습니다.

30.1.13. *According to . . .* with *. . .*-에 의하면

64. 오늘 신문에 의하면 한국경제가 점점 좋아지고 있다고 합니다.

65. 저희 아버지의 말씀에 의하면 한국전쟁 후에 한국은 굉장히 가난했다고 하셨습니다.

66. 일기예보에 의하면 곧 장마가 진다고 합니다.

30.1.14. 달라(고) 하- to Quote 주-

67. 친구한테 내가 목욕을 하는 동안 전화를 좀 받아 달라고 부탁을 했습니다.

68. 엄마가 동생한테 차를 좀 빌려 주라고 하십니다.

69. 웨이터한테 맥주를 3병 더 갖다 달라고 했습니다.

30.1.15. The Particle (으)로: More Meanings

70. 이 병은 나이가 드신 분들한테 흔한 병으로 고칠 수는 없습니다.

71. 저 교수는 한국학 교수로 우리 대학에 방문 교수로 오셨습니다.

72. 우리 지하실 방을 내 사무실로 씁니다.

30.1.16. Retrospective Aspect

73. 장마철에 한국에 가니까 어떻던가요?

74. 이 교수님 연구실에 가니까 교수님이 벌써 집에 가셨더군요.

75. 저 가수는 거의 20년 전에 아주 유명했던 가수에요.

76. 전에 우리가 퇴근하고 가던 술집이 없어졌어요.

30.1.17. -던데(요)

77. 어제 교통사고로 다친 사람은 죽겠던데요.

78. 한국 시골에 가면 아직도 한국의 고유풍습을 볼 수 있던데요.

79. 대통령 후보들이 모두 다 법대를 나왔던데요.

30.1.18. Retrospective Conditionals in -더라면

80. 내가 어렸을 때부터 한국어를 공부했더라면 지금쯤은 아주 유창했을 거에요.

81. 중국에 갔을 때 중국어를 할 수 있었더라면 얼마나 좋았겠습니까!

82. 그 사람은 그런 스캔들이 없었더라면 국회의원으로 당선이 됐겠지요.

30.1.19. -더라고(요)

83. 독일에 갔을 때 독일어를 못 하니까 아주 불편하더라고요.

84. 상류사회 사람들은 대부분 너무 거만하더라고요.

85. 상철이가 10년 안에 꿈을 이루겠다고 했는데 정말 7년 만에 꿈을 이루더라고요.

30.1.20. *To the Extent that . . .* with -(으)ㄹ 정도(로)

86. 몸살이 날 정도로 운동을 한꺼번에 많이 했습니다.

87. 부페에 가서 배가 아플 정도로 많이 먹었습니다.

88. 주말에도 사무실에 나올 정도로 일이 밀렸습니다.

30.1.21. -고 나서: *after VERBing . . .*

89. 민수는 성공을 하고 나서 고향을 찾았습니다.

90. 나는 직장을 구하고 나서 결혼을 할 예정입니다.

91. 하느님을 믿고 나서 마음이 편안하고 즐겁습니다.

30.1.22. *for the sake of . . .* with (을/를) 위해(서)

92. 부모님들을 위해서 공부하지 말고 여러분들 자신을 위해서 공부를 하십시오.

93. 건강을 위해서 야채와 과일을 많이 먹고 운동을 하십시오.

94. 전쟁이 없는 세계를 위해서 항상 기도를 합시다.

30.1.23. -기도 하-, -기는 하-, -기만 하-

95. 음악회에 사람들이 많이 오기도 했네요.

96. 이 컴퓨터가 1000불이면 싸기도 하네요.

97. 7월인데 무덥기도 하네요.

98. 주말에 등산을 가기도 하고 낚시를 가기도 합니다.

99. 친구한테 이메일을 띄우기도 하고 편지를 보내기도 합니다.

100. 이곳은 겨울에 춥기도 하고 바람이 불기도 합니다.

101. 매운 음식을 먹기는 하지만 즐겨 먹지는 않습니다.

102. 외식을 하기는 하지만 집에서 먹는 것을 더 좋아합니다.

103. 고유의 결혼풍습이 있기는 하지만 요즘은 별로 인기가 없습니다.

104. 동생이 아파서 요즘은 자기만 합니다.

105. 요즘 시간이 많으니까 집에서 먹기만 합니다.

106. 아기가 밤에 자지 않고 울기만 해요.

30.1.24. *Is on the . . .ing side* with -(으)ㄴ/-는 편이-

107.　만호 씨는 약속을 잘 지키는 편입니까?

108.　저 학생은 게으른 편이라서 항상 야단쳐 줘야 된다.

30.1.25. *[TIME] since* with -(으)ㄴ 지

109.　한국어를 공부한 지 오래됐지만 아직 한국말을 유창하게 못 합니다.

110.　원고를 갖다 준 지 석 달이 됐는데도 원고료를 아직 못 받았습니다.

111.　제일 친했던 고등학교 친구하고 헤어진 지 벌써 5년이나 됐습니다.

30.1.26. Oblique Questions in -(으)ㄴ지, -는지, -(으)ㄹ지

<u>-(으)ㄴ지</u>

112.　저 야당의원은 어떤 사람인지 모르겠습니다.

113.　서울의 날씨가 추운지 어떤지 좀 물어봐 주십시오.

114.　그 사람이 거만한지 거만하지 않은지 아십니까?

<u>-는지</u>

115.　사촌 동생이 건강하게 잘 지내는지 궁금합니다.

116.　생선은 어디에 가야 좋은 것을 살 수 있는지 아십니까?

117.　시카고에서 오는 비행기가 얼마나 연착이 되는지 알아봅시다.

118.　저 거만한 사장이 전에는 얼마나 겸손했는지 모릅니다.

119.　내가 늦게 제출한 논문을 교수님이 받으셨는지 모르겠습니다.

-(으)ㄹ지

120. 내 친구한테 나하고 유럽여행을 같이 갈지 물어봐야겠습니다.

121. 제가 감기에 걸려서 이 일을 내일까지 끝낼 수 있을지 모르겠습니다.

122. 대전에 우선 급행열차로 갈지 완행열차로 갈지 결정합시다.

30.1.27. Polite Questions with . . . 가요 and . . . 나요

-(으)ㄴ가요
123. 저 사람이 대통령후보인가요?

124. 홍 교수님은 자녀분이 많으신가요? (= 많으시나요?)

125. 날씨가 많이 더운가요? (= 덥나요?)

126. 생일파티에 쓸 술이 충분한가요? (= 충분하나요?)

-는가요
127. 무슨 과목에 흥미가 있는가요? (= 있나요?)

128. 한국에서는 설날에 무엇을 하는가요? (= 하나요?)

129. 산 속에 가서 있는 동안 무엇을 깨달았는가요? (= 깨달았나요?)

-나요
130. 이 꽃집에서 어떤 꽃이 제일 예쁘나요? (= 예쁜가요?)

131. 새벽 4시에 떠나면 너무 이르지 않나요? (= 않은가요?)

132. 약속시간을 내 마음대로 정해도 되나요? (= 되는가요?)

133. 서양 사람들은 집 안에서 신을 안 벗나요? (= 벗는가요?)

134. 폭풍우 때문에 피해가 많았나요? (= 많았는가요?)

30.2. Verb Forms: Summary

Any Korean verb form used in a Korean sentence has two parts to it: a BASE and an ENDING. A base is not complete, ready for use, until it is finished off with an ending; and obviously, an ending must be attached to something before it can be put into a sentence (just as you don't use the English endings *-ing* or *-ed* in mid-air). When we summarize verb forms, then, we can most conveniently split our discussion into the two large categories BASES and ENDINGS.

30.2.1. Verb Bases

Here is a complete list of all the pure Korean verbs that have appeared so far in Lessons 16–29, classified according to type (vowel base, consonant base).

BASE   **GLOSS**

Vowel-base verbs

가지–	possess, hold, take
갈아타–	change (transport, lines, etc.)
개–	it clears up
건너–	cross (the street)
건네–	hand over, turn over, transfer
걸리–	catch (a sickness, disease)
고치–	fix it, repair it
그러–	say (so); think (so)
그만두–	quit, stop doing it
그치–	[rain/snow] stops
깨–	wake up (intransitive)
깨–	break it
깨우–	awaken sb, wake sb up
깨지–	get broken
꺼내–	broach (a subject); take out
끓이–	boil it; make [a stew]
끼–	(clouds/fog) form, gather
끼–	fasten (a snap)
나–	exit, come out, appear
나누–	share, divide
나오–	[a subject] comes up
나타나–	appear, put in an appearance; show up
내–	hand in, turn in
내다 보–	look out (at)
내려다 보–	look down at/upon

Lesson Thirty / 360

내리-	*get off (a bus, train); let sb off/out*
넘어지-	*fall down*
놀라-	*be surprised*
놀러 가-	*go on an outing; go [to sb's house] to visit*
놀리-	*make fun of, tease*
놓치-	*miss (bus, plane)*
느리-	*be slow*
닫히-	*get closed/ shut*
당기-	*pull it*
더듬거리-	*stutter or speak haltingly*
데리-	*take (person) along*
돌려 주-	*give back*
두-	*put, place; leave (behind)*
드려다 보-	*look in (through), peep in (through)*
들리-	*stop by, drop in*
따-	*be different*
때리-	*hit, strike, beat*
떨어지-	*fall; run out of s.th.*
띄우-	*send (email)*
막히-	*get/be blocked, congested*
맞추-	*have (clothes) made to order*
멋지-	*be stylish, cool, elegant*
모시-	*(humble) take (sb) along, accompany sb*
못 되-	*be bad, bad-natured, evil, wicked, good-for-nothing*
못 생기-	*ugly*
밀리-	*be backed up, congested (cars, traffic)*
바꾸-	*(ex)change it, trade it*
바치-	*offer up, sacrifice*
밝히-	*make bright or clear; clarify, explain*
보이-	*be visible, "shows"; show it*
붉히-	*make it red, redden it*
비키-	*get out of the way*
빌려 주-	*lend*
빌리-	*borrow; rent (a car)*
빠지-	*fall (into); come out/ fall off (hair, etc.); lose (weight)*
뿌리-	*sprinkle it*
삼키-	*swallow it*
생기-	*come about, happen*
서-	*stop, come to a stop*
세우-	*bring it to a stop*
숨기-	*hide it, conceal it*
시-	*be sour*
싸우-	*quarrel, argue with*
알리-	*let somebody know; inform*

Lesson Thirty / 361

어기-	break (a promise)
어울리-	spend time with, hang around with, associate with
어울리-	fit, go well with, match with
없어지-	disappear
여기-	consider
여쭈-	asks sb esteemed
여쭤 보-	asks sb esteemed
열리-	open, be opened
웃기-	be (act) funny; make one laugh
이기-	win; beat
이루-	achieve, bring about
잃어버리-	lose something
자라-	it grows
잡숴 보시-	[sb esteemed] eat s.th., try s.th.
재-	take measurements of, measure
재-	take (sb's pulse)
졸리-	be sleepy; feel sleepy
죽이-	kill
지-	lose (to)
지나가-	pass by
지키-	keep (appointment/promise); abide by, stick to
짜-	be (too) salty
찌-	steam it; gain (weight)
차리-	prepare, make ready; collect, concentrate
찾아 가-	call on; visit, go calling on
찾아 오-	call on; visit, come calling on
치-	reckon, calculate
켜-	turn on, switch on
터지-	it bursts
튀기-	deep-fry it
틀리-	be different; be wrong, incorrect
팔리-	be sold, get sold, "sell (well)"
편찮으시-	be ill, not well (honorific)
헤어지-	separate from, part with, split up with
혼(을) 내-	give sb a hard time; give a good scolding
혼(이) 나-	have a hard time of it, have an awful time/experience
화(가) 나-	get angry
화(를) 내-	get angry
훔치-	steal it, swipe it
흐리-	be cloudy, overcast
흘리-	spill it; shed (tears)

○-DROPPING VOWEL-BASE VERBS

고프-	be hungry, feel hungry
기쁘-	be happy, content
끄-	turn off, switch off; extinguish
들르-	drop in, drop by
모으-	gather (it), collect
못 쓰-	be no good, worthless
슬프-	feel sad, sorrowful
쓰-	be bitter
잠그-	fasten (buttons, snaps); lock (door, window)

ㄹ-DOUBLING VOWEL-BASE VERBS

게으르-	be lazy
기르-	breed, raise, grow
마르-	dry up; be/get dry
마르-	be thirsty, feel thirsty
바르-	apply, smear it
서두르-	hurry, hasten, make haste
이르-	be early
자르-	cut (one's hair)
조르-	pester for, keep after for

ㄹ-EXTENDING VOWEL-BASE VERBS

기-ㄹ-	be long
끄-ㄹ-	drag; pull, draw
다-ㄹ-	be sweet
도-ㄹ-	turn, spin; make a round; go around
미-ㄹ-	push it
버-ㄹ-	earn, make (money)
부-ㄹ-	blow
빠-ㄹ-	wash (clothes), launder
여-ㄹ-	have/host (a party)
우-ㄹ-	cry, weep
조-ㄹ-	doze

CONSONANT-BASE VERBS

감-	wash (hair)
귀찮-	be a pain in the neck, be a nuisance, be annoying
깊-	be deep
깎-	cut (one's hair)
끊-	break it off; hang up [phone]
낡-	get old (things)
남-	remain, be left over
낮-	be low

낳–	*give birth to; have (baby)*
넓–	*be wide, broad; spacious*
넘–	*exceed, be more than; pass beyond*
높–	*be high, tall*
늙–	*get old (people)*
다듬–	*trim, spruce up; give final embellishments to*
맑–	*be clear*
맞–	*get (a shot, injection)*
믿–	*believe*
밝–	*be bright, light, clear*
볶–	*cook in a skillet or frying pan*
붉–	*be red; crimson*
뽑–	*take out, extract*
삶–	*boil it*
삼–	*make s.th. of (a person or thing)*
숨–	*hide, conceal oneself*
씹–	*chew it*
씻–	*wash*
얕–	*be shallow*
얻–	*get, obtain*
옅–	*be light (color); thin (fog)*
웃–	*smile; laugh*
잡–	*catch, grasp, take hold of*
점잖–	*be well-behaved, decent, respectable*
짙–	*be deep, rich, dark (color); thick (fog)*
짚–	*take (sb's pulse)*
짧–	*be short*

W - ㅂ VERBS

귀여w–	*be cute*
더러w–	*be filthy, dirty*
도w–	*help*
뜨거w–	*be hot to the touch*
만나 뵈w–	*meet [with] sb esteemed; see sb esteemed*
무더w–	*be hot and muggy*
미끄러w–	*be slippery*
반가w–	*be pleased to see/hear sb/s.th.*
뵈w–	*humbly see or meet; have an audience/ interview with*
부끄러w–	*feel embarrassed, ashamed*
부러w–	*be envious*
새로w–	*be new*
시끄러w–	*be noisy, loud*
싱거w–	*be bland, not salted enough*
아름다w–	*be beautiful*

어두w-	*be dark*
차가w-	*be cold to the touch*
찾아 뵈w-	*call on sb esteemed; visit, come calling on sb esteemed*

ㄹ-ㄷ Verbs
깨달- (ㄹ~ㄷ)	*realize, come to realize*

ㅅ-Ø Verbs
나(ㅅ)-	*be preferable, better than*
부(ㅅ)-	*pour it*
지(ㅅ)-	*build (house); make (rice)*

ㅎ- Irregular Verbs
그렇-	*be so, be like that, be that way*
까맣-	*be black, dark*
노랗-	*be yellow*
빨갛-	*be red*
새까맣-	*be jet-black*
새노랗-	*be vivid yellow*
새빨갛-	*be bright red*
새파랗-	*be vivid deep blue*
새하얗-	*be bright white*
파랗-	*be blue*
하얗-	*be white*

30.2.2. Verb Endings

Endings, added to bases, make the verb form complete. In addition to this function, they often perform another job at the same time: they tell whether or not you have come to the end of a sentence.

Broadly speaking, there are two types of verb ending in Korean: some are FINAL (the ending completes a sentence), and some are NONFINAL (the ending does not complete a sentence; many of this type are CONNECTIVE). In this latter category are the infinitive ending -어/ -아, etc. (except in the Intimate Style, where it can end a sentence), the suspective ending -지 (except in the Intimate Style, where it can end a sentence), connective -고, and the conditional ending in -(으)면) endings.

Here are all the endings you have learned in *Continuing Korean*, grouped according to whether they are Final or Nonfinal.

FINAL ENDINGS

[as Intimate Style]	-어/-아; -지
[. . . , *you see*]	-거든요
[First Realization]	-(는)군요!
[Mild Surprise]	-네요
[Imminent Elaboration]	-는데(요), -은데(요), -ㄴ데(요)
[Plain Style Statements]	-다, -ㄴ다, -는다
[Plain Style Questions]	-(으)냐, -느냐; -니
[Plain Style Suggestions]	-자
[Plain Style Commands]	-(으)라; -어라, -아라, -여라
[Retrospective Aspect]	-습디다/-ㅂ디다, -습디까?/-ㅂ디까?; -더군(요)!
	-데요, -더라고(요), -던가요? -던데요
	-더라, -더냐?, -디?, -더군!
[Polite Questions]	-(으)ㄴ가(요)?/ -는가(요)?
[Polite Questions]	-나요

NONFINAL ENDINGS

[the -고 Form]	-고
[Infinitive (followed by particles)]	-어/-아
[Nominalizer Form]	-기
[Modifiers]	-(으)ㄹ; -(으)ㄴ; -는; -던
[*and; while*]	-(으)며
[Conditional]	-(으)면
[Intentive]	-(으)려(고)
[*if one intends to DO*]	-(으)려면
[*While*]	-(으)면서(도)
[Transferentive]	-다(가)
[*In spite of . . .ing*]	-는/-은/-ㄴ데도
[*was going to . . . , but*]	-(으)려다가
[Adverbative]	-게
[*Because of . . .ing*]	-느라(고)
[Retrospective Conditionals]	-더라면
[*after VERBing . . .*]	-고 나서

Nearly all of these NONFINAL endings enter into a wide variety of patterns that have already been introduced in the lesson notes. Check the Korean-to-English Pattern Glossary for a full list.

As you learned in *Elementary Korean*, Korean verb endings can be classified another way, according to the number of alternate shapes they have. Here are all the endings you have learned in *Continuing Korean*, grouped according to whether they are one-shape or two-shape or three-shape.

ONE-SHAPE ENDINGS

[the -고 Form]	-고
[Nominalizer Form]	-기
[Processive Modifier]	-는
[Retrospective Modifier]	-던 (also -던가요? and -던데요)
[Transferentive]	-다(가)
[Adverbative]	-게
[*Because of . . .ing*]	-느라(고)
[Retrospective Conditional]	-더라면
[*after VERBing . . .*]	-고 나서
[Intimate Style]	-지
[. . . , *you see*]	-거든요
[Mild Surprise]	-네요
[Plain Style Questions]	-니
[Plain Style Suggestions]	-자
[Retrospective Apperceptive]	-더군(요)!
[Retrospective Aspect]	-데요; -더라고(요); -더라; -더냐?; -디?
[(Polite) Questions]	-나(요)?

Several peculiarities must be mentioned about one-shape endings.

1. The base 잡수시- *eat* can abbreviate to 잡숫- before one-shape endings:

잡수시고	→	잡숫고	*[sb esteemed] eats, and . . .*
잡수시지만	→	잡숫지만	*[sb esteemed] eats, but . . .*
잡수시겠어요	→	잡숫겠어요	*[sb esteemed] will eat*

2. One-shape endings are attached to the EXTENDED BASES of L-extending verbs:

아-ㄹ-	*know*	알지만	*knows, but . . .*
		알고	*knows, and . . .*
		알겠어요	*knows* or *will know*

The only exceptions are the endings that begin with ㄴ: Mild Exclamations in -네요, Plain Style Questions in -니, (Polite) Questions in -나(요), -느라(고), and the Processive Modifier -는:

잘 아네요!	*I see you know this stuff!*
아니?	*Do you know?*
아나요?	*Do you know?*
차를 파느라고	*In the course of selling the car . . .*
차를 파는 사람	*the person selling the car*

3. When a one-shape ending that begins with ㄷ, ㅈ, or ㄱ is attached to a consonant base that ends in ㅎ, the strings -ㅎ.ㄷ-, -ㅎ.ㅈ-, and -ㅎ.ㄱ- are pronounced -ㅌ-, -ㅊ-, and -ㅋ-:

좋- *be good*	좋지	〔조치〕
	좋고	〔조코〕
	좋던가요?-	〔조턴가요〕

This is true also of ㅀ and ㄶ:

많- *be much/many*	많지	〔만치〕
	많고	〔만코〕
	많던가요?	〔만턴가요〕
싫- *be disliked*	싫지	〔실치〕
	싫고	〔실코〕
	싫던가요?	〔실턴가요?〕

If the ending begins with some other consonant—the only common case is ㄴ—the final ㅎ after a vowel is pronounced as if it were ㄴ: 좋네요! *Gee, it's good!* is pronounced 존네요, just as 못 받네요! *He just can't catch it!* is pronounced 반네요. The clusters ㄶ and ㅀ reduce to ㄴ and ㄹ: 많네요! is pronounced 만네요, 싫네요! is pronounced 실레요.

4. When a one-shape ending is attached to a consonant base that ends in /w/, the /w/ changes to ㅂ:

도 w- *help*	돕지	〔돕찌〕
	돕고	〔돕꼬〕
	돕던가요?	〔돕떤가요〕
	돕네요	〔돔네요〕

Were it not for the other forms (도와, 도우면, 도우시-) we would not know that such bases are different from the usual bases ending in ㅂ like 입- *wear*: 입지, 입고, 입겠-, 입네요; 입어, 입으면, 입으시-. In traditional Korean grammar, the /w/-verbs are called "irregular ㅂ- verbs."

5. When a one-shape ending is attached to a consonant base that ends in ㄹ, the ㄹ changes to ㄷ:

들-	*hear*	들지	〔드찌〕
		들고	〔드꼬〕
		들던가요?	〔드떤가요〕
		들네요	〔든네요〕

Notice the difference between the behavior of these bases and the L-extending vowel bases: 드-ㄹ- *lift; cost* has the forms 들지, 들고, 들겠-, 드네요. The infinitives are the same; both 드-ㄹ- and 들- come out as 들어.

But the conditional forms are different: 들면 is from 드-ㄹ- *cost; enter,* 들으면 is from 들- *hear, listen.* And the honorific forms are also different: 드시면 is from 드-ㄹ-, 들으시면 is from 들-. In traditional Korean grammar, the consonant bases that end in ㄹ are called "irregular ㄷ-verbs." (Note that a "regular" ㄷ-verb like 닫- "close it" will have similar forms when attaching most one-shape endings (닫지, 닫고, 닫겠-) but different forms when attaching two-shape endings (닫으면, 닫으시-) or forming the infinitive (닫아)).

6. The usual automatic sound changes take place when a base ending in a consonant attaches an ending shape that begins with a consonant. First, if the base ends in a consonant or cluster other than ㅂ, ㄷ, ㄱ, ㅁ, ㄴ, ㄹ, in pronouncing the resulting form you reduce the consonant or cluster to one of those: ㅄ and ㅍ are treated like ㅂ; ㄲ and usually ㄺ are treated like ㄱ; ㄻ is treated like ㅁ; ㄵ is treated like ㄴ; ㅅ, ㅆ, ㅈ, and ㅊ are all treated like ㄷ.

TWO-SHAPE ENDINGS

	AFTER VOWEL	AFTER CONSONANT
[Prospective Modifier]	-ㄹ	-을
[Modifier]	-ㄴ	-은
[*and; while*]	-며	-으며
[Conditional]	-면	-으면
[Intentive]	-려(고)	-으려고
[*if one intends to DO*]	-려면	-으려면
[*While*]	-면서(도)	-으면서(도)
[*was going to . . . , but*]	-려다가	-으려다가
[Plain Style Commands]	-라	-으라
[Retrospective Aspect]	-ㅂ디다	-습디다
	-ㅂ디까?	-습디까?
[First Realization]	-(는)군요!	
[Infinitive]	-어/-아	
[Plain Style Commands]	-어라, -아라, -여라	

The only special feature about two-shape endings is that the endings -(으)며, -(으)면, -(으)면서(도), -(으)려(고), -(으)려다(가), -(으)려면 and -(으)라 are attached to the EXTENDED base of L-extending bases:

노-ㄹ-	*play*	놀며,	놀면,	놀면서(도),
		놀려고,	놀려다가,	놀려면,
		놀라		

PATTERNS BASED ON THE INFINITIVE

[infinitive] -어/-아

["even if, even though"] -어도/-아도
 Asking and Giving Permission
 -어도 좋-, -어도 괜찮-, -어도 되-

 Doesn't have to. . .
 -지 않아도 좋-, -지 않아도 괜찮-, -지 않아도 되-

["only if"] -어야/-아야
 -어야 되-, -어야 하-

['and so; and then'] -어서/-아서
 I'm glad that . . . ; Good thing that . . .
 -어서 좋아요

 so . . . I could die
 -어서 죽겠어요:

["get/become"] -어 + 져요 (지-)

[sensory verbs, 3rd Person] -어 해요
[compound verbs] -어 가- , -어 오-
[resultant states] -어 있-
[exploratory pattern] -어 봐요
[favors] -어 줘요

THREE-SHAPE ENDINGS

Finally, you have learned the following three-shape endings.

1. the "Imminent Elaboration" forms built on Circumstantial -데:

      Descriptive Vowel Base: -ㄴ데(요)
      Descriptive Consonant Base: -은데(요)

      Processive Bases,
      Past and Future Bases, and   -는데(요)
      있- and 없-

2. *In spite of . . .ing* with -는/-은/-ㄴ데도:

      Descriptive Vowel Base: -ㄴ데도
      Descriptive Consonant Base: -은데도

      Processive Bases,
      Past and Future Bases, and   -는데도
      있- and 없-

3. Polite Questions in -(으)ㄴ가(요)?/ -는가(요)?:

      Descriptive Vowel Base: -ㄴ가(요)?
      Descriptive Consonant Base: -은가(요)?

      Processive Bases,
      Past and Future Bases, and   -는가(요)?
      있- and 없-

4. Plain Style Questions in -(으)냐, -느냐:

      Descriptive Vowel Base: -냐?
      Descriptive Consonant Base: -으냐?

      Processive Bases,
      Past and Future Bases, and   -느냐?
      있- and 없-

5. Plain Style statements in -다, -ㄴ다, -는다:

Processive Vowel Bases:	-ㄴ다
Processive Consonant Bases:	-는다

All Descriptive Bases, Past and Future Bases, and 있- and 없-	-다

30.3. Particles, Particle Phrases, Postnouns, and Suffixes: Summary

Here is a list of the particles, particle phrases, postnouns and suffixes covered in *Continuing Korean*. In short, any "particle-like" thing that can attach to a noun.

NOUN -네
NOUN보다
NOUN말고
NOUN에 관해서   *about, concerning*
NOUN에 대해서   *about, concerning*
NOUN으로
NOUN (을/를) 위해(서)   *for the sake of NOUN*
NOUN에 의하면   *According to . . .*
NOUN에다(가)
NOUN -이   (Diminutive)

Note also that, technically speaking, the 하고 and -(이)라고 used for verbatim quotations are a kind of (quotation) particle, as is the -고 used for indirect quotations. Likewise, this book treats the 야, 도, and 서 in the patterns -어야, -어도 and -어서 as particles, too.

30.4. Auxiliary Verbs: Summary

For our purposes here, we can define "auxiliary verb" as any verb that occurs with (and follows) another primary (and preceding) verb to produce a discrete pattern.

You have encountered the following auxiliary verbs:

가-	as in compound verbs like 돌아가-, etc.
마-르-	as in -지 말아요, -지 마세요, etc.
보-	as in the exploratory pattern in -어 봐요
싶-	as in the "want to" pattern in -고 싶-
주-	as in the favor pattern in -어 줘요
않-	as in -지 않아요, etc.
오-	as in compound verbs like 돌아오-, etc.
-있-	as in resultant states in -어 있어요
지-	as in -어져요 *get/become*
하-	as in 3rd person sensory verbs in -어해요
하-	as in -기도 해요, -기만 해요, -기는 해요

REVIEW EXERCISES

Grammar Practice

Exercise 1: Convert to Plain Style

The following short statements should all be translated using the Plain Style.

1. That hospital is too small.
2. There is a bag in my room.
3. I don't know.
4. It's getting late.
5. Does he buy clothes often?
6. I waited for my friend.
7. Does he live here?
8. It's a long way to Pusan.
9. Can you do it this way?

10. I'm not tired.
11. He'll be better by tomorrow.
12. let's buy this one!
13. Will he go to school?
14. Is it too sweet?
15. My doctor is very kind.
16. He drives dangerously.
17. His wife will die tomorrow?
18. I don't lie down during the day time.
19. It costs 15,000 won.
20. I'm staying at school this afternoon.

Exercise 2: Convert to Quotations

The following English sentences all contain quotations. Translate each one into Korean twice over, once using a direct quotation, once using an indirect quotation pattern.

1. My brother asked why you were going out.
2. My mother said "you can come to visit us tonight."
3. He suggested that we eat together.
4. He said that his brother is a famous singer.
5. Mr. Kim thinks that old women are often fat.
6. My brother says that Dad reads too much.
7. My wife asked her friend if she could buy her some apples.
8. He says he'll clean his room tomorrow.
9. I asked "Is this Mr. Kim's house?"
10. He told me to study harder.

Exercise 3: Convert to Retrospectives

Translate the following sentences into Korean using the Retrospective Aspect construction that you learned in Lesson 28. Be sure to use the style indicated.

Using the Formal Style:

1. (I noticed) Mr. Kim was sending a telegram this morning.
2. They say it usually rains on Tuesday.
3. Does he love her?
4. He repaired his bike before going to school.
5. Next week will be the start of the rainy season.
6. What's the beer like?

Using the Plain Style:

7. They say he died yesterday.
8. My wife is studying in her room at the moment.
9. It's going to be cold tomorrow.
10. When did it begin to get warmer?
11. Many valuables were stolen from the jewelry shop.
12. Did she buy those shoes in town?

Using the Polite Style (or *it's a fact that . . .*)

13. The doctor was going to the airport.
14. (It's a fact that) he will not go tomorrow.
15. He's singing again!
16. The king doesn't want his son to be a rock star.
17. Did you give a lecture yesterday?
18. I heard she had a big fight with her boyfriend.

Exercise 4: Convert to Questions in . . .가요 and
. . .나요

Translate the following questions into Korean. Use the Type 1 question forms of Lesson 29 for the first five and the Type 2 forms from the same Lesson for the second five.

1.   Is that thing he's reading a magazine?
2.   Is there plenty of food for supper?
3.   Is that car fast?
4.   Is that painter very famous?
5.   Is he studying?
6.   Will you be late tonight?
7.   Is my brother telling jokes again?!
8.   How many times have you seen that musician play?
9.   Did you have a drought in England last summer?
10.   Is that the room you used to read in?

Korean to English Translation

Translate the following Korean sentences into English.

Exercise 5

1.   어제 밤 우리와 같이 저녁식사를 하신 분이 우리 아버지에요.
2.   비싼 시계도 좋아요.
3.   비가 왔기 때문에 새 구두를 신을 수 없었지요.
4.   방학이어서 내일 집에 갈 거에요.
5.   내 옆에 앉을 사람이 와요. [*Here comes* . . .]
6.   영미가 신문을 읽는 동안(에), 나는 숙제를 마치겠어요.
7.   영미가 말 한 것을 듣지 못 했어요.
8.   오늘은 외식하지 않고 집에서 먹겠어요.
9.   김 선생 옆에 앉은 사람이 유명한 음악가지요.
10.   일기예보에 의하면, 날씨가 좋을 거라고 했어요.

11. 우리 밭에 꽃을 심은 사람이 김 선생의 밭에도 심었어요.
12. 저 간호사는 환자들한테 너무 불친절해요.
13. 다방에 같이 가서 차 좀 마실까요?
14. 밤에 눈이 왔으면 좋겠어요.
15. 저렇게 높은 산을 보신 일이 있어요?
16. 일기예보를 좀 듣지요. 듣기는 듣지만 잘 안 맞아요.
17. 운동장에 있었을 때, 학생들이 운동을 하는 것을 봤어요.
18. 나는 이 일을 빨리 마치고 싶은데 떠나시기 전에 도와주실 수 있으세요?
19. 편지를 매일 우체국에 가지고 가는 사람이 있어요.
20. 어제 저녁을 먹고 있을 때 손님이 오셨어요.
21. 날이 너무 추워서 집에 있는 게 낫겠어요.
22. 내년에 대학을 졸업하기 위해서 최선을 다하겠어요.
23. 일어는 잘 읽을 수 없지만, 중국어는 좀 읽을 수 있어요.
24. 그 아이가 걸을 수도 없으면서 뛰려고 해요.
25. 우리가 테니스를 치는 동안에 비가 오기 시작했어요.
26. 우리 팀이 내일 축구시합에 이겼으면 좋겠어요.
27. 아침에 너무 바빴기 때문에 은행에 갈 시간이 없었어요.
28. 음악회에 걸어 가지 말고 택시를 부를까요?
29. 그 상점에 비싼 옷도 있고, 싼 옷도 있어요.
30. A. 에릭씨 보기에 이 두 색깔이 같지요?
    B. 아니오, 달라요.
31. 우리에게 영어를 가르쳐 주시는 분이 김 선생(에게)도 가르쳐 드려요.
32. 그 사람은 게으르지도 않지만, 부지런하지도 않아요.
33. 제가 아침을 먹을 때 손님이 오면 없다고 하세요.
34. 박 선생의 녹음기를 제가 좀 들을 수 있어요?
35. 그 여자는 노래 부르기도 좋아하지도 않고, 피아노 치기도 좋아하지 않아요.
36. 어젯밤에 김 선생이 자전거를 타는 것을 봤어요.
37. 극장에 저녁을 먹은 후에 가지 말고 저녁을 먹기 전에 갈까요?
38. 어제 밤 본 영화는 좋지 않았어요.
39. 참 재미 있는 이야기였지요?
40. 이렇게 재미 있는 이야기를 들으신 일이 있어요?
41. 어제 밤에 들은 노래를 부른 사람은 유명한 성악가에요.
42. 핑계만 대는 것은 좋지 않아요.
43. 바람 부는 것을 들을 수 있어요?
44. 저 선생님 뒤에 앉은 사람이 누구에요?
45. 어제 밤 음식점에서 저녁을 먹을 때 김 선생을 봤어요.
46. 내가 사고 싶은 양복은 대단히 비싸요.

47. 내가 숙제를 해 주면 내 방 청소를 해 줄래요?

48. 영국에 가 본 일은 없지만 미국에 가 본 일은 있어요.

49. 저는 미국서 태어났지만 어렸을 때 한국에 왔어요.

50. 내년 여름에 유럽 여행을 가기 위해서 돈을 모으고 있습니다.

English to Korean Translation

Translate the following sentences into Korean.

Exercise 6

1. I suppose the books in this store are pretty expensive?

2. Do you know Mr. Kim's maternal aunt who lives in Pusan?

3. I've never been this sick before.

4. Can you see the tall green trees on that mountain?

5. He told me a story, but I didn't understand it.

6. How about playing tennis with me?

7. I've decided not to go out this evening.

8. The food we had last night was delicious.

9. You do nothing but eat!

10. People who live in Korea eat a lot of rice.

11. He plays baseball well, and also plays the piano well.

12. The house in back of ours is blue.

13. A. You like music, don't you?

    B. Of course!

14. Before we go play soccer, let's rest a little.

15. Did you see the man who went into that low building over there?

16. I don't like to study, but I have to if I want to get good marks.

17. It's exam time, so I can't fool around these days.

18. I don't like days when it's raining.

19. What are you planning to do after you graduate from high school?

20. I'm sorry you got sick and couldn't go to the concert last night.

21. Did the burglar who stole your watch get away by the gate?

22. Who's that man standing in front of the bank?

23. It looks as if it's beginning to snow.

24. How about talking to me while you eat?
25. A. What kind of weather do you like?

    B. I like sunny days and I also like cloudy days.
26. Whose textbook is that on the chair?
27. Do you like to take walks in the rain (= while it's raining)?
28. This bookstore is nice and big, isn't it?
29. In my opinion, this is a very cheap dress.
30. It looks as if we won't have time to finish our game before it gets dark.
31. They were playing tennis while I was doing my homework.
32. If you'd like, you may bring a friend to the soccer game with you.
33. I hope our team will win the soccer game!
34. See that man? He's a famous novel writer.
35. The movie theater is so far from here that I think we'd better take a taxi.
36. My brother plays tennis well and studies hard too.
37. We'd better take a taxi so we can get home before it rains.
38. I hope to learn to play tennis next year.
39. I'm doing my best to finish reading this book before it's time to go to bed.
40. I can read English, but I can't read Russian.
41. You're going to the tennis court again? You do nothing but play tennis all the time!
42. My mother promised to buy me a blue dress.
43. Do you ever have breakfast in bed?
44. It looked like rain, so I decided not to go downtown.
45. According to the papers, the famous singer is sick and can't come to our school tomorrow.
46. A. Why don't you read this book?

    B. I *did* read it, but I didn't understand it.
47. The sun tried to come out, but then it turned cloudy.
48. That student has a fine attitude, but he seems to be lazy.
49. You must hate having to get up so early in the morning, don't you?
50. It snowed while we were asleep.

KOREAN to ENGLISH VOCABULARY

가난하- be poor, indigent (18)

가루 powder (26)

가만히 quietly; still; cautiously (22)

가정의 family doctor (26)

가져가-/가져오- take/bring (thing) along (24)

가족제도 family system (28)

가지- possess, hold, take (24)

가지고 가- take (thing) along (24)

가지고 오- bring (thing) along (24)

가지고 있- have, have in one's possession (21)

간 the saltiness of a dish or food (22)

간(을) 보- check the saltiness of a dish or food (22)

간장 soy sauce (22)

간호사 nurse (26)

갈비 ribs (16)

갈색 the color brown; brown (21)

갈아타- change (transport, lines, etc.) (16)

감- wash (hair) (16)

감기 a cold (21)

감기몸살 severe cold; flu (21)

감사 magistrate, auditor (29)

감자국 [-꾹] potato soup (22)

강연 lecture (a special lecture) (16)

강의 lecture (in a series or course) (16)

강의(를) 하- lecture, give a lecture (16)

갖고 있- have s.th. with one, have (24)

개- it clears up (21)

개울 stream, brook (19)

개인 individual person (26)

거리 street (18)

거리 distance (26)

거만하- be arrogant (28)

거실 living room (23)

거의 nearly, almost, well-nigh (16)

거절(을) 하- refuse sb/s.th. (24)

거짓말 lie, fib (21)

거짓말쟁이 liar (21)

건너(에) across [from NOUN] (27)

건너- cross (the street) (16)

건네- hand over, turn over, transfer (29)

걸리- catch (a sickness, disease) (19)

검사 inspection, test (26)

검사(를) 하- inspect, test, examine (26)

게으르- be lazy (16)

게으름뱅이 lazybones, lazy person (21)

결국 ultimately, as a result, in the end, in the final analysis (24)

결석(을) 하- be absent (from school) (21)

결승전 the finals (29)

결정 decision (18)

결정(을) 하- decide it (18)

결혼식	wedding ceremony (17)	공기	air (22)
결혼식장	wedding venue (17)	공부벌레	nerd; somebody who does nothing but study (27)
겸손하–	be modest (28)		
경제발전	economic development (24)	공산주의	communism (28)
		공평하–	be fair (23)
경찰	policeman (24)	공항	airport (18)
경찰서	police station (24)	공해	pollution (21)
경치	scenery (21)	–과	department (18)
경험	experience (28)	–과	lesson (18)
경험(을) 하–	experience it (28)	과자	biscuit(s), cookie(s) (21)
계란	(chicken-) egg (22)		
계속(해서)	continuously, still [at it], without interruption (21)	과장(님)	Head of Dept., dept. chairman (18)
		과학	science (24)
계속하–	continues it/it continues (21)	관객	spectator, audience (28)
계절	season (23)	교과서	textbook (21)
계획	plan (24)	교류	interchange (24)
고구마	sweet potato (22)	교민	resident overseas Korean(s) (23)
고단하–	be tired, fatigued, weary (21)	교정(을) 하–	proofread it (29)
고등학교	high school (28)	교통	traffic (22)
고생(을) 하–	suffer hardship(s), suffer (29)	교통사고	traffic accident (26)
		교통위반(을) 하–	commit a driving/ traffic infraction (29)
고약하–	be ugly, wicked, nasty, hard to deal with (24)	교포	overseas Korean(s) (23)
고약한 놈	S. O. B. [term of abuse] (24)	구름	cloud (21)
고유...	indigenous, inherent (28)	구운 밤	roasted chestnuts (21)
		구체적으로	concretely, specifically (24)
고유풍습	indigenous customs (28)	구하–	look for [work, a job]; buy, get, obtain (26)
고장(이) 나–	s.th. breaks, breaks down, gets out of order (28)	구하–	save it, rescue it (28)
		국	soup (22)
고전	an old book; a classic (29)	국제–	international (24)
고전소설	Korean traditional novel (29)	국제관계	international relations (24)
고추	(red) pepper (22)	국제교류	international [human] exchange (24)
고추가루	red pepper powder (26)	국회의원 후보	candidate for member of the national assembly (28)
고치–	fix it, repair it (24)		
고프–	be hungry, feel hungry (16)	궁금하–	be/feel curious about (17)
고향	hometown (22)		
곧	any moment now, right away, before long, at once (21)	권사	(church) Elder [female] (24)
		귀여w–	be cute (19)
골뱅이	snail; "@" in email addresses (28)	귀중품	valuables (28)

귀찮-	be a pain in the neck, be a nuisance, be annoying (16)
그	he, that person [male] (26)
그대로	intact, just as it is (28)
그러-	say (so); think (so) (27)
그러-, 그래요	do so, do like that (21)
그런 NOUN	such a/that sort of NOUN (19)
그렇-, 그래요	be so, be like that, be that way (21)
그릇	bowl, dish, vessel; plate (24)
그리	so, to that extent, in that way (16)
그만두-	quit, stop doing it (18)
그만하-	quit, stop doing it (18)
그저 그렇-	be so-so (22)
그치-	[rain/snow] stops (24)
글피	3 days from now (21)
금강산	Diamond Mountains, Kŭmgang Mountains (28)
급하-	be urgent (26)
급행	express (train, bus) (19)
급행 버스	express bus (19)
급행열차	express train (19)
급히	hastily, in a rush (26)
기-ㄹ-	be long (18)
기간	time period, interval (28)
기고(를) 하-	submit an article (29)
기꺼이	with pleasure (23)
기도	prayer (24)
기도(를) 하-	pray (24)
기르-	breed, raise, grow (27)
기름	oil; gasoline, petrol (18)
기름(을) 넣-	get gas, put in gas (18)
기분전환	change of mood (22)
기쁘-	be happy, content (16)
기사 (아저씨)	driver, chauffeur (23)
기생	a "kisaeng," Korean geisha (29)
기억(을) 하-	remember (19)\
기억(이) 나-	remember (19)
기운(이) 없-	have no energy (26)
기입(을) 하-	fill in (a form) (17)

기침(을) 하-	cough (24)
기타	guitar (18)
기타(를) 치-	play the guitar (18)
길거리 [	main road, thoroughfare (18)
김치	kimchee (16)
김치찌개	kimchee stew (22)
깊-	be deep (19)
까만(색)	(the color) black; black (21)
까맣-, 까매요	be black, dark (22)
깎-	cut (one's hair) (16)
깜빡	(forgot) totally (29)
깨-	wake up (intransitive) (17)
깨-	break it (29)
깨달- (ㄹ ~ ㄷ)	realize, come to realize (28)
깨우-	awaken sb, wake sb up (17)
깨지-	get broken (29)
꺼내-	bring up, broach (a subject); take out (e.g. from pocket) (28)
껌	chewing gum (22)
껌(을) 씹-	chew gum (22)
꽤	rather, quite (28)
꿈(을) 이루-	achieve/realize one's dream (28)
끄-	turn off, switch off; extinguish (22)
끄-ㄹ-	drag; pull, draw (26)
끊-	break it off; hang up [phone] (27)
끓이-	boil it; make [a stew] (22)
끝으로	finally, lastly (24)
끼-	(clouds/fog) form, gather (21)
끼-	fasten (a snap) (21)

ㄴ

나(ㅅ)-	be preferable, better [than = 보다] (23)
나-	exit, come out, appear (17)
나누-	share, divide (16)

나쁜 놈	S. O. B. [term of abuse] (24)	논문	(academic) paper; thesis (27)
나오-	[a subject] comes up (23)	놀라-	be surprised (24)
나이 드신 분	old person, oldster [respectful] (19)	놀러 가-	go on an outing, excursion or picnic; go [to sb's house] to visit (22)
나중에	later, afterward (22)		
나타나-	appear, put in an appearance; show up (19)	놀리-	make fun of, tease (23)
		-놈	[usually abusive] "guy," S. O. B. (24)
낙제(를) 하-	fail, flunk (17)	농구 선수	basketball player (23)
난방 장치	heating (17)	농담	joke, something said in jest (21)
날씬하-	be thin, slim (22)		
낡-	get old (things) (19)	농담(을) 하-	joke, jest (21)
남	others, strangers (29)	높-	be high, tall (19)
남-	remain, be left over (19)	놓치-	miss (bus, plane) (16)
		눈물	tears (24)
남색	the color [navy] blue (21)	눈물(을) 흘리-	cry, shed tears (24)
		눈병 〔눈뼝〕	eye disease (19)
낭만	(being) romantic (29)	느리-	be slow (19)
낭만소설	a romance (i.e., novel in the romance genre) (29)	늙-	get old (people) (19)
		늙은이	old person, oldster [somewhat disrespectful] (19)
낮-	be low (19)		
낮잠(을) 자-	nap, take a nap (22)	늦잠(을) 자-	sleep late, wake up late (22)
낳-	give birth to; have (baby) (16)		
내-	hand in, turn in (17)		
내과	internal medicine (26)		
내다 보-	look out (at) (26)	**ㄷ**	
내려다 보-	look down at/upon (26)		
내리-	get off (a bus, train); let sb off/out (17)	다-르-	be sweet (26)
		다듬-	trim, spruce up; give final embellishments to (17)
냄새(가) 나-	it smells (24)		
냉방 장치	air-conditioning (17)	다행	luck, fortunate (24)
넓-	be wide, broad; spacious (22)	다행히(도)	fortunately, as [good] luck would have it (24)
넘-	exceed, be more than; pass beyond (29)	단거리	short-distance (26)
		단골	regular (customer/ place) (27)
넘어지-	fall down (22)		
-네	-'s place (23)	단골손님	regular customer (27)
네거리	crossroads; intersection (17)	단어	word; vocabulary item (18)
노란(색)	(the color) yellow; yellow (21)	단추	button; snap (21)
		단추를 끼-	fasten a snap (21)
노랗-, 노래요	be yellow (22)	단추를 잠그-	do up a button (21)
노력	efforts, hard work (24)	단편소설	short story (28)
노력(을) 하-	makes efforts (24)	닫히-	get closed/ shut (17)
녹색	the color green; green (21)	달걀	(chicken-) egg (22)

당기-	pull it (21)	도w-	help (17)
당연하-	stand to reason, make perfect sense, be natural (23)	도둑	thief, burglar (24)
		도둑(을) 맞-	be burgled, robbed (24)
당연히	naturally, as a matter of course (23)	도둑놈	thief, burglar (24)
당장	immediately, straight away, on the spot (18)	도착시간	arrival time (19)
		독감	flu (26)
대가족	large family (28)	독방	single room (17)
대가족 제도	extended family system (28)	독신자	unmarried person (by choice) (26)
대기실	waiting room (22)	독하-	be strong (drinks) (22)
대단히	very (17)	돌	stone, rock (27)
대답	answer, response (17)	돌려 주-	give back (28)
대답(을) 하-	answer, respond (17)	동기동창	classmate (same school, same year) (18)
대도시	big city, metropolis (28)	동시	same time; simultaneously (29)
대부분	the most part, the greater part; for the most part (28)	동시통역(을) 하-	do simultaneous interpreting (29)
대자연	the Great Outdoors, Mother Nature (24)	동양	East Asia (18)
		동양화	Oriental painting (23)
대접(을) 하-	treat somebody, host somebody (17)	동창	classmate, graduate of same school (18)
대통령	president (of country) (27)	동창회	alumni society; club for graduates of same school (18)
대통령 후보	candidate for president (28)	된장찌개	*toenjang* stew (22)
대하소설	epic novel; multi-volumed novel (28)	두-	put, place; leave (behind) (29)
대학생	college student, university student (23)	둘째로	secondly, second of all (24)
대합실	waiting room [in, e.g., a station or terminal] (22)	드디어	finally, at last (16)
		드려다 보-	look in (through), peep in (through) (26)
더듬거리-	stutter or speak haltingly (23)	들르-	drop in, drop by (18)
더러w-	be filthy, dirty (19)	들리-	stop by, drop in (23)
덜	less, little (21)	등록	registration (23)
데려가-	take (person) along (23)	등록(을) 하-	register (23)
		등산	hiking (21)
데려오-	bring (person) along (23)	등산(을) 가-	go hiking (21)
데리-	take (person) along (23)	등산(을) 하-	engage in hiking (21)
		따-	be different (22)
데리고 가-	take (person) along (23)	따뜻하-	be warm (18)
		따로	separately (18)
데리고 오-	bring (person) along (23)	딴 것	something different (22)
-도	degrees (of temperature) (26)	딴 사람들	others (22)
		때리-	hit, strike, beat (18)
도-ㄹ-	turn, spin; make a round; go around (17)	떡국	ricecake soup (22)
		떨어지-	fall; run out of s.th. (27)

또한	moreover, furthermore, what's more (16)	매연	exhaust fumes (21)
뚱뚱하–	be fat, chubby (16)	매우	very, exceedingly (21)
뜨거w–	be hot to the touch (16)	매월	every month (23)
뜻	meaning (27)	매주	every week (21)
띄우–	send (email) (28)	매콤하–	be somewhat spicy-tasting (22)
		맥(을) 짚–	take sb's pulse (26)
		맥	pulse (26)

ㄹ

		맥박	pulse (26)
로비	lobby (19)	맥박(을) 재–	take sb's pulse (26)
록키산맥	Rocky Mountains (28)	머리(를) 깎–	cut one's hair, get one's hair cut (16)
		머리(를) 자르–	cut one's hair, get one's hair cut (16)
		머리(를) 하–	do one's hair [used by women] (16)

ㅁ

		멋	(good) taste, elegance, style (19)
		멋(이) 있–	be stylish, cool, elegant (19)
마감	deadline (29)	멋쟁이	stylish person, sb who always dresses well (21)
마감일	deadline (29)		
–마디	counter for words (29)		
마르–	dry up; be/get dry (16)	멋지–	be stylish, cool, elegant (19)
마음껏	to one's heart's content (22)		
마음에 드–ㄹ–	be to one's liking (21)	면도(를) 하–	shave (16)
마일	mile (18)	면도기	electric shaver (16)
마일수	mileage (18)	면도칼	razor blade (16)
막히–	get/be blocked, congested (16)	면도크림	shaving cream (16)
		면허증	license, certificate (18)
만나 뵈w–	meet [with] sb esteemed; see sb esteemed (18)	명령	order, command (27)
		명령(을) 하–	order, command (27)
		모든 NOUN〔들〕	all NOUNs (17)
만두	dumplings (22)	모셔가–	take (person) along (23)
만두국	dumpling soup (22)		
말썽꾸러기	troublemaker (child), rascal (26)	모셔오–	bring (person) along (23)
		모시–	[HUMBLE] take (sb) along, accompany sb (23)
말씀(을) 드리–	tell sb (humble for 말(을) 하–) (16)		
말하자면	as it were; so to speak (23)	모시고 가–	take (sb) along (23)
		모시고 오–	bring (sb) along (23)
맑–	be clear (22)	모양	shape, appearance, style, design (21)
맞–	get (a shot, injection) (26)		
		모으–	gather (it), collect (16)
맞추–	order (to specifications), have (clothes) made to order (21)	모임	gathering, meeting (18)
		목	throat (16)
매년	every year (21)	목(이) 마르–	be thirsty, feel thirsty (16)
매달	every month (21)	목소리	voice (27)
		목욕(을) 하–	have a bath (16)

목욕탕	public bath; bathroom (16)	미용실	beauty parlor; hairdresser's (16)
목적	goal, objective (28)	미팔군	U.S. Eighth Army (26)
목적(을) 이루-	achieve one's goal (28)	민주주의	democracy (28)
몸	body (18)	믿-	believe (27)
몸살	general fatigue (from overwork) (21)	밀리-	be backed up, congested (cars, traffic) (22)
몸살(이) 나-	suffer from general fatigue (from overwork) (21)		
몸살감기	severe cold or flu brought on by exhaustion (21)	**ㅂ**	
몸조리(를) 하-	take care of one's health; recuperate (27)	바꾸-	(ex)change it, trade it (18)
몹시	very, awfully (18)	바닷가	seashore, seaside; beach (24)
못 되-	be bad, bad-natured, evil, wicked, good-for-nothing (22)	바둑	game of "Go" (24)
		바둑(을) 두-	play *paduk* (24)
못 생겼-	ugly (24)	바람	wind (19)
못 쓰-	be no good, worthless (22)	바르-	apply, smear it (17)
		바보	fool; idiot; dummy (27)
무궁화	Rose of Sharon (19)		
무기	weapon(s), arm(s) (28)	바치-	offer up, sacrifice (28)
		바퀴벌레	cockroach (27)
무더w-	be hot and muggy (18)	박수	applause (28)
무리(를) 하-	overdo it; work or play too hard (22)	박수(를) 치-	applaud (28)
		반가w-	be pleased to see/hear sb/s.th. (22)
무스	mousse for hair (17)		
무식하-	be ignorant (19)	반대	opposition (29)
무조건	unconditionally (28)	반대(를) 하-	oppose (29)
문법	grammar (18)	반말	Intimate Style (29)
문병(을) 가-	visit (a sick person) (26)	반주	accompaniment (24)
문병(을) 하-	visit (a sick person) (26)	반주(를) 하-	accompany (musically) (24)
문장	sentence (26)	반주자	accompanist (24)
문학	literature (23)	발전 [-쩐]	development (24)
문화	culture (24)	발전(을) 시키-	develop it (24)
물고기	[live] fish (22)	발전(을) 하-	it develops (24)
물만두	boiled dumplings (22)	발코니	balcony (17)
뭐니뭐니 해도	say what you like (21)	발표	announcement; public presentation (27)
미-ㄹ-	push it (21)	발표(를)하-	announce; make a presentation; present (a paper) (27)
미군	American army (26)		
미끄러w-	be slippery (29)		
미리	in advance, ahead of time (26)	밝-	be bright, light, clear (27)
		밝히-	make bright or clear; clarify, explain (27)
미식축구 선수	American football player (23)	밤	chestnut (21)

밤 늦도록	until late in the night (24)
밤(을) 새-	stay up all night (29)
밤색	the color chestnut brown; chestnut brown (21)
방문	a visit (24)
방문(을) 하-	visit, make a visit (24)
방문학자	visiting scholar (24)
방해	disturbance, obstruction (26)
방해(가) 되-	get in the way (26)
방해(를) 하-	disturb someone (26)
배(가) 고프-	be hungry, feel hungry (16)
배(가) 나오-	get a big belly (24)
배구 선수	volleyball player (23)
배꼽	navel, belly button (28)
배꼽(이) 빠지-	navel falls out (w/ laughter) (28)
배달(을) 하-	deliver (21)
배달부	delivery man (21)
배탈(이) 나-	get an upset stomach, get sick to one's stomach (24)
버-르-	earn, make (money) (19)
번역	translation (29)
번역(을) 하-	translates it (29)
번역가	translator (29)
벌레	bug, insect (27)
벨소리	"bell sound" = ringing (23)
벼슬	a government post, official rank (29)
벽	wall (27)
변비	constipation (26)
변하- 〔-으로〕	change; turn/ metamorphose into (27)
병	sickness, disease (19)
병(이) 나-	get sick (19)
병원	hospital (16)
보고(를) 하-	report (22)
보고서	(written) report (22)
보라색	the color purple; purple (21)
보석상	jewelry shop (28)
보이-	be visible, "shows" (28)

보이-	show it (17)
보증금	deposit (18)
보험	insurance (18)
보험(을) 드-르-	take out insurance, insure (18)
보험료	insurance fee, insurance charge (18)
복습	review, revision (24)
복습(을) 하-	review, revise (24)
복잡하-	be complicated; crowded (18)
볶-	cook in a skillet or frying pan (22)
볶음밥	fried rice (22)
볼륨	volume (24)
봉급	salary, wages (24)
뵈w-	humbly see or meet; have an audience/ interview with (18)
-부	copy (counter for books, etc.) (28)
부(ㅅ)-	pour it (19)
부-르-	blow (19)
부끄러w-	feel embarrassed, ashamed (17)
부러w-	be envious (17)
부부	husband and wife couple (29)
부분	portion, part, section (29)
부분적으로	partially, in part(s) (29)
부지런하-	be diligent (22)
부지런하-	be hard working, diligent (16)
부지런히	diligently (22)
분명하-	be clear, obvious (23)
분명히	clearly, obviously (23)
분홍색	the color pink; pink (21)
불(이) 나-	a fire breaks out (22)
불공평하-	be unfair (23)
불꽃놀이	fireworks (27)
불쌍하-	be pitiful; "poor thing" (18)
불어	French language (21)
불친절하-	be unkind (26)
불행	unhappiness, misfortune (24)
불행하-	be unfortunate, unhappy (24)
불행하게(도)	unfortunately, as [bad]

불행히(도)	luck would have it (24) unfortunately, as [bad] luck would have it (24)
붉-	be red; crimson (27)
붉히-	make it red, redden it (27)
비둘기	pigeon (19)
비로소	for the first time (28)
비서	secretary (17)
비지네스맨	businessman (28)
비키-	get out of the way (26)
빌려 주-	lend (17)
빌리-	borrow; rent (a car) (16)
빠-르-	wash (clothes), launder (22)
빠지-	fall (into); come out/ fall off (hair, etc.) (28); lose (weight) (27)
빨간(색)	(the color) red; red (21)
빨갛-, 빨개요	be red (22)
빨래	laundry, dirty clothes (16)
뺨	cheek(s) (27)
뽑-	take out, extract (19)
뿌리-	sprinkle it (22)

ㅅ

사건 [사껀]	scandal, notorious event (28)
사계절	the four seasons (23)
사고	an accident (24)
사고(가) 나-	an accident happens/ occurs (24)
사과	apology (21)
사귀-	make friends with, get to know (24)
사랑	love (24)
사랑에 빠지-	fall in love (24)
사은회 파티	party in honor of one's teacher (23)
사이즈	size (21)
사전	dictionary (18)
사진	photo (22)
사진(을) 찍-	take photos (22)
사탕	sweets, candy (21)

사형	capital punish- ment, death penalty (29)
사형(을) 하-	execute (29)
사회	society (28)
사회주의	socialism (28)
사회학	sociology (28)
사회학자	sociologist (28)
산꼭대기	mountain top, peak (27)
산맥	mountain range (28)
산부인과	obstetrics and gyne- cology (26)
살	flesh (27)
살(이) 빠지-	lose weight (27)
살(이) 찌-	get fat, gain weight (27)
삶-	boil it (22)
삼-	make s.th. of (a person or thing) (29)
삼계탕	Korean ginseng chicken soup (17)
삼키-	swallow it (22)
상관(이) 없-	not to care, not to be concerned; be of no concern (19)
상당히	quite (17)
상류사회	high society, polite society (28)
상하-	spoil, go off, go bad (24)
새까맣-	be jet-black (22)
새노랗-	be vivid yellow (22)
새로	newly, anew (27)
새로w-	be new (19)
새마을	New Village (rural development move- ment in 1960s) (19)
새빨갛-	be bright red (22)
새파랗-	be vivid deep blue (22)
새하얗-	be bright white (22)
색	color (21)
색깔	color (21)
생각	thought, idea (19)
생각(을) 하-	think (22)
생각(이) 나-	it comes to mind; think of s.th. (19)
생기-	come about, happen (28)
생선	fish [for human consumption] (22)

샤워(를) 하-	take a shower (24)	성공	success (28)
샴푸	shampoo (19)	성공(을) 하-	be successful (28)
서-	stop, come to a stop (19)	성명	full name, surname + given name (17)
서기	secretary, clerk (24)	성서	Bible (24)
서두르-	hurry, hasten, make haste (22)	성적	marks, grades (23)
서로	mutually, to each other (29)	성적표	report card (23)
		세계	world, the world (28)
서류	document (18)	세상	the world (22)
서비스	service (e.g., in a restaurant); s.th. unexpected you get for free as part of a transaction (17)	세상에!	Oh, my! My goodness! You don't say! (22)
		세수(를) 하-	wash face (16)
		세우-	bring it to a stop (17)
		소극적으로	passively, in a feeble or unaggressive way (24)
서양	the West; Western countries; Western (18)	소금	salt (22)
서양사람	a Westerner (29)	소나기	cloudburst, shower (21)
선거	election (28)		
선배	senior from school (18)	소도시	small city (28)
		소리	noise, sound (27)
선선하-	be cool, fresh (21)	소리(를) 지르-	shout, cry out (27)
선약	a previous appointment or engagement (17)	소설	a work of fiction; novel (28)
선언	pronouncement, declaration (27)	소식	news, word of/from sb (17)
선언(을) 하-	pronounce, declare (27)	소아과	pediatrics (26)
선택(을) 하-	select, choose (24)	소용	use; utility, usefulness (18)
섣달	December (28)		
섣달 그믐	New Year's Eve (28)	소용(이) 없-	be useless (18)
설교	sermon (24)	소위 NOUN	a so-called NOUN (27)
설교(를) 하-	give a sermon (24)	소풍	a [school] outing, [school] picnic (22)
설날	New Year's Day (28)	소풍(을) 가-	go on a [school] outing or picnic (22)
설명	explanation (16)		
설명(을) 하-	explain, give an explanation (16)	소화	digestion (26)
		소화(가) 안 되-	has indigestion (26)
설명서	brochure, pamphlet, piece of explanatory literature (18)	소화제	digestive tablet(s); medicine to help digestion (26)
설악산	Mount Sŏrak (21)	속(이) 나쁘-	have a sore stomach, feel sick in the stomach (22)
섬유	textiles (22)		
섭섭하-	feel sad and/or empty about, feel wistful about (17)	속(이) 상하-	be distressing; feel distressed (16)
섭씨	Celsius (26)	속도	speed (19)
성가대	(church) choir (24)	속도위반(을) 하-	commit a speeding violation; speed (29)
성가대원	member of (church) choir (24)	수구 선수	water polo player (23)
성경	Bible (24)	수단	a way or means; a measure; a trick (29)
성경 공부	Bible Study (24)		

수술	an operation (medical) (23)
수술(을) 받-	have an operation (23)
수술(을) 하-	perform an operation; have an operation (23)
수술실	operating theatre (23)
수입(을) 하-	import something (24)
수첩	small notebook; pocket memo-book (22)
수출(을) 하-	export something (24)
수학	mathematics, math (24)
숙박	lodging (17)
숙박(을) 하-	lodge at, put up at (17)
숙박부	lodging [registration] form (17)
순간	moment, instant (29)
숟가락	spoon (22)
숨-	hide, conceal oneself (29)
숨기-	hide it, conceal it (29)
슈퍼	supermarket (22)
스캔들	scandal (often sexual) (28)
슬프-	feel sad, sorrowful (16)
시-	be sour (26)
시간표	time table, schedule (24)
시계	watch, clock (17)
시끄러w-	be noisy, loud (19)
시원하-	be refreshing, reviving; fresh, cool; feel relieved (16)
시작(이) 되-	it begins (17)
시장	mayor (26)
시절	time, era; days when; a time in the past (19)
시집(을) 가-	(woman) get married (27)
시집(을) 보내-	marry, marry off (woman) (27)
시차	time difference; jet lag (29)
시합	a match, contest, game (sport) (26)
식당차	dining car (19)
식사(를) 하-	eat a meal (16)
신경	nerve, nerves (23)
신경(을) 쓰-	be nervous, worried (23)
신경(이) 쓰이-	be nervous, worried (23)

신랑	the groom (17)
신부	the bride (17)
신분	social status, station in life (29)
신분증 〔-쯩〕	ID card (29)
신사	gentleman (21)
실망(을) 하-	be disappointed, feel disappointed (23)
실수	a mistake, blunder (22)
실수(를) 하-	make a mistake (22)
실컷	to one's heart's content, to the point where one is sick of it (22)
심판	umpire, referee (29)
심판(을) 하-	umpire, referee (29)
심하-	be severe, intense, extreme (21)
싱거w-	be bland, not salted enough (22)
싸우-	quarrel, argue with (19)
싸움	fight, struggle (28)
싹	entirely, completely (24)
쌀쌀하-	be cool, chilly (18)
쓰-	be bitter (26)
씹-	chew it (22)
씻-	wash (16)

아름다w-	be beautiful (17)
아무 NOUN(이)나	any NOUN at all, any NOUN whatsoever (23)
아무 NOUN도	no NOUN at all, no NOUN whatsoever (23)
아무것도	nothing at all (24)
아무리	however much [one VERBs]; at the very [(ADJ-est)] (18)
아이스 하키 선수	ice hockey player (23)
안개	fog (21)
안색	one's complexion (22)
알리-	let somebody know; inform (24)
암	cancer (19)
암행어사	secret inspector-general, undercover agent of the king (29)

애(를) 쓰-	make efforts, try hard (26)
애인	steady girlfriend/ boyfriend (19)
야끼 만두	pan-fried dumplings (22)
야단(을) 맞-	be scolded, get a scolding (18)
야단(을) 치-	scold, give a scolding to (18)
야당	opposition party (28)
야유회	[company] outing, picnic (22)
야유회(를) 가-	go on an outing, picnic (22)
약간	some, a little, a few; somewhat (27)
약국	pharmacy, drugstore (18)
약사	pharmacist (18)
약속	an appointment; a promise (16)
약속(을) 하-	make an appointment; promise (16)
얌전하-	be of good upbringing; be well-behaved and quiet (27)
양반	yangban (traditional Korean gentry or nobility) (29)
얕-	be shallow (19)
어기-	break (a promise) (16)
어두w-	be dark (24)
어떤 때는	sometimes (22)
어린 아이	small child, infant (19)
어린이	a young one, child (19)
어서	right away, quickly (16)
어울리-	spend time with, hang around with, associate with (18)
어울리-	fit, go well with, match with (21)
어쨌든	anyhow, in any case, at any rate (22)
어차피	anyhow, in any case, at any rate (22)
얻-	get, obtain (29)
얼굴	face (17)
얼굴(을) 붉히-	turn red (in the face) (27)
얼른	quickly, immediately, at once (22)
없어지-	disappear (18)
없이	without (adv) (17)
엉덩이	rump, bottom, derriere (28)
엉망	a mess, a wreck (24)
여권	passport (24)
여기-	consider (27)
여당	government party (28)
여러분	all of you; you all; y'all (21)
여쭈-	asks sb esteemed (23)
여쭤 보-	asks sb esteemed (23)
여행	travel; a journey (17)
여행(을) 하-	travel (17)
여-ㄹ-	have/host (a party) (23)
역사	history (24)
역시	sure enough (28)
연결(이) 되-	be/get connected with (19)
연기	smoke (21)
연봉	annual salary (24)
연습	practice (16)
연습(을) 하-	practice, do exercises (16)
연애(를) 하-	fall in love; "date" (17)
연착(이) 되-	be/get delayed (19)
연휴	a long weekend (21)
열	fever (high temperature) (26)
열(이) 높-	have a high temperature, run a high fever (26)
열(이) 있-	have a fever (high temperature) (26)
열리-	open, be opened (17)
열쇠	key (17)
염려(를) 하-	worry (22)
영문(을) 모르-	not understand what is going on, have no idea why (28)
영수증	receipt (23)
옅-	be light (color); thin (fog) (21)
예	example (28)
예를 드-ㄹ-	give an example (28)
예를 든다면	for example (28)
예를 들면	for example (28)

예를 들자면	for example (28)
예배	church service (24)
예배(를) 드리-	attend a church service; worship (24)
예보	forecast, prediction (26)
예습	preparation (of lessons), preview (24)
예습(을) 하-	prepare (lessons), preview (24)
예약석	reserved seats (19)
예정	plan, prearrangement, schedule (24)
옛날	old days, ancient times; in the past (19)
오래	for a long time (16)
오래 가-	go/last a long time (27)
오래간만에	after a long interval, for the first time in a long while (16)
오랫동안	for a long time (16)
오렌지색	the color orange; orange (21)
오자	typo, misprint (21)
오페라	opera (19)
오해	a misunderstanding (18)
오해(를) 하-	misunderstand s.th. (18)
오히려	rather (than), sooner (than); actually; on the contrary, contrary to what one expects (22)
온 세상	the whole world (24)
온도	atmospheric temperature (26)
온몸	one's entire body (24)
완행	stopper (train, bus); the local (train, bus) (19)
완행버스	slow bus, stopping bus (19)
완행열차	slow train, stopping train (19)
왕	king (28)
외과	surgery (26)
외과의사	surgeon (26)
외무부	Ministry of Foreign Affairs (24)
외식(을) 하-	dine out, eat out (29)
외우-	memorize it (18)
요금	fee; fare (17)

욕실	bathroom, room with a bath (17)
욕조	bathtub (16)
용돈	pocket money (26)
우-ㄹ-	cry, weep (16)
우물쭈물하-	waffle, prevaricate, beat around the bush (27)
우선	first, firstly; as a matter of priority (24)
우연히	by chance, by coincidence (24)
우표	postage, stamp (17)
운동 선수	athlete (23)
운전(을) 하-	drive, operate a vehicle (16)
운전면허증	driver's license (18)
웃-	smile; laugh (16)
웃기-	be (act) funny; make one laugh (28)
원고	a manuscript, draft (29)
원고료	manuscript fee (29)
원고지	manuscript paper (29)
원래	originally; actually (27)
원하-	want, desire, wish for (19)
월급	monthly salary (24)
위반	transgression; foul (29)
위험하-	be dangerous (16)
유럽	Europe (17)
유럽공동체	European Community (17)
유명하-	be famous (18)
유식하-	be learned, knowledgeable, refined (19)
유전자	gene (23)
유창하게	fluently (18)
유학	study abroad (24)
유학(을) 시키-	send somebody to study abroad (24)
유학생	international student, student studying abroad (24)
유행	s.th. popular, s.th. in vogue (19)
유행이-	be the vogue, the fashion (19)
유행하-	be popular, in vogue (19)

육개장	spicy chopped beef soup (17)
육교	pedestrian overpass (16)
으레	customarily, usually, habitually (28)
음식(을) 차리-	prepare food (27)
응급차	ambulance (26)
응급치료	first-aid treatment (26)
응접실	reception room [in a home] (22)
의과 대학	medical school (26)
이기-	win; beat (29)
이런 NOUN	such a/that sort of NOUN (19)
이루-	achieve, bring about (28)
이르-	be early (18)
이리	this way, this direction, here (16)
이메일	email (28)
이민	immigration (23)
이민(을) 가-	emigrate (23)
이민(을) 오-	immigrate (23)
이민자	immigrant (23)
이발(을) 하-	get a haircut (usually used by males) (16)
이발사	barber (16)
이발소	barbershop (16)
이비인후과	ear/nose/throat specialist (26)
이세	second generation (23)
이튿날	second day, next day, day after (28)
이해	understanding (18)
이해(가) 가-	one understands it; it is understandable (18)
이해(를) 하-	understand something (18)
이호선	Line 2 (on Seoul subway) (19)
인기(가) 있-	be popular, well-liked (19)
인사	greeting, a formal hello or good-bye (17)
인턴	intern (26)
인형	doll (26)
일기	the weather (26)
일기예보	weather forecast (26)
일어서-	stand up (24)
일점오세	1.5 generation (23)

잃어버리-	lose something (24)
입맛	one's appetite, one's desire to eat (24)
입원(을) 하-	be/get hospitalized, go into hospital (24)
입장	position, standpoint, stand (on an issue) (24)
잎	leaf (21)

ㅈ

자꾸(만)	incessantly, constantly (often annoyingly) (21)
자라-	it grows (24)
자르-	cut (one's hair) (16)
자리	seat, place (18)
자식	child(ren), offspring (29)
자연	nature (24)
자연스럽게	naturally; fluently, freely (18)
자주색	the color burgundy; burgundy (21)
작가	writer, author (19)
잔디	lawn (21)
잘못	a mistake, error, blunder; by mistake, wrongly, erroneously (21)
잘못 거-ㄹ-	dials a wrong number (23)
잠그-	fasten (buttons, snaps); lock (door, window) (21)
잡-	catch, grasp, take hold of (21)
잡숴 보시-	[sb esteemed] eat s.th., try s.th. (17)
장(을) 보-	go shopping (for food) (21)
장가(를) 가-	get married (of a man) (27)
장가(를) 보내-	marry, marry off (man) (27)
장거리	long-distance (26)
장기	Korean chess (24)
장기(를) 두-	plays *changgi* (24)
장난꾸러기	mischief maker, little monkey (child) (26)

장로	(church) Elder [male] (24)
장마철	rainy season (28)
장소	place, venue (27)
장편소설	full-length novel (28)
장학금	scholarship (24)
재–	take measurements of, measure (21)
재–	take (sb's pulse) (26)
재미	resident in the United States (23)
재미교포	Korean American (23)
재일	resident in Japan (23)
재일교포	Korean Japanese (23)
저런 NOUN	such a/that sort of NOUN (19)
저리	that way, that direction, over there (16)
적극적으로	positively, actively, in an outgoing way (24)
전경	the view (17)
전날	previous day (28)
전문	specialty (24)
전문가	specialist, expert (24)
전문지식	specialized knowledge, expertise (24)
전보	telegram (28)
전보(를) 치–	sends a telegram (28)
전염병	contagious disease/illness (26)
전쟁	war (24)
젊은이	young person, a youth (19)
점	point, dot, mark (28)
점수	grade mark (28)
점잖–	be well-behaved, decent, respectable (27)
점점	gradually, little by little, by degrees (18)
접대실	reception room (22)
젓가락	chopstick(s) (22)
정당하–	be legitimate, rightful (29)
정도	extent, degree (28)
정부	government (27)
정신	spirit, mind, nerves (17)
정신(을) 차리–	collect one's senses, keep one's presence of mind (27)

정신(이) 없–	be preoccupied with s. th. such that one is unable to cope with other things (17)
정월	January (28)
정치가	politician (21)
정하–	settle upon, decide upon, fix (17)
제–	ordinalizer (for "1st," "2nd," etc.) (18)
제대로	as it should/ought be done, properly, in proper fashion (18)
제도	system, institution (28)
제목	title (of book/work) (27)
제안	suggestion, proposal (24)
제출(을) 하–	turn in, submit, hand in (27)
조–ㄹ–	doze (21)
조르–	pester for, keep after for (27)
조심하–	be careful about (24)
조용하–	be quiet (18)
조용히	quietly (18)
조촐하–	be small and neat (23)
존경	respect (29)
존경(을) 받–	be respected (29)
존경(을) 하–	respect someone (29)
존댓말	Polite or Formal Style; respectful speech (29)
졸리–	be sleepy; feel sleepy (21)
종강 파티	end-of-term party (23)
주미 . . .	in the U.S. (e.g., Embassy) (24)
주사	a shot, an injection (26)
주사(를) 놓–	give a shot, administer an injection (26)
주사(를) 맞–	get a shot, have an injection (26)
주유소	gas station (18)
주인공	"star"; protagonist; person of honor at a party (23)
주차	parking (29)
주차(를) 하–	park the car (29)
주차위반(을) 하–	commit a parking infraction (29)

주차장	parking lot (29)
주한 미국 대사관	U.S. embassy in Korea (24)
주황색	the color orange; orange (21)
죽이–	kill (29)
준결승전	semifinals (29)
준비	preparations (16)
준비(를) 하–	prepare, make preparations (16)
줄	line (of text); line (that you stand in) (26)
줄(을) 서–	stand in line (26)
줄거리	plot (29)
–중	the middle; during, in the middle of (21)
중(에서)	among (NOUNs) (19)
중년	middle age (19)
중년들	middle-aged people (19)
중류사회	the middle classes, middle-class society (28)
중심	center, core, crux (24)
중심적으로	primarily, with s.th. as one's main focus (24)
중요하–	be important (21)
중편소설	novella (28)
중학교	middle school (28)
즐겁게	enjoyably, happily (18)
지(ㅅ)–	build (house); make (rice) (19)
지– (–한테)	lose (to) (29)
지각(을) 하–	arrive late (29)
지갑	wallet; purse (26)
지나가–	pass by (19)
지도	map (26)
지루하–	be boring, tedious (17)
지방	the country(side), the provinces (28)
지식	knowledge (19)
지연(이) 되–	be/get delayed (19)
지키–	keep (appointment/ promise); abide by, stick to (16)
지휘자	conductor, director [of a musical group] (24)
직장	job, work, workplace (27)

직장(을) 구하–	look for work, look for a job (27)
직접	direct(ly); immediate-(ly); personally, in person (21)
직책	duties, responsibilities of office (24)
진단	diagnosis (26)
진담	s.th. said in all seriousness (21)
진찰	a checkup, medical examination (26)
진찰(을) 받–	have a checkup; consult a doctor (26)
진찰(을) 하–	examine sb medically (19)
진찰실	(medical) consultation room (26)
진하–	be thick (of liquid or makeup) (22)
질문(을) 하–	ask a question (28)
집사	(church) deacon (24)
짙–	be deep, rich, dark (color); thick (fog) (21)
짚–	take (sb's pulse) (26)
짜–	be (too) salty (22)
–짜리	–'s worth (17)
짧–	be short (18)
찌–	steam it (22); gain (weight) (27)
찌개	stew (22)
찐 만두	steamed dumplings (22)

ㅊ

차키	(car-)key (17)
차가w–	be cold to the touch (16)
차리–	prepare, make ready; collect, concentrate (27)
차이	difference (29)
착실하–	be steadfast, thorough (26)
창피하–	be/feel embarrassed (23)
찾아 가–	call on; visit, go calling on (18)

찾아 뵈w-	call on sb esteemed; visit, come calling on sb esteemed (18)
찾아 오-	call on; visit, come calling on (18)
처자식	wife and children (28)
천장	ceiling (27)
천하-	be of low birth; be lowly, ignoble (29)
첩	concubine; mistress (29)
첫눈에	at first sight (24)
첫째로	firstly, first of all (24)
체온	body temperature (26)
체온(을) 재-	takes sb's temperature (26)
체크인(을) 하-	check in (17)
쳐다 보-	look up at; stare at (26)
초등학교	elementary school (28)
초하루(날)	first day (28)
촉진(을) 시키-	expedite, promote, facilitate (24)
총각	unmarried young man (26)
총장	president (university) (28)
최근	latest, most recent (19)
최근에	recently, lately (19)
최선을 다 하-	do one's best (28)
추방(을) 하-	expel, drive out' banish (26)
추진(을) 시키-	promote s.th., propel s.th. forward (24)
추진(을) 하-	promote s.th., propel s.th. forward (24)
추측	conjecture, guess, inference (27)
추측(을) 하-	surmise, guess, infer (27)
축구 선수	soccer player (23)
축하(를) 하-	congratulate (27)
출근(을) 하-	go/come to work; report for work (22)
출근시간	time when one leaves home for work (22)
출발(을) 하-	set off, depart (24)
출발시간	departure time (19)
출장(을) 가-	go away on business, make a business-related journey (24)
출퇴근(을) 하-	commute to work (22)

출판(을) 하-	publish it (28)
출판사	publishing company (28)
충분하-	be enough, plenty, sufficient (28)
충분히	enough (adv.), sufficiently (28)
취소(가) 되-	get cancelled (24)
취소(를) 하-	cancel it (24)
치-	reckon, calculate (28)
치과 〔-꽈〕	dentistry (26)
치과의사	dentist (26)
치료	medical treatment (26)
치료(를) 받-	receive/undergo medical treatment (26)
친절하-	be kind (26)
친하-	be close (19)

칼	knife (16)
캐나다교포	Korean Canadian (23)
컴퓨터	computer (16)
켜-	turn on, switch on (22)
코스	course (23)
코피	nosebleed (24)
코피(가) 나-	get a nosebleed (24)
큰일(이) 나-	s.th. serious happens; get in big trouble (22)
키	height (17)
키	(car-)key (17)
키(가) 크-	be tall (17)

태도	attitude (17)
태백산맥	T'aebaek Mountains (28)
태풍	typhoon (21)
택시요금	taxi fare (18)
택하-	select, choose (24)
터지-	it bursts (24)
토하-	vomit, throw up (26)
-통	counter for letters (22)

통역	(simultaneous) interpreting (29)
통역(을) 하-	do (simultaneous) interpreting (29)
통역사	interpreter (29)
통일	unification (19)
통화중이에요	(phone) is busy; (sb) is on the phone (23)
퇴근(을) 하-	go/come home from work; leave the office (22)
퇴근시간	time when one leaves work for home (22)
퇴원(을) 하-	get out of hospital (24)
튀기-	deep-fry it (22)
튀긴 만두	deep-fried dumplings (22)
특별하-	be special, particular (29)
특별히	especially, particularly (29)
특히	especially, in particular (17)
틀리-	be different; be wrong, incorrect (19)

포크	fork (22)
포함(을) 하-	include it (17)
포함(이) 되-	be/get included (17)
폭풍우	a storm (29)
표현	[verbal] expression (23)
표현(을) 하-	express (23)
푸른(색)	(the color) blue; blue; (the color) green; green (21)
푹	(sleep) deeply; (rest) soundly (26)
풍습	custom(s), habit(s) (28)
피	blood (26)
피검사	blood-test (26)
피부	skin (27)
피해	damage, harm (29)
피해(를) 입-/받-	suffer damage, harm (29)
필요	need, necessity (21)
필요하-	be necessary, needed (21)
핑크색	the color pink; pink (21)

ㅍ

파란(색)	(the color) blue; blue; (the color) green; green (21)
파랗-	be blue (22)
파마(를) 하-	get a perm (16)
파산(이) 되-	go bankrupt (27)
파출부	maid (26)
파티(를) 여-ㄹ-	have/host a party (23)
팔리-	be sold, get sold, "sell (well)" (28)
팝콘	popcorn (19)
팩스	fax (23)
팩스번호	fax number (23)
퍽(이나)	very, quite, rather (28)
편리하-	be convenient (26)
편찮으시-	be ill, not well (honorific) (18)
평화	peace (28)
포기(를) 하-	give up, give up on (23)

ㅎ

하나님	God (Protestant) (18)
하느님	God (Catholic) (18)
하늘	heaven; sky (18)
하늘색	the color light ["sky"] blue (21)
하루종일	all day long (16)
하류사회	the lower classes, lower class society (28)
하얀(색)	white (21)
하얗-	be white (22)
하여튼	anyhow, in any case, at any rate (22)
하품	yawn (28)
하품(을) 하-	yawn (28)
학생시절	one's student days (19)
학자	scholar (27)
학장	dean (28)
한미	Korea-U.S. (24)

한미간	between Korea and the United States (24)
한미간의	pertaining to Korea and the U.S. (24)
한자	Chinese character (18)
한턱	a treat, a feast (17)
한턱(을) 내-	treat, stand treat, give as a treat to (17)
할 수 없이	unavoidably, without having any other recourse (29)
할인	discount (17)
할인(을) 받-	get/receive a discount (17)
할인(을) 해 주-	give a discount (17)
해결	solution (to a problem) (27)
해결(을) 하-	resolve (a problem) (27)
해결(이) 되-	be/get resolved (27)
핵	nucleus (28)
핵가족	nuclear family (28)
핵무기	nuclear weapons (28)
행복	happiness (21)
행복하-	be happy [in life] (21)
행사	happening, formal event, function (27)
허락	permission (26)
허락(을) 받-	get permission (26)
허락(을) 하-	permit, allow (26)
헌 NOUN	old/used NOUN (19)
헌책방	secondhand bookshop (19)
헤어지-	separate from, part with, split up with (19)
현관	entrance vestibule (26)
혈압	blood pressure (26)
혈압(을) 재-	take sb's blood pressure (26)
-호	number ___ (17)
혼(을) 내-	give sb a hard time; teach sb a lesson, give a good scolding (23)
혼(이) 나-	have a hard time of it, have an awful time/experience (22)
혼인	wedding, matrimony (29)
혼인(을) 하-	get married, enter into matrimony (29)
화(가) 나-	get angry (27)
화(를) 내-	get angry (27)

화씨	Fahrenheit (26)
화장(을) 하-	put on one's makeup (16)
환자	patient; a sick person (23)
회복(이) 되-	recover (e.g., from illness) (26)
회복(을) 하-	recover (e.g., from illness) (26)
회색	the color grey; grey (21)
회의	conference (23)
-후	afterwards, later, later on (16)
후배	junior from school (18)
후보	candidate (28)
후추	(black) pepper (22)
후추가루	black pepper powder (26)
훌륭하-	be great, admirable (23)
훔치-	steal it, swipe it (24)
훨씬	much (. . .-er), by far (19)
휘발유	gasoline, petrol (18)
휴가	holiday, leave from work (17)
흐리-	be cloudy, overcast (18)
흔하-	be common (26)
흔히	often, commonly (26)
흘리-	spill it; shed (tears) (24)
흠	flaw, defect (21)
흥미(가) 없-	be uninteresting, dull, not at all amusing (28)
흥미(가) 있-	be interesting, amusing (28)
흰(색)	white (21)

ENGLISH to KOREAN VOCABULARY

A

abide by   지키- (16)
absent (from school)   결석(을) 하-
                               (21)
accident happens   사고(가) 나-
                               (24)
accompaniment   반주 (24)
accompanist   반주자 (24)
accompany (musically)   반주(를) 하-
                               (24)
accompany sb (humble)   모시- (23)
achieve   이루- (28)
achieve one's dream   꿈(을) 이루-
                               (28)
achieve one's goal   목적(을)
                               이루- (28)
across from   건너(에) (27)
actively   적극적으로
                               (24)
actually   원래 (27);
                               오히려 (22)
admirable   훌륭하- (23)
after a long interval   오래간만에
                               (16)
afterward   나중에 (22);
                               -후 (16)
ahead of time   미리 (26)
air   공기 (22)
air-conditioning   냉방 장치
                               (17)
airport   공항 (18)
all day long   하루종일
                               (16)
all NOUNs   모든 NOUN
                               (들) (17)
all of you   여러분 (21)
allow   허락(을) 하-
                               (26)

almost   거의 (16)
alumni club/society   동창회 (18)
ambulance   응급차 (26)
American army   미군 (26)
American football   미식축구
                               (23)
among NOUNs   NOUN 중(에
                               서)(19)
amusing   흥미(가) 있-
                               (28)
ancient times   옛날 (19)
anew   새로 (27)
angry (get)   화(를) 내-,
                               화(가) 나-
                               (27)
announce   발표(를) 하-
                               (27)
announcement   발표 (27)
annoying   귀찮- (16)
annual salary   연봉 (24)
answer   대답, 대답
                               (을) 하-
                               (17)
any moment now   곧 (21)
any NOUN at all   아무 NOUN
                               (이)나 (23)
anyhow/anyway   하여튼,
                               어쨌든,
                               어차피 (22)
apology   사과 (21)
appear   나- (17);
                               나타나- (19)
appearance   모양 (21)
appetite   입맛 (24)
applaud   박수(를) 치-
                               (28)
applause   박수 (28)
apply   바르- (17)

appointment	약속 (16)	
argue with	싸우- (19)	
arm(s)	무기 (28)	
arrival time	도착시간 (19)	
arrive late (school, work)	지각(을) 하- (29)	
arrogant	거만하- (28)	
as a matter of course	당연히 (23)	
as a matter of priority	우선 (24)	
as it ought to be done	제대로 (18)	
as it were	말하자면 (23)	
as (bad) luck would have it	불행하게 (도) 불행히 (도) (24)	
ashamed	부끄러w- (17)	
ask a question	질문(을) 하- (28)	
ask sb esteemed	여쭈-, 여쭤 보- (23)	
associate with	어울리- (18)	
"at" (@ for email)	골뱅이 (28)	
at first sight	첫눈에 (24)	
at last	드디어 (16)	
at once	얼른 (22); 곧 (21)	
at the very [(ADJ-est)]	아무리 (...-어도) (18)	
athlete	운동 선수 (23)	
atmospheric temperature	온도 (26)	
attend a church service	예배(를) 드리- (24)	
attitude	태도 (17)	
audience	관객 (28)	
auditor	감사 (29)	
author	작가 (19)	
awaken sb	깨우- (17)	
awful experience	혼(이) 나- (22)	
awfully	몹시 (18)	

B

backed up (cars, traffic)	밀리- (22)	
bad	못 되- (22)	
balcony	발코니 (17)	
banish	추방(을) 하- (26)	
bankrupt (go/become)	파산(이) 되- (27)	
barber	이발사 (16)	
barbershop	이발소 (16)	
basketball	농구 (23)	
bathe	목욕(을) 하- (16)	
bathroom	목욕탕 (16); 욕실 (17)	
bathtub	욕조 (16)	
beach	바닷가 (24)	
beat	때리- (18)	
beat (in a game)	이기- (29)	
beat around the bush	우물쭈물하- (27)	
beautiful	아름다w- (17)	
beauty parlor	미용실 (16)	
before long	곧 (21)	
begin (it begins)	시작(이) 되- (17)	
believe	믿- (27)	
"bell sound"	벨소리 (23)	
belly button	배꼽 (28)	
better than	나(ㅅ)- (23)	
between Korea and the U.S.	한미간 (24)	
beyond	넘- (29)	
Bible	성서 (24), 성경 (24)	
Bible study	성경 공부 (24)	
big belly (get)	배(가) 나오- (24)	
big city	대도시 (28)	
big trouble	큰일(이) 나- (22)	
biscuit(s)	과자 (21)	
bitter	쓰- (26)	
black	까만(색), 까맣- (22)	
black pepper	후추 (22)	

black pepper powder	후추가루 (26)	build (house)	지(ㅅ)- (19)
		burglar	도둑(놈) (24)
bland	싱거w- (22)		
blocked (be/get)	막히- (16)	burgled (be/get)	도둑(을) 맞- (24)
blood	피 (26)		
blood test	피검사 (26)	burgundy	자주색 (21)
blood pressure	혈압 (26)	burst	터지- (24)
blow	부-ㄹ- (19)	business trip	출장(을) 가- (24)
blue	푸른(색), 파란(색), 푸른(색) (21); 파랗- (22)		
		businessman	비지네스맨 (28)
		busy (phone)	통화중이에요 (23)
blue (navy)	남색 (21)	button	단추 (21)
blunder	실수 (22); 잘못 (21)	buy	구하- (26)
		by chance	우연히 (24)
body	몸 (18)	by coincidence	우연히 (24)
body temperature	체온 (26)	by degrees	점점 (18)
boil it	끓이- (22), 삶- (22)	by far	훨씬 (19)
		by mistake	잘못 (21)
boiled dumplings	물만두 (22)		
boring	지루하- (17)		
borrow	빌리- (16)	**C**	
bowl	그릇 (24)		
break (a promise)	어기- (16)	calculate	치- (28)
break down	고장(이) 나- (28)	call on	찾아 오-, 찾아 가- (18)
break it	깨- (29)	call on sb. esteemed	찾아 뵈w- (18)
break it off	끊- (27)		
breed	기르- (27)	cancel	취소(를) 하- (24)
bride	신부 (17)		
bright	밝- (27)	cancelled (be/get)	취소(가) 되- (24)
bright red	새빨갛- (22)		
bright white	새하얗- (22)	cancer	암 (19)
bring (sb) along	데리고 오-, 데려오- (23)	candidate	후보 (28)
		candidate for president	대통령 후보 (28)
bring (sb) along (humble)	모시고 오-, 모셔오- (23)		
		candy	사탕 (21)
bring (thing) along	가지고 오-, 가져오- (24)	capital punishment	사형 (29)
		careful	조심하- (24)
bring about	이루- (28)	catch	잡- (21)
bring to a stop	세우- (17)	catch (sickness, disease)	걸리- (19)
bring up (subject)	꺼내- (28)	cautiously	가만히 (22)
broach (subject)	꺼내- (28)	ceiling	천장 (27)
broad	넓- (22)	Celsius	섭씨 (26)
brochure	설명서 (18)	center	중심 (24)
broken (get)	깨지- (29)	certificate	면허증 (18)
brook	개울 (19)	change into	변하- (27)
brown	갈색 (21)	change (transport)	갈아타- (16)
bug	벌레 (27)		

change it	바꾸- (18)	cockroach	바퀴벌레 (27)
change of mood	기분전환 (22)	cold	감기 (21)
chauffeur	기사 (아저씨) (23)	cold to the touch	차가w- (16)
		collect	모으- (16)
check in	체크인(을) 하- (17)	collect one's senses	정신(을) 차리- (27)
check saltiness of food	간(을) 보- (22)	college student	대학생 (23)
checkup	진찰, 진찰 (을) 받- (26)	color	색깔, 색 (21)
		come about	생기- (28)
cheek(s)	뺨 (27)	come calling on	찾아 오- (18)
chemist (pharmacist)	약사 (18)	come out	나- (17)
chestnut	밤 (21)	come out (hair, etc.)	빠지- (28)
chestnut brown	밤색 (21)	come to a stop	서- (19)
chew	씹- (22)	come to mind	생각(이) 나- (19)
chew gum	껌(을) 씹- (22)		
		come to realize	깨달- (ㄹ ~ ㄷ) (28)
chewing gum	껌 (22)		
child	어린이 (19)	come to work	출근(을) 하- (22)
child(ren)	자식 (29)		
chilly	쌀쌀하- (18)	come up (a subject)	나오- (23)
Chinese character	한자 (18)	command	명령, 명령 (을)하- (27)
choir (church)	성가대 (24)		
choir member	성가대원 (24)	commit a parking infraction	주차위반(을) 하- (29)
choose	택하-; 선택 (을) 하- (24)	commit a speeding violation	속도위반(을) 하- (29)
chopstick(s)	젓가락 (22)	commit a traffic infraction	교통위반(을) 하- (29)
chubby	뚱뚱하- (16)		
church choir	성가대 (24)	common	흔하- (26)
church service	예배 (24)	commonly	흔히 (26)
clarify	밝히- (27)	communism	공산주의 (28)
classic	고전 (29)		
classmate	동기동창, 동창 (18)	commute	출퇴근(을) 하- (22)
clear	밝- (27); 맑- (22); 분명하- (23)	completely	싹 (24)
		complexion	안색 (22)
		complicated	복잡하- (18)
clear up (weather)	개- (21)	computer	컴퓨터 (16)
clearly	분명히 (23)	conceal it	숨기- (29)
clerk	서기 (24)	conceal oneself	숨- (29)
clock	시계 (17)	concentrate	차리- (27)
close (to a friend)	친하- (19)	concretely	구체적으로 (24)
closed (get)	닫히- (17)		
cloud	구름 (21)	concubine	첩 (29)
cloudburst	소나기 (21)	conductor	지휘자 (24)
cloudy (be/get)	흐리- (18)	conference	회의 (23)
		congested (be/get)	막히- (16); 밀리- (22)

congratulate	축하(를) 하- (27)	custom(s)	풍습 (28)
conjecture	추측 (27)	customarily	으레 (28)
connected with (be/get)	연결(이) 되- (19)	cut one's hair	머리(를) 깎-, 머리(를) 자르- (16)
consider	여기- (27)	cute	귀여w- (19)
constantly	자꾸(만) (21)		
constipation	변비 (26)		
consult a doctor	진찰(을) 받- (26)		

D

consultation room (medical)	진찰실 (26)	damage	피해 (29)
contagious disease	전염병 (26)	dangerous	위험하- (16)
content	기쁘- (16)	dark	어두w- (24); 까맣- (22)
contest	시합 (26)	dark (color)	짙- (21)
continues it/it continues	계속하- (21)	date	연애(를) 하- (17)
continuously	계속(해서) (21)	day after	이튿날 (28)
contract (sickness, disease)	걸리- (19)	days when	시절 (19)
contrary to expectation	오히려(22)	deacon (church)	집사 (24)
convenient	편리하- (26)	deadline	마감일, 마감 (29)
cook in a frying pan	볶- (22)	dean (at university)	학장 (28)
cookie(s)	과자 (21)	death penalty	사형 (29)
cool	시원하- (16); 쌀쌀하- (18); 선선하- (21)	December	섣달 (28)
		decent	점잖- (27)
cool	멋(이) 있-, 멋지- (19)	decide it	결정(을) 하- (18)
copy (counter)	-부 (28)	decide upon	정하- (17)
core	중심 (24)	decision	결정 (18)
cough	기침(을) 하- (24)	declaration	선언 (27)
		declare	선언(을) 하- (27)
counter for letters	-통 (22)		
counter for words	-마디 (29)	deep	깊- (19); 짙- (21)
country(side)	지방 (28)		
couple (husband & wife)	부부 (29)	deep-fried dumplings	튀긴 만두 (22)
course	코스 (23)		
crimson	붉- (27)	deep-fry	튀기- (22)
cross (the street)	건너- (16)	deeply (sleep)	푹 (26)
crossroads	네거리 (17)	defect	흠 (21)
crowded	복잡하- (18)	degree	정도 (28)
crux	중심 (24)	degrees (of temperature)	-도 (26)
cry	눈물(을) 흘리- (24); 우-ㄹ- (16)	delayed (be/get)	연착(이) 되- 지연(이) 되- (19)
cry out	소리(를) 지르- (27)	deliver	배달(을) 하- (21)
culture	문화 (24)	delivery man	배달부 (21)
curious about	궁금하- (17)		

democracy	민주주의 (28)	distressed	속(이) 상하- (16)
dentist	치과의사 (26)	disturb sb	방해(를) 하- (26)
dentistry	치과 (26)		
depart	출발(을) 하- (24)	disturbance	방해 (26)
department	-과 (18)	divide	나누- (16)
departure time	출발시간 (19)	do exercises	연습(을) 하- (16)
deposit	보증금 (18)	do like that	그러- (21)
Dept. chairman	과장(님) (18)	do one's best	최선을 다 하- (28)
derriere	엉덩이 (28)	do one's hair	머리(를) 하- (16)
design	모양 (21)	do so	그러- (21)
desire	원하- (19)	do up a button	단추를 잠그- (21)
desire to eat	입맛 (24)		
develop	발전(을) 하- 발전(을) 시키- (24)	document	서류 (18)
		doll	인형 (26)
development	발전 (24)	dot	점 (28)
diagnosis	진단 (26)	doze	조-ㄹ- (21)
dial a wrong number	잘못 거-ㄹ- (23)	draft	원고 (29)
		drag	끄-ㄹ- (26)
Diamond Mountains	금강산 (28)	draw	끄-ㄹ- (26)
dictionary	사전 (18)	drive	운전(을) 하- (16)
difference	차이 (29)		
different	따- (22); 틀리- (19)	driver	기사 (아저씨) (23)
digestion	소화 (26)		
digestive tablet(s)	소화제 (26)	driver's license	운전면허증 (18)
diligent	부지런하- (22)	drop by/in	들르- (18); 들리- (23)
diligently	부지런히 (22)	drugstore	약국 (18)
dine out	외식(을) 하- (29)	dry (be/get)	마르- (16)
		dull	흥미(가) 없- (28)
dining car	식당차 (19)		
direct(ly)	직접 (21)	dummy	바보 (27)
director (of musical group)	지휘자 (24)	dumpling soup	만두국 (22)
dirty	더러w- (19)	dumplings	만두 (22)
dirty clothes	빨래 (16)	dumplings (boiled)	물만두 (22)
disappear	없어지- (18)	dumplings (deep-fried)	튀긴 만두 (22)
disappointed (be/get)	실망(을) 하- (23)	dumplings (pan-fried)	야끼 만두 (22)
discount	할인 (17)	dumplings (steamed)	찐 만두 (22)
disease	병 (19)	during	-중 (21)
dish	그릇 (24)	duties	직책 (24)
distance	거리 (26)		

E

each other	서로 (29)
ear specialist	이비인후과 (26)
early	이르- (18)
earn (money)	버-ㄹ- (19)
East Asia	동양 (18)
eat a meal	식사(를) 하- (16)
eat out	외식(을) 하- (29)
eat s.th. (honorific)	잡숴 보시- (17)
economic development	경제발전 (24)
efforts	노력 (24)
efforts (make)	노력(을) 하- (24); 애(를) 쓰- (26)
egg (chicken)	달걀, 계란 (22)
Elder (church) (female)	권사 (24)
Elder (church) (male)	장로 (24)
election	선거 (28)
electric shaver	면도기 (16)
elegance	멋 (19)
elegant	멋(이) 있-, 멋지- (19)
elementary school	초등학교 (28)
e-mail	이메일 (28)
embarrassed	창피하- (23)
emigrate	이민(을) 가- (23)
end-of-term party	종강 파티 (23)
energy	기운 (26)
engage in hiking	등산(을) 하- (21)
enjoyably	즐겁게 (18)
enough	충분하- (28)
enough (adv.)	충분히 (28)
enter into matrimony	혼인(을) 하- (29)
entire body	온몸 (24)
entirely	싹 (24)
entrance vestibule	현관 (26)
envious	부러w- (17)

epic novel	대하소설 (28)
era	시절 (19)
erroneously	잘못 (21)
error	실수 (22); 잘못 (21)
especially	특별히 (29); 특히 (17)
Europe	유럽 (17)
European Community	유럽공동체 (17)
every month	매월 (23); 매달 (21)
every week	매주 (21)
every year	매년 (21)
evil	못 되- (22)
examine	검사(를) 하- (26)
examine sb medically	진찰(을) 하- (19)
example	예 (28)
exceed	넘- (29)
exceedingly	매우 (21)
exchange it	바꾸- (18)
excursion	놀러 가- (22)
execute	사형(을) 하- (29)
exercises (do)	연습(을) 하- (16)
exhaust fumes	매연 (21)
exit	나- (17)
expedite	촉진(을) 시키- (24)
expel	추방(을) 하- (26)
experience	경험, 경험 (을) 하- (28)
expert	전문가 (24)
expertise	전문지식 (24)
explain	밝히- (27); 설명(을) 하- (16)
explanation	설명 (16)
explanatory literature	설명서 (18)
export something	수출(을) 하- (24)
express	표현(을) 하- (23)

express (train, bus)	급행 (19)	feebly	소극적으로 (24)
express bus	급행 버스 (19)	feel disappointed	실망(을) 하- (23)
express train	급행열차 (19)	feel distressed	속(이) 상하- (16)
expression (verbal)	표현 (23)	feel embarrassed	부끄러w- (17); 창피하- (23)
extended family	대가족 (28)		
extended family system	대가족 제도 (28)	feel hungry	배(가) 고프- (16)
extent	정도 (28)		
extinguish	끄- (22)	feel relieved	시원하- (16)
extract	뽑- (19)	feel sad	슬프- (16)
extreme	심하- (21)	feel sad and/or empty about	섭섭하- (17)
eye disease	눈병 (19)	feel sick in the stomach	속(이) 나쁘- (22)

F

		feel sleepy	졸리- (21)
		feel thirsty	목(이) 마르- (16)
face	얼굴 (17)	feel wistful about	섭섭하- (17)
facilitate	촉진(을) 시키- (24)	fever	열(이) 있- (26)
Fahrenheit	화씨 (26)	few	약간 (27)
fail	낙제(를) 하- (17)	fib	거짓말 (21)
		fight	싸움 (28)
fair	공평하- (23)	fill in (a form)	기입(을) 하- (17)
fall	떨어지- (27)		
fall (into)	빠지- (28)	filthy	더러w- (19)
fall down	넘어지- (22)	finally	끝으로 (24); 드디어 (16)
fall in love	사랑에 빠지- (24); 연애 (를) 하- (17)	finals	결승전 (29)
fall out (hair)	빠지- (28)	fire breaks out	불(이) 나- (22)
family doctor	가정의 (26)		
family system	가족제도 (28)	fireworks	불꽃놀이 (27)
famous	유명하- (18)	first	우선 (24)
fare	요금 (17)	first day	초하루(날) (28)
fashionable	유행이- (19)		
fasten (buttons, snaps)	잠그-; 끼- (21)	first of all	첫째로 (24)
		first-aid treatment	응급치료 (26)
fat	뚱뚱하- (16)		
fat (get)	살(이) 찌- (27)	firstly	첫째로 (24); 우선 (24)
		fish (live)	물고기 (22)
fatigued	고단하- (21)	fish (to eat)	생선 (22)
fax	팩스 (23)	fit	어울리- (21)
fax number	팩스번호 (23)	fix	정하- (17)
		fix it	고치- (24)
feast	한턱 (17)	flaw	흠 (21)
fee	요금 (17)		

flesh	살 (27)	game of "Go"	바둑 (24)
flu	독감 (26); 몸살감기, 감기 몸살 (21)	gas station	주유소 (18)
		gasoline	휘발유, 기름 (18)
fluently	유창하게; 자연스럽게 (18)	gather (clouds/fog)	끼- (21)
		gather (it)	모으- (16)
		gathering	모임 (18)
flunk	낙제(를) 하- (17)	gene	유전자 (23)
fog	안개 (21)	general fatigue	몸살 (21)
fool	바보 (27)	gentleman	신사 (21)
for a long time	오랫동안, 오래 (16)	gentry	양반 (29)
		get	얻- (29); 구하- (26)
for example	예를 든다면, 예를 들면, 예를 들자면 (28)	get a big belly	배(가) 나오- (24)
		get a discount	할인(을) 받- (17)
for first time in a long while	오래간만에 (16)	get a haircut	이발(을) 하- (16)
for the first time	비로소 (28)	get a nosebleed	코피(가) 나- (24)
for the most part	대부분 (28)	get a perm	파마(를) 하- (16)
forecast	예보 (26)		
fork	포크 (22)	get a scolding	야단(을) 맞- (18)
form (clouds/fog)	끼- (21)		
formal event	행사 (27)	get a shot	주사(를) 맞- (26)
Formal or Polite Style	존댓말 (29)		
fortunate	다행 (24)	get an upset stomach	배탈(이) 나- (24)
fortunately	다행히(도) (24)		
		get angry	화(를) 내-, 화(가) 나- (27)
foul	위반 (29)		
four seasons	사계절 (23)		
freely	자연스럽게 (18)	get broken	깨지- (29)
		get delayed (train, plane)	연착(이) 되- (19)
French language	불어 (21)		
fresh	시원하- (16); 선선하- (21)	get discharged (from hospital)	퇴원(을) 하- (24)
fried rice	볶음밥 (22)	get fat	살(이) 찌- (27)
full name	성명 (17)		
full-length novel	장편소설 (28)	get gas	기름(을) 넣- (18)
funny	웃기- (28)	get in big trouble	큰일(이) 나- (22)
furthermore	또한 (16)		
		get in the way	방해(가) 되- (26)
		get married	혼인(을) 하- (29)
G			
		get married (man)	장가(를) 가- (27)
gain weight	살(이) 찌- (27)		
game (sport)	시합 (26)		

get married (woman)	시집(을) 가- (27)	go hiking	등산(을) 가- (21)
get off (bus, train)	내리- (17)	go home from work	퇴근(을) 하- (22)
get old (people)	늙- (19)		
get old (things)	낡- (19)	go into hospital	입원(을) 하- (24)
get one's hair cut	머리(를) 깎- 머리(를) 자르- (16)	go on an outing/picnic	야유회(를) 가- (22)
get out of hospital	퇴원(을) 하- (24)	go on a (school) outing	소풍(을) 가- (22)
get out of the way	비키- (26)	go on an excursion	놀러 가- (22)
get permission	허락(을) 받- (26)	go shopping (for food)	장(을) 보- (21)
get resolved	해결(이) 되- (27)	go to work	출근(을) 하- (22)
get sick to one's stomach	배탈(이) 나- (24)	go well with	어울리- (21)
get to know	사귀- (24)	go (to sb's house) to visit	놀러 가- (22)
ginseng chicken soup	삼계탕 (17)	"G o"	바둑 (24)
give a sermon	설교(를) 하- (24)	goal	목적 (28)
give a discount	할인(을) 해 주- (17)	God	하느님 (Catholic), 하나님 (Protestant) (18)
give a lecture	강의(를) 하- (16)		
give a scolding	혼(을) 내- (23); 야단 (을) 치- (18)	good taste	멋 (19)
		good upbringing	얌전하- (27)
give a shot to	주사(를) 놓- (26)	good-for-nothing	못 되- (22)
give an example	예를 드-ㄹ- (28)	government	정부 (27)
		government party	여당 (28)
give an explanation	설명(을) 하- (16)	government post	벼슬 (29)
give back	돌려 주- (28)	grade	점수 (28)
give birth to	낳- (16)	grades	성적 (23)
give final embellishments to	다듬- (17)	gradually	점점 (18)
give sb a hard time	혼(을) 내- (23)	graduate of same school	동창 (18)
		grammar	문법 (18)
give up (on)	포기(를) 하- (23)	grasp	잡- (21)
		great	훌륭하- (23)
go a long time	오래 가- (27)	Great Outdoors	대자연 (24)
go around	도-ㄹ- (17)	greater part	대부분 (28)
go away on business	출장(을) 가- (24)	green	푸른(색) (21), 파란 (색), 녹색 (21)
go bad (food/one's mood)	상하- (24)		
go bankrupt	파산(이) 되- (27)	greeting	인사 (17)
		grey	회색 (21)
go calling on	찾아 가- (18)	groom	신랑 (17)
		grow (intr.)	자라- (24)

grow it	기르- (27)
guess	추측, 추측 (을) 하- (27)
guitar	기타 (18)
gum	껌 (22)
guy	-놈 (24)

H

habit(s)	풍습 (28)
habitually	으레 (28)
hairdresser's	미용실 (16)
hand in	제출(을) 하- (27); 내- (17)
hand over	건네- (29)
hang around with	어울리- (18)
hang up (telephone)	끊- (27)
happen	생기- (28)
happening	행사 (27)
happily	즐겁게 (18)
happiness	행복 (21)
happy	기쁘- (16); 행복하- (21)
hard time (give)	혼(을) 내- (23)
hard time (have)	혼(이) 나- (22)
hard to deal with	고약하- (24)
hard work	노력 (24)
hard working	부지런하- (16)
harm	피해 (29)
hasten	서두르- (22)
hastily	급히 (26)
have	갖고 있- (24); 가지고 있- (21)
have (baby)	낳- (16)
have a bath	목욕(을) 하- (16)
have a checkup	진찰(을) 받- (26)
have a hard time of it	혼(이) 나- (22)
have a party	파티(를) 여-ㄹ- (23)
have an audience with	뵈w- (18)

have in one's possession	갖고 있- (24); 가지고 있- (21)
have made to order	맞추- (21)
have s.th. with one	갖고 있- (24); 가지고 있- (21)
he	그 (26)
head of department	과장(님) (18)
heating	난방 장치 (17)
heaven	하늘 (18)
height	키 (17)
help	도w- (17)
here	이리 (16)
hide	숨- (29)
hide it	숨기- (29)
high	높- (19)
high school	고등학교 (28)
high society	상류사회 (28)
high temperature	열(이) 높- (26)
hiking	등산 (21); 등산(을) 하- (21)
history	역사 (24)
hit	때리- (18)
hold	가지- (24)
holiday	휴가 (17)
hometown	고향 (22)
hospital	병원 (16)
hospitalized (be/get)	입원(을) 하- (24)
host a party	파티(를) 여-ㄹ- (23)
host sb	대접(을) 하- (17)
hot and muggy	무더w- (18)
hot to touch	뜨거w- (16)
however much (one VERBs)	아무리 [... -어도] (18)
humbly see or meet	뵈w- (18)
hungry	배(가) 고프- (16)
hurry	서두르- (22)
husband & wife couple	부부 (29)

I

ice hockey	아이스 하키 (23)
ID card	신분증 (29)
idea	생각 (19)
idiot	바보 (27)
ignoble	천하- (29)
ignorant	무식하- (19)
ill (honorific)	편찮으시- (18)
immediate(ly)	직접 (21); 당장 (18); 얼른 (22)
immigrant	이민자 (23)
immigrate	이민(을) 오- (23)
immigration	이민 (23)
import	수입(을) 하- (24)
important	중요하- (21)
in a rush	급히 (26)
in advance	미리 (26)
in any case	하여튼, 어쨌든, 어차피 (22)
in part(s)	부분적으로 (29)
in particular	특히 (17)
in person	직접 (21)
in proper fashion	제대로 (18)
in that way	그리 (16)
in the middle of	-중 (21)
in the past	옛날 (19)
in the way	방해(가) 되- (26)
in vogue	유행하- (19)
incessantly	자꾸(만) (21)
include it	포함(을) 하- (17)
included (be/get)	포함(이) 되- (17)
incorrect	틀리- (19)
indigenous	고유 (28)
indigenous customs	고유풍습 (28)
indigent	가난하- (18)

indigestion	소화(가) 안 되- (26)
individual person	개인 (26)
infant	어린 아이 (19)
infer	추측(을) 하- (27)
inference	추측 (27)
inform	알리- (24)
injection	주사, 주사 (를) 맞-, 주사(를) 놓- (26)
insect	벌레 (27)
inspect	검사(를) 하- (26)
inspection	검사 (26)
instant	순간 (29)
institution	제도 (28)
insurance	보험 (18)
insurance charge	보험료 (18)
insurance fee	보험료 (18)
insure	보험(을) 드-ㄹ- (18)
intact	그대로 (28)
intense	심하- (21)
interchange	교류 (24)
interesting	흥미(가) 있- (28)
intern	인턴 (26)
internal medicine	내과 (26)
international	국제- (24)
international student	유학생 (24)
international exchange	국제교류 (24)
international relations	국제관계 (24)
international student	유학생 (24)
interpreter	통역사 (29)
interpreting (simultaneous)	통역 (29)
intersection	네거리 (17)
interval	기간 (28)
Intimate Style	반말 (29)

J

January	정월 (28)
jest	농담(을) 하- (21)
jet-black	새까맣- (22)
jet lag	시차 (29)
jewelry shop	보석상 (28)
job	직장 (27)
joke	농담, 농담 (을) 하- (21)
journey	여행 (17)
junior from school	후배 (18)
just as it is	그대로 (28)

K

keep (appointment/promise)	지키- (16)
keep after for	조르- (27)
keep one's presence of mind	정신(을) 차리- (27)
key	열쇠 (17)
key (car-)	(차)키 (17)
kill	죽이- (29)
kimchee	김치 (16)
kimchee stew	김치찌깨 (22)
kind	친절하- (26)
king	왕 (28)
kisaeng	기생 (29)
knife	칼 (16)
knowledgeable	유식하- (19)
knowledge	지식 (19)
Korea-U.S.	한미 (24)
Korean American	재미교포 (23)
Korean Canadian	캐나다교포 (23)
Korean chess	장기 (24)
Korean *geisha*	기생 (29)
Korean gentry	양반 (29)
Korean Japanese	재일교포 (23)
Korean national flower	무궁화 (19)
Korean traditional novel	고전 소설 (29)
Kŭmgang Mountains	금강산 (28)

L

large family	대가족 (28)
last long	오래 가- (27)
lastly	끝으로 (24)
lately	최근에 (19)
later (on)	-후 (16); 나중에 (22)
latest	최근 (19)
laugh	웃- (16)
launder	빠-르- (22)
laundry	빨래 (16)
lazy	게으르- (16)
lazy person	게으름뱅이 (21)
lazybones	게으름뱅이 (21)
learned	유식하- (19)
leave (behind)	두- (29)
leave from work	휴가 (17)
leave the office	퇴근(을) 하- (22)
lecture	강의, 강의 (를) 하-; 강연 (16)
left over	남- (19)
legitimate	정당하- (29)
lend	빌려 주- (17)
less	덜 (21)
lesson	-과 (18)
let sb know	알리- (24)
let sb off/out	내리- (17)
liar	거짓말쟁이 (21)
license	면허증 (18)
lie	거짓말 (21)
light	밝- (27)
light (color)	옅- (21)
like that	그렇- (21)
line	줄 (26)
Line 2 (on Seoul subway)	이호선 (19)
literature	문학 (23)
little	약간 (27)
little by little	점점 (18)
little monkey (child)	장난꾸러기 (26)
living room	거실 (23)
lobby	로비 (19)
local (train, bus)	완행 (19)

lock (door, window)	잠그- (21)	make a stew	찌개 (를)
lodge at	숙박(을) 하-		끓이- (22)
	(17)	make a visit	방문(을) 하-
lodging	숙박 (17)		(24)
lodging form	숙박부 (17)	make an appointment	약속(을) 하-
long	기-ㄹ- (18)		(16)
long weekend	연휴 (21)	make bright	밝히- (27)
long-distance	장거리 (26)	make clear	밝히- (27)
long-lasting	오래 가- (27)	make efforts	노력(을) 하-
look down at/upon	내려다 보-		(24); 애(를)
	(26)		쓰- (26)
look for a job/work	직장(을)	make friends with	사귀- (24)
	구하- (27)	make fun of	놀리- (23)
look in (through)	드려다 보-	make haste	서두르- (22)
	(26)	make it red	붉히- (27)
look out at	내다 보- (26)	make laugh	웃기- (28)
look up at	쳐다 보- (26)	make perfect sense	당연하- (23)
lose (game)	지- (29)	make preparations	준비(를) 하-
lose s.th.	잃어버리-		(16)
	(24)	make ready	차리- (27)
lose weight	살(이) 빠지-	make s.th. of	삼- (29)
	(27)	make to order	맞추- (21)
loud	시끄러w-	manuscript	원고 (29)
	(19)	manuscript fee	원고료 (29)
love	사랑 (24)	manuscript paper	원고지 (29)
low	낮- (19)	map	지도 (26)
low birth (of)	천하- (29)	mark	점수; 점 (28)
lower-class society	하류사회	marks	성적 (23)
	(28)	marry	시집(을)
lower classes	하류사회		보내- (27)
	(28)	marry off (man)	장가(를)
lowly	천하- (29)		보내- (27)
luck	다행 (24)	marry off (woman)	시집(을)
			보내- (27)
		match	시합 (26)
M		match with	어울리- (21)
		mathematics	수학 (24)
		matrimony	혼인 (29)
M.P.	국회의원	mayor	시장 (26)
	(28)	meaning	뜻 (27)
magistrate	감사 (29)	measure	재- (21)
maid	파출부 (26)	measure	수단 (29)
main road	길거리 (18)	medical examination	진찰 (26)
make (a stew)	끓이- (22)	medical school	의과 대학
make (money)	버-ㄹ- (19)		(26)
make (rice)	지(ㅅ)- (19)	medical treatment	치료 (26)
make a mistake	실수(를) 하-	medicine to help digestion	소화제 (26)
	(22)	meet (with) sb esteemed	만나 뵈w-
make a presentation	발표(를)하-		(18)
	(27)	meeting	모임 (18)

member of church choir	성가대원 (24)
memorize	외우- (18)
mess	엉망 (24)
metamorphose into	변하- (27)
metropolis	대도시 (28)
middle	-중 (21)
middle age	중년 (19)
middle-class society	중류사회 (28)
middle school	중학교 (28)
middle-aged people	중년들 (19)
mile	마일 (18)
mileage	마일수 (18)
mind	정신 (17)
Ministry of Foreign Affairs	외무부 (24)
mischief maker	장난꾸러기 (26)
misfortune	불행 (24)
misprint	오자 (21)
miss (bus, plane)	놓치- (16)
mistake	실수 (22); 잘못 (21)
mistress	첩 (29)
misunderstand	오해(를) 하- (18)
misunderstanding	오해 (18)
modest	겸손하- (28)
moment	순간 (29)
monthly salary	월급 (24)
more than	넘- (29)
moreover	또한 (16)
most recent	최근 (19)
Mother Nature	대자연 (24)
Mount Sŏrak	설악산 (21)
mountain range	산맥 (28)
mountain top	산꼭대기 (27)
mousse for hair	무스 (17)
much (. . .-er)	훨씬 (19)
multivolumed novel	대하소설 (28)
mutually	서로 (29)
My goodness!	세상에! (22)

N

nap	낮잠(을) 자- (22)
nasty	고약하- (24)
natural	당연하- (23)
naturally	당연히 (23); 자연스럽게 (18)
nature	자연 (24)
navel	배꼽 (28)
navel falls out (w/ laughter)	배꼽(이) 빠지- (28)
navy blue	남색 (21)
nearly	거의 (16)
necessary	필요하- (21)
necessity	필요 (21)
need	필요 (21)
needed	필요하- (21)
nerd	공부벌레 (27)
nerve (s)	신경 (23); 정신 (17)
nervous	신경(이) 쓰이-, 신경 (을) 쓰- (23)
new	새로w- (19)
New Village	새마을 (19)
New Year's Day	설날 (28)
New Year's Eve	섣달 그믐 (28)
newly	새로 (27)
news	소식 (17)
next day	이튿날 (28)
no concern (of)	상관(이) 없- (19)
no energy	기운(이) 없- (26)
no idea	영문(을) 모르- (28)
no NOUN at all	아무NOUN도 (23)
no-good	못 쓰- (22)
nobility	양반 (29)
noise	소리 (27)
noisy	시끄러w- (19)

nose specialist	이비인후과 (26)	old NOUN	헌 NOUN (19)
nosebleed	코피 (24)	old person	늙은이 (19)
not at all amusing	흥미(가) 없- (28)	old person (honorific)	나이 드신 분 (19)
not be concerned	상관(이) 없- (19)	oldster	늙은이 (19)
not care	상관(이) 없- (19)	oldster (respectful)	나이 드신 분 (19)
not have a clue	영문(을) 모르- (28)	on the contrary	오히려(22)
not salted enough	싱거w- (22)	on the phone	통화중이에요 (23)
not understand	영문(을) 모르- (28)	on the spot	당장 (18)
not well (honorific)	편찮으시- (18)	one's best (do)	최선을 다 하- (28)
nothing at all	아무것도 (24)	one-point-five generation	일점오세 (23)
notorious event	사건 (28)	opened (be/get)	열리- (17)
novel	소설 (28)	opera	오페라 (19)
novella	중편소설 (28)	operate a vehicle	운전(을) 하- (16)
nuclear family	핵가족 (28)	operating theatre	수술실 (23)
nuclear weapons	핵무기 (28)	operation (medical)	수술(을) 하- 수술(을) 받- (23)
nucleus	핵 (28)	oppose	반대(를) 하- (29)
nuisance	귀찮- (16)	opposition	반대 (29)
number ___	-호 (17)	opposition party	야당 (28)
nurse	간호사 (26)	orange	오렌지색; 주황색 (21)
		order	명령, 명령 (을)하- (27)

O

objective	목적 (28)	order (to specifications)	맞추- (21)
obstetrics and gynecology	산부인과 (26)	ordinalizer	제- (18)
obstruction	방해 (26)	Oriental painting	동양화 (23)
obtain	얻- (29); 구하- (26)	originally	원래 (27)
obvious	분명하- (23)	others	딴 사람들 (22); 남 (29)
obviously	분명히 (23)	out of order	고장(이) 나- (28)
offer up	바치- (28)	outgoingly	적극적으로 (24)
official post	벼슬 (29)	outing (company)	야유회 (22)
offspring	자식 (29)	outing (school)	소풍 (22)
often	흔히 (26)	over there	저리 (16)
Oh, my!	세상에! (22)	overwork	무리(를) 하- (22)
oil	기름 (18)	overcast	흐리- (18)
old (people)	늙- (19)		
old (things)	낡- (19)		
old days	옛날 (19)		

overdo it	무리(를) 하- (22)	personally	직접 (21)
overpass	육교 (16)	pester for	조르- (27)
overseas Korean(s)	교민 (23)	petrol	휘발유, 기름 (18)
overseas Korean(s)	교포 (23)	pharmacist	약사 (18)
		pharmacy	약국 (18)
		phone is busy	통화중이에요 (23)

P

pain in the neck	귀찮- (16)	picnic (company)	야유회 (22)
pamphlet	설명서 (18)	picnic (school)	소풍 (22)
pan-fried dumplings	야끼 만두 (22)	pigeon	비둘기 (19)
paper (academic)	논문 (27)	pink	핑크색; 분홍색 (21)
park the car	주차(를) 하- (29)	pitiful	불쌍하- (18)
parking	주차 (29)	place	두- (29)
parking infraction	주차위반 (29)	place	장소 (27); 자리 (18)
parking lot	주차장 (29)	plan	예정; 계획 (24)
part	부분 (29)	plate	그릇 (24)
part with	헤어지- (19)	play *changgi*	장기(를) 두- (24)
partially	부분적으로 (29)	play *paduk*	바둑(을) 두- (24)
particular	특별하- (29)	play the guitar	기타(를) 치- (18)
particularly	특별히 (29)	play too hard	무리(를) 하- (22)
party to honor one's teacher	사은회 파티 (23)	pleased to see/hear	반가w- (22)
pass beyond	넘- (29)	plenty	충분하- (28)
pass by	지나가- (19)	plot	줄거리 (29)
passively	소극적으로 (24)	pocket memo-book	수첩 (22)
passport	여권 (24)	pocket money	용돈 (26)
patient	환자 (23)	point	점 (28)
peace	평화 (28)	police station	경찰서 (24)
peak	산꼭대기 (27)	policeman	경찰 (24)
pedestrian	육교 (16)	Polite or Formal Style	존댓말 (29)
pediatrics	소아과 (26)	polite society	상류사회 (28)
peep in (through)	드려다 보- (26)	politician	정치가 (21)
pepper (black)	후추 (22)	pollution	공해 (21)
pepper (red)	고추 (22)	poor	가난하- (18)
perform an operation	수술(을) 하- (23)	popcorn	팝콘 (19)
perm	파마 (16)	popular	인기(가) 있-; 유행하- (19)
permission	허락 (26)	portion	부분 (29)
permit	허락(을) 하- (26)	position (on an issue)	입장 (24)
person of honor at a party	주인공 (23)	positively	적극적으로 (24)
		possess	가지- (24)

postage	우표 (17)	propel s.th. forward	추진(을) 하-
potato soup	감자국 (22)		/시키- (24)
pour it	부(ㅅ)- (19)	properly	제대로 (18)
powder	가루 (26)	proposal	제안 (24)
practice	연습, 연습	protagonist	주인공 (23)
	(을) 하- (16)	provinces	지방 (28)
pray	기도(를) 하-	public bath	목욕탕 (16)
	(24)	public presentation	발표 (27)
prayer	기도 (24)	publish it	출판(을) 하-
prearrangement	예정 (24)		(28)
prediction	예보 (26)	publishing company	출판사 (28)
preferable	나(ㅅ)- (23)	pull	끄-ㄹ- (26);
preoccupied	정신(이) 없-		당기- (21)
	(17)	pulse	맥; 맥박 (26)
preparation (of lessons)	예습 (24)	purple	보라색 (21)
preparations	준비 (16)	purse	지갑 (26)
prepare	준비(를) 하-	push	미-ㄹ- (21)
	(16)	put	두- (29)
prepare (lessons)	예습(을) 하-	put in an appearance	나타나- (19)
	(24)	put in gas	기름(을) 넣-
prepare food	음식(을)		(18)
	차리- (27)	put on one's makeup	화장(을) 하-
present (a paper)	발표(를)하-		(16)
	(27)	put up at	숙박(을) 하-
president (of country)	대통령 (27)		(17)
president (of university)	총장 (28)		
presidential candidate	대통령 후보		
	(28)		
prevaricate	우물쭈물하-	**Q**	
	(27)		
preview	예습, 예습	quarrel	싸우- (19)
	(을) 하- (24)	quickly	어서 (16);
previous appointment	선약 (17)		얼른 (22)
previous day	전날 (28)	quiet	조용하- (18)
previous engagement	선약 (17)	quietly	가만히 (22);
primarily	중심적으로		조용히 (18)
	(24)	quit	그만하-;
promise	약속, 약속		그만두- (18)
	(을) 하-	quite	꽤; 퍽(이나)
	(16)		(28); 상당히
promote	촉진(을)		(17)
	시키-; 추진		
	(을) 하-/		
	시키- (24)	**R**	
pronounce	선언(을) 하-		
	(27)	rainy season	장마철 (28)
pronouncement	선언 (27)	raise	기르- (27)
proofread it	교정(을) 하-	rascal	말썽꾸러기
	(29)		(26)

rather	꽤; 퍽(이나) (28)	report (written)	보고서 (22)
		report card	성적표 (23)
rather (than)	오히려(22)	report for work	출근(을) 하- (22)
razor blade	면도칼 (16)		
realize	깨달- (ㄹ ~ ㄷ) (28)	rescue it	구하- (28)
		reserved seats	예약석 (19)
realize one's dream	꿈(을) 이루- (28)	resident in Japan	재일 (23)
		resident in the U.S.	재미 (23)
receipt	영수증 (23)	resident overseas Korean(s)	교민 (23)
receive a discount	할인(을) 받- (17)	resident/staying (in)	주... (24)
		resolve (a problem)	해결(을) 하- (27)
receive medical treatment	치료(를) 받- (26)		
recently	최근에 (19)	resolved (be/get)	해결(이) 되- (27)
reception room	접대실 (22)		
reception room (in home)	응접실 (22)	respect	존경, 존경 (을) 하- (29)
reckon	치- (28)	respectable	점잖- (27)
recover (e.g., from illness)	회복(을) 하- 회복(이) 되- (26)	respected (be/get)	존경(을) 받- (29)
		respectful speech	존댓말 (29)
recuperate	몸조리(를) 하- (27)	respond	대답(을) 하- (17)
red	빨간(색) (21); 빨갛- (22)	response	대답 (17)
		responsibilities of office	직책 (24)
red pepper	고추 (22)	review	복습, 복습 (을) 하- (24)
red pepper powder	고추가루 (26)	revision	복습 (24)
redden it	붉히- (27)	reviving	시원하- (16)
referee	심판; 심판 (을) 하- (29)	ribs	갈비 (16)
		ricecake soup	떡국 (22)
refined	유식하- (19)	rich (color)	짙- (21)
refreshing	시원하- (16)	right away	얼른 (22); 어서 (16); 곧 (21)
refuse	거절(을) 하- (24)		
register	등록(을) 하- (23)	rightful	정당하- (29)
		ringing sound (of bell)	벨소리 (23)
registration	등록 (23)	roasted chestnuts	구운 밤 (21)
regular (customer/place)	단골 (27)	robbed (be/get)	도둑(을) 맞- (24)
regular customer	단골손님 (27)		
relieved	시원하- (16)	rock	돌 (27)
remain	남- (19)	Rocky Mountains	록키산맥 (28)
remember	기억(이) 나- 기억(을) 하- (19)	ROK embassy in the USA	주미대한민국 대사관 (24)
		romance (genre)	낭만소설 (29)
rent (a car)	빌리- (16)	romantic	낭만적 (29)
repair it	고치- (24)	room with a bath	욕실 (17)
report	보고(를) 하- (22)	Rose of Sharon	무궁화 (19)
		rump	엉덩이 (28)

run a high fever	열(이) 높- (26)	secret inspector-general	암행어사 (29)
run out of s.th.	떨어지- (27)	secretary	비서 (17); 서기 (24)
		section	부분 (29)

S

		see s.b. esteemed	만나 뵈w- (18)
S. O. B.	-놈; 고약한 놈; 나쁜 놈 (24)	select	선택(을) 하-택하- (24)
		sell (well)	팔리- (28)
s.th. different	딴 것 (22)	semi-finals	준결승전 (29)
s.th. said in all seriousness	진담 (21)		
sad	슬프- (16)	send a telegram	전보(를) 치- (28)
sad and/or empty about	섭섭하- (17)		
salary	봉급 (24)	send abroad to study	유학(을) 시키- (24)
salary (annual)	연봉 (24)		
salary (monthly)	월급 (24)	send an (email)	띄우- (28)
salt	소금 (22)	senior from school	선배 (18)
saltiness of food	간 (22)	sentence	문장 (26)
salty (too salty)	짜- (22)	separate from	헤어지- (19)
same time	동시 (29)	separately	따로 (18)
save it	구하- (28)	serious happening	큰일(이) 나- (22)
say what you like	뭐니뭐니 해도 (21)		
		sermon	설교; 설교 (를) 하- (24)
say (so)	그러- (27)		
sb who dresses well	멋쟁이 (21)	service	서비스 (17)
sb's place	-네 (23)	service (in church)	예배 (24)
scandal	사건 (28)	set off	출발(을) 하- (24)
scandal (sexual)	스캔들 (28)		
scenery	경치 (21)	settle upon	정하- (17)
schedule	예정 (24); 시간표 (24)	severe	심하- (21)
		severe cold or flu	몸살감기, 감기몸살 (21)
scholar	학자 (27)		
scholarship	장학금 (24)	shallow	얕- (19)
science	과학 (24)	shampoo	샴푸 (19)
scold	혼(을) 내- (23); 야단 (을) 치- (18)	shape	모양 (21)
		share	나누- (16)
		shave	면도(를) 하- (16)
scolded (be/get)	야단(을) 맞- (18)		
scolding	야단 (18)	shaving cream	면도크림 (16)
seashore	바닷가 (24)	shed tears	눈물(을) 흘리- (24)
season	계절 (23)		
seat	자리 (18)	short	짧- (18)
second day	이튿날 (28)	short story	단편소설 (28)
second generation	이세 (23)		
second of all	둘째로 (24)	short-distance	단거리 (26)
second-hand bookshop	헌책방 (19)	shot	주사 (26)
secondly	둘째로 (24)		

shout	소리(를) 지르- (27)	so-called NOUN	소위 NOUN (27)
show it	보이- (17)	so-so	그저 그렇- (22)
show up	나타나- (19)	soccer	축구 (23)
shower	소나기 (21)	social status	신분 (29)
shut (get)	닫히- (17)	socialism	사회주의 (28)
sick (get)	병(이) 나- (19)	society	사회 (28)
sick in the stomach	속(이) 나쁘- (22)	sociologist	사회학자 (28)
sick person	환자 (23)	sociology	사회학 (28)
sick to one's stomach	배탈(이) 나- (24)	sold (be/get)	팔리- (28)
sickness	병 (19)	solution (to a problem)	해결 (27)
simultaneous interpreting	동시통역(을) 하- (29)	some	약간 (27)
simultaneously	동시 (29)	sometimes	어떤 때는 (22)
single room	독방 (17)	somewhat	약간 (27)
size	사이즈 (21)	somewhat spicy-tasting	매콤하- (22)
skin	피부 (27)	sooner (than)	오히려 (22)
sky	하늘 (18)	sore stomach	속(이) 나쁘- (22)
sleep late	늦잠(을) 자- (22)	sorrowful	슬프- (16)
sleepy	졸리- (21)	sound	소리 (27)
slim	날씬하- (22)	soundly (rest)	푹 (26)
slippery	미끄러w- (29)	soup	국 (22)
slow	느리- (19)	sour	시- (26)
slow bus	완행버스 (19)	soy sauce	간장 (22)
slow train	완행열차 (19)	spacious	넓- (22)
small and neat	조촐하- (23)	speak haltingly	더듬거리- (23)
small child	어린 아이 (19)	special	특별하- (29)
small city	소도시 (28)	specialist	전문가 (24)
small notebook	수첩 (22)	specialized knowledge	전문지식 (24)
smear (mousse, cream)	바르- (17)	specialty	전문 (24)
smells	냄새(가) 나- (24)	specifically	구체적으로 (24)
smile	웃- (16)	spectator	관객 (28)
smoke	연기 (21)	speed	속도; 속도 위반(을) 하- (29)
snail	골뱅이 (28)	speeding violation	속도위반 (29)
snap	단추 (21)	spend time with	어울리- (18)
so	그렇- (21); 그리 (16)	spicy chopped beef soup	육개장 (17)
so to speak	말하자면 (23)	spill it	흘리- (24)
		spin	도-ㄹ- (17)
		spirit	정신 (17)
		split up with	헤어지- (19)

spoil (food/one's mood)	상하- (24)	study abroad	유학(을) 가- (24)
spoon	순가락 (22)	stutter	더듬거리- (23)
sprinkle it	뿌리- (22)	style	멋 (19); 모양 (21)
spruce up	다듬- (17)		
stamp	우표 (17)	stylish	멋(이) 있-, 멋지- (19)
stand (on an issue)	입장 (24)		
stand in line	줄(을) 서- (26)	stylish person	멋쟁이 (21)
stand to reason	당연하- (23)	submit	제출(을) 하- (27)
stand treat	한턱(을) 내- (17)	submit an article	기고(를) 하- (29)
stand up	일어서- (24)	success	성공 (28)
standpoint (on an issue)	입장 (24)	successful (become)	성공(을) 하- (28)
stare at	쳐다 보- (26)		
station in life	신분 (29)	such a NOUN	그런 NOUN, 이런, 저런 NOUN (19)
stay up all night	밤(을) 새- (29)		
steadfast	착실하- (26)	suffer	고생(을) 하- (29)
steady girlfriend/boyfriend	애인 (19)		
steal	훔치- (24)	suffer damage	피해(를) 입-/받- (29)
steam	찌- (22)		
steamed dumplings	찐 만두 (22)	suffer from general fatigue	몸살(이) 나- (21)
stew	찌개 (22)		
stick to	지키- (16)	suffer hardship(s)	고생(을) 하- (29)
still	가만히 (22)		
stone	돌 (27)	suffer harm	피해(를) 입-/받- (29)
stop	서- (19)		
stop (rain/snow)	그치- (24)	sufficient	충분하- (28)
stop by	들리- (23); 들르- (18)	sufficiently	충분히 (28)
		suggestion	제안 (24)
stop doing it	그만두-; 그만하- (18)	supermarket	슈퍼 (22)
		sure enough	역시 (28)
stopper (train, bus)	완행 (19)	surgeon	외과의사 (26)
stopping bus	완행버스 (19)		
		surgery	외과 (26)
stopping train	완행열차 (19)	surmise	추측(을) 하- (27)
storm	폭풍우 (29)	surprised	놀라- (24)
straight away	당장 (18)	swallow it	삼키- (22)
strangers	남 (29)	sweet	다-ㄹ- (26)
stream	개울 (19)	sweet potato	고구마 (22)
street	거리 (18)	sweets	사탕 (21)
strike	때리- (18)	swipe it	훔치- (24)
strong (drinks)	독하- (22)	switch off	끄- (22)
struggle	싸움 (28)	switch on	켜- (22)
student days	학생시절 (19)	system	제도 (28)
student studying abroad	유학생 (24)		

T

T'aebaek Mountains 태백산맥 (28)

take 가지- (24)

take (sb) along 데리-, 데려가-, 데리고 가- (23)

take (sb) along (humble) 모시-, 모셔 가-, 모시고 가- (23)

take sb's blood pressure 혈압(을) 재- (26)

take (thing) along 가져가-, 가지고 가- (24)

take a nap 낮잠(을) 자- (22)

take a shower 샤워(를) 하- (24)

take care of one's health 몸조리(를) 하- (27)

take hold of 잡- (21)

take measurements of 재- (21)

take out 뽑- (19)

take out (from pocket) 꺼내- (28)

take photos 사진(을) 찍- (22)

take sb's pulse 맥(을) 짚-, 맥박(을) 재- (26)

take sb's temperature 체온(을) 재- (26)

take out insurance 보험(을) 드-ㄹ- (18)

tall 높- (19); 키가 크- (17)

taxi fare 택시요금 (18)

teach sb a lesson 혼(을) 내- (23)

tears 눈물 (24)

tease 놀리- (23)

tedious 지루하- (17)

telegram 전보 (28)

tell sb (humble) 말씀(을) 드리- (16)

terribly 몹시 (18)

test 검사(를) 하- (26)

textbook 교과서 (21)

textiles 섬유 (22)

that direction 저리 (16)

that person (male) 그 (26)

that sort of NOUN 그런 NOUN, 이런 NOUN, 저런 NOUN (19)

that way 그렇- (21); 저리 (16)

thesis (academic) 논문 (27)

thick (liquid or makeup) 진하- (22)

thief 도둑(놈) (24)

thin 날씬하- (22)

thin (fog) 엷- (21)

think 생각(을) 하- (22)

think (so) 그러- (27)

think of s.th. 생각(이) 나- (19)

thirsty 목(이) 마르- (16)

this direction 이리 (16)

this way 이리 (16)

thorough 착실하- (26)

thoroughfare 길거리 (18)

thought 생각 (19)

three days from now 글피 (21)

throat 목 (16)

throat specialist 이비인후과 (26)

throw a party 파티(를) 여-ㄹ- (23)

throw up 토하- (26)

time 시절 (19)

time difference 시차 (29)

time in the past 시절 (19)

time period 기간 (28)

time table 시간표 (24)

tired 고단하- (21)

title (of book/work) 제목 (27)

to one's heart's content 마음껏; 실컷 (22)

to one's liking 마음에 드-ㄹ- (21)

to point where one is sick of it 실컷 (22)

to that extent	그리 (16)
toenjang stew	된장찌개 (22)
totally (forgot)	깜빡 (29)
trade it	바꾸- (18)
traffic	교통 (22)
traffic accident	교통사고 (26)
traffic infraction	교통위반 (29)
transfer	건네- (29)
transgression	위반 (29)
translate it	번역, 번역 (을) 하- (29)
translator	번역가 (29)
travel	여행, 여행 (을) 하- (17)
treat	한턱, 한턱 (을) 내- (17)
treat sb (to a meal)	대접 (을) 하- (17)
trick	수단 (29)
trim	다듬- (17)
troublemaker	말썽꾸러기 (26)
try hard	애 (를) 쓰- (26)
try s.th. (honorific)	잡숴 보시- (17)
turn	도-ㄹ- (17)
turn in	내- (17); 제출 (을) 하- (27)
turn into	변하- (27)
turn off	끄- (22)
turn on	켜- (22)
turn over	건네- (29)
turn red (in face)	얼굴 (을) 붉히- (27)
typhoon	태풍 (21)
typo	오자 (21)

U

ugly	고약하-; 못 생겼- (24)
ultimately	결국 (24)
umpire	심판, 심판 (을) 하- (29)
unaggressively	소극적으로 (24)
unavoidably	할 수 없이 (29)
unconditionally	무조건 (28)
undercover agent of king	암행어사 (29)
undergo medical treatment	치료 (를) 받- (26)
understand	이해 (를) 하-, 이해 (가) 가- (18)
understandable	이해 (가) 가- (18)
understanding	이해 (18)
unfair	불공평하- (23)
unfortunate	불행하- (24)
unfortunately	불행하게(도) 불행히(도) (24)
unhappiness	불행 (24)
unhappy	불행하- (24)
unification	통일 (19)
uninteresting	흥미 (가) 없- (28)
university student	대학생 (23)
unkind	불친절하- (26)
unluckily	불행하게(도) 불행히(도) (24)
unmarried person	독신자 (26)
unmarried young man	총각 (26)
until late in the night	밤 늦도록 (24)
upset stomach	배탈 (이) 나- (24)
urgent	급하- (26)
U.S. army	미군 (26)
U.S. Eighth army	미팔군 (26)

U.S. embassy in Korea	주한 미국 대사관 (24)
use	소용 (18)
used NOUN	헌 NOUN (19)
usefulness	소용 (18)
useless	못 쓰- (22); 소용(이) 없- (18)
usually	으레 (28)
utility	소용 (18)

V

valuables	귀중품 (28)
venue	장소 (27)
very	대단히 (17); 퍽(이나) (28); 매우 (21); 몹시 (18)
vessel	그릇 (24)
view	전경 (17)
visible	보이- (28)
visit	놀러 가- (22); 방문, 방문(을) 하- (24); 찾아 오-, 찾아 가- (18)
visit (a sick person)	문병(을) 하-, 문병 (을) 가- (26)
visit sb esteemed	찾아 뵈w- (18)
visiting scholar	방문학자 (24)
vivid deep blue	새파랗- (22)
vivid yellow	새노랗- (22)
vocabulary item	단어 (18)
vogue	유행, 유행이- (19)
voice	목소리 (27)
volleyball player	배구 선수 (23)
volume	볼륨 (24)
vomit	토하- (26)

W

waffle	우물쭈물하- (27)
wages	봉급 (24)
waiting room	대기실; 대합실 (22)
wake sb up	깨우- (17)
wake sb up	깨우- (17)
wake up (intr.)	깨- (17)
wake up late	늦잠(을) 자- (22)
wall	벽 (27)
wallet	지갑 (26)
want	원하- (19)
war	전쟁 (24)
warm	따뜻하- (18)
wash	씻- (16)
wash (clothes)	빠-르- (22)
wash (hair)	감- (16)
wash face	세수(를) 하- (16)
watch	시계 (17)
water polo	수구 (23)
way or means	수단 (29)
weapon(s)	무기 (28)
weary	고단하- (21)
weather	일기 (26)
weather forecast	일기예보 (26)
wedding	혼인 (29)
wedding ceremony	결혼식 (17)
wedding venue	결혼식장 (17)
weep	우-르- (16)
well-behaved	점잖- (27)
well-behaved and quiet	얌전하- (27)
well-liked	인기(가) 있- (19)
well-nigh	거의 (16)
West (the)	서양 (18)
Western (as modifier)	서양 (18)
Western countries	서양 (18)
Westerner	서양사람 (29)
what's more	또한 (16)

white	하얀(색); 흰 (색) (21); 하얗- (22)	yellow	노랗- (22); 노란(색) (21)
whole world	온 세상 (24)	you all	여러분 (21)
wicked	고약하- (24); 못 되- (22)	You don't say!	세상에! (22)
wide	넓- (22)	young one	어린이 (19)
wife and children	처자식 (28)	young person	젊은이 (19)
win (a game)	이기- (29)	youth	젊은이 (19)
wind	바람 (19)		
wish for	원하- (19)		
wistful about	섭섭하- (17)		
with pleasure	기꺼이 (23)		
with s.th. as one's main focus	중심적으로 (24)		
without NOUN (adv)	NOUN 없이 (17)		
without other recourse	할 수 없이 (29)		
word	단어 (18)		
word of/from sb	소식 (17)		
work	직장 (27)		
work of fiction	소설 (28)		
workplace	직장 (27)		
world	세계 (28); 세상 (22)		
worried	신경(이) 쓰이-; 신경 (을) 쓰- (23)		
worry	염려(를) 하- (22)		
worship	예배(를) 드리-(24)		
worth (-'s)	-짜리 (17)		
worthless	못 쓰- (22)		
wreck	엉망 (24)		
writer	작가 (19)		
wrong number (dial)	잘못 거-ㄹ- (23)		
wrong	틀리- (19)		
wrongly	잘못 (21)		

Y

yangban	양반 (29)
yawn	하품, 하품 (을) 하- (28)

KOREAN to ENGLISH
PATTERN GLOSSARY

Korean Pattern	**English Gloss**	**Section**

ㄱ

Korean Pattern	English Gloss	Section
-거든요	*. . . , you see? I hasten to give you an explanation or rationale for what I just said (or implied) in perhaps too crude, obscure or blunt a fashion*	16.6
것	*the fact of . . .ing; . . .ing*	19.8
것 같아요	*seems; looks as if*	22.8
-게	adverbative form	24.4
-게 돼요	*gets so that . . . ; turns out so that . . .*	24.6
-게 해요	causative; *causes [him/it] to do s.th.* or *causes [him/it] to be some way*	24.5
-고	*does [so-and-so], and . . . ; is [so-and-so], and . . . ; having done [so-and-so], and . . . ; having been [so-and-so], and . . .*	16.1
-고	indirect quotations	27.1
-고	additional uses of the quotation pattern	28.5
-고 나서	*after VERBing . . . ; after doing [it]*	28.8
-고요	unfinished sentences and afterthoughts	16.3
관해 (서)	*about, concerning, with respect to*	16.5
-군요	first realizations	21.9
-기	nominalizer form *the act of doing, the state of being, the act of having done, the state of having been, the act of going-to-do, the state of going-to-be*	17.5
-기 전에	*before, before [sb] does*	17.9
-기(가) 귀찮-	*not feel like doing, not be in the mood to do*	17.6
-기(가) 싫-	*not want to do*	17.6

K-E Pattern Glossary / 426

ㄴ

ㄷ

ㄹ

-ㄹ 때까지	*until*	23.8
-ㄹ 때마다	*every time; whenever*	23.8
-ㄹ 때부터	*ever since*	23.8
-ㄹ 수 없-	*cannot do*	18.5
-ㄹ 수 있-	*can do*	18.5
-ㄹ 정도(로)	*to the extent that . . .*	28.7
-ㄹ지	oblique questions	29.4
-(이)라(고)	quoted copula statements	27.5
-(이)라고	direct quotations	27.1
-(이)라도	*even though it be*	18.2
-라	Plain Style commands	26.4
-라(고)	quoted commands	27.4
-래요	quoted commands	27.4
-려(고)	*intending to*	21.6
-려다가	*was going to . . . , but*	23.10
-려면	*if one intends to; if one is fixing to do, if one wants to do*	21.7
로	*is* [such-and-such a noun], *and; as or for* (= *in the capacity/function of*)	27.9
를 위해서	*for the sake of NOUN*	28.9
를 통해(서)	*through (the agency of); by way of*	18.7

▣

말고	pseudo-particle; *not being*	22.6
말아요	auxiliary verb; *avoid, refrain, desist from doing*	22.6
-며	*and, while, and [simultaneously/ at the same time]*	18.6
-면	conditional form;	21.1
	if . . . ; when(ever);	21.2
	hopes and wishes	21.3
	polite requests	21.4
-면서(도)	*while*	22.1
-면 안 돼요	denial of permission	21.5
-(이)면	contrasted topics	22.2

ㅂ

ㅅ

ㅇ

ㅈ

ENGLISH to KOREAN
PATTERN GLOSSARY

English Gloss	**Korean Pattern**	**Section**

A

abbreviated verbs of manner and color		22.4
about, concerning	에 관해/대해(서)	16.5
according to	에 의하면	27.7
adverbative form	-게	24.4
after doing [it]	-고 나서	28.8
	-(으)ㄴ 후에	24.1
after thoughts	-고요; -어서요/-아서요)	16.3
agree to do	-기로 하-	18.8
and	-(으)며	18.6
	-고	16.1
and then (sequence)	서 (-어서/-아서)	16.2
apperceptive retrospectives	-더군, etc.	28.1.2
as, in the capacity of	-(으)로	27.9
as a result of . . .ing	-느라(고)	26.7
as long as you're at it	-(으)ㄴ/는 김에	22.7
as soon as	-(으)ㄴ/는 대로	24.9
avoid	말아요	22.6

B

because	-기 때문에	17.8
because of . . .ing	-(으)ㄴ/는 바람에	24.3
	-느라(고)	26.7
become	-어 져요 (지-)	18.4
before . . .ing	-기 전에	17.9
begin to do	-기(를) 시작하-	17.6
best to	-는 게 좋겠어요	24.7

both x and y	-기도 하-	29.1
but	-(으)ㄴ/는데(요)	23.1
but even so	-아도/ -어도	18.2
by way of NOUN	NOUN(을) 통해(서)	18.7

C

can do	-(으)ㄹ 수 있-	18.5
cannot do	-(으)ㄹ 수 없-	18.5
causative	-게 해요	24.5
cause and/or sequence	-아서/-어서	16.2
cause [him/it] to be/to do	-게 해요	24.5
circumstance	데	23.3
concerning	에 관해/대해(서)	16.5
conditional form	-(으)면	21.1
consequence (of) doing~being	-(으)ㄴ/는 바람에	24.3
contrasted topics	-(이)면	22.2
copula + 서	-(이)라서	16.2
copula in quotations	-(이)라고	27.5
copula transferentive	다/-아다/-어다	26.8

D

decide to do	-기로 하-	18.8
denial of permission	-(으)면 안 돼요	21.5
desist from doing	말아요	22.6
difficult to do	-기(가) 힘(이) 드-ㄹ-	17.6
diminutive suffix	-이	23.4
direct quotations	-(이)라고/하고	27.1
directional particle	에다(가)	26.8
doing favors	-어 주어요/-어 줘요	17.4
does both x and y	-기도 하-	29.1
does, but	-기는 하지만	29.1
does indeed	-기도 하-	29.1
does nothing but . . .	-기만 하-	29.1
does only . . .	-기만 하-	29.1

does [so-and-so], and	-고	16.1
does it to see	-아 봐요/ -어 봐요	17.3
doesn't have to	-지 않아도 되-	18.2
don't . . . !	말아요	22.6

E

easy to do	-기(가) 쉬w-	17.6
errand-type request	-아다 주-/-어다 주-	26.8
even though	-아도/-어도	18.2
even though it be	-(이)라도	18.2
ever does	-는 일이 있어요	
	-는 적이 있어요	19.4
ever since	-(으)ㄹ 때부터	23.8
every time	-(으)ㄹ 때마다	23.8
exploratory pattern	-아 봐요/-어 봐요	17.3

F

fact of . . .ing	것	19.8
fairly ~ pretty . . .	-(으)ㄴ/-는 편이-	29.2
first realizations	-(는)군요	21.9
for the sake of NOUN	(을/를) 위해서	28.9
for the sake of VERBing	-기(를) 위해서	28.9
fun to do	-기(가) 재미(가) 있-	17.6

G

get to be	-어 져요 (지-)	18.4
get so that	-게 돼요	24.6
give me (in quotes)	달라(고) 하-	27.8
good thing that . . .	-아/-어서 좋아요	16.2

H

hard to do	-기(가) 어려w-	17.6
has ever done	-(으)ㄴ 일이 있어요	
	-(으)ㄴ 적이 있어요	19.4
has never done	-(으)ㄴ 일이 없어요	
	-(으)ㄴ 적이 없어요	19.4
have to	-어야 되-, -어야 하-	18.1
having been/done . . . , and . . .	-고	16.1
hopes and wishes	-(으)면 좋-	21.3
how is it to . . . ?	-기(가) 어때요	17.6

I

I feel so . . . that I could die	-아/-어서 죽겠어요	16.4
I'm glad that . . .	-아/-어서 좋아요	16.2
incredibly . . .	-아/어서 죽겠어요	16.2
if	-더라면	28.4
	-(으)면	21.2
if one intends/wants to . . .	-(으)려면	21.7
imminent elaboration	-(으)ㄴ/는데(요)	23.1
in accordance with	-(으)ㄴ/는 대로	24.9
in order to VERB	-기(를) 위해서	28.9
in spite of . . .ing	-(으)ㄴ/는 데도	23.2
in spite of the fact that	-아도/-어도	18.2
in the middle of . . .ing	-(는)도중(에); -(는)동안(에);	
	-(는)사이에	24.2
indirect quotations	-고	27.1
. . .ing	것	19.8
instead of . . .ing	-지 말고	22.6.1
instead of NOUN	말고	22.6
intending to	-(으)려(고)	21.6
intentions		24.8
Intimate Style	-아/-어	26.6
is both x and y	-기도 하-	29.1
is, but . . .	-기는 하지만	29.1
is indeed	-기도 하-	29.1

is it all right . . . ?	-어/-아도 돼요/좋아요?	18.2
is [so-and-so], and	-고	16.1
is [such-and-such a NOUN],		
and . . .	-(으)로	27.9
it would be best to	-는 게 좋겠어요	24.7

J

| just | 좀 | 21.8 |

L

Let's . . .	-자	26.3
like to do	-기(가) 좋-	17.6
likely to do	-기(가) 쉬w-	17.6
look as if	것 같아요	22.8; 23.9

M

may I?	-어도 괜찮아요?	18.2
mild exclamations	-네요	22.3
modifier clauses		19.3
modifiers	-(으)ㄴ	19.1
	-는	19.2
	-(으)ㄹ	23.5
more than	보다	19.6
must	-어야 되-, -어야 하-	18.1

N

never did	-(으)ㄴ 일이 없어요	
	-(으)ㄴ 적이 없어요	19.4
never does	-는 일이 없어요	
	-는 적이 없어요	19.4

sure does/is	-기도 하-	29.1

T

than (in comparisons)	보다	19.6
through (the agency of) NOUN	NOUN(을) 통해(서)	18.7
time since	지	29.3
time when	-(으)ㄹ 때	23.8
to be sure, but . . .	-기는 하지만	29.1
to the extent that	-(으)ㄹ 정도(로)	28.7
tough to do	-기(가) 힘(이) 드-ㄹ-	17.6
transferentive	-다(가)	22.5
tries doing	-아 봐요/-어 봐요	17.3
turning descriptive verbs into processive verbs	-아/-어 해요	17.1
turn out so that	-게 돼요	24.6

U

unfinished sentences and	-고요; -어서요/-아서요)	16.3
unlikely to do	-기(가) 어려w-	17.6
until	-(으)ㄹ 때까지	23.8

W

was going to . . . , but	-(으)려다가	23.10
what is it like to . . . ?	-기(가) 어때요?	17.6
when	-(으)ㄹ 때	23.8
when(ever)	-(으)면	21.2
whenever	-(으)ㄹ 때마다	23.8
while	-(으)며;	18.6
	-(으)면서(도)	22.1
while . . .ing	-(는)도중(에); -(는)동안(에);	
	-(는)사이에	24.2
what with . . .ing	-느라(고)	26.7
with respect to	에 관해/대해(서)	16.5
without . . .ing	-지 말고	22.6.1

words for young and old 19.7

. . . , you see?   - 거든요   16.6

English Equivalents
to the
Korean Dialogues

Lesson Sixteen
Dialogue 1

Eric	*Sorry I'm late.*
Song	*No problem. Do come in. So, why are you late?*
Eric	*Last night I was drinking and went to bed late.*
	I got up late this morning and missed the bus.
Song	*Do you drink every day?*
Eric	*No, I don't drink every day—it's expensive and it's bad for your health.*
Song	*What about your homework?*
Eric	*I didn't have time to do it. Sorry.*
Song	*All you did yesterday was drink instead of doing your homework?*
Eric	*Yes, I went to a bar and talked with my Korean friends about politics. In Korean, of course!*
Song	*It really burns me up that the students are all lazy like this.*

Korean Text - A Monologue

I get up at 8 in the morning.
First I wash my face and eat breakfast.
At about 9 o'clock I go to school to learn Korean.
After Korean language class finishes, I study in the library until 5.
But since today is Saturday I don't have class.
In the evenings I usually meet with Korean friends and go to a bar to drink.
My friends can't speak English well, but we always have fun and have interesting things to talk about.
Lately, thanks to those friends, I am also learning a lot about Korean politics.
And I am also practicing a lot of Korean.
Right now I can only speak a little Korean, but I want to speak well soon.
I'll study real hard starting from tomorrow.

Lesson Seventeen
Dialogue 1

Miss Lee	*Do you like Korean food?*
Eunice	*Yes, I especially like **kalbi** and **pibimpap**. I ate [Korean food] quite a bit before coming to Korea.*
Miss Lee	*So, have you also tried **yukkaejang** and **kimchee**?*

Eunice	*I've tried them, but I don't particularly like them.*
Miss Lee	*They're hard to handle because they're so spicy, right? Well, how about if we go out sometime to eat samgyet'ang or something?*
Eunice	*Sure, let's do that.*
Miss Lee	*But say, I have another engagement tomorrow, so how's the day after tomorrow or so?*
Eunice	*Sure. My husband always wants to eat Korean food, too, so I'll ask him and then we'll settle on a day, OK?*

Dialogue 2

Chris	*Hello. I've made a reservation.*
Young lady	*May I have your name please?*
Chris	*My name is Chris Murphy. Last month I made a reservation for two double rooms.*
Young lady	*I've found it. That will be room 304 and room 305. They're on the third floor.*
Chris	*It has a balcony, right?*
Young lady	*Of course. It has a balcony, and the view is also lovely.*
Chris	*And are all three meals included?*
Young lady	*No, you get just the morning meal.*
Chris	*Say, is there a discount for students? These guys are college students.*
Young lady	*Yes, we'll give you a discount. First please fill in this lodging form and then go up to your room. Here is the key.*
Chris	*Thank you.*

Reading Passage

Today my friend's older brother got married.
Before going to the wedding venue, I had a bath and went to the barber.
The barber trimmed my hair and put some mousse on it for me.
I went to the wedding venue and paid my respects to the bride and groom.
Because the bride was very beautiful and tall, everybody was envious of the groom.
My friend's father was also very happy that his son was getting married.
As a wedding present, I gave my friend's brother a book.
Some day ["one time"] I, too, would like to try the falling-in-love thing.

Lesson Eighteen
Dialogue 1

Eric	*I've been drinking so much lately that my health has deteriorated ["become bad"].*
	I drink every day and wake up late so I can't eat breakfast.
Song	*No matter how much you might drink, you absolutely have to eat breakfast. And you should sleep properly, too, you know.*

Eric	*Is it all right if I go home a bit early today?*
Song	*Go ahead. And why don't you try dropping in at the school infirmary?*
Eric	*Even should I want to go, I haven't any money, so I can't.*
Song	*In that case, even if you can't go to the infirmary, you should at least go to a pharmacy and take some medicine.*

Dialogue 2

Chris	*Where can I rent a car?*
Young lady	*We can arrange ["do"] it for you. Here is a brochure.*
Chris	*Is mileage also included in this?*
Young lady	*Mileage is included, but you have to pay gasoline and an insurance fee separately.*
Chris	*Do I also have to pay a deposit?*
Young lady	*Since you're renting through our hotel, you don't have to pay a deposit. Just show me your driver's license, and I'll prepare all the documents for you.*
Chris	*Thank you.*

Reading Passage

Because Korean is difficult, you should study it at least three hours per day and you should study it every day. Even though Koreans do not study [their] grammar separately, they understand the grammar naturally and can speak freely, but foreigners have to know grammar properly if they are to learn Korean well. In the beginning you do not have to consult the dictionary, but you have to memorize many words. For some people, because they know no vocabulary, even though they know a lot of grammar, they are unable to speak well. And of course, if you hang out often with Koreans, this is good practice for your Korean, and you can also learn a lot through television, so watch TV often.

That's the only way learning Korean becomes fun. Even though Korean is a bit difficult, study hard!

Lesson Nineteen
Dialogue 1

Yŏngch'ŏl	*Eric! What's the music you're listening to?*
Eric	*It's a pop-song tape I borrowed from my Korean teacher.*
Yŏngch'ŏl	*Let me see. Geez, this is old! These are songs that were popular ten years ago.*
Eric	*I, for one, have never heard them before, so I wouldn't know. So the singer who sang these songs isn't popular anymore?*
Yŏngch'ŏl	*Well, I suppose he's popular with middle-aged people who went to college ten years ago. Let's go—I know a good store just nearby, so I'll buy you a much more recent tape than this one.*

Dialogue 2

Chris	*What time is the next train for Pusan?*
Young lady	*There are four different Pusan-bound trains. Which one would you like?*
Chris	*I'm not really sure. What are the different kinds?*
Young lady	*They're all different depending on the speed. The Dove is a slow train, and the Unification is a bit faster and also has reserved seats. The Rose of Sharon and the New Village are express trains, and the New Village is the most expensive and the most comfortable.*
Chris	*Actually, what I want is a train that connects through Taegu. I guess I'll have to go with the Unification, right?*
Young lady	*Yes, that's right. The next Unification train leaves at 3 o'clock, but it is running a bit late. Would that be OK?*
Chris	*It doesn't matter. I guess I'll take that one.*

Reading Passage

*As today they weren't quite so busy as yesterday, Eric and Sandy went downtown ["to play"]. Sandy wanted to see any old movie, and because Eric had never seen a Korean movie, he wanted to see a Korean film. There were lots of people waiting at the cinema. The cinema was terribly crowded, with people reading the newspaper, people eating popcorn, people talking with their friends, and people listening to their Walkmen. Eric and Sandy sat down together on a chair in the lobby and waited for the movie to finish. It was a boring movie, but the music was beautiful. After the movie finished, the two of them went to a restaurant in the vicinity of the theater, had a delicious meal, and then stopped in at a **noraebang** on the way home.*

Lesson Twenty-one
Dialogue 1

Eric	*I'm thinking of going swimming in the ocean if the weather is good this long weekend. Would you like to go with me?*
Yŏngch'ŏl	*Hmm. Don't you think the ocean will be a bit cold? I'd like to go to the mountains.*
Eric	*Which mountains do you suppose would be best [to go to]?*
Yŏngch'ŏl	*The scenery at Mt. Sŏrak is nice.*
Eric	*But if we want to go to Mt. Sŏrak, we have to get up early in the morning, don't we?*
Yŏngch'ŏl	*Lazy bum! In that case, I'll wake you up early in the morning. That works out, doesn't it?*
Eric	*Sure, let's do that. I just hope it doesn't rain.*

Dialogue 2

Chris	*I'd like to have a pair of shoes made, please.*
Man	*Yes, of course. What's your size?*
Chris	*I'm not really sure. Every country has different sizes, so how about if you measure me?*

(The salesman measures Chris's feet.)

Man	*What color and style would you like?*
Chris	*I need shoes that go with the suit I'm wearing now. Do you have something in this style in brown?*
Man	*Of course. But don't you think a darker color would be better? How's this?*
Chris	*Yes, that's fine. Let's go with that.*
Man	*When do you need them by?*
Chris	*How about if I come to collect them on Friday?*
Man	*You don't have to come pick them up yourself—we'll deliver them to your home.*
Chris	*Say, pretty good service!*

Reading Passage

Happiness

What is most important for a person to be[come] happy?
Do you think you would be happy if you had lots of money?
Do you think you would be happy if you ate lots of good food?
Or will you be happy if you become a famous person?
But however much money you might have, however much good food you might eat, and however famous a person you might become, if you are not happy in yourself, you cannot be happy.
Say what you like, but because you can't do anything at all if you're not healthy, one's health is more important than anything else.

Lesson Twenty-two
Dialogue 1

Because he was out last night drinking until late, Chairman Murphy slept in. Even after hurrying off to the office after drinking a quick cup of coffee, he was a good forty minutes late. Miss Lee is waiting for Mister Murphy to appear.

Miss Lee	*Mister Murphy! What happened? I was worried.*
Murphy	*Pretty useless if the boss is late like this, eh? Last night was a disaster.*
Miss Lee	*Really? It seems you're overdoing it lately. You probably haven't even had breakfast.*
Murphy	*My stomach's so bad I can't eat anyway. [checking his diary] Hey—isn't today the day that Chairman Kang of Han'guk Sŏmyu is coming?*
Miss Lee	*He's already waiting for you. He's in the reception room having a cup of coffee.*
Murphy	*Man am I in big trouble.*

Chairman Murphy checks some documents for a moment, then goes into the reception room. Chairman Kang is reading some documents while drinking his coffee.

Murphy	*Chairman Kang! I'm so sorry. You've been waiting long, haven't you? I'm so sorry, I don't know what to say.*
Kang	*Don't mention it. Actually, it turns out well, since I*

English Equivalents / 449

	hadn't read this report yet. Now I've read it through.
Murphy	Really? Actually, I haven't read it myself yet.
Kang	Say, Chairman Murphy—you don't look so good. Maybe you should take a break before we talk?

Dialogue 2

Yuko	Whenever night comes, I get homesick. And whenever I get homesick, I have a drink while listening to music.
Sandy	I sometimes miss my friends back home, too. When I start to miss my friends, I write letters. I wrote three of them yesterday.
Yuko	How sad! Let's not talk of such things anymore, and for a change of mood, let's go out and get some coffee ["tea"] or something.
Sandy	Sure, why not. Let's drop by the post office than go to this **tabang** I know.

A short while late, at the *tabang*

| Yuko | Want something other than tea? |
| Sandy | Hmm. Long as we're out on the town, might as well have a drink, I suppose! |

Reading Passage

On Sundays our family sometimes goes to the countryside for a change of pace.
Last Sunday our family went out to the outskirts of the city where the air is clear and it is quiet.
For the first time in ages we went to the countryside, drank in the clean air and ate delicious meat to our hearts' content.
Father cooked the meat and mother boiled up a fish stew while talking with father.
I had an enjoyable time [while] playing with my younger brothers and sisters.
Seeing as we were in the city outskirts, we took lots of photos, too.
Whenever I go out to the city outskirts with my family members like that, I'm in such a good mood it seems like I've come to a different world.
Next month, too, we mustn't forget to go off to the city outskirts with the family.

Lesson Twenty-three
Dialogue 1

Nam	I'm planning on having a little party tomorrow night. Won't you please come?
Murphy	Oh, really? We'd love to. What time should we arrive [by]?
Nam	It [seems it]'ll be difficult if you plan to come on your own, so I'll [come and] bring myself.
Murphy	Oh, by the way—we have a friend here staying from England; would it be OK to take him?
Nam	Of course! I'll come to your place at 6:30 tomorrow.

Dialogue 2

As soon as her husband says they've been invited to a party, Eunice starts worrying. Every time Eunice gets invited, she always endeavors to wear new clothes. And so, she has met up with Mrs. Kim.

Eunice	*I have to go to this party tomorrow, but have no clothes to wear; what should I do?*
Mrs. Kim	*The clothes you're wearing now are just fine! After all, there's no need to wear new clothes all the time, right?*
Eunice	*Still, I want to wear something better than this. Know any nice places that sell nice, cheap clothes?*
Mrs. Kim	*Of course. They sell nice clothes at the department stores, but if you want to go now, it's probably too late.*
Eunice	*Then won't you go with me tomorrow morning when I go to the department store?*
Mrs. Kim	*I'd like to go with you, but when exactly are you going?*
Eunice	*I'm thinking of going at lunchtime; shall we meet at your place?*
Mrs. Kim	*Sure, sounds good.*

Reading Passage

Suyŏng is a Korean American college student born in Korea.
Because she immigrated to the United States with her parents when she was a child, she is, you might say, a "One-point-five Generation."
The year before last she was going to travel to Korea but couldn't go because she didn't have enough money, so when she saved up money for a year and finally went to Korea during last year's summer vacation, she had a lot of difficulties because she couldn't speak Korean well.
Whenever she met the Korean friends she had made in Korea, they would ask her like this:
    "Suyŏng, why can't you speak Korean even though you're Korean?"
At first, when she was asked questions like these, Suyŏng felt bad and had nothing to say, but later she began to answer like this:
    "But there's no separate Korean language gene, right? Because I grew up in the United States since I was little, it is only natural for me not to speak Korean well."
Even when she rode in taxis, there were taxi drivers who made fun of her because she fumbled in Korean, and the embarrassment was terrible.
At first Suyŏng was disappointed and was about to give up learning Korean, but then she reconsidered and henceforth registered in a Korean language course at university to learn Korean.
And Suyŏng made up her mind inside to study Korean really hard until she can speak it fluently.

Lesson Twenty-four
Dialogue 1

Eunice	*Do you mind watching the house for me while I go to the police station?*
halmŏni	*Why, is something the matter?*
Eunice	*Just now while I was taking a shower a burglar came in and stole our television.*
halmŏni	*Really? I didn't see anybody . . . Wouldn't it be better to just call them instead of going in person?*
Eunice	*Say, I guess it would be better to call them. I'm so flustered I'm not in my right mind right now.*
halmŏni	*After you've called the police station, don't forget to inform the insurance company, too. You're lucky all they stole was the television. From now on you should be more careful.*
Eunice	*Yes, halmŏni, I'll be sure to do that. Thanks!*

Dialogue 2

Reporter	*When are you scheduled to depart for the United States?*
Diplomat	*I intend to leave as soon as I get my passport from the Ministry of Foreign Affairs.*
Reporter	*In what official function is it that you will be going to the United States?*
Diplomat	*I'm going as the Secretary of the Korean Embassy in the United States.*
Reporter	*What projects will you be focussing on promoting?*
Diplomat	*I want to promote cultural exchange between Korea and the United States.*
Reporter	*So, concretely speaking, what plans do you have?*
Diplomat	*Firstly, I intend to send many Korean students to the United States to study. In addition, I plan to take positive steps to introduce Korean culture to the United States through organizations like the Korea Foundation.*

Reading Passage

After graduating from college, Suyŏng intends to work for a big insurance company in Korea. Lately, she is studying Korean very hard.
Even while eating, she reads the Korean newspaper, and even while bathing she is memorizing vocabulary. Even during the summer vacation she did not go anywhere and only studied instead. Lately she is also making efforts to speak in Korean to her parents at home, too. Yesterday, because she had been studying late into the night, she got a nosebleed in the morning. Last month she got to know a student from Korea at a party. Suyŏng's Korean boyfriend teaches her Korean and always has her speak in Korean. Of course, for her part, Suyŏng sometimes teaches her boyfriend English. As a result, the two of them came to love each other. Whenever Suyŏng's boyfriend speaks Korean to her, he speaks slowly so that she can understand. The two of them plan to go to Korea next year and get married. So, even though she grew up in the United States, Suyŏng ended up living in Korea.

Lesson Twenty-six
Dialogue 1

On the train:

Pohŭi	[looking out the window] *What station is this?*
Kyŏngsuk	*Yŏkkok Station, I guess.*
Pohŭi	*How much further to Seoul, I wonder?*
Kyŏngsuk	*The next station after Yŏkkok is Onsu, so we're almost in Seoul.*
Pohŭi	*So, about how many more minutes does it take to get to downtown [Seoul]?*
Kyŏngsuk	*I don't know, probably about thirty more minutes. What should we do downtown?*
Pohŭi	*I want to check out both Ch'anggyŏng Palace and Tŏksu Palace, and go shopping at Lotte Department Store, too.*
Kyŏngsuk	*That's fine, too, but the first thing we have to do is go to Ewha University and meet Chinyŏng.*
Pohŭi	*Do you think we'll have that much time? Then I guess we'll look up Chinyŏng first!*
Kyŏngsuk	*The train's stopping! It's City Hall Station! Hurry and get off!*

Inside City Hall Station:

Pohŭi	*Just a second—Ewha University is in Sinch'on, see? We can take the subway from here, but which is the right way to go? Let's go ask at that information booth over there.*

At the information booth:

Pohŭi	*Excuse me—can I get a subway map, please? If you have them, two please.*

In Chinyŏng's dormitory room:

Chinyŏng	*Good to see you! But you should have called first before you set off . . .*
Kyŏngsuk	*We were going to call you, but got sidetracked wandering around in the subway . . . But lucky you were here.*

Dialogue 2

Father	*What're you doing in there ["in the room"]?*
Chinsŏp	*I'm studying.*
Father	*That's enough now—let's eat.*
Chinsŏp	*OK, I'll be right there.*

A few moments later, at the dinner table:

Mother	*Be sure to chew your food thoroughly!*
Chinsŏp	*Yes, mother.*
Mother	*Got some time after supper?*
Chinsŏp	*Why? I have to go out for a little while . . .*
Mother	*In that case make sure you come home early, OK? I've got a bone to pick with you.*

Reading Passage

For several days now Kyŏngsuk has been running a fever, has no energy, and whenever she eats anything throws it up right away, so she went to the university hospital near her house to get checked up. There were many sick people, so she had to wait quite a long time. In the examination room, first the nurse took Kyŏngsuk's pulse, temperature, and blood pressure. Then she waited for about another hour, after which the doctor came into the examination room and spoke to her kindly while conducting his examination. In the end, the diagnosis received from the doctor was "severe cold," so Kyŏngsuk got a shot and went home again.

Because Kyŏngsuk had already had a shot there was no need to worry, but nonetheless she was worried about her health the next day, and so she just stayed at home and rested instead of contemplating [doing] anything. But strangely, even after taking a good rest at home for several days, Kyŏngsuk kept throwing up, had indigestion, and ached all over. So she had no choice but to go back to the hospital.

Just like last time, the same nurse went so far as to take a blood test this time and the same doctor examined her, but this time the resulting diagnosis was "flu." So Kyŏngsuk got yet another shot and on her way home, thought to herself:

"That doctor and nurse are quacks. Next time I'll have to go to a different hospital."

Fortunately, after a few more days' rest, Kyŏngsuk recovered completely.

Lesson Twenty-seven
Dialogue 1

Because there is a conference next week on Cheju Island, Chairman Nam is planning to take his family and his secretary Miss Kim to Cheju Island this weekend to have a short holiday.

Wife	*Did you ask the kids if they're going to go with us to Cheju Island tomorrow?*
Nam	*Yep. They said they're going.*
Wife	*What time did you tell the kids to get home by today?*
Nam	*I told them to get home by six, but Number One said he'd be a bit late.*
Wife	*Miss Kim said she was going to think about it, so what does she say?*
Nam	*I told her to think about it and call us this evening.*
Wife	*I told her to come with us if at all possible.*
Nam	*She wants to go, but I heard she has a prior engagement this weekend. Anyway, she'll call.*

Dialogue 2

Yesterday Chinyŏng called Sandy late at night and told her there was something she wanted to meet and talk to her about. And so they are eating breakfast together at a restaurant near school.

Chinyŏng	*Sorry I called you suddenly so late at night!*
Sandy	*No problem, it's OK. So anyway, what's so urgent?*
Chinyŏng	[turning slightly red] *Actually, it looks like Ch'ŏlsu and I are going to get married. You've met him, right?*
Sandy	*Wow, really? Congratulations!*
Chinyŏng	*But Ch'ŏlsu says I should stop school once we get married.*
Sandy	*Really? So are you really going to quit school and get married?*
Chinyŏng	*I just told Ch'ŏlsu I'd think about it. But as a matter of fact, I want to continue with my studies.*
Sandy	*Of course you should! Hey, wait a minute, Chinyŏng— this guy is too much. Did you tell him you want to keep studying?*
Chinyŏng	*Yeah, of course I did.*
Sandy	*So what's he say?*
Chinyŏng	*He says stop joking around. It's like talking to a brick wall. He says what's the point of a married woman continuing with her studies.*
Sandy	*What do your parents say?*
Chinyŏng	*I haven't told them yet.*
Sandy	*You're in serious trouble. Hurry up and get a grip, and find another guy!*

Reading Passage

I decided to go hiking ["to the mountain"] today with my friends. But because according to the weather report yesterday they said it would rain today, I was a bit worried. As soon as I got up this morning, I asked my brother if it was raining. Replying that the weather was fine, my brother suggested we play tennis today. I told him I couldn't play tennis with him because I had an engagement to go hiking with my friends, but he kept insisting that I play tennis with him instead of going hiking. I had no choice but to ask him to come hiking with us. All my friends had arrived and were already waiting for me at the prearranged meeting place. Telling us to hurry up, they asked my brother if it wouldn't be difficult for him to go all the way to the top of the mountain. My brother replied that he had gone hiking often before, and told them to stop worrying and hurry up and get going. But in the end, because of my brother, we weren't able to make it all the way to the top. After we got home I kept teasing him by calling him a dolt.

Lesson Twenty-eight
Dialogue 1

Chris	*Mr. Kim, have you read the novel called* T'aebaek Sanmaek *which came out recently?*
Kim	*Yes, it was quite interesting.*
Chris	*I heard it was interesting but haven't read it yet.*
Kim	*I borrowed it from a friend and read it. I shouldn't have returned it to him. But it's probably a bit difficult for you to read. After all, it's a good ten volumes.*
Chris	*Are they still selling it in bookstores these days?*
Kim	*As I recall, it was already all sold out at the Kyobo Book Center.*
Chris	*If a ten-volume epic novel sells well enough to sell out in bookstore, the author must have made a lot of money.*
Kim	*Ever the businessman! But as I recall, it would have been the publisher rather than the author that made more money. I mean, it's already sold around a million copies.*

Dialogue 2

At a high-society gathering.

Eunice	*Isn't that man the politician we met the last time we went to party?*
Mrs. Kim	*I think you're right. But that time he came with a different woman . . .*
Eunice	*You're right. Shall we go over and ask him to introduce us?*
Mrs. Kim	*Because of all the scandals which came up during this last election period, I've become absolutely fed up with politicians.*
Eunice	*But still, aren't there those who do their utmost for the country? Let's have a glass wine then go on over.*
Mrs. Kim	*Well, that's true enough. If you insist . . .*

Reading Passage

A Page from Chris Murphy's Diary
This past Christmas and New Year's our family took a little trip to the Korean countryside. While traveling in the countryside we came to realize that the Korean countryside is different from Seoul in many respects. As the children put it, "When we got to the countryside, it finally felt like we had come to the real Korea."

Seoul is not particularly different from [any other] foreign metropolis, but it seemed there were many indigenous customs remaining unchanged in the provinces. Moreover, whereas the family system in Seoul is gradually changing to the nuclear family system, in the countryside it seemed they were still clinging to the extended family system to a surprising extent. If I were to give what I think was the most interesting example from among the things we learned on this last trip, it would be as follows.

We saw a child be born and then turn two the next day. Somebody had invited us to their home on the first day of the lunar calendar so we went over and one of the people there started talking about his son. My wife asked how old the child was, whereupon the man replied that he was two, and had been born the previous day. Not getting it, my wife asked for an explanation, and he explained that since the child was born on the last day of the last lunar month, he was one year old [then], and that because the next day was the first day of the lunar new year, he [thereby] gained another year in age, and thus was two years old.

And so we learned the following important point. To wit, in Korea age is not calculated by one's birthday; instead, as soon as a child is born it customarily gains one year of age, and once the lunar new year passes, the child comes to gain another year in age. Thus, although it had only been two days since the child we met in the first month of the lunar calendar had been born, he was two years old. If the child had been born one day later, it would have been one year old.

Lesson Twenty-nine
Dialogue 1

Today the Murphys have invited the Kims to supper. Thus, they have arranged to go to the Murphys' by seven o'clock.

Mr. Kim	*Honey, do you know where the car keys are?*
Mrs. Kim	*There's no time, honey, so let's just take a taxi.*
Mr. Kim	*We're late because of you putting on your makeup—I'll never understand why it takes women so long to put on their makeup.*

The Kims have arrived at the Murphys' house, at 7:30.

Mr. Kim	*I'm really sorry we're late.*
Eunice	*Did you have any trouble finding our house?*
Mr. Kim	(handing over a bottle of wine) *No, the house was easy to find, but traffic was bad, so we were held up a bit.*
Eunice	*You should just come as you are—you didn't need to bring this!*
Chris	*Supper is already served, so why don't you proceed to the dining room?*

In the dining room

Mrs. Kim	*What sort of food do you usually eat at home?*
Eunice	*We eat both Korean food and Western food. My husband cooks the Chinese dishes.*
Mrs. Kim	*Korean food is such a hassle to make you probably don't make it often, do you? Do you also eat out sometimes?*
Chris	*We **do** eat out sometimes, but we're so busy it's been over a month since we went out for a meal together.*
Eunice	*But you know, with no time for exercise because of work, my husband has gained too much weight.*

Dialogue 2

Chris	*Mr. Kim, what's the Koreans' most popular traditional story?*
Mr. Kim	*The traditional story that we Koreans like the most is probably the* Tale of Ch'unhyang.
Chris	*Who wrote it?*
Mr. Kim	*It's a traditional novel, so there is no way to know who the original author is.*
Chris	*What kind of plot is it?*
Mr. Kim	*In a word, it's a love story. If you like romantic stories, you should read it once.*

Reading Passage

The Tale of Ch'unhyang

Long, long ago, there lived a kisaeng's daughter named Ch'unhyang, and she was both noble of character and beautiful. She and Mongnyong, the son of the magistrate, came to love each other, and the two of them decided to get married. But because of the difference in social status between a lowly kisaeng and the son of a lofty yangban, they were unable to conduct a proper wedding ceremony and lived for some months together in secret.

Unfortunately, on account of Mongnyong's father obtaining a higher government post, Mongnyong, too, ended up having no choice but to follow his father back to Seoul. Of course, he had wanted to take Ch'unhyang with him, but due to his parents' opposition, he just left Ch'unhyang there and promised to come back in three years.

Not long after Mongnyong had left, a new magistrate came to the region. Pyŏn Hakto, the newly arrived magistrate, tried all kinds of tricks to make Ch'unhyang his concubine. But because Ch'unhyang absolutely would not give in, Pyŏn Hakto decided to kill Ch'unhyang. Just at the moment when Pyŏn Hakto was about to kill Ch'unhyang, Mongnyong, who had become a royal secret inspector, appeared and saved her. And so the two of them had a son and a daughter and lived happily ever after.

Answer Key to Written Exercises

Lesson Sixteen

Exercise 1: Using -고

(1). 진섭 씨는 한국사람이고 에릭 씨는 영국사람이에요.
 진섭 is Korean, and Eric is English.
(2). 한 사람은 도서관에 갔고 또 한 사람은 기숙사에 돌아 갔어요.
 One person went to the library, and another person went back to the dorm.
(3). 아침에 일어나서 먼저 세수를 하고 머리를 감아요.
 I wake up in the morning, and first I wash my face and [then] my hair.
(4). 옷을 입고 아침을 먹지요.
 I get changed, and [then] I eat.
(5). 식사 후 이를 닦고 버스 정류장으로 나가요.
 After eating, I brush my teeth and [then] go out to the bus stop.
(6). 학교에 와서 도서관에서 숙제를 마치고 수업에 들어 가요.
 I come to school, finish my homework at the library, and [then] go to class.
(7). 오후에는 피아노를 연습하고 운동장에 나가요.
 In the afternoon, I practice piano and [then] go out to the playground.
(8). 옷을 갈아 입고 운동을 좀 하지요.
 Why don't we get changed, and do a bit of exercise.
(9). 저녁에는 집에 와서 쉬고 부엌에서 저녁식사를 준비해요.
 In the evening, I come home and rest, then prepare dinner in the kitchen.
(10). 공부를 조금 더 하고 자요.
 Study a little more, and then rest.
(11). 나는 이발소에 가고 그분은 목욕탕에 가요.
 I go to the barber shop, and he goes to the public bath.
(12). 나는 면도를 했고 우리 집사람은 화장을 했어요.
 I shaved, and my wife did her make-up.
(13). 이것은 싸고 저것은 비싸요.
 This is cheap, and that is expensive.
(14). 비행기는 빠르고 자동차는 빠르지 않아요.
 Planes are fast, and cars are not.
(15). 중국음식은 싸고 맛이 있어요.
 Chinese food is cheap and tastes good.
(16). 여름에는 덥고 비가 많이 와요.
 In the summer it's hot and it rains a lot.
(17). 겨울에는 춥고 눈이 많이 와요.
 In the winter it's cold and it snows a lot.

Exercise 2: Using -고 with Long Negatives

(1). 나는 공부하지 않고 부엌을 청소했어요.
(2). 나는 이발소에 가지 않고 목욕탕에 갔어요.

(3).   나는 수진 씨를 만나지 않고 그 동생을 만날 거에요.
(4).   우리 아들이 밖에 나가지 않고 집에서 책만 읽어요.
(5).   우리는 여기서 살지 않고 우체국 옆에 살아요.
(6).   우리는 버스를 서울역에서 갈아타지 않고 시청에서 갈아탔어요.
(7).   숙제를 하지 않고 다방에 갈래요.
(8).   이 옷을 입지 않고 다른 옷으로 갈아 입을래요.
(9).   테레비를 보지 않고 피아노 연습을 할래요.
(10).   지하철을 타지 않고 걸어 왔습니다.

Exercise 3: Using -고 with Negative Commands

(1).   자지 말고 공부나 하세요.
(2).   그냥 놀지 말고 일 좀 하세요.
(3).   내일 가지 말고 오늘 가세요.
(4).   공부하지 말고 주무세요.
(5).   식사를 하지 말고 그냥 가세요.
(6).   일만 하지 말고 좀 쉬세요.
(7).   옷을 벗지 밀고 입으세요.
(8).   아직 가지 말고 나하고 같이 좀 더 있어요.
(9).   도서관에 가지 말고 술집에 가서 술이나 마십시다.
(10).   지하철을 타지 말고 택시로 오세요.
(11).   혼자만 먹지 말고 나눠서 먹읍시다.
(12).   걸어 가지 말고 지하철로 갑시다.
(13).   나한테 물어 보지 말고 선생님한테 물어 보세요.

Exercise 4: Fill in the Blank

(1).   기분이 좋아서 노래를 부릅니다.
(2).   시간이 없어서 택시를 탔습니다.
(3).   책을 많이 읽어서 눈이 아픕니다.
(4).   오래간만에 친구를 만나서 기분이 좋습니다.
(5).   공부를 많이 해서 피곤합니다.
(6).   술을 많이 마셔서 배가 아픕니다.
(7).   하루종일 일을 해서 피곤합니다.
(8).   비가 많이 와서 야구를 못 했습니다.
(9).   늦어서 미안합니다.
(10).   숙제를 마쳐서 기분이 좋습니다.
(11).   만나서 반갑습니다.
(12).   점심을 못 먹어서 배가 고파요.
(13).   영화가 너무 길어서, 끝까지 못 봤어요.
(14).   사과는 이것만 있으니깐, 나누어서 먹읍시다.

Exercise 5: Using Infinitive + 서

(1). 편지를 써서 우체국에 갔습니다.
  I wrote a letter and then went to the Post Office.
(2). 집을 팔아서 미국에 갔습니다.
  I sold my house, and then went to the United States.
(3). 도서관에 가서 친구를 찾겠습니다.
  I will go to the library to look for my friend.
(4). 교실에 들어 가서 선생님한테 물어보세요.
  Go into the classroom and ask the teacher.
(5). 나와서 잠깐 기다리세요.
  Please come out and wait a minute.
(6). 공원에 가서 운동을 하시지요.
  Why don't we go to the park to exercise.
(7). 밖에 나가서 담배 피우세요.
  Please go outside and smoke.
(8). 일어나서 아침을 잡수세요.
  She wakes up and then eats breakfast.
(9). 여기 앉아서 기다리세요.
  Please sit here and wait.
(10). 일어나서 노래를 부르세요.
  Please stand up and sing.
(11). 누워서 좀 쉬세요.
  Please lie down and rest a little.
(12). 선생님을 만나서 말씀 드리지요.
  We should meet the teacher and tell him.
(13). 머리가 아파서 죽겠어요.
  I have an incredible headache.
(14). 더워서 죽겠어요.
  It's boiling hot.
(15). 피곤해서 죽겠어요.
  I'm so tired [I could die].
(16). 배가 고파서 죽겠어요.
  I'm starving.
(17). 어제 우리 집 개가 죽어서 좀 슬프지요.
  Our dog died last night, so I'm kind of sad.

Exercise 6: Using -거든요

(1). 어제 하나도 못 잤어요. 언니하고 밤 늦게까지 남자들에 대해서
  이야기 했거든요.
  Yesterday I couldn't sleep at all. I was talking about men with my sister until late at night.
(2). 배가 고파서 죽겠어요. 점심을 못 먹고 왔거든요.
  I'm starving. I came without having had lunch.
(3). 빨리 오세요. 준비가 다 됐거든요.
  Please come quickly. Everything is ready.
(4). 교수님은 지금 안 계십니다. 강의를 하러 들어 가셨거든요.
  The professor isn't here now. She went to give a lecture.

(5). 요즘 너무 바빠서 죽겠어요. 지난 주일에 개학을 했거든요.
  These days I'm terribly busy. Last week I started school, you see.
(6). 다음 주에 못 가겠어요. 우리 할아버님이 돌아가셨거든요.
  I won't be able to go next week. My grandfather passed away.
(7). 손이 아파서 죽겠어요. 어제 다쳤거든요.
  My hand is killing me. I injured it yesterday.
(8). 일요일은 안 되겠어요. 그날 친척이 오거든요.
  Sunday won't do. My relatives are coming that day.
(9). 나는 바다에 가지 않고, 산에 갈래요. 수영을 못 하거든요.
  I won't go to the ocean, but [instead] I'd like to go to the mountain.—I can't swim.
(10). 손이 차갑지요? 밖이 춥거든요.
  My hands are cold, aren't they?—It's cold outside.
(11). 걱정하지 마세요. 시간이 아직 있거든요.
  Don't worry. We still have time.
(12). 거기 가지 마세요. 위험하거든요.
  Please don't go there. It's dangerous.
(13). 기다리지 마세요. 아직 멀었거든요.
  Please don't wait. There's still a long way to go.
(14). 못 먹겠습니다. 방금 뭘 많이 먹고 왔거든요.
  I can't eat it. I just had lots to eat.
(15). 요즘 매일 수영을 해요. 수영장이 우리 집에서 가깝거든요.
  These days I swim everyday. The pool is near our house, you see.

Exercise 7: English to Korean Translation

(1). 어제 시장에 가서 사과를 샀어요.
(2). 오늘 아침에 백화점에 가서 어머니한테 선물을 사 드렸어요.
(3). 우리 아버지는 자동차에 대해서 많이 아세요.
(4). 어제 남동생이 와서 좋아요.
(5). 지난 화요일에 시내에 가서 영화를 봤어요.
(6). 어제 친구가 우리 집에 와서 같이 저녁을 먹었어요.
(7). 다방에 가서 커피 한 잔 마실까요?
(8). 오래간만에 운전해서 좋아요.
(9). 요즘 한국 정치에 대해서 많이 배우고 있어요.
(10). 면도를 해서 기분이 좋아요.
(11). 손과 팔이 아파서 같이 테니스를 칠수 없을 거에요.
(12). 면도를 하고 세수를 해서 이제는 시원해요.
(13). 먼저 준비하고 쉽시다.
(14). 우리 집은 서점에서 가까워요.
(15). A. 이 문제를 풀 수 없어요.
  B. 그럼 김 교수님한테 말하세요.
(16). 선생님한테 시험에 대해서 물어보자.
(17). 나는 지금 집에 빨리 가서 식사를 준비할게요.
(18). 그 교수님은 강의를 너무 잘 하셔서 사람이 많이 와요.
(19). 여기서 내리지 말고 다음 역에서 갈아타요.

Lesson Seventeen

Exercise 1: *I'm glad that . . .*

(1). 선생님이 오셔서, (나는) 좋아요.
I'm glad the teacher came.
(2). 아버지가 자동차를 팔아서 (나는) 좋아요.
I'm glad father sold the car.
(3). 시험이 너무 어렵지 않아서 (나는) 좋아요.
I'm glad the test wasn't very hard.
(4). 오늘은 바쁘지 않아서 (나는) 좋아요.
I'm glad I'm not busy today.
(5). 음악회 표를 사서 (나는) 좋아요.
I'm glad I bought tickets for the music concert.
(6). 음식이 아주 매워서 (나는) 좋아요.
I'm glad the food is very spicy.
(7). 네거리에서 차를 갑자기 세웠지만, 애기가 안 깨서 (나는) 좋아요.
I'm glad the baby didn't wake up, even though I suddenly stopped the car at the intersection,
(8). 동생이 시험에 합격해서 (나는) 좋아요.
I'm glad my younger brother (sister) passed the test.
(9). 아내가 아들을 낳아서 (나는) 좋아요.
I'm glad that my wife had a boy.
(10). 우리 딸이 좋은 사람하고 결혼해서 (나는) 좋아요.
I'm glad that our daughter married a nice person.
(11). 내일부터 휴가가 시작돼서 (나는) 좋아요.
I'm glad the vacation will be starting (from) tomorrow.
(12). 저 학생의 태도가 좋아서 (나는) 좋아요.
I'm glad that student has a good attitude.
(13). 오늘 해가 드디어 나서 (나는) 좋아요.
I'm glad that the sun finally came out today.

Exercise 2: Practice with Sensory Verbs

(1). 수미 씨는 냉면을 좋아해요.
(2). 수미 씨는 삼계탕이 안 매워서 좋아해요.
(3). 수미 씨는 오빠가 유럽으로 자주 여행을 가서 부러워해요.
(4). 수미 씨는 어제 파티에서 교수님 옆에 앉아 있어서 좀 어려워했어요.
(5). 수미 씨는 무스를 바르고 싶어하지 않아요.
(6). 수미 씨는 친구가 도와줘서 고마워해요.
(7). 수미 씨는 방학이 돼서 좋아해요.
(8). 수미 씨는 친구가 외국어를 많이 해서 부러워해요.
(9). 수미 씨는 애기때문에 정신이 없어서, 나가고 싶어해요.
(10). 수미 씨는 다른 사람한테 부탁하기 싫어해요.

Exercise 3: Practice with -기 때문에

(1). 수진 씨가 일찍 오지 않았기 때문에, 나는 수진 씨를 못
만났지요.
(2). 나는 돈이 조금 밖에 없기 때문에, 컴퓨터를 사지 못 하고
있어요.
(3). 어제 날씨가 너무 추웠기 때문에, 나는 집에 있었어요.
(4). 약혼자가 꽃을 좋아하기 때문에, 나는 꽃을 많이 사 줘요.
(5). 나는 그 영화가 너무 좋기 때문에, 2번이나 봤어요.
(6). 그 안경이 비싸기 때문에, 나는 못 샀어요.
(7). 우리는 내일 저녁에 약속이 없기 때문에, 음악회에 가서
음악을 들을 거에요.
(8). 오늘은 피곤하기 때문에, 운전하지 않겠어요.
(9). 내일 밤에 손님이 오기 때문에, 어머니가 음식을 많이 준비 하고 계세요.
(10). 내일 아침에 수업이 8시부터 시작하기 때문에, 오늘 밤에 일찍 잘래요.
(11). 집에 400원짜리 우표가 없었기 때문에, 200원짜리
2장을 사서 편지를 부쳤어요.

Exercise 4: The Exploratory Pattern

(1). 만호씨가 일본에 가 봤어요.
(2). 나는 한국 음식을 먹어 봤어요.
(3). 나는 서울에 기차를 타고 가 보고 싶어요.
(4). 한국 목욕탕에 가 볼래요.
(5). 버스를 한번 운전해 봤어요.
(6). 나는 이 책을 읽어 보고 싶어요.
(7). 유럽 여행을 해 봤어요.
(8). 나는 시내를 구경해 보고 싶어요.
(9). 사무실에 올라가 봤어요.
(10). 나는 안경을 써 보고 싶어요.

Exercise 5: Practice with -기 전에

(1). 김 선생님을 만나기 전에, 표를 2장 샀어요.
(2). 박 선생님 부인이 오시기 전에, 박 선생님이 벌써 오셨지요.
(3). 아이들은 밥을 먹기 전에, 놀았어요.
(4). 선생님이 방에서 나가기 전에, 그 학생이랑 이야기 하셨어요.
(5). 할아버지한테 사진을 보여 드리기 전에, 어머니한테 보여 드렸어요.
(6). 수업 시간이 끝나기 전에, 영어로 말하지 마세요.
(7). 한국을 떠나기 전에, 박 교수님께 인사를 드리고 싶습니다.
(8). 집 안으로 들어가기 전에, 어머니하고 같이 이야기를 좀 해 주세요.
(9). 옷을 입기 전에, 세수하고 면도를 빨리 하세요.
(10). 주무시기 전에, 창문 좀 닫아 주세요.

(11). 아버지가 집에 돌아 오시기 전에, 저녁 준비를 합시다.

(12). 택시에서 내리기 전에, 돈을 냈어요.

Exercise 6: English to Korean Translation

(1). 그 잡지를 어머니 한테 보이지 말아요!
(2). 비가 오니까 저 육교 밑에서 잠시 기다립시다.
(3). 삼계탕 먹어 봤어요?
(4). 200원짜리 우표 2장을 주시겠어요?
(5). 미스터 김이 오시기 전에, 아버지는 벌써 떠나셨어요.
(6). 300원짜리 우표 6장을 사고 싶어요.
(7). 10000원에 표 3장을 주세요.
(8). 우표를 모으세요?
(9). 할아버지는 위층에 누워 계십니다.
(10). 사람을 먼저 깨워 주시겠어요?
(11). 이 편지를 한국에 보내 주실래요?
(12). 유럽에 가기 전에, 외국어를 해 보지 않았어요.
(13). 이 책은 정말 어려워요. 읽어 주시겠어요?
(14). 어제 20000불짜리 컴퓨터를 샀어요.
(15). 중국에 가 봤어요?
(16). 그 영화를 보기 전에, 내일 콘서트 표를 샀어요.
(17). 나는 라디오 듣기를 좋아해요.
(18). 표가 없기 때문에 우리는 못 가요.
(19). 이 선생님 조카는 유럽여행을 하고 싶어해요.
(20). 그 사람은 작년에 그 책을 쓰기 시작했지만, 아직 끝내지 않았어요.

Exercise 7: Korean to English Translation

Translate the following sentences into English.

(1).   *The Japanese test is so long and hard that is it easy to fail.*
(2).   *Since there's been no news from younger sister, mother is anxious to hear from her.*
(3).   *[At the hotel] Is breakfast also included here?*
(4).   Sujin: *You're still eating just bread and (drinking just) coke?*
      Thomas: *No, recently I've started eating Korean food often, too.*
(5).   영진: *Sujin, your clock is so cool! Was it a birthday present?*
      수진: *Yes, my father bought it for me.*
(6).   *[At the reception party]*
      진호: *The food is good, isn't it?*
      수진: *Yes, but it's uncomfortable eating, because there's no chairs.*
(7).   *Our four-year-old child has finally started attending school.*
(8).   현철: *How is it learning Chinese?*
      수미: *Speaking is easy, but reading and writing are difficult.*
(9).   *[In the car]*
      철호: *Which road do you think is faster?*
      만호: *This road gets crowded easily, so let's go by that road.*
(10). *When I said "hello" in English, the child starting crying.*

(11). 철호: *Why would he be so late? Does that person keep his promises?*
수진: *Yes, but he's probably late because of the rain.*
(12). *Our sixteen-year-old child has recently started learning how to drive.*
(13). 철호: *Could you lend me just 10000 wŏn?*
수진: *But (remember) I lent you 10000 wŏn just last week?!*
(14). 수진: *Your hairstyle is so pretty! Where did you get it done?*
미나: *My mother's friend cut it for me. Isn't it cool?*

Exercise 8: Vocabulary Drill

(1). _____ (나는) 좋아요.

a. 친구가 와서
b. 형이 결혼해서
c. 내일 약속이 있어서
d. 일요일이라서
e. 어머니가 지금 바쁘지 않으셔서

(2). 만호씨는 _____.

a. 넥타이를 매고 있어요.
b. 안경을 쓰고 있어요.
c. 새 신을 신고 있어요.
d. 모자를 쓰고 있어요.
e. 한복을 입고 있어요.

(3). _____걸었어요.

a. 가게까지
b. 공원 안에서
c. 3층까지
d. 우체국에서 은행까지
e. 집에서 학교까지

(4). 만호씨는 _____ 싶어해요.

a. 이를 닦고
b. 이발을 하고
c. 세수를 하고
d. 머리를 감고
e. 면도를 하고

(5). 에릭은 _____ 보고 있어요.

a. 신을 신어
b. 셔츠를 입어
c. 장갑을 껴
d. 새 옷을 입어
e. 새 안경을 써

(6). 숙희는 _____ 줬어요.

a. 애들을 봐
b. 모자를 사
c. 2시간 기다려
d. 휴지와 수건을 사
e. 편지 6통을 보내

(7). 상호 씨는 내 부모님한테 ____

a. 손목시계를 사 드렸어요.
b. 은행에 가서 돈을 찾아 드렸어요.
c. 택시를 불러 드렸어요.
d. 숙박부를 기입해 드렸어요.

(8). 나는 ____고 싶어요.

a. 모자를 많이 사
b. 자동차를 팔
c. 지금 집에 가
d. 일본과 한국을 보
e. 기차로 유럽을 여행하

Lesson Eighteen

Exercise 1: Practice with -어도

(1). 비가 와도 가고 싶습니다.
Even though it rains, I would like to go.

(2). 한국말이 어려워도 재미있어질 거에요.
Even though Korean is hard, it will get interesting.
(3). 멀어도 꼭 가야겠습니다.
Even though it's far, I absolutely must go.
(4). 바빠도 모임에 가야 합니다.
Even though I'm busy, I must go to the meeting.
(5). 그 분이 찾아 오지 않으셔도 나는 찾아 가야지요.
Even though that person doesn't come calling, I must go find him.
(6). 돈은 있어도 사지 않을래요.
Even though I have money, I don't feel like buying it.
(7). 한국말이 재미없어도 열심히 공부하세요.
Event though Korean isn't interesting, please study hard.
(8). 이 책을 읽고 있어도 이해가 안 갑니다.
Even though I'm reading this book, I don't understand it.
(9). 영국에서 5년 살았어도 영어를 잘 못 합니다.
Even though I lived in England for five years, I can't speak English well.
(10). 할머니는 좀 편찮으셔도, 꼭 오실 거에요.
Even though grandmother is a little unwell, she will come for sure.
(11). 하늘이 흐렸어도, 비는 안 올 거에요.
Even though the sky is cloudy, it won't rain.
(12). 한국학 전공이어도, 말은 아직 잘 못 합니다.
Even though my major is Korean Studies, I can't speak well yet.
(13). 약은 먹어도, 소용이 없어요.
Even though I take medicine, it's no use.
(14). 병원에 들러 봤어도, 소용이 없었어요.
Even though I dropped by the hospital, there was no use.

Exercise 2: More Practice with -어도

(1). 한국에서도 이 구두를 신어도 좋아요?
(2). 내가 아기한테 이 음식을 줘도 돼요?
(3). 애들이 개와 같이 놀아도 괜찮아요.
(4). 언니의 친구가 오늘 점심 먹으러 와도 좋아요.
(5). 선생님이 학생을 야단쳐도 돼요.
(6). 문을 닫지 않아도 괜찮아요?
(7). 지금 전화하지 않아도 돼요?
(8). 보증금을 안 내도 좋아요.
(9). 약국에 들르지 않아도 괜찮아요.
(10). 과장님을 잠깐 안 뵈어도 좋아요.
(11). 호텔을 통해서 차를 빌리지 않아도 돼요.
(12). 기타를 안 쳐도 괜찮아요.
(13). 동창회 모임에 가지 않아도 좋아요.

Exercise 3: *Need not/Don't have to*

(1). 내일 아침은 우리가 일찍 일어나지 않아도 좋아요.
We don't have to get up early tomorrow.

(2). 과장님을 안 찾아 뵈어도 괜찮아요.
I don't have to call on the head of the department.

(3). 양복을 입고 가지 않아도 좋아요.
You don't need to go wearing a suit.

(4). 딸이 그 남자와 결혼하지 않아도 괜찮아요.
Our daughter need not marry that man.

(5). 오늘은 넥타이를 안 매도 좋아요.
I don't have to wear a tie today.

(6). 숙박부에 기입하지 않아도 괜찮아요.
We don't have to fill in a registration form.

(7). 이발을 안 해도 좋아요.
I don't have to get my hair cut.

(8). 라디오를 듣지 않아도 괜찮아요.
I don't have to listen to the radio.

(9). 전화를 안 걸어도 좋아요.
I don't have to call.

(10). 불고기를 더 안 구워도 괜찮아요.
We don't have to cook any more pulgogi.

Exercise 4: *Has to/Must do*

(1). 우리는 친구를 기다려야 해요.
We have to wait for our friends.

(2). 방학 동안에 아르바이트를 해야 돼요.
I have to work during the vacation.

(3). 떠나기 전에 교수님한테 인사를 드려야 해요.
I have to say good-bye to the professor before she leaves.

(4). 어머니는 아기와 같이 많이 놀아야 돼요.
Mothers should play a lot with their babies.

(5). 선생님은 이 의자에 앉으셔야 해요.
You should sit in this chair.

(6). 친구한테 결혼 선물을 줘야 돼요.
I have to give a wedding gift to my friend.

(7). 혼자 살아야 해요.
I have to live alone.

(8). 병원에 들러야 돼요.
I have to drop by the hospital.

(9). 내일 날씨가 더워야 해요.
The weather has to be hot tomorrow.

(10). 라디오를 들어야 돼요.
I have to listen to the radio.

Exercise 5: *Can(not)* *do*

(1). 호텔을 통해서는 차를 빌릴 수 없어요.
You can't rent a car through the hotel.
(2). 한국에서도 미국음식을 많이 먹을 수 있어요?
Can you eat lots of American food in Korea, too?
(3). 형님이 영어를 가르칠 수 있어요?
Can your older brother teach English?
(4). 수영을 잘 할 수 있어요.
I can swim well.
(5). 나는 외국에서 살아서, 한국음식을 먹을 수 없었어요.
Since I lived abroad, I couldn't eat Korean food.
(6). 우리 남편이 운전할 수 있어요.
My husband can drive.
(7). 담배를 피울 수 없었어요.
I wasn't able to smoke.
(8). 아이들이 저 공원에서 놀 수 있어요.
The children can play at that park over there.
(9). 우리가 택시를 부를 수 없어요.
We can't call a taxi.
(10). 어제는 제가 모임에 올 수 없었어요.
I wasn't able to come to the meeting yesterday.
(11). 기타를 칠 수 있어요.
I can play the guitar.

Exercise 6: Practice with -(으)며

(1). 진섭 씨는 내 선배이며 만호 씨는 내 후배입니다.
(2). 한 사람은 병원에 갔으며 또 한 사람은 동창회 모임에 갔습니다.
(3). 아침에 일어나서 먼저 단어를 외우며 아침을 먹습니다.
(4). 수진 씨는 노래를 잘 부르며 기타도 잘 칩니다.
(5). 이 호텔 방은 난방장치가 돼 있으며 발코니도 있습니다.
(6). 크리스 씨는 차를 빌려서 갔으며 우리는 기차로 갔습니다.
(7). 보증금을 안 내도 되며 휘발유 값은 따로 내야 됩니다.
(8). 오늘은 하늘이 좀 흐리며 몹시 무덥습니다.
(9). 오늘은 대단히 추우며 눈이 옵니다.

Exercise 9: English to Korean Translation

(1). 오늘 저녁에 찾아 가도 괜찮아요? 오늘 저녁에 찾아 뵈어도 괜찮아요?
(2). 손님을 만나러 곧 역에 나가야 돼요.
(3). 오늘 밤에 숙제를 안 해도 좋아요.
(4). 이 자동차는 너무나 천천히 가서 바꿔야 되겠어요.
(5). 이 수업이 재미 없어도 배워야 돼요.
(6). 몹시 무더워도 나는 기분이 좋아요.
(7). 밤마다 늦게 집에 들어와도 부모님이 야단치지 않으세요.
(8). 할머니는 편찮으시기 때문에 꽃을 사 드리겠어요.

(9).   오늘 오후에는 아마 더워질 거예요.
(10).   한국에서는 날씨가 무더워도, 셔츠를 벗을 수 없어요.

Exercise 10: Korean to English Translation

(1).   *I have to go to church tomorrow.*
(2).   *Even if it rains, I would like to meet you (for sure).*
(3).   *Even if it's a little cloudy, it won't rain so I don't have to buy an umbrella.*
(4).   *No matter how many times I've tried eating Korean food, I want to try eating more.*
(5).   *I'll have to cut my hair before going to the wedding ceremony.*
(6).   *Even though she's so famous, she is very nice.*
(7).   *From our house to teacher's house it will take three hours at the farthest.*
(8).   *Even though this work isn't that difficult, my younger brother/sister isn't too bright, so he/she will find it a bit difficult.*
(9).   *No matter how distressed you are, you must eat.*
(10).   *No matter how much that person eats his belly doesn't stick out, so I'm jealous.*

Exercise 11: Vocabulary Drill

(1).   _____ 야 해요.

a. 병원에 가
b. 숙제를 끝내
c. 한영사전을 사
d. 이 옷을 바꿔
e. 면도를 해

(2).   _____ 지 않아도 괜찮아요.

a. 돈이 많
b. 택시로 가
c. 오늘 밤에 전화하
d. 지금 신을 벗
e. 내일 약국에 들르

(3).   지금 _____ 야 돼요.

a. 머리를 빗어
b. 양말을 신어
c. 옷을 입어
d. 넥타이를 매
e. 손을 씻어

(4).   나는 _____ 수 있어요.

a. 테니스를 칠
b. 수영을 할
c. 운전할
d. 자동차를 빌릴
e. 내일 찾아 갈

Lesson Nineteen

Exercise 1: Modifying Subjects

(1).   옆 방에서 잡지를 보는 사람은 언제 왔어요?
(2).   여기서 영어를 가르치는 분은 영국사람이 아니에요.
(3).   날마다 술집에 가는 친구는 공부를 못 해요.
(4).   큰 자동차가 진호 씨 것이에요?
(5).   크고 좋은 집이 수진 씨 집이지요?
(6).   라디오를 듣는 아이들은 우리 조카들이에요.
(7).   어린 애기는 우유만 먹어요.
(8).   먼 학교는 좋지 않아요.

(9).　담배를 피우고 있는 사람은 우리 영미 씨에요.
(10).　한국에 사는 사람들은 친절해요.
(11).　아까 도착한 열차는 급행열차였어요.
(12).　지금 듣고 있는 노래는 10년 전에 유행했어요.

Exercise 2: Modifying Objects

(1).　제가 그 일을 한 사람을 만났어요.
(2).　제가 노래를 부른 아이를 찾고 있어요.
(3).　제가 책상 위에 있는 넥타이를 매고 싶어요.
(4).　제가 책상 위에 있는 모자를 썼어요.
(5).　제가 예쁜 고양이가 보고 싶어요.
(6).　제가 한국말을 배우는 영국 사람을 만났어요.
(7).　우리가 맛 없는 음식을 먹어 본 적이 있어요.
(8).　친구가 그 재미있는 노래를 불렀어요.
(9).　그 유명한 가수를 한번 만나고 싶어요.
(10).　어머니가 요즘 보시는 책을 나도 봤어요.
(11).　제가 닫은 문을 열어 주시겠어요?
(12).　제가 산 컴퓨터를 쓰실래요?
(13).　이모부도 이모가 좋아하는 영화를 좋아해요.
(14).　선생님이 만나신 사람을 제가 잘 알아요.
(15).　형님이 매고 있는 넥타이를 나도 한번 매 봤어요.
(16).　아버지가 저한테 주신 선물을 보셨어요?
(17).　우리가 먹지 않는 음식을 개한테 줘도 좋아요?
(18).　제가 부른 노래를 선생님도 아세요?
(19).　아들이 쓴 돈을 누구한테 받았지요?
(20).　우리가 한국에서 매일 들은 음악을 기억하세요?

Exercise 3: More Practice with Modifiers

(1).　가까운 극장에 가고 싶어요.
(2).　슬픈 영화를 보고 싶지 않아요.
(3).　저는 학교 옆에 있는 도서관에서 주말마다 잡지를 읽어요.
(4).　우리가 한국에서 온 학생과 같이 차를 1잔 마셨어요!
(5).　저는 은행에서 일을 하는 사람의 집에서 살아요.
(6).　저는 어제 저한테 책을 준 학생하고 같이 이야기하고 있었어요.
(7).　저는 우리 집에서 살고 계시는 김 교수님한테 생신 선물을 드리겠어요.
(8).　더러운 옷을 입고 있는 어린이한테 돈을 주고 싶었어요.
(9).　물이 너무 깊은 수영장에서는 수영하고 싶지 않아요.
(10).　저도 아주 멋진 애인을 만나고 싶어요.
(11).　우리가 너무 시끄러운 술집에서 나왔어요.
(12).　저 아주머니가 보는 책은 한국말 책일 거예요.

(13). 제가 산 자동차는 크고 좋아요.
(14). 제가 산 책은 재미있어서 좋아요.
(15). 우리 아이가 벗은 옷은 어디 있어요?
(16). 우리 아들이 신은 새 신은 참 예쁘지요?
(17). 제가 아까 마신 것은 물이 아니었지요!
(18). 가수가 버는 돈은 많지요?
(19). 수업에 들어가기 전에 제가 읽은 책은 한국말 책이었어요.
(20). 제가 사고 싶은 자동차는 값이 너무 비싸서, 사지 못 하겠어요.
(21). 제가 날마다 타는 지하철은 2호선이에요.

Exercise 4: Yet More Modifiers

(1). 제가 잡지를 보는 도서관은 가까워요.
(2). 장 선생님이 가르치는 과부터 시작합시다!
(3). 제가 어젯밤에 만난 은행원 집에서 학생 1명이 살고 있어요.
(4). 오빠가 오늘 아침에 지나간 학교에 제가 다녀요.
(5). 제가 좋아하는 가수한테 편지를 써 봤어요.
(6). 제가 날마다 가는 학교는 멀어요.
(7). 우리가 사는 집은 작아요.
(8). 사장님이 전화를 건 사람은 누구였지요?
(9). 우리가 결혼을 한 교회를 한 선생님이 구경하시겠어요?
(10). 나는 수진 씨가 사는 집을 잘 알아요.
(11). 서 선생님이 제가 일요일마다 나가는 성당을 못 찾으셨어요?
(12). 제가 수진 씨를 만난 음악회는 서울에서 열렸어요.
(13). 제가 공부를 하는 대학을 구경하시겠어요?

Exercise 5: Retrospective Modifiers

(1). 어제 왔던 사람이 또 왔어요.
  The person who was here yesterday has come again.
(2). 1시간 전에 공원에서 신문을 읽던 수진 씨가 아직도 신문을 읽고
  있어요.
  Sujin, who was reading the paper at the park an hour ago, is still reading (the paper).
(3). 어제 하던 일을 아직까지 마치지 못 했어요.
  I still haven't been able to finish the work I was doing yesterday.
(4). 날마다 우리 집 앞으로 지나가던 사람이 오늘은 안 지나가요.
  The person who has been passing in front our house every day isn't passing by today.
(5). 지난 주에 이 교실에서 강의하셨던 김 선생님이 오늘은 안 나타나셨어요.
  Mr. Kim, who gave a lecture in this classroom last week, didn't show up today.
(6). 오랫동안 보고 싶던 친구를 오늘 드디어 만났어요.
  I finally met today the friend I've been wanting to see for a long time.
(7). 어제 저녁에 먹던 밥이 아직도 남아 있어요.
  There is still some rice left over from what we ate last night.

(8).   대학 시절 때 친했던 그 여자를 아직도 가끔 만나고 있어요.
        I sometimes still meet with a girl I was close to in my university days.
(9).   100년 전에 인기가 있었던 그 오페라는 오늘까지도 인기가 있어요.
        That opera which was popular 100 years ago is still popular today.

Exercise 6: English to Korean Translation

(1).   한국에 가 본 적이 있어요?
(2).   나는 일본에서 한 번 아픈 일이 있어요.
(3).   남자친구하고 싸워 본 적이 없어요?
(4).   리비아에 편지를 보내 본 일이 있어요?
(5).   나는 이를 빼 본 적이 없어요.
(6).   교회에 나오는 일이 있어요.
(7).   여자친구하고 싸우는 일이 있어요.
(8).   이 편지를 보냅시다.
(9).   우리는 저 헌 책들을 안 팔아도 되는데 새 책들을 사야 되겠습니다.
(10).   나는 이를 닦기와 머리를 빗기를 싫어해요.

Exercise 7: Korean to English Translation

(1).   *Have you ever tried washing your hair with beer?*
(2).   *My nephew who left for a trip to Europe last month got sick, but I'm sure he'll recover soon.*
(3).   *I don't want to go to such an expensive and noisy bar.*
(4).   *The singer who is singing that song is a tall and cool woman.*
(5).   *The man who is sitting over there is a movie actor who used to be popular in the past.*
(6).   *The girl who married my friend is quite cute.*
(7).   *Although I am quite close to that friend, I sometimes fight with her.*
(8).   *This year I'll have to borrow some money.*
(9).   *I tried writing a letter to the person who wrote that book.*
(10).   *Were the universities you visited in Seoul good, famous schools?*
(11).   *Take a look at that lady wearing clothes that were in fashion 20 years ago. Weird, eh?*
(12).   *Is it very windy in the summer in Korea?*

Lesson Twenty

English to Korean Translation

(1).   A.   오늘 저녁에 어느 미스터 리를 만났어요?
        B.   은행에서 일을 하는 미스터 리를 만났어요.
(2).   내가 먹은 사과 때문에 병이 났습니다.
(3).   우리 개가 노는 공원은 가까워요.
(4).   그 노래를 들어 본 적 있어요?
(5).   우리 조카는 나 보다 나이가 많아요.
(6).   그 시장에서 좋고 싼 옷을 본 일 있어요?
(7).   어젯밤에 파티에서 우리 아내가 아름다운 노래를 불렀습니다.
(8).   그 사람이 독일에 간 날은 금요일이었습니다.
(9).   비행기를 타 본 적이 있어요?
(10).   내가 더 바쁘잖아요!

(11). 나한테 그 돈을 빌려 주신 선생님을 특별히 좋아해요.
(12). 늦어도 10시까지 집에 돌아가야 돼요.
(13). 나는 수영도 못 치고 테니스도 못 쳐요.
(14). 그 남자는 몹시 가난해도 항상 행복해요.
(15). 오늘 밤에 돌아와도 상관 없고 안 돌아와도 상관없어요.
(16). 내일 해야겠어요.
(17). 3월에는 아마 따뜻할 거에요.
(18). 부인이 돌아오기 전에 의사를 봐야 되겠어요.
(19). 가게가 가까워도 시내에 갈까 해요.
(20). 문제가 쉬워도 2시간 걸렸거든요!
(21). 놀기만 하면 안 좋아요.
(22). 내가 내 방을 청소해서 어머니는 좋아하세요.
(23). 주말에 연습하기가 싫어요.
(24). 우리 형은 우표를 모으지만 아직 많지 않아요.
(25). A.   이 문제의 답을 알려주세요.
      B.   너무 바빠서 못 하겠어요.
(26). 나는 공부가 싫어요.
(27). 그 여자는 화장을 하고 나갔어요.
(28). A.   실례지만 화장실이 어디에 있어요?
      B.   모르겠어요. 그 할아버지한테 여쭤 보세요.
(29). 기차가 너무 늦어서 친구와 나는 비행기를 놓쳤어요.
(30). A.   김치를 좀 먹어 보지 않을래요?
      B.   아니오. 저는 배도 고프지 않고 너무 매워요.
(31). 미스터 오는 서 있지 않아요. 저기 앉아 있어요.
(32). 비가 너무 많이 와서 서울에 못 갔어요.
(33). 저 노인은 유명한 작가에요. 몰랐지요?

Korean to English Translation

(1).   *I can't eat meat even if I'm hungry.*
(2).   *Can I hit the dog?*
(3).   *I want to go to the airport by 3 o'clock at the latest.*
(4).   *Can I come home a bit late this evening?*
(5).   *We received a letter from the Japanese student who was staying at our house for four weeks last fall.*
(6).   *You've probably never seen anything like that.*
(7).   *Teacher's house is much bigger than our house.*
(8).   *Why is Manho eating the bread that I was eating?*
(9).   *Who was the guy who fought with Mr. Lee's wife a little while ago?*
(10).   *We are going to buy that big, nice house.*
(11).   *He went to the store to buy bread and meat.*
(12).   *There is a big clock across the street from the post office.*
(13).   *The weather was good so I came on foot.*
(14).   *Let's not read comics; let's play baseball instead.*
(15).   *Professor Kim is probably younger than you.*
(16).   *Could we learn Chapter 19 at home on our own?*
(17).   *Have you tried on this hat, too?*
(18).   *She went into the kitchen to prepare breakfast.*
(19).   *To speak Korean well is very difficult.*
(20).   *The eyes of those who watch a lot of television slowly get bad.*
(21).   *That person is someone who has fought with me a lot, so I don't like him.*
(22).   *There aren't any taxis so we'll have to walk.*
(23).   *My aunt had a daughter six months ago, so she's happy.*

(24). *Since 석준 went back to Korea, his father who was living alone must be glad.*
(25). A. *Could you watch the baby [for me] tonight?*
      B. *Why?*
      A. *Because I want to go out for a bit.*
(26). *You shouldn't just study—you have to do some exercise, too!*
(27). A. *Who is the oldest?*
      B. *I am one year older.*
(28). *Since I did all of my homework, it is okay to rest a bit today.*
(29). *I think the letter I sent yesterday probably still hasn't gone yet.*
(30). *Could you buy me that umbrella as a gift?*
(31). A. *Could you wake me up around 8 o'clock?*
      B. *Why?*
      A. *I have an appointment with someone, you see?*
(32). *Have you ever tried driving your father's car?*
(33). *I'm glad that we can eat naengmyŏn for lunch.*
(34). *The letter I received a little while ago has disappeared!*
(35). *Even though I've finished all of my work, I'm not tired.*
(36). *I drank so much last night, so I slept until late.*

Lesson Twenty-One

Exercise 1: Conditionals in -(으)면

(1). 방학이 되면 집에 갈 거에요.
     When the vacation comes, I will go home.
(2). 감기에 걸리면 물을 많이 마셔야 해요.
     If you catch a cold, you have to drink a lot of water.
(3). 비가 계속 오면 등산을 못 가겠어요.
     If it keeps raining, we won't be able to go hiking.
(4). 마음에 들면 많이 사겠어요.
     If it's to my liking, I will buy a lot.
(5). 날씨가 개면 밖에 나갈 거에요.
     If the weather clears up, I will go outside.
(6). 위험하면 하지 마세요.
     If it's dangerous, please don't do it.
(7). 애기가 울면 저를 불러 주세요.
     If the baby cries, please call me.
(8). 흠이 있으면 사지 마세요.
     If there's a defect, please don't buy it.
(9). 글피에 도착하면 더 좋아요.
     It will be better if you arrive three days from now.
(10). 해가 나면 더워질 거에요.
      If the sun comes out, it will get hot.
(11). 서울에 오래 있으면 몸살이 나요.
      If you are in Seoul for a long time, you suffer from general fatigue.

Exercise 2: Expressing Wishes with -(으)면

(1). 그 사람이 우리 친구가 되면 좋겠어요.
I wish he would become our friend.

(2). 나는 돈을 많이 벌면 좋겠어요.
I hope I will make a lot of money.

(3). 그 친구가 나한테 전화를 걸면 좋겠어요.
I wish that friend would call me.

(4). 태풍이 불지 않으면 좋겠어요.
I hope there won't be a typhoon.

(5). 그 상점의 물건이 싸면 좋겠어요.
I hope the things at that store will be cheap.

(6). 아이들이 말을 잘 들으면 좋겠어요.
I wish the children would listen well.

(7). 어머니가 동생을 낳으면 좋겠어요.
I hope my mother will have a baby brother or sister.

(8). 이번 주말이 연휴면 좋겠어요.
I wish this weekend were a long weekend.

(9). 멋쟁이 남자친구가 있으면 좋겠어요.
I wish I had a cool-looking boyfriend.

(10). 학교에 걸어 갈 수 있으면 좋겠어요.
I wish I could walk to school.

(11). 날씨가 선선하면 좋겠어요.
I hope the weather will be cool.

(12). 감기에 자주 걸리지 않으면 좋겠어요.
I wish I wouldn't catch colds so often.

(13). 이 교과서에 오자가 많지 않았으면 얼마나 좋을까요?
How wonderful it would be if there weren't many typos in this textbook!

(14). 여자친구가 내일 도착했으면 얼마나 좋겠어요?
How wonderful it would be if my girlfriend arrived tomorrow!

(15). 불어를 잘 했으면 얼마나 좋겠어요?
How wonderful it would be if I could speak French well!

(16). 위험하지 않았으면 얼마나 좋겠어요?
How wonderful it would be if it weren't dangerous!

(17). 매일 등산했으면 얼마나 좋겠습니까?
How wonderful it would be if we went hiking every day!

(18). 우리 애기가 자꾸만 울지 말고 더 웃었으면 얼마나 좋겠어요?
How wonderful it would be if our baby didn't constantly cry, but laughed more instead!

(19). 정치가들이 자꾸만 거짓말을 하지 않았으면 얼마나 좋겠어요?
How wonderful it would be if our politicians didn't constantly lie.

(20). 매주 시험을 보지 않았으면 얼마나 좋겠어요?
How wonderful it would be if we didn't haven't to take a test every week.

Exercise 3: Denial of Permission with -(으)면

(1). 아이들이 개와 같이 놀면 안 돼요.
The children mustn't play with the dog.

(2). 우리 아들이 그 여자와 결혼하면 안 돼요.
      Our son shouldn't marry that girl.
(3). 나는 새 옷을 또 사면 안 돼요.
      I shouldn't buy more new clothes.
(4). 애기에게 사탕을 주면 안 돼요.
      You mustn't give candies to the baby.
(5). 성당에서 춤을 추면 안 돼요.
      You mustn't dance in church.
(6). 수업 시간에 졸면 안 돼요.
      You shouldn't doze off in class.
(7). 도서관에 가서 음악을 들으면 안 돼요.
      You mustn't listen to music at the library.
(8). 여기서 신발을 벗으면 안 돼요.
      You mustn't take off your shoes here.
(9). 선생님한테 농담하면 안 돼요.
      You shouldn't joke with the teacher.
(10). 그 핑크색 바지를 입고 나가면 안 돼요.
       You shouldn't go out wearing those pink pants.
(11). 정치가는 거짓말을 하면 안 돼요.
       Politicians shouldn't lie.

Exercise 4: Obligation with -(으)면

(1). 선생님은 이 책을 보시지 않으면 안 돼요.
      You have to read this book.
(2). 물을 많이 마시지 않으면 안 돼요.
      You have to drink a lot of water.
(3). 우리는 10분쯤 쉬지 않으면 안 돼요.
      We should rest for 10 minutes or so.
(4). 학교에 자동차를 타지 않으면 안 돼요.
      I have to ride my bike to school.
(5). 선생님은 그 사람을 만나지 않으면 안 돼요.
      The teacher has to meet that person.
(6). 우리는 서울에 살지 않으면 안 돼요.
      We have to live in Seoul.
(7). 오늘 저녁에 넥타이를 매지 않으면 안 돼요.
      I have to wear a tie tonight.
(8). 우리는 그 영화를 구경하지 않으면 안 돼요.
      We have to watch that movie.
(9). 오늘 저녁에 우리는 라디오를 듣지 않으면 안 돼요.
      We have to listen to the radio this evening.
(10). 새 구두를 맞추지 않으면 안 돼요.
       I have to have some new shoes made.
(11). 이 편지를 1시까지 배달 안 하면 안 돼요.
       I have to deliver this letter by one o'clock.
(12). 이 책을 보지 않으면 안 돼요.
       I have to read this book.
(13). 문을 잠그지 않으면 안 돼요.
       You have to lock the door.

Exercise 5: Polite Requests

(1).   내일 와 주시면 고맙겠어요.
       I'd like you to come tomorrow.
(2).   점심을 사 주시면 고맙겠어요.
       I would be grateful if you buy me lunch.
(3).   우리 아들을 찾아 주시면 고맙겠어요.
       I would be grateful if you could find our son.
(4).   한국말을 가르쳐 주시면 고맙겠어요.
       I'd like you to teach me Korean.
(5).   저한테 편지를 써 주시면 고맙겠어요.
       I would be grateful if you could write me a letter.
(6).   이 서류를 읽어 주시면 고맙겠어요.
       I would appreciate it if you would read this document.
(7).   이 쪽으로 나가 주시면 고맙겠어요.
       I would appreciate it if you would leave from this side.
(8).   노래를 불러 주시면 고맙겠어요.
       I would appreciate it if you would sing a song.
(9).   양복 단추를 잠궈 주시면 고맙겠어요.
       I would be appreciate it if you would button your suit.
(10). 수업 시간에 졸지 않아 주시면 고맙겠어요.
       I would be grateful if you would not doze in class.
(11). 이 책은 흠이 있으니까, 다른 것으로 바꿔 주시면 고맙겠어요.
       This book has a defect, so I would appreciate it if you would change it.

Exercise 6: Practice with -(으)려고

(1).   한국말을 배우려고 고려대학교에 다닙니다.
       I'm attending Korea University so as to learn Korean.
(2).   새 양복을 맞추려고 백화점에 가는 길입니다.
       I'm on my way to the department store so as to have a new suit made.
(3).   등산 하려고 설악산에 갑니다.
       I'm going to Mt. Sŏrak to go hiking.
(4).   음식을 좀 만들려고 이것 저것 샀어요.
       I bought a few things wih the intention of making some food.
(5).   청소를 하려고 문을 잠시 열었어요.
       I opened the door for a moment because I intend to clean up.
(6).   돈을 찾으려고 은행에 가요.
       I am going to the bank to withdraw money.

Exercise 8: Practice with -(는)군요

(1).   피아노를 잘 치시는군요.
(2).   눈이 많이 오는군요.
(3).   바람이 많이 부는군요.
(4).   이 하얀 꽃이 참 예쁘군요.
(5).   피곤하군요.
(6).   몸살이 났군요.

(7). 집이 가깝군요.
(8). 내일 춥겠군요.
(9). 애인이랑 싸우셨군요.
(10). 맥주 1잔 하니까, 시원하군요.
(11). 머리를 깎으니까, 기분이 좋군요.
(12). 요즘 좀 선선해졌군요.
(13). 그 남자가 마음에 드는군요.
(14). 빨간 색을 싫어 하는군요.

Exercise 9: English to Korean Translation

(1). 돈이 있으면 좀 빌려 주세요.
(2). 선생님한테 농담을 하면 안 돼요.
(3). 마음에 들면 사세요.
(4). 해가 나면 공원에 나갑시다.
(5). 날씨가 흐려지면 들어갑시다.
(6). 글피에 도착하지 않으면 안 돼요.
(7). 혼자서 등산하러 가면 위험해요.
(8). 수업 시간에 졸면 안 돼요.
(9). 그 정치가를 도와주지 않으면 안 돼요.
(10). 밖에서 놀려면 늦게까지 놀지 마세요.
(11). 한국말을 잘 하려면, 김치를 많이 먹지 않으면 안 돼요.

Exercise 10: Korean to English Translation

(1). *If you hit me, I will cry.*
(2). *If it's dangerous, I won't go.*
(3). *I wish the sun would come out.*
(4). *I want to keep playing tennis until 5 o'clock.*
(5). *If you intend to become a bank clerk, you'll have to take a test.*
(6). *I would be grateful if you would read this textbook.*
(7). *Yesterday it was very windy, and today there will probably be a typhoon.*
(8). *If my friend comes, I intend to go to church with her.*
(9). *How wonderful it would be if the baby didn't cry all day!*
(10). *If you intend to be here a little longer, you'll have to wait in the next room.*
(11). *If the living is good there, shall we go live there?*
(12). *If the weather is bad, we won't be able to go hiking.*
(13). *I'm so tired [I could die], so don't joke around!*
(14). *I wish my girlfriend were a stylish person.*
(15). *I intend to go swimming at the beach three days from now.*
(16). *Manho jokes a lot if he is in a good mood.*
(17). *I like light purple better than dark purple.*
(18). *You must be tired from delivering pizza all day long.*
(19). *I'm so tired [I could die] because I couldn't sleep last night.*
(20). *The weather is cool now, but it will get more and more chilly.*
(21). *I must rest during the long weekend because of my severe cold.*
(22). *I like the shape and size of my table.*
(23). *I heard that directly from Manho.*
(24). *If you intend to learn Korean well, it is very important to study every day.*

Lesson Twenty-Two

Exercise 1: Practice with -(으)면서

(1). 사장님을 수첩을 보시면서 접대실 안으로 들어오셨습니다.
Looking at his diary, the company president entered the reception room.

(2). 나는 오늘 밤에 라디오를 들으면서 공부하겠어요.
Tonight I will study while I listen to the radio.

(3). 우리는 공원에 가서 산보하면서 꽃을 구경하겠어요.
We will go to the park look at the flowers while we go for a stroll.

(4). 아버지는 신문을 읽으시면서 음악을 들으세요.
Father is listening to music while reading the paper.

(5). 나는 집 생각을 하면서 어머니한테 편지를 썼어요.
Thinking of home, I wrote a letter to my mother.

(6). 그 학생이 저녁을 먹으면서 테레비를 봐요.
That student is watching television while eating dinner.

(7). 친구를 기다리면서 신문을 읽었어요.
I read the paper while I was waiting for my friend.

(8). 영화를 보면서 울었어요.
I cried while I was watching the movie.

(9). 제임스는 껌을 씹으면서 담배를 피워요.
James smokes while he chews gum.

(10). 어머니는 생선을 구우면서 소금을 뿌리세요.
Mother sprinkles salt on the fish while she broils it.

Exercise 2: Practice with -(으)면서도

(1). 그 남자는 그 여자를 사랑하면서도 그 여자와 결혼을 하지 못 했습니다.
Even though that man loves that woman, he couldn't marry her.

(2). 그분은 웃으면서도 기뻐하지 않습니다.
Though he is smiling, he isn't happy.

(3). 그 사람은 돈이 많으면서도 잘 쓰지 않습니다.
Though that person has lots of money, he doesn't spend much.

(4). 젓가락을 잘 쓰면서도 포크로 먹는 것을 더 좋아해요.
Even though I can use chopsticks well, I prefer eating with a fork.

(5). 일본 음식은 좀 싱거우면서도 맛이 있습니다.
Though Japanese food is a bit bland, it's delicious.

(6). 저는 돈이 없으면서도 잘 씁니다.
Though I haven't got any money, I spend a lot.

(7). 그 학생은 똑똑하면서도 실수를 많이 합니다.
Even while that student is bright, she makes many mistakes.

(8). 열심히 공부하면서도 어떤 때는 수업에 안 옵니다.
While it's true that she studies hard, sometimes she doesn't come to class.

(9). 그분은 부지런하면서도 어떤 때는 일을 안 합니다.
Even while he works diligently, at times he doesn't do his work.

(10). 값이 싸면서도 물건이 좋습니다.
Though the thing is cheap, it's good.

Exercise (3): Practice with -네요

(1). 시험을 잘 봤네요.
My, you sure did well on your test!

(2). 한국말 잘 하시네요.
My, you sure speak Korean well!

(3). 일본말도 배우네요.
My, you're learning Japanese as well!

(4). 그분이 벌써 약속 시간을 결정했네요.
My, he's already decided an appointment time.

(5). 이 커피가 진하네요.
My, this coffee sure is strong!

(6). 길이 넓네요.
My, the road sure is wide!

(7). 오늘 날씨가 굉장히 덥네요.
Oh dear, the weather is very hot today!

(8). 아이구, 실수했네요.
Oh dear, I've really committed a blunder!

(9). 따님이 아주 예쁘네요.
My, your daughter is very pretty!

(10). 약속을 잊어버렸네요.
Oh dear, I've forgotten my appointment!

(11). 돈을 다 썼네요.
Oh dear, I've used up all of my money!

(12). 내일 선생님이랑 얘기해야겠네요.
My, I had better talk with the teacher tomorrow.

(13). 대합실이 참 크네요.
My, the waiting room is really big!

(14). 매운 거 잘 먹네요.
My, you eat spicy food so well!

(15). 오히려 잘 된 것 같네요.
Actually, it seems like things have turned out rather well.

Exercise 4: Practice with -다가

(1). 접대실에서 한 시간 기다렸다가 그냥 갔어요.
I waited for an hour in the reception room and then left.

(2). 수진 씨는 밥을 먹다가 갑자기 안색이 이상해졌어요.
Sujin's complexion suddenly became weird while she was eating.

(3). 젓가락을 쓰다가 포크로 바꿨어요.
I was using chopsticks, and then switched to a fork.

(4). 밤 늦게까지 보고서를 쓰다가 잤어요.
I fell asleep in the middle of writing my report until late at night.

(5). 버스에서 내리다가 넘어졌어요.
I fell down when I was getting off the bus.

(6). 생선만 며칠동안 먹다가 병이 났어요.
After eating only fish for a few days, and got sick.

(7). 뉴스를 보다가 너무 지루해서 테레비를 그냥 껐어요.
I was watching the news but then it was so boring, I just turned off the television.

(8). 집에 가다가 도서관에 들러야겠어요.
I'll have to drop by the library on my way home.

(9). 학교에 오다가 영진 씨를 만났어요.
I met Yŏngjin on my way to school.

(10). 비가 쏟아지다가 갑자기 개었어요.
It was raining hard and then it suddenly cleared up.

(11). 한국에서 회사에 다니다가 캐나다에 왔습니다.
I was working for a company in Korea, and then I came to Canada.

(12). 야유회를 가다가 친구를 만났어요.
I met a friend on an outing.

(13). 사무실을 청소하다가 이 사진을 찾았어요.
I was cleaning the office when I found this picture.

(14). 운동을 하다가 다리를 다쳤어요.
I hurt my leg when I was exercising.

(15). 음악을 듣다가 여자친구 생각이 났어요.
I suddenly thought of my girlfriend as I was listening to music.

Exercise 5: Practice with -(으)ㄴ/-는 것 같아요

(1). 수진 씨는 튀긴 만두 말고 찐 만두를 좋아하는 것 같아요.
It seems Sujin likes steamed dumplings, and not pan-fried ones.

(2). 만호 씨는 부엌에서 계란을 삶는 것 같아요.
Manho seems to be boiling an egg in the kitchen.

(3). 고추를 너무 많이 넣은 것 같아요.
Seems you put in too much red pepper.

(4). 철호 씨는 안색이 갑자기 나빠진 것 같아요.
It looks like Ch'ŏrho's complexion has suddenly become bad.

(5). 손님은 응접실에서 기다리고 계신 것 같아요.
It seems the guest is waiting in the reception room.

(6). 오늘 차가 별로 밀리지 않는 것 같아요.
It seems the traffic isn't so congested today.

(7). 어머님이 찌개를 맛있게 끓이시는 것 같아요.
It seems your mother makes delicious stew.

(8). 사장님이 벌써 결정을 하신 것 같아요.
It seems the boss has already made a decision.

(9). 할아버지는 기분전환으로 밖에 나가신 것 같아요.
It seems grandfather has gone outside for a change in mood.

(10). 서울의 공기가 아주 안 좋은 것 같아요.
It seems the air in Seoul is really bad.

(11). 애들이 실컷 논 것 같아요.
It seems the children played to their heart's content.

(12). 이 생선은 너무 짠 것 같아요.
It seems this fish is too salty.
그래요? 나한테는 오히려 너무 싱거운 것 같아요.
Is that so? To me it actually seems very bland.

(13). 그 분은 매일 지하철로 출퇴근하시는 것 같아요.
It seems that person commutes to work every day by subway.

(14). 그렇지요? 네, 그런 것 같아요.
Isn't that so? Yes, it seems so.

(15). 선생님은 요즘 너무 무리하시는 것 같아요.

It seems the teacher is really overdoing it these days.

Exercise 6: Practice with -(으)ㄴ/-는 김에

(1). 시내에 나온 김에 백화점에 들러서 쇼핑이나 할까요?

Seeing as we're downtown, shall we dropby a department store and do some shopping?

(2). 생각이 난 김에 그 사람한테 전화나 겁시다.

Seeing as we've thought of it, what say we try to give him a call.

(3). 이왕 준비를 하는 김에 보고서를 잘 씁시다.

Now that we're preparing it anyway, let's write a good report.

(4). 이왕 사는 김에 괜찮고 보기 좋은 것 을 삽시다.

Seeing that we're buying one anyhow, let's buy a decent, nice-looking one.

(5). 영국까지 가는 김에 프랑스 구경도 좀 하고 옵시다.

Seeing that were going all the way to England, let's visit France, too.

(6). 도서관에 온 김에 신문이나 보고 가야겠어요.

As long as I'm at the library, I might as well read the paper or something.

(7). 우리 집에 오신 김에 점심이나 드시고 가시지요.

Now that you've come to our house, you might as well have some lunch before you go.

(8). 청소를 하는 김에 내 방도 좀 청소할래요?

While you're at it [cleaning], could you clean my room, too?

(9). 빨래를 하는 김에 이 바지도 좀 빨아 줄래요?

As long as you're at it [doing the laundry], could you wash these trousers, too?

(10). 한국말을 배우는 김에 한자도 좀 배워야겠어요.

Seeing as I'm learning Korean, I'd better learn some Chinese characters, too.

(11). 일어선 김에 그 창문 좀 닫아 줄래요?

Seeing as you're up, could you please close that window?

(12). 말이 나온 김에 이 문제에 대해서 좀 더 이야기합시다.

Seeing that we've brought it up, let's talk about this problem a little more.

(13). 친구의 생일 선물을 사는 김에 내 것도 하나 살까요?

As long as I'm buying a birthday gift for my friend, shall I buy one for myself, too?

(14). 우체국에 가는 김에 이 편지도 부쳐 주실래요?

As long as you're going to the post office could you also mail this letter for me?

Exercise 7: Korean to English Translation

(1). *Don't forget to broil the fish.*
(2). *Don't just stand there, please help me out a bit!*
(3). *My, you've bought a new car!*
(4). *My, your daughter is very cute! It seems she has grown a lot.*
(5). *My, your son is diligent!*
(6). *Even while I spend lots of money, I can't make very much.*
(7). *Don't think like that, just rest at your ease.*
(8). A.   *How was the movie?*
    B.   *It was so-so.*
(9). A.   *You're making so much money; why are you doing that?*
    B.   *Does it seem as though I make a lot of money?*
(10). A.   *How did you know?*
    B.   *Yesterday, I both heard it on the radio, and read it in the paper.*

(11). A. *Shall we eat fish today?*
     B. *Yes, let's do that.*
(12). A. *You won't have time if you drop by the library, right?*
     B. *I guess so.*
(13). *[To the guest] Please stay a bit more before going.*
(14). *I put on my shirt, and then took it off.*
(15). *It seems Sumi keeps crying, then laughing. Is there something the matter?*
(16). A. *Aren't you going now?*
     B. *I'll rest a bit, then go.*
(17). *Stop pacing like that, and just sit still.*
(18). A. *What did you do yesterday evening?*
     B. *I watched television, then slept.*
(19). *I was learning golf, but it was too expensive, so I stopped.*
(20). *The prices are fluctuating.*
(21). A. *The weather is so nice lately that it'd be nice to go out somewhere for a bit.*
     B. *Seeing that we've brought it up, let's go to Pusan next weekend.*

Exercise 8: English to Korean Translation

(1). 나는 그 책을 읽으면서 음악을 들어요.
(2). 나는 낮이면 기쁘지만 밤이면 슬퍼요.
(3). 한국에 가는 김에 일본도 구경합시다.
(4). 이 생선은 맛이 없네요!
(5). 그렇게 부끄러워하면 안 돼요.
(6). 아이구, 나는 친구의 책을 또 잊어버렸네요!
(7). 젓가락으로 먹고 싶으면 이렇게 먹어야 돼요.
(8). A. 이리 오세요.
     B. 저리 가요!
(9). 그렇게 많은 돈을 어떻게 벌었어요?
(10). 우리 어머니는 가끔 음식을 그렇게 준비하세요.
(11). 김 선생님이 우리집에 들르시면 서로 싸우지 맙시다.
(12). 잊지 말고 이 물을 끓이세요.
(13). 우리 언니는 날씬하지만 나는 돼지처럼 뚱뚱해요.
(14). 소금을 조금 뿌립시다.
(15). 잊지 말고 가게에 가세요. 가게에 가는 김에 이 편지를 부치세요.
(16). 그분은 왔다 갔다 하세요.
(17). 나는 호주에 갔다 왔어요.
(18). 어떤 때는 이가 아팠다가 머리가 아팠다가 해요.

Lesson Twenty-Three

Exercise 1: Practice with -(으)ㄴ/-는데

(1). 그 학생은 공부하는데, 수진이는 왜 공부하지 않아요?
   That student studies, but why doesn't Sujin study?
(2). 나는 시계가 없는데 하나 살까요?
   I don't have a watch; should I buy one?
(3). 그분을 만나야겠는데 어디 가셨지요?
   I have to meet that person, but where did she go?
(4). 그게 좋은데 사지 못 하겠어요.
   That's good, but I'm afraid I won't be able to buy it.

(5). 그분이 집에 돌아가셨는데 왜 오셨지요?
That person went back home, so why did you come?

(6). 그분이 자주 나오시는데 한번 만나 보세요.
That person often comes, so why don't you meet her once.

(7). 눈이 오는데 가시겠어요?
It's snowing; do you still want to go?

(8). 바람은 많이 부는데 별로 춥지 않아요.
It's very windy, but it's not all that cold.

(9). 저는 학교에 가는데 그분은 가지 않으세요.
I'm going to school, but that person isn't going.

(10). 샌디 씨는 한국에서 태어났는데 한국말을 잘 못 해요.
Sandy was born in Korea, but she can't speak Korean well.

Exercise 2: More Practice with -(으)ㄴ/-는데

(1). A. 배가 고파요.
B. 나도 배가 고픈데 밥 먹을까요?
I'm hungry, too, so shall we eat?

(2). A. 커피 1잔 주세요.
B. 커피는 없는데 홍차 안 마실래요?
There's no coffee, but would you like some tea?

(3). A. 누구를 기다려요?
B. 영진 씨를 기다리는데 아직 안 와요.
I'm waiting for Youngjin, but she hasn't come yet.

(4). A. 버스를 탔는데 늦었어요.
B. 다음에는 지하철을 타고 오세요.
Next time take the subway.

(5). A. 어제 갈비를 먹었는데 굉장히 맛있었어요.
B. 어디에서 먹었는데요?
So, where was it that you ate?

(6). A. 어제 시험을 봤는데 아주 어려웠어요.
I took a test yesterday, but it was very difficult.
B. 열심히 공부해야지요.
You have to study hard.

Exercise 3: Practice with -(으)ㄹ

(1). 우리가 살 집은 시골에 있어요.
The house where we're going to live is in the country.

(2). 내가 쓸 편지가 많아요.
There are lots of letters I have to write.

(3). 김 선생님이 내년부터 가르칠 학교를 아세요?
Do you know the school at which Mr. Kim is going to teach next year?

(4). 오늘 저녁에 우리가 먹을 음식은 한국 음식이겠지요?
The food we're going to eat tonight will be Korean food, yes?

(5). 우리 아들이 전화를 걸 친구는 박 사장님 아들이지요.
The friend my son is going to call is company president Park's son, right?

(6). 의사가 내일 수술할 환자는 운동선수에요.

The patient on which the doctor will perform an operation tomorrow is an athlete.

(7). 내일 아침 장 선생을 만날 사람은 미국에서 온 선교사지요?

The person who will meet Mr. Chang tomorrow morning is a missionary from America, right?

(8). 오늘 밤에 그 유명한 가수가 부를 노래는 무슨 노랠까요?

What do you suppose the song is that that famous singer will sing tonight?

(9). 내일 오실 손님은 할아버지 친구분이시지요.

The guest who is coming tomorrow is grandfather's friend.

(10). 내가 책을 빌릴 도서관은 우리 집에서 가까워요.

The library from which I will borrow a book is close to our house.

(11). 형님이 내일부터 나갈 회사는 보험회사에요.

The company at which our elder brother will work starting tomorrow is an insurance company.

(12). 이번 주말에 우리가 초대할 손님들은 국회의원들이에요.

The guests we will invite this weekend are members of the National Assembly.

Exercise 4: Practice with Modifiers

(1). 내일 볼 영화는 "드라큐라"에요.

The movie we will see tomorrow is "Dracula".

(2). 일요일에 만날 친구는 대학생입니다.

The friend I'm going to meet on Sunday is a university student.

(3). 바쁜 일이 그렇게 많으세요?

Do you really have so many things to do?

(4). 노래를 부를 사람은 손을 드시지요.

Those who want to sing a song, please raise your hands.

(5). 커피랑 홍차가 있는데, 커피 드실 분은 손을 드십시오.

There's both coffee and tea; those who would like coffee, please raise your hands.

(6). 사진 찍을 데는 덕수궁입니다.

The place I'm going to take pictures at is Tŏksu palace.

(7). 그런데, 파티에 갈 때 입을 옷이 하나도 없어요.

But, I don't have any clothes to wear to the party.

Exercise 5: Practice with -(으)ㄹ 때

(1). 우리가 노래를 불렀을 때 친구가 왔어요.

My friend came when we were singing songs.

(2). 우리가 미국에서 살았을 때 한국 음식을 먹을 수 없었어요.

When we lived in America, we couldn't eat Korean food.

(3). 내가 친구 집에 전화를 걸었을 때 통화중이었어요.

The line was busy when I called my friend's house.

(4). 내가 심 선생님을 찾았을 때 심 선생님이 집에 안 계셨어요.

When I looked for Mr. Shim, he wasn't at home.

(5). 부모님이 젊으셨을 때 음악회에 자주 가셨어요.

When my parents were young, they went to concerts often.

(6). 한국에 살았을 때 친구들과 술을 많이 마셨어요.

When I lived in Korea, I drank a lot with my friends.

(7). 우리가 돈이 많았을 때 일을 너무 안 했어요.
      When we had a lot of money, we didn't do a lot of work.
(8). 작년에 한국에 갔을 때 좋은 친구를 많이 만났어요.
      When I went to Korea last year, I made a lot of good friends.
(9). 우리가 그 한국 노래를 불렀을 때 아이들이 참 좋아 했어요.
      The children really liked it when we sang that Korean song.
(10). 내가 대학교를 졸업했을 때 우리 집은 가난했어요.
      My family was poor when I graduated from university.
(11). 날씨가 좋을 때 갑시다.
      Let's go when the weather is good.
(12). 시간이 있을 때 여행을 많이 하세요.
      Please travel a lot when you have time.
(13). 물건 값이 쌀 때 많이 사겠어요.
      When the price of things is cheap, I will buy a lot.

Exercise 6: Exclamatory -(으)ㄴ/-는데요

(1). 밖이 추운데요!
      My, it's cold outside!
(2). 그 여자가 예쁜데요!
      My, how pretty that girl is!
(3). 한국 경치가 좋은데요!
      My, what fine scenery there is in Korea!
(4). 우리가 만난 선생님은 무서운데요!
      The teacher we met is so scary!
(5). 이 길이 나쁜데요!
      What a bad road this is!
(6). 이 소설은 재미있는데요!
      My, such an interesting book!
(7). 도서관이 가까운데요!
      The library is so close!
(8). 김 선생님 댁이 큰데요!
      My, how big Mr. Kim's house is!
(9). 비가 많이 왔는데요!
      What a lot it rained!
(10). 이 책은 어려운데요!
      My, but this book is so difficult!

Exercise 7: Practice with -(으)려다가

(1). B. 아니오, 등산을 가려다가 너무 피곤해서 포기했어요.
      No, we were going to go hiking, but then we were too tired, so we gave up.
(2). B. 아니오, 오늘 아침에 전화를 하려다가 손님이 찾아와서 못 했습니다.
      No, I was going to call this morning but I had company so I couldn't.
(3). B. 넥타이를 매려다가 너무 더울 것 같아서 그만뒀어요.
      I was going to wear a necktie, but it seemed like it would be very hot, so I didn't.

(4). B. 아니오, 극장에서 보려다가 시간이 없어서 놓쳤어요. 비디오가 나올 때까지 기다려야겠어요.

No, I was going to go see it at the movie theatre, but I had no time, so I missed it. I'll have to wait until it comes out on video.

(5). B. 아니오, 버스를 타려다가 늦을 것 같아서 택시를 타고 왔지요.

No, I was going to take the bus, but then it seemed as though I was going to be late, so I came by taxi.

(6). B. 아니오, 택하려다가 너무 어려울 것 같아서 다른 과목으로 바꿨어요.

No, I was going to take it, but it seemed too hard, so I changed to another subject.

(7). B. 네, 캐나다로 이민을 오려다가 미국이 더 나을 것 같아서 다들 뉴욕으로 갔어요.

Yes, they were going to immigrate to Canada, but they thought America would be better, so they all went to New York..

(8). B. 데리고 오려다가 동생이 재미없어 할 것 같아서 혼자 왔어요.

I was going to bring her, but it looked like she would be bored, so I came alone.

(9). B. 네, 다음 주일 일요일로 정하려다가 수진 씨한테는 불편할 것 같아서, 토요일로 바꿨어요.

Yes, we were going to settle on next Sunday, but it seemed it would be inconvenient for Sujin, so we changed it to Saturday.

(10). B. 아니오, 어머니를 모시고 가려다가 요즘 좀 편찮으셔서 안 모시고 가는 게 좋을 것 같아요.

No, we were going to take mother with us, but these days she's been a bit ill, so it looks like it would be better not to take her along.

Exercise 8: Korean to English Translation

(1). *I was going to call Mr. Kim, but the line was always busy.*
(2). *Even though I missed the flight, I was able to go to Seattle.*
(3). *Seeing as I had visited Mr. Pak for the first time in ages, I took a picture of him, too.*
(4). *Last night I went to Eric's place.*
(5). *The test I'll write tomorrow seems difficult.*
(6). *When you have to have an operation, you get very nervous.*
(7). *My, that mountain is quite high!*
(8). *If you buy that book, please be sure to lend it to me.*
(9). *That place sells cheap, stylish clothes, so shall we drop by a minute and then go?*
(10). *I was planning not to talk, but now that it's been brought up, I'll have to say what I wanted to say.*

Exercise 9: English to Korean Translation

(1). 내가 대학교를 다녔을 때 운동을 많이 했어요.
(2). 선생님이 오실 때까지 기다리세요.
(3). 한국에 가려면 한국말을 공부할 필요가 있어요.
(4). 가방을 샀어요?
    사려다가 좋은 것이 없어서 안 샀어요.
(5). 점심 먹었어요?
    먹으려다가 배가 좀 아파서 안 먹었어요.
(6). 편지를 쓰려다가 팩스를 보냈어요.
(7). 그 편지를 쓸 때 머리가 아팠어요.
(8). 너는 러시아에 가 본적이 없는데 왜 러시아에 안 가요?

(9).   그 양복을 입을 때마다 어머니는 좋아하세요.
(10).   혼자서 가려다가 친구도 갔어요.

Lesson Twenty-Four

Exercise 1: Practice with -(으)ㄴ 후에~다음에

(1).   저녁을 잘 먹은 후에 산보를 했어요.
        After eating a good dinner, I took a walk.
(2).   도서관에 가서 책을 1권 빌린 다음에 집에 돌아가서 읽었어요.
        After going to the library and borrowing a book, I went home and read it.
(3).   선생님은 다방에서 차 1잔 마신 후에 어디로 가셨어요?
        After the teacher drank a cup of tea at the tabang, where did she go?
(4).   아버지가 은행에서 돈을 많이 찾으신 다음에 멋 있는 자동차를 사셨어요.
        After father went to the bank and withdrew a lot of money, he bought a cool car.
(5).   음악회가 끝난 후에 우리는 공원에 가서 친구들을 만날까요?
        After the concert is over, shall we go to the park and meet our friends?
(6).   할아버지가 신문을 보신 후에 학교에 전화를 거셨어요 .
        After grandfather read the paper, he called the school.
(7).   복동이가 머리를 빗은 후에 모자를 쓰고 나갔어요.
        After Poktong combed his hair, he put on a hat and went out.
(8).   아주머니가 그릇을 씻은 다음에 애기를 데리고 가게에 가서 뭘 샀어요.
        After aunty washed the dishes, she took the baby to the store to buy something.
(9).   영화가 끝난 후에 술을 마시러 술집에 갈래요?
        After the movie is over, do you want to go to a bar to have a drink?
(10).   할머니가 병이 나신 후에 바닷가로 가서 쉬셨어요.
        After grandmother got sick, she went to the beach to rest.
(11).   전화를 건 다음에 이야기하지요, 뭐.
        After you make your call, what say we have a talk.
(12).   고친 다음에 고장이 1번도 안 났습니다.
        After we fixed it, it hasn't broken even once.
(13).   복습하신 다음에 좀 쉬세요.
        After you review, please take a rest.

Exercise 2:   Practice with -는 동안~사이에

(1).   저는 이를 닦는 동안 동생의 이야기를 듣지 못 했어요.
(2).   한국말을 공부하는 동안에 영어로 말하면 안 되지요.
(3).   재미있는 책을 보고 있는 동안에 도둑이 들어왔어요.
(4).   교수님이 예쁜 여자하고 이야기를 하고 계시는 사이에 부인이 왔다 갔어요!
(5).   도둑이 집에 들어온 동안에 우리 개가 잠을 잤어요.
(6).   아버지가 외국에 가신 동안에 어머니가 동생을 낳으셨어요.
(7).   내가 편지를 쓰고 있는 동안에 동생은 우표를 사러 나갔어요.
(8).   우리가 영화를 보고 있는 동안에 밖에 눈이 많이 왔어요.
(9).   형님이 미국에서 공부하고 있는 동안에 나는 결혼했어요.

(10). 한국에서 전쟁이 일어나는 동안에 일본은 많이 발전했어요.
(11). 한국에 사는 동안에 재미있는 사람을 많이 만나봤어요.
(12). 우리가 재미 있게 노는 동안에 만호 씨는 혼자서 일을 했어요.

Exercise 3: Practice with - 는 중이에요

(1). 나는 한국말 공부를 하는 중이었어요.
(2). 아이들이 음악을 듣는 중에요.
(3). 그 사람이 소설을 읽는 중에요?
(4). 저 2사람이 장기를 두는 중이었어요.
(5). 아들이 복습을 하는 중이었어요.
(6). 아내가 물건을 사는 중이에요.
(7). 동생이 피아노를 치는 중이었어요.
(8). 저녁을 먹는 중이었어요.
(9). 2사람은 싸우는 중이었어요.
(10). 선생님은 외국 여행을 하시는 중이었어요.

Exercise 4: Practice with - 는 중에

(1). 내가 공부하는 중에 손님이 오셨어요.
(2). 선생이 편지를 쓰는 중에 전화가 왔어요.
(3). 아내가 전화를 거는 중에 애기가 문을 열고 방에서 나갔어요.
(4). 내가 어제 밤에 신문을 보는 중에 이상한 소리를 들었어요.
(5). 우리가 그 영화를 보는 중에 도둑이 들어왔어요.
(6). 제가 설거지를 하는 중에 전기가 나갔어요.
(7). 바둑을 두는 중에 날이 어두워졌어요.
(8). 도둑하고 싸우는 중에 코피가 터졌어요.
(9). 저는 예습을 하는 중에 불이 났어요.
(10). 한국을 방문하는 중에 학생들이 데모하는 것을 봤어요.
(11). 한동안 운동을 못하는 중에 배가 나왔어요.
(12). 오랫동안 외국생활을 하는 중에 한국 경제가 많이 발전했어요.

Exercise 5: Intentions

(1). 친구들과 같이 등산을 갈 예정입니다.
(2). 내일은 그 대학교를 방문할 예정입니다.
(3). 조금 이따가 회의를 할 예정입니다.
(4). 약혼식은 서울에서 할 생각입니다.
(5). 그리고 결혼식은 캐나다에서 할 계획입니다.
(6). 입원할 생각입니다.
(7). 한국에 나와 있는 동안에 장기를 배울 생각입니다.
(8). 성경 공부를 좀 할 작정입니다.
(9). 그분의 제안을 거절할 작정입니다.

(10). 앞으로는 예배를 한국말로 드릴 생각입니다.
(11). 여러 가지 물건을 수출할 계획입니다.

Exercise 6: Practice with -게 되-

(1). 그분 얼굴이 빨갛게 됐습니다.
(2). 만호 씨는 장학금을 받게 됐습니다.
(3). 팔을 다쳐서 농구를 못하게 됐습니다.
(4). 교통이 복잡하게 됐습니다.
(5). 한국신문을 읽을 수 있게 됐습니다.
(6). 그것이 하얗게 됐습니다.
(7). 내일의 회의는 취소하게 됐습니다.
(8). 이번 일요일에 교회에서 반주를 하게 됐습니다.
(9). 내년에 런던대학에 방문학자로 가게 됐습니다.
(10). 내년부터는 외무부에서 근무하게 됐습니다.
(11). 언니는 내년부터 유학을 가게 됐습니다.
(12). 내일 종강 파티에 못 가게 됐습니다.
(13). 회사 일로 한국에 오게 됐습니다.
(14). 그분의 입장을 이해하게 됐습니다.
(15). 전에는 고생을 많이 했지만 이제는 잘 살게 됐습니다.

Exercise 7: Practice with Causatives in -게 하-

(1). 수미 씨는 할머니한테 경찰서에 전화를 거시게 했습니다.
   Sumi had grandmother call the police station.
(2). 수미 씨는 박 선생님을 대사관에 들리시게 했어요.
   Sumi had Mr. Park drop by the embassy.
(3). 수미 씨는 아들한테 바둑을 못 두게 합니다.
   Sumi doesn't let her son play paduk.
(4). 수미 씨는 딸한테 하루종일 복습을 하게 합니다.
   Sumi makes her daughter review the whole day long.
(5). 수미 씨는 애들한테 밤늦도록 예습을 하게 합니다.
   Sumi makes her children practice until late in the night.
(6). 수미 씨는 아들한테 수학숙제를 끝까지 하게 했어요.
   Sumi made her daughter finish her math homework until the end.
(7). 수미 씨는 만호 씨를 내일의 성경 공부에 못 가게 해요.
   Sumi won't let Manho go to tomorrow's Bible study.
(8). 수미 씨는 애들한테 날마다 자기 전에 기도를 하게 해요.
   Sumi has her children pray every day before they go to sleep.
(9). 수미 씨는 자기 딸한테 반주를 해 주게 했어요.
   Sumi had her daughter accompany her.
(10). 수미 씨는 만호 씨를 성가대원이 되게 했어요.
   Sumi had Manho become a member of the church choir.
(11). 수미 씨는 방문교수한테 1학기 동안 강의를 하게 했어요.
   Sumi had the visiting professor lecture for one semester.

(12). 수미 씨는 딸한테 유학을 못 가게 했어요.
Sumi didn't let her daughter study abroad.
(13). 수미 씨는 아들한테 좀 더 적극적으로 공부를 하게 했어요.
Sumi made her daughter study a little more positively.
(14). 수미 씨는 애들을 제대로 앉게 해요.
Sumi makes her children sit properly.
(15). 수미 씨는 아들한테 자동차를 고치게 했어요.
Sumi had her son fix the car.
(16). 수미 씨는 만호 씨한테 커피를 흘리게 했어요.
Sumi made Manho spill the coffee.
(17). 수미 씨는 수진 씨한테 약속을 취소하게 했어요.
Sumi had Sujin cancel the appointment.
(18). 수미 씨는 남편한테 출장을 못 가게 했어요.
Sumi wouldn't let her husband go away on business.
(19). 수미 씨는 아이들을 일찍 자게 해요.
Sumi makes her children go to bed early.
(20). 수미 씨는 남편한테 술을 못 마시게 해요.
Sumi doesn't let her husband drink.
(21). 수미 씨는 아이들한테 껌을 못 씹게 해요.
Sumi doesn't let her children chew gum.
(22). 거기는 위험하니까, 수미 씨는 아이들을 거기서 못 놀게 해요.
That place is dangerous, so Sumi won't let the children play there.
(23). 수미 씨는 어머니를 기뻐하게 해요.
Sumi makes her mother happy.
(24). 수미 씨는 방을 좀 더 따뜻하게 해요.
Sumi makes the room a little more warm.
(25). 수미 씨는 그 사람을 화가 나게 했어요.
Sumi made that person angry.
(26). 수미 씨는 유학생들을 일찍 등록하게 했어요.
Sumi had the foreign students register early.

Exercise 8: Practice with -(으)ㄴ/-는 대로

(1).   선생님이 시키시는 대로 하세요.
(2).   일을 끝나는 대로 갈 거에요.
(3).   생각이 나는 대로 말을 했어요.
(4).   아버지가 한국에서 도착하시는 대로 바로 이사갈 예정입니다.
(5).   가르쳐 주신 대로 집을 찾았어요.
(6).   제가 부르는 대로 한번 써보세요.
(7).   회의가 끝나는 대로 얼른 집에 와요.
(8).   내일 수업이 끝나는 대로 점심을 먹으러 갑시다.
(9).   소식이 들어오는 대로 알려 드릴게요.
(10). 고향에 도착하는 대로 편지를 쓰겠습니다.
(11). 준비가 다 되는 대로 떠납시다.
(12). 눈이 그치는 대로 출발할까요?

Exercise 9: Practice with 바람에

(1). 안경을 잃어버리는 바람에 영화를 제대로 못 봤지요.
(2). 버스가 늦게 오는 바람에 저도 늦었지요.
(3). 애기가 자꾸 기침을 하는 바람에 잠을 제대로 못 잤어요.
(4). 남편이 갑자기 출장을 가는 바람에 파티를 취소했습니다.
(5). 옆 집에서 이상한 소리가 나는 바람에 밤중에 깼어요.
(6). 부엌에서 이상한 냄새가 나는 바람에 입맛이 싹 없어졌어요.
(7). 갑자기 비가 쏟아지는 바람에 온몸이 젖었어요.
(8). 시내에서 사고가 나는 바람에 차가 많이 밀렸어요.
(9). 깜짝 놀라는 바람에 넘어졌어요.
(10). 상한 음식을 먹는 바람에 배탈이 났어요.
(11). 애기가 정신없이 노는 바람에 온 집안이 엉망이에요.

Exercise 10: Practice with -는 게 좋겠어요

(1). 오늘은 집에서 쉬시는 게 좋겠어요.
(2). 나는 배탈이 나서, 밥을 안 먹는 게 좋겠어요.
(3). 저는 할 일이 많거든요. 혼자 가시는 게 좋겠어요.
(4). 매운 것을 잘 못 드시니까, 냉면을 드시지 마시는 게 좋겠어요.
(5). 저는 많이 마시지는 않았지만, 만호 씨가 운전을 하시는 게 좋겠어요.
(6). 머리가 아프시면 일찍 주무시는 게 좋겠어요.
(7). 목사님, 설교를 영어로 하시는 게 좋겠어요.
(8). 그런 것은 장로님께 여쭈어보시는 게 좋겠어요.
(9). 집사님께서 기도를 하시는 게 좋겠어요.
(10). 코피가 났으면 좀 누워 계시는 게 좋겠어요.

Vocabulary Drill

지난 봄	내년 봄
last spring	*next spring*
어려워요	쉬워요
difficult	*easy*
일해요	놀아요
work	*play*
게을러요	부지런해요
lazy	*hard-working*
높아요	낮아요
high	*low*
비싸요	싸요
expensive	*cheap*
시골	도시
countryside	*city*
울어요	웃어요
cry	*laugh*

달라요	같아요
different	*same*
이야기를 해요	이야기를 들어요
talk	*listen*

Lesson Twenty-Five

Exercise 1: Korean to English Translation

(1).   *If I travel a lot I become tired.*
(2).   *You have to do your homework by tomorrow.*
(3).   *Could you lend me a pencil?*
(4).   *How wonderful it would be if I could rest all day at the beach!*
(5).   *It would be best to leave by 12 o'clock.*
(6).   *I'm sorry to trouble you, but it would be best if we could leave as soon as possible.*
(7).   *I was going to buy those shoes, but it looked like they had a defect so I bought something else.*
(8).   *When is that person planning to arrive?*
(9).   *How wonderful it would be if it were winter again.*
(10). *If you are cold, please button up.*
(11). *You must take the test by next Monday.*
(12). *It seems like it's bad for your body if you eat a lot right before going to sleep.*
(13). *If you like beautiful, natural scenery, try going hiking in Vancouver sometime. Yes, I will..*
(14). *I'm on my way downtown now to visit the doctor.*
(15). *My, this pulgogi is bland!*
(16). *This coffee is good and dark.*
(17). *I'll have to drop by the embassy a little later on.*
(18). *My, how dangerous it would be if there were a fire here!*
(19). *you shouldn't chew gum during class. You get in trouble from the teacher.*
(20). *Don't worry; try having fun to your heart's content sometime.*
(21). *I'm very sorry for the trouble, but would it be all right if we do today's conference another time?*
(22). *Did you remember to lock the car doors?*
(23). *Seeing that you've come all the way to London, why don't you stay a few days at our house?*
(24). *I've decided to keep chewing gum, even if the teacher gets angry.*
(25). *How are your Korean studies going these days? They're so-so.*
(26). *Let's have a drink, and then not go by car, but take a taxi.*
(27). *How happy your son must be to have graduated university!*
(28). *Don't have any reservations; feel free to go ask the professor directly.*
(29). *If the sun comes out, I intend to go for a walk or something for a change of mood.*

Exercise 2: English to Korean Translation

(1).   홍 교수님한테 전화를 걸려고 했는데 잘못 걸었어요.
(2).   작년에 졸업을 했는데도 하나도 똑똑하지 않아요.
(3).   남 선생님 댁은 아주 큰데 나는 그 곳을 별로 안 좋아해요.
(4).   내일 회의가 있는데 걱정이에요.
(5).   오늘 밤에 우리를 위해서 노래를 부를 사람을 만났어요?
(6).   그 가게에는 싸게 살 것이 없어요.
(7).   동양화를 살 때 조심해야 돼요.

(8). 걱정이 될 때는 독한 술을 마셔야지요.
(9). 전화를 걸 때마다 통화중이었어요.
(10). 제임스가 한국에 갈 때까지 기다리세요.
(11). 그 외교관을 만날 때 사진을 찍어 줄게요.
(12). 작년에 테니스를 쳤을 때 운동 선수가 되고 싶어졌어요.
(13). 수술을 했을 때 1달 동안 출근을 안 해도 됐어요.
(14). 날씨가 흐려지는데 집에 갑시다.
(15). 이번 가을에 일본에 갈 예정인데 어떤 선물을 사야 될까요?

Lesson Twenty-Six

Exercise 1: Plain Style Statements

(1). 김 사장님 사모님도 오신다.
Mr. Kim's wife is coming too.

(2). 시장의 장모가 유명한 정치가다.
The mayor's mother-in-law is a famous politician.

(3). 독감에 걸려서 대학병원에서 치료를 받아야겠다.
I caught the flu, so I'll have to receive medical treatment from the university hospital.

(4). 몸살이 나서 온 몸이 아프고 기운이 없다.
I am fatigued, so my whole body aches and I have no energy.

(5). 그 사람의 딸은 아직도 어리다.
That person's daughter is still young.

(6). 일기예보가 잘 안 맞는다.
The weather forecast is often wrong.

(7). 박 선생님이 우리 아버지한테 전화를 거실 것이다.
Mr. Park will call our father.

(8). 선생님께서 그 사람한테 재미있는 편지를 쓰셨다.
The teacher wrote that person an interesting letter.

(9). 그 사람의 아이들이 다니는 학교가 집에서 멀지 않다.
The school that person's children attend isn't far from their home.

(10). 뉴스를 봐야 하는데 우리 장난꾸러기가 자꾸 방해를 한다.
I have to watch the news, but our little monkey keeps disturbing us.

(11). 귀가 아프면 이비인후과에서 진찰을 받아야 한다.
If your ear hurts, you have to have a check-up at the ear, nose, and throat specialist.

(12). 그 강은 짧고 얕다.
That river is short and shallow.

(13). 운동한 후에 맥주를 마시면 시원하다.
It's refreshing to drink beer after exercising.

(14). 아이들은 일찍 자고 싶어하지 않는다.
The children don't want to go to sleep early.

(15). 그 부인이 밥을 할 때 남편도 돕는다.
When that wife prepares a meal, her husband helps, too.

(16). 그 생선은 한국에 흔하다.
That fish is common in Korea.

Exercise 2: Plain Style Questions

(1). 우리 아버지가 병이 나셨(느)냐?
Is our father ill?

(2). 그 우체국은 가까우냐?
Is the post office close?

(3). 학생들이 점심을 어디서 먹(느)냐?
Where do the students eat lunch?

(4). 그분의 부인은 열이 높으냐?
Is that person's wife's temperature high?

(5). 간호사가 불친절했(느)냐?
Was the nurse unkind?

(6). 그 산부인과 의사는 착실하냐?
Is that obstetrics and gynecology doctor thorough?

(7). 의사 선생님이 어디서 사시냐?
Where does the doctor live?

(8). 누구를 불렀느냐?
Who did you call?

(9). 밖이 춥지 않으냐?
Is it not cold outside?

(10). 내일 무엇을 하고 싶으냐?
What do you want to do tomorrow?

(11). 친구가 퇴원하기 전에 문병을 갔(느)냐?
Did you go to visit your friend before she got out of hospital?

(12). 왜 그렇게 기운이 없느냐?
Why do you have so little energy?

(13). 간호사가 체온을 재는 것을 잃어버렸느냐?
Did the nurse forget to check my temperature?

(14). 그 전염병에 걸리면 토하고 열이 심하게 나(느)냐?
If you catch that contagious disease do you vomit and get a severe fever?

(15). 그 말썽꾸러기가 홍역에 걸렸(느)냐?
Did that trouble-maker catch measles?

(16). 교통사고가 나서 길이 복잡하지 않으냐?
Are the roads not congested because of a traffic accident?

(17). 운전할 때 응급차가 오면 길 어느 쪽으로 비켜야 되(느)냐?
To which side of the road do you have to pull over if an ambulance comes when you're driving?

(18). 오늘은 몇 도인데 이렇게 시원하냐?
What's the temperature today that it is so cool?

(19). 섭씨 영(0)도는 화씨 몇 도냐?
How many degrees Fahrenheit is zero degrees Celcius?

Exercise 3: Plain Style Suggestions

(1). 일찍 일어나서 산보하자.
Let's get up early and take a walk.

(2). 선생님한테 곧 허락을 받자.
Let's get permission from the teacher right away.

(3). 수지 씨가 떠나지 못하게 방해를 하자.
Let's obstruct Suzy so she can't leave.

(4). 좀 쉬자.
Let's rest a bit.

(5). 고춧가루를 그만 치자.
Let's stop sprinkling the red pepper powder.

(6). 인턴한테 주사를 맞자.
Let's get a shot from the intern.

(7). 이 연필을 깎자.
Let's sharpen this pencil.

(8). 체온을 먼저 재고 맥박을 재자.
First let's take your temperature, and then your pulse.

(9). 꽃을 좀 사 가지고 가자.
Let's go buy some flowers. and bring them along

(10). 문을 좀 열자.
Let's open the door.

(11). 회사에 전화를 걸자.
Let's call the company.

(12). 소화가 잘 안 되면 곧 검사를 해 보자.
If you have indigestion let's get it tested right away.

Exercise 4: Plain Style Commands

(1). 여기 앉아라!
Sit here!

(2). 그 책을 학교에 가지고 와라!
Bring that book to school!

(3). 새 구두를 신어라!
Wear your new shoes!

(4). 옷을 벗어라!
Take off your clothes!

(5). 집에 있어라!
Stay at home!

(6). 그 책을 읽어라!
Read that book!

(7). 오늘 밤에 넥타이를 매라!
Wear your necktie tonight!

(8). 의사한테 전화를 걸어라!
Phone the doctor!

(9). 돈을 많이 쓰지 말아라!
Don't spend lots of money!

(10). 영어를 하지 말아라!
Don't speak English!

(11). 그렇게 큰 소리로 부르지 말아라!
Don't yell so loud!

Exercise 5: English to Korean (Plain Style)

(1).   나는 선생님을 도와 드린다~도와 드렸다~도와 드리겠다.
(2).   나는 출근할 때 운전한다~운전했다~운전하겠다.
(3).   나는 저녁에 피곤하다~피곤했다~피곤하겠다.
(4).   그는 항상 그렇다~그랬다~그렇겠다.
(5).   나는 음악을 듣는다~들었다~듣겠다.
(6).   런던은 깨끗하다~깨끗했다~깨끗하겠다.
(7).   할아버지가 집에 안 계신다~안 계셨다~안 계시겠다.
(8).   나는 형을 찾아간다~찾아갔다~찾아가겠다.
(9).   나는 개 2마리와 고양이 1마리가 있다~있었다~있겠다.
(10). 그분은 내 친구와 계신다~안 계셨다~안 계시겠다.
(11). 만호는 수진이보다 키가 크다~컸다~크겠다.
(12). 책상 밑에 종이가 없다~없었다~없겠다.
(13). 이 영화는 너무 재미없다~재미없었다~재미없겠다.
(14). 나는 자주 공부하지 않는다~공부하지 않았다~공부하지 않겠다.~

Exercise 7: More English to Korean (Plain Style)

(1).   그 개는 너무 크다~컸다~크겠다.
(2).   나는 이렇게 한다~했다~하겠다.
(3).   나는 여기서 혼자 있지 않는다~않았다~않겠다.
(4).   나는 어머니한테 책을 드린다~드렸다~드리겠다.
(5).   그는 여자 친구한테 매일 전화를 건다~걸었다~걸겠다.
(6).   그 의자 위에 인형이 있다~있었다~있겠다.
(7).   우리 집은 여기서 멀지 않다~않았다~않겠다.
(8).   저녁에 나는 내 방에 있는다~있었다~있겠다.
(9).   나는 그 의자에 앉지 않다~않았다~않겠다.
(10). 나는 그 책이 없다~없었다~없겠다.
(11). 그 음식은 그렇게 좋지 않다~않았다~않겠다.
(12). 나는 매일 다른 신발을 신는다~신었다~신겠다.
(13). 내 여동생은 개와 같이 논다~놀았다~놀겠다.
(14). 너무 춥다~추웠다~춥겠다.

Exercise 8: Practice with -어다/-아다

(1).   엄마, 빵 좀 사다 주세요.
(2).   수진 씨, 이 젓가락 좀 씻어다 주세요.
(3).   만호 씨, 비디오를 하나 좀 빌려다 줘요.
(4).   에릭 씨, 이 가방 좀 들어다 줄래요?
(5).   샌디 씨, 저것 좀 받아다 줘요.
(6).   수영 씨, 은행에 가서 돈 좀 찾아다 줘요.
(7).   너무 늦었으니까 내가 데려다 줄게요.
(8).   커피 1잔 타다 드릴까요?
(9).   손님을 지하철역까지 모셔다 드렸어요.
(10). 들어다 드릴까요? 네, 들어다 주세요.

Exercise 9: Yet More English to Korean (Plain Style)

(1).   좋으냐?
(2).   그는 화요일에 대학교에 가(느)냐?
(3).   우리 집을 팔자!
(4).   추웠(느)냐?
(5).   빨리 경찰을 불러라!
(6).   그 사람은 미국에 살아 본 적이 있(느)냐?
(7).   이 책들은 흔하냐?
(8).   가서 면도를 해라!
(9).   오늘 저녁에 같이 먹자.
(10). 그는 그 빵을 먹겠(느)냐?

Exercise 10: Korean to English Translation

(1).   *I don't want to be disturbed when I'm eating lunch.*
(2).   *Don't forget to lock the door when you go out!*
(3).   *Didn't you put too much red pepper powder in this kimchee? It's so hot I could die!*
(4).   *Even though I was hospitalized one month ago, I don't seem to have recovered.*
(5).   *I'm not all that bright, but I am conscientious.*
(6).   *Get out of this house at once!*
(7).   *Yesterday, for the first time in a long time, I met my former university classmate.*
(8).   *This subway station is close to my house, so it's really convenient.*
(9).   *Where did you buy that doll? Was it expensive?*
(10). *It's because she's good at business that she became such a rich woman.*
(11). *Yesterday I lost my bag again.*
(12). *Which medical school did that person graduate from?*
(13). *The wind is blowing refreshlingly today.*
(14). *Are you going to keep living as a single person? Are you thinking of marriage?*
(15). *There were many customers at the department stores on the weekend.*
(16). *That student isn't preparing at all.*
(17). *It's grandmother's birthday so let's buy her dinner or something.*
(18). *Do you want to go with me to Tokyo during the long weekend this September?*
(19). *While I was out visiting my sick grandfather, a thief came in and stole the maid's purse.*

Vocabulary Drill

(1).   수진 씨 남편은 감기에 걸렸다 ~ 머리가 아프다 ~ 지난 주에 진찰을 받았다.
(2).   만호 씨 아들은 작년에 의과대학을 졸업했다 ~ 소아과를 공부하고 있다 ~ 병원에서 인턴으로 일하고 있다.
(3).   친구와 나는 박 선생님을 문병했다 ~ 선생님한테 꽃을 드렸다 ~ 길이 복잡해도 운전을 한다.
(4).   의과 대학생이 ~ 인턴이 ~ 이비인후과 의사가 나를 진찰했다.
(5).   용호 씨는 이제 완전히 회복했(느)냐? ~ 열이 아직도 높으냐? ~ 이제 퇴원했(느)냐?
(6).   간호사가 방금 수술실에서 나왔다 ~ 진찰실 안에 들어갔다 ~ 환자한테 주사를 놓아 줬다
(7).   내가 받은 수술 ~ 응급치료 ~ 피검사에 대해서 이야기 해 줄까요?
(8).   아이는 전염병에 걸렸냐? ~ 열이 있냐? ~ 학교에서 문학을 공부하냐?

Lesson Twenty-Seven

Exercise 1: Quoted Statements

(1). 진희가 호철한테 다음 주에 미국에 간다고 했어요.
진희 *told* 호철 *she's going to the United States next week.*

(2). 진희가 호철한테 그 술집은 우리 단골집이라고 했어요.
진희 *told* 호철 *that that bar is our regular bar.*

(3). 진희가 호철한테 내일 눈이 올 거라 했어요.
진희 *told* 호철 *that it's going to snow tomorrow.*

(4). 진희가 호철한테 전쟁때 고생을 많이 한 것 같다고 했어요.
진희 *told* 호철 *that it seemed people suffered a lot during the war.*

(5). 진희가 호철한테 그런 영화는 보기 싫다고 했어요.
진희 *told* 호철 *that she doesn't like watching those kinds of movies.*

(6). 진희가 호철한테 에릭 씨 아버님이 유명한 학자시라고 했어요.
진희 *told* 호철 *that Eric's father is a famous scholar.*

(7). 진희가 호철한테 아버지가 수영하러 가고 싶어하신다고 했어요.
진희 *told* 호철 *that her father wants to go swimming.*

(8). 진희가 호철한테 밖에서 가방을 들고 있겠다고 했어요.
진희 *told* 호철 *that she'd be waiting outside, holding her bag.*

(9). 진희가 호철한테 수철 씨가 교통사고로 죽었다고 했어요.
진희 *told* 호철 *that* 수철 *died in a traffic accident.*

(10). 진희가 호철한테 김치 없으면 못 산다고 했어요.
진희 *told* 호철 *that she couldn't live without kimchee.*

(11). 진희가 호철한테 회사가 파산이 돼서 화가 났다고 했어요.
진희 *told* 호철 *that she got angry that the company went bankrupt.*

(12). 진희가 호철한테 병이 나았지만 몸조리를 잘 못하고 있다고 했어요.
진희 *told* 호철 *that she's recovered, but she hasn't been taking care of her health so well.*

(13). 진희가 호철한테 대통령을 모시러 간다고 했어요.
진희 *told* 호철 *that she was going to go accompany the president.*

(14). 진희가 호철한테 결국에는 오래 가지 못하고 파산을 선언했다고 했어요.
진희 *told* 호철 *that that ultimately they couldn't go on for long and that they declared bankruptcy.*

(15). 진희가 호철한테 친구가 장가를 간다고 했어요.
진희 *told* 호철 *that her friend is getting married.*

(16). 진희가 호철한테 저 학생은 아주 얌전하다고 했어요.
진희 *told* 호철 *that that student is a 'very nice young man.'*

(17). 진희가 호철한테 4월에 논문을 제출해야 한다고 했어요.
진희 *told* 호철 *that she has to hand in her thesis in April.*

Exercise 2: Quoted Questions

(1). 진호가 진주한테 왜 그러느냐고 물어봤어요.
Chinho asked Chinju why she was doing that.

(2). 진호가 호철한테 서울에 언제 도착했느냐고 물어봤어요.
Chinho asked 호철 *when she arrived in Seoul.*

(3). 진호가 호철한테 어디에 가고 싶으냐고 물어봤어요.
Chinho asked 호철 *where she wanted to go.*

(4). 진호가 호철한테 오늘 아침에 일찍 일어났느냐고 물어봤어요.
Chinho asked 호철 *if she woke up early this morning.*

(5). 진호가 호철한테 학생이냐고 물어봤어요.
Chinho asked 호철 *if she was a student.*

(6). 진호가 호철한테 같이 영화 보러 가지 않겠느냐고 물어봤어요.
Chinho asked 호철 *if she didn't want to go see a movie together.*

(7). 진호가 호철한테 생일날에 뭘 할 것이냐고 물어봤어요.
Chinho asked 호철 *what she was going to do on her birthday.*

(8). 진호가 호철한테 짐이 무거우냐고 물어봤어요.
Chinho asked 호철 *if his luggage was heavy.*

(9). 진호가 호철한테 요즘 영국 날씨가 좋으냐고 물어봤어요.
Chinho asked 호철 *if the weather in England was good these days.*

(10). 진호가 호철한테 내일 오겠느냐고 물어봤어요.
Chinho asked 호철 *if she was coming tomorrow.*

(11). 진호가 호철한테 자기를 바보로 여기느냐고 물어봤어요.
Chinho asked 호철 *if she considered him a fool.*

(12). 진호가 호철한테 왜 그렇게 살이 빠졌느냐고 물어봤어요.
Chinho asked 호철 *why he lost so much weight.*

(13). 진호가 호철한테 소리를 지르려면 산꼭대기로 올라가야겠느냐고 물어봤어요.
Chinho asked 호철 *if they wouldn't have to go to the top of the mountain if they wanted to scream*

(14). 진호가 호철한테 그 소설 제목이 뭐냐고 물어봤어요.
Chinho asked 호철 *what the title of that novel was.*

(15). 진호가 호철한테 저 가게는 단골이 많으냐고 물어봤어요.
Chinho asked 호철 *if there were many regulars at that store.*

Exercise 3: Quoted Suggestions

(1). 진희가 호철한테 시청역에서 내리자고 했어요.
진희 *suggested to* 호철 *that they get off at City Hall station.*

(2). 진희가 호철한테 돼지 1마리 기르자고 했어요.
진희 *suggested to* 호철 *that they raise a pig.*

(3). 진희가 호철한테 산꼭대기까지 올라 가지 말자고 했어요.
진희 *suggested to* 호철 *that they don't go up to the top of the mountain.*

(4). 진희가 호철한테 담배를 끊자고 했어요.
진희 *suggested to* 호철 *that they quit smoking.*

(5). 진희가 호철한테 고기를 굽자고 했어요.
진희 *suggested to* 호철 *that they roast the meat.*

(6). 진희가 호철한테 다음 주에 떠나지 말자고 했어요.
진희 *suggested to* 호철 *that they not leave next week.*

(7). 진희가 호철한테 선생님께 이야기하자고 했어요.
진희 *suggested to* 호철 *that they talk to the teacher.*

(8). 진희가 호철한테 창문을 좀 열자고 했어요.
진희 *suggested to* 호철 *that they open the window a bit.*

(9). 진희가 호철한테 박 선생님께 편지를 쓰자고 했어요.
진희 *suggested to* 호철 *that they write a letter to Mr. Pak.*

(10). 진희가 호철한테 시험 날짜를 발표하자고 했어요.
진희 *suggested to* 호철 *that they announce the date of the exam.*

(11). 진희가 호철한테 벽과 천장은 흰색으로 하자고 했어요.
진희 *suggested to* 호철 *that they make the walls and ceiling white.*

Exercise 4: Quoted Commands

(1). 박 선생님이 장 선생님한테 예수님을 믿으시라고 했어요.
Mr. Pak told Mr. Chang to believe in Jesus.

(2). 박 선생님이 장 선생님한테 밖에서 잠깐만 기다리시라고 했어요.
Mr. Pak told Mr. Chang to wait outside a minute.

(3). 박 선생님이 장 선생님한테 이번 주일에는 오지 마시라고 했어요.
Mr. Pak told Mr. Chang not to come this week.

(4). 박 선생님이 장 선생님한테 그 여자한테 장가 가지 마시라고 했어요.
Mr. Pak told Mr. Chang not to marry that woman.

(5). 박 선생님이 장 선생님한테 좀 더 일찍 출근하시라고 했어요.
Mr. Pak told Mr. Chang to report to work a little earlier.

(6). 박 선생님이 장 선생님한테 이 책의 제목을 바꾸시라고 했어요.
Mr. Pak told Mr. Chang to change the title of this book.

(7). 박 선생님이 장 선생님한테 저렇게 큰 소리로 떠들지 마시라고 했어요.
Mr. Pak told Mr. Chang not to carry on in such a loud voice.

(8). 박 선생님이 장 선생님한테 영어로 발표하지 마시라고 했어요.
Mr. Pak told Mr. Chang not to present in English.

(9). 박 선생님이 장 선생님한테 빨리 앉으시라고 했어요.
Mr. Pak told Mr. Chang to quickly take a sit.

(10). 박 선생님이 장 선생님한테 이를 닦으시라고 했어요.
Mr. Pak told Mr. Chang to brush his teeth.

(11). 박 선생님이 장 선생님한테 사실을 밝히시라고 했어요.
Mr. Pak told Mr. Chang to reveal the truth.

(12). 박 선생님이 장 선생님힌테 명령하지 마시라고 했어요.
Mr. Pak told Mr. Chang not to order him around.

(13). 박 선생님이 장 선생님한테 추측하지 마시라고 했어요.
Mr. Pak told Mr. Chang not to guess.

(14). 박 선생님이 장 선생님한테 바퀴벌레를 잡으시라고 했어요.
Mr. Pak told Mr. Chang to catch the cockroach.

Exercise 5: Quoted Requests for Favors

(1). 홍빈이 호철한테 새로 산 양복을 보여 달라고 했어요.
Hongbin asked 호철 to show him the new suit he bought.

(2). 홍빈이 호철한테 집 주소 좀 가르쳐 달라고 했어요.
Hongbin asked 호철 to tell him his home address.

(3). 홍빈이 호철한테 시계를 잠깐만 빌려 달라고 했어요.
Hongbin asked 호철 to lend him his watch for a minute.

(4). 홍빈이 호철한테 내일 교수님께 연락을 해 달라고 했어요.
Hongbin asked 호철 to contact the professor tomorrow.

(5). 홍빈이 호철한테 내일 공항에 나와 달라고 했어요.
Hongbin asked 호철 to come out to the airport tomorrow.

(6). 홍빈이 호철한테 후추를 달라고 했어요.
Hongbin asked 호철 to give him the pepper.

(7). 홍빈이 호철한테 시간이 있으면, 오늘 좀 도와 달라고 했어요.
Hongbin asked 호철 to help him today if he has time.

(8). 홍빈이 호철한테 잠깐만 기다려 달라고 했어요.
Hongbin asked 호철 to please wait a minute.

(9). 홍빈이 호철한테 형이 있으면, 전화 좀 바꿔 달라고 했어요.
      Hongbin asked 호철 to put his older brother on the phone if he was there.
(10). 홍빈이 호철한테 10000원만 달라고 했어요.
      Hongbin asked 호철 to give him just 10000 wŏn.
(11). 홍빈이 선생님한테 자기가 쓴 논문을 한번 봐 달라고 했어요.
      Hongbin asked the teacher to look over the thesis that he wrote.

Exercise 6: Quotes, Direct and Indirect

(1). 선생님이 나한테 "숙제를 했어요?" 라고 물어보셨어요.
      선생님이 나한테 숙제를 했느냐고 물어보셨어요.
(2). 만호가 나한테 "많이 자면 안 돼요" 라고 했어요.
      만호가 나한테 많이 자면 안 된다고 했어요.
(3). 우리 아버지가 "오늘 밤에 술 마시러 간다" 라고 해요.
      우리 아버지가 오늘 밤에 술 마시러 가신다고 해요.
(4). 진호가 "날씨는 어때요?" 라고 물어봐요.
      진호가 날씨는 어떠냐고 물어봐요.
(5). 어머니가 나한테 "집에 일찍 들어 와라" 라고 했어요.
      어머니가 나한테 집에 일찍 들어 오라고 했어요.
(6). 수진이 나한테 "너무 뚱뚱해요" 라고 했어요.
      수진이 나한테 너무 뚱뚱하다고 했어요.
(7). 그 여자가 나한테 "부산에 사십니까?" 라고 물어봤어요.
      그 여자가 나한테 부산에 사느냐고 물어봤어요.
(8). 우리 남동생이 "아버지가 편찮으세요" 라고 했어요.
      우리 남동생이 아버지가 편찮으시다고 했어요.
(9). 미나는 아마 나한테 "다른 여자 친구를 찾아봐요" 라고 할 거에요.
      미나는 아마 나한테 다른 여자 친구를 찾아보라고 할 거에요.
(10). 그 여자는 나한테 "박 목사님께 드리세요" 라고 했어요.
      그 여자는 나한테 박 목사님께 드리고 했어요.

Exercise 7: Indirect Quotes, Three Ways

(1). 그 학생은 나한테 너무 빨리 말하지 말라고 했어요~말하지 말라 했어요~
      말하지 말랬어요.
(2). 만호가 사장을 도둑이라고 여겨요~도둑이라 여겨요~도둑이래요.
(3). 수진이가 김 선생님한테 그 책은 자기 것이라고 했어요~것이라 했어요~
      것이랬어요.
(4). 의사선생님이 나한테 더 쉬어야 한다고 했어요~한다 했어요~한댔어요.
(5). 만호가 사과를 다 먹었다고 했어요?~먹었다 했어요?~먹었댔어요?
(6). 상호는 올해가 작년보다 나쁘다고 믿어요~나쁘다 믿어요~나쁘대요.
(7). 어머니는 나한테 내년에 졸업한 후에 일본에 가라고 했어요~가라 했어요
      ~가랬어요.
(8). 미아가 그 건물이 상호가 일했던 곳이냐고 물어봤어요~곳이냐 물어봤어요
      ~곳이ㄴㅐㅆ어요. [NB: remarkably, the Apple Korean Language Kit does not
      allow the combination ㄴ + ㅐ + ㅆ as one syllable!]
(9). 우리 어머니는 내가 너무 많이 먹는다고 생각하시지만~먹는다 생각하지만
      ~먹는다지만, 나는 살이 빠졌다고 생각해요.
(10). 그 여자가 새 일을 찾는다고 했어요~찾는다 했어요~찾는댔어요.

Exercise 8: Korean to English Translation

(1). My younger sister asked me if it was okay if she could borrow some pants to wear tomorrow.
(2). My girlfriend told me not to see other women.
(3). That old gentleman thinks all politicians are liars.
(4). I'll have to tell my homestay mother to make the kimchee less spicy.
(5). What does the word "조르다" mean?
(6). You mean to say such a lazy student became a Japanese professor?
(7). I suggested we leave early so we could meet with Mr. Park's wife for a minute.
(8). My father told me that I shouldn't have too much fun.
(9). I heard that that person, a company employee, lives in the house next door.
(10). Mr. Kim's wife complains that Mr. Kim leaves early for work every morning, and comes home late every evening.
(11). Let's confirm whether this train is the train going to Seoul.
(12). The doctor said that even though I didn't take the medicine every day, I would get better soon.
(13). What does the title of this book mean? How should I translate it in English?
(14). [At the party]
       Umm, this is Professor 이현희 from Seoul University; please introduce yourself.
(15). That student tries hard for an American student.
(16). Shall I ask what time the performance will start this evening?
(17). A. Did Mr. & Mrs. Nam say they had a 'love marriage' or did they say they had an arranged marriage?
       B. They said they were originally what you might call a campus couple.
(18). My mother told me to sleep at Manho's house if it gets too late.
(19). 형: What did father say?
       동생: He asked if I needed more pocket money.
       형: So what did you answer?
       동생: Of course I said I need more—do you think I'd say I didn't need any?

Exercise 9: From Contracted to Expanded Quotations

강의실에 가는 길에 석만이는 에릭을 만났습니다.
Sŏngman met Eric on his way to the lecture room.

석만   저, 에릭씨, 어디 가요?
            Say, Eric, where are you going?
에릭   수업이 끝나서 집에 가요. 참, 진영이가 전화 좀 해 달라고 했어요.
            My class is over, so I'm going home. Oh yes, 진영 asked if you could phone her.
            저녁 9시쯤 하라고 했어요.
            She said to phone around 9 o'clock this evening.
석만   그래요? 알았어요. 영철이가 이번 주말에 뭐 하느냐고 물었어요?
            영화 보러 가자고 했어요.
            Really? Okay. Did 영철 ask what you were doing this weekend? He suggested that we go see a movie.
에릭   무슨 영화를 보자고 했어요?
            Which movie did he suggest we watch?
석만   잘 모르겠는데 대한극장에서 한다고 했어요.
            I'm not sure, but he said it's playing at Taehan Theatre.
에릭   그래요? 주말에 특별히 할 일도 없는데 가지요, 뭐. 근데 무슨 영화
            냐고 물어 봐요.

	Really? I don't have anything special to do on the weekend, so I guess I'll go. But ask him which movie it is.
석만	알았어요. 그럼 5시에 대한극장 앞에서 만나자고 할게요.
	Okay. Then I'll tell him we'll meet in front of Daehan *theatre at five o'clock.*
에릭	만나는 김에 저녁을 같이 먹고 영화를 보자고 하죠.
	Tell him that while we're at it, we can have dinner together and then go watch the movie.
석만	그래요, 영철이한테 물어 보고 전화를 해 줄게요.
	Okay, I'll ask 영철, *and then I'll call you.*
에릭	영철이 만나면 나한테 전화 좀 해 달라고 해 줘요.
	If you meet 영철, *tell him to call me.*
석만	알았어요, 나중에 보죠.
	All right, I'll see you later.

Lesson Twenty-Eight

Exercise 1: Practice with Retrospectives

(1). 김 선생은 하던 일을 빨리 마치고 갔데요.
Mr. Kim quickly finished the work he was doing and left.

(2). 동생이 우체국에 혼자 가고 있었데요.
My brother was going to the post office alone.

(3). 학장이 총장한테 전보를 쳤었데요.
The dean had sent the president a telegram.

(4). 베이커 선생이 김 선생한테 한국말로 이야기했었데요.
Mr. Baker had apparently spoken in Korean to Mr. Kim.

(5). 한국에서는 고등학교 때는 열심히 공부하지만, 대학교에서는 주로 놀던데요.
As I recall, in high school in Korea they study hard, but in university they mostly have fun.

(6). 관객들이 모두 서서 오랫동안 박수를 쳤었던가요?
Did the audience give a long standing ovation?

(7). 에릭은 학생시절에는 사회주의를 꽤 좋아했던가요?
Did Eric prefer socialism during his student years?

(8). 그 교수의 강의는 굉장히 지루했던가요?
Was that professor's lecture really boring?

(9). 지난 번 소풍을 갔을 때 날씨가 굉장히 쌀쌀했겠더라고요.
When you last went out on an outing the weather must have been very chilly.

(10). 여당후보가 야당후보를 공산주의자라고 하던데요.
The government party candidates said the opposition party candidates were communists.

(11). 집에 있는 모든 귀중품을 다 팔았데요?
Did they sell all the valuables that were in their house?

(12). 신부님의 자동차가 고장났디?
Did the Catholic priest's car break down?

(13). 그 사람이 처자식을 위해서 최선을 다하고 있던데요.
He was doing his best for his wife and children.

(14). 장마철에는 우산을 들고 나가도 소용이 없더군요!
There was no use going out with an umbrella during the rainy season, I recall.

(15). 보석상에 퍽 좋은 금시계가 있었던가요?
Was there a very nice gold watch at the jewelry shop?
(16). 제 친구는 여자친구하고 벌써 헤어졌더군요!
My friend had already broken up with his girlfriend.
(17). 어제 극장에는 빈 자리가 하나도 없었더냐?
There weren't any [empty] seats at the theatres yesterday?
(18). 대통령의 자동차가 참 크고 좋더라고요.
The president's car was really big and nice.
(19). 그 비서가 꽤 거만더하군!
The secretary was rather arrogant!

Exercise 2: Korean to English Translation

(1). *Let's raise our glasses for the sake of our success.*
(2). *The new president said "I will do my best for the sake of economic development."*
(3). *The doctors are working hard for the sake of the patient.*
(4). *You have to be modest for the sake of becoming a great person.*
(5). *Are all the preparations for the operation ready?*
(6). *I want to work part-time to make money.*
(7). *He struggled a lot in order not to separate from his wife.*
(8). *The singer sang old songs for the audience.*
(9). *I did a lot of research in order to write that novel.*
(10). *In communist society there is no art for art's sake.*

Exercise 3: Practice with -고 나서

(1). 자동차가 고장이 나고 나서 걸어다니기 시작했어요.
I started walking after the car broke down.
(2). 총장님이 학생들하고의 모임을 마치고 나서 학장들하고 만났어요.
After conducting the meeting with the students, the president met with the deans.
(3). 선거가 끝나고 나서 대통령이 테레비에 나왔어요.
After the election had finished, the president appeared on TV.
(4). 공산주의가 생기고 나서 세계 경제가 복잡해졌어요.
After the appearance of communism, the world's economy became complicated.
(5). 신부님이 전보를 치시고 나서 성당에 나가셨어요.
The Catholic priest went to church after sending a telegram.
(6). 공항에 갔다오고 나서 또 공항에 가야 했어요.
After having made a trip to the airport and back, I had to go to the airport again.
(7). 그 지루한 강의를 다 듣고 나서 박수도 안 쳤어요.
After having listened to that boring lecture, I didn't even applaud.
(8). 고등학교 친구들하고 술을 마시고 나서 바로 집에 돌아갔어요.
After drinking with my high school friends, I went straight home.
(9). 그 여자 친구하고 헤어지고 나서 오랫동안 혼자 있었어요.
After breaking up with that girlfriend, I was alone for a long time.
(10). 어제 아르바이트를 하고 나서 심심해서 영화를 보러 갔어요.
After working part time yesterday I was bored so I went to see a movie.
(11). 그 회사가 파산이 되고 나서 사장님이 갑자기 없어졌어요.
After that company went bankrupt, the president suddenly disappeared.
(12). 장가를 가고 나서 살이 쪘어요.
I gained weight after I got married.

(13). 대학을 졸업하고 나서 그 사람이 유명한 학자가 됐어요.
After graduating university that person became a famous scholar.

Exercise 4: Korean to English Translation

(1). *These days I've been having problems with my girlfriend, but it's not to the extent that we would break up.*
(2). *I rather loved that man, but not to the extent that I would marry him.*
(3). *This kimchee is so hot it makes your mouth hurt.*
(4). *That comedian was so funny. I laughed so hard my stomach hurt.*
(5). *That movie was so sad it made me cry.*
(6). *Is that friend's condition severe? She says it's so severe she'll have to have an operation.*
(7). *How far is it from here? Too far to walk. ("It's so far you can't walk.")*
(8). *That American woman was surprisingly good at Japanese.*
(9). *It's so foggy you can't see the road.*
(10). *The subway was so crowded you could hardly ride it.*
(11). *My back hurts so much I haven't been able to get up for four days.*
(12). *The business at that store is so slow it should close.*
(13). *These days I'm so busy I've lost my senses.*
(14). *That person was joking around so much he made us feel bad.*
(15). *That lecture was so boring it makes you yawn.*

Exercise 7: Manipulating Retrospectives
The Formal Style
(1). 질문을 많이 하는 학생들이 제일 똑똑합디다. (똑똑하더군요)
The students asking lots of questions were the smartest.
(2). 만호 씨는 동생하고 밖에서 야구를 합디다. (하더군요)
Manho was playing baseball with his brother outside.
(3). 대부분의 한국 남자들은 양주를 좋아합디다. (좋아하더군요)
Most Korean men seemed to like foreign/imported spirits.
(4). 러시아말로 쓴 책이었습디까? (책이었던가요?)
Was it a book written in Russian?
(5). 집에 들어 왔을 때도 계속 머리가 아팠습디까? (아팠던가요?)
Did you still have a headache even when you came home?

The Plain Style
(6). 매주마다 그 여자한테서 선물을 받더냐?
Was he getting gifts from that girl every week?
(7). 아버지는 밭에서 일을 하셨더냐?
Was father working in the field?
(8). 관객들이 박수를 오래 쳐 줬디?
Did the audience applaud for a long time?
(9). 그 사람의 집에 귀중품이 많았더냐?
Did that person's house have lots of valuables?
(10). 은행에 언제 가신다고 그랬디?
When did he say he would go to the bank?

The Polite Style
(11). 집 주위에는 꽃들이 다 피었던가요?
Had all the flowers around the house bloomed?

(12). 그 작가는 최근에 소설을 쓴댔던가요?
   Did that author say he was writing a novel recently?
(13). 의사 선생님은 오늘 넥타이를 안 매고 계셨던가요?
   Was the doctor not wearing a necktie today?
(14). 책상 위에 성냥을 못 봤던가요?
   Did you not see any matches on the desk?
(15). 저녁을 먹고 나서 싸움을 했던가요?
   Did they have a fight after eating dinner?

Exercise 8: Practice with -(으)ㄹ 정도(로)

(1). 어느 정도로 짧게 잘라 드릴까요? 귀가 나올 정도로 잘라 주세요.
(2). 지난 겨울에 눈이 많이 왔어요? 네, 밖에 못 나갈 정도로 많이 왔어요.
(3). 어제 술을 많이 마셨어요? 네, 너무 취해서 걸을 수 없을 정도로 마셨어요.
(4). 밖에 비가 많이 와요? 네, 우산이 있어도 소용이 없을 정도로 많이 와요.
(5). 김치 맛이 어때요? 눈물이 나올 정도로 매워요.
(6). 손이 아직도 아픕니까? 네, 잠을 못 잘 정도로 아파요.
(7). 만호 씨한테 야단쳤어요? 네, 목이 아플 정도로 소리 질렀어요.
(8). 한국말을 어느 정도 할 수 있어요? 전화로 이야기를 주고 받을 수 있을 정도로 해요.
(9). 샌디 씨는 한국말이 많이 늘었지요? 네, 놀랄 정도로 늘었어요.
(10). 수진 씨는 가끔 말을 더듬거리지요? 네, 어떨 때는 나도 못 알아들을 정도로 더듬거려요.

Exercise 9: English to Korean Translation

(1). 학교에서 돌아오는 길에 매우 피곤해 보이던 러시아말 선생님을 만났어요.
(2). 사람들이 그분의 강의는 너무 지루하다던데요.
(3). 이 시계를 금요일까지 고쳐 주시겠습니까?
(4). A. 너희네 집은 크니?
   B. 뭐라고?
   A. 너희네 집이 크냐고...
(5). 학교 가는 길에 교통사고를 봤습니다.
(6). A. 가고 싶지 않으면 안 가도 돼.
   B. 뭐라고?
   A. 가고 싶지 않으면 안 가도 된다고...
(7). 아침을 먹고 있는 중에 전보를 받았습니다.
(8). A. 어디 있었냐?
   B. 뭐라고?
   A. 어디 있었느냐고...
   B. 미안해. 부산에.
(9). 보스턴에서 돌아오는 길에 런던이 훨씬 더 좋다고 아내에게 말했어요.
(10). 어제 만난 친구가 오늘 저녁에 같이 술집에 가자고 하더군요.
(11). A. 정치를 좋아하니?
   B. 뭐라고?
   A. 정치를 좋아하느냐고...
   B. 당연히 싫지!

(12).   장마철에는 소풍을 많이 안 가는 게 좋겠어요.
(13).   한국사람들은 보통 음식에 후추를 뿌려 먹던가요?
(14).   A. 너무 장난하지 말아라.
        B. 뭐라고?
        A. 너무 장난하지 말라고...

Lesson Twenty-Nine

Exercise 1: Practice with -기만 해요

(1).   우리 개가 늘 짖기만 해요.
(2).   어머니가 라디오를 듣기만 해요.
(3).   아들이 밖에 나가지 않고, 집에 있기만 해요.
(4).   할아버지가 날마다 신문을 보시기만 해요.
(5).   우리 남편이 담배를 피우기만 해요.
(6).   우리 친구가 말하지 않고, 앉아 있기만 해요.
(7).   애기가 먹기만 해요.
(8).   너는 왜 늘 쉬기만 하니?
(9).   너는 왜 항상 놀기만 하니?

Exercise 2: Practice with -기도 해요

(1).   그 꽃이 좋기도 하네요.
(2).   나는 영화 구경을 가고 싶기도 하네요.
(3).   그 사람은 돈이 많기도 하네요.
(4).   아들이 돈을 잘 쓰기도 하네요.
(5).   학교가 집에서 가깝기도 하네요.
(6).   우체국이 교회에서 멀기도 네요.
(7).   그 사람은 편지 쓰기를 좋아하기도 하네요.
(8).   그 애기가 어리기도 하네요.
(9).   우리 사장님이 젊기도 하시네요.
(10).   애기가 밤에 잘 자기도 하네요.
(11).   날이 춥기도 하네요.
(12).   이 편지가 무겁기도 하네요.
(13).   그 여자가 통역을 잘 하기도 하네요.
(14).   통역사의 태도가 이상하기도 하네요.

Exercise 3: Practice with -기는 . . . 지만

(1).   원고료는 받기는 받았지만, 원고는 아직 못 쓰고 있어요.
(2).   그 회의에는 가기는 가겠지만, 가기 싫어요.
(3).   그 사람도 초대하기는 했지만, 안 오면 좋겠어요.
(4).   컴퓨터를 사기는 샀지만, 잘 안 써요.

(5). 폭풍우가 있기는 있었지만, 큰 피해는 없었어요.
(6). 졸리기는 하지만, 끝까지 봐야지요.
(7). 지각을 하기는 했지만, 온 김에 일이나 해야지요.
(8). 귀찮기는 하지만, 처자식을 위해서 하는 거니까 해야지요.
(9). 맛이 없기는 없지만, 많이 잡수세요.
(10). 번역가가 번역하기는 했지만, 엉터리였어요.

Exercise 4: Practice with -(으)ㄴ/-는 편이다

(1). 금년의 독감은 작년 것보다 심한 편입니다.
(2). 할아버지는 소화가 잘 안 되시는 편이세요.
(3). 우리 아들은 남을 적극적으로 도와 주는 편이에요.
(4). 잘 생긴 편인데요.
(5). 수진이는 친구를 쉽게 사귀는 편입니다.
(6). 질문을 많이 하는 편이에요.
(7). 최선을 다 하는 편이에요.
(8). 잘 팔리는 편입니다.
(9). 점잖은 편이에요.
(10). 친절한 편인데요.

Exercise 5: Practice with -(으)ㄴ/-는가요 and -나요

(1). 다음 달에 한국에 가나요?
(2). 요즘 무엇을 하시나요?
(3). 마감이 언제인가요?
(4). 원고료가 얼마였나요?
(5). 가방이 가벼운가요?
(6). 그렇게 하면 좀 귀찮지 않은가요?
(7). 교정을 다 보셨나요?
(8). 누가 이 그릇을 깼나요?
(9). 이 번역은 잘 됐나요?
(10). 호철 씨 약혼자가 예쁜가요?
(11). 그분이 사장님이신가요?
(12). 김치가 너무 매운가요?

Exercise 6: More Practice with -(으)ㄴ/-는가요

(1). 먼가요?
(2). 내일 같이 놀 수 있겠는가요?
(3). 방은 너무 더운가요?
(4). 그 건물은 우리 집보다 높은가요?
(5). 그 교과서는 박 교수님이 쓰신 것인가요?
(6). 한국의 경치는 아름다운가요?
(7). 그것은 연필인가요?

(8). 그분의 자동차는 멋있는가요?
(9). 서울 시내의 공기는 좋은가요?
(10). 또 통화중인가요?

Exercise 7: More Practice with -나요

(1). 그 차는 사고 싶던 차였나요?
(2). 그는 외국에서 방금 돌아왔나요?
(3). 작년에 시험을 봤나요?
(4). 그 아이가 한 일을 보면 그분이 화를 내시겠나요?
(5). 그 선물을 그분한테 드렸을 때 웃으셨나요?
(6). 이곳은 그분이 사실 곳이나요?
(7). 아침을 먹었나요?
(8). 시내에 갔다 온 후에 같이 나가겠나요?
(9). 그는 토론토에서 새 모자를 샀나요?
(10). 언제 졸업하나요?

Exercise 8: Korean to English Translation

(1). *I've decided to wake up early from tomorrow.*
(2). *I've decided to marry that girl.*
(3). *Let's decide to leave on the 3 o'clock flight.*
(4). *I promised to give the computer I used to my friend.*
(5). *I've decided to quit drinking from now.*
(6). *Let's agree on using panmal with each other from now on, OK?*
(7). *I promised my mother I wouldn't drink.*
(8). *I've decided to use this book for teaching in class.*
(9). *Where did you decide to meet?*
(10). *I decided not to translate this part.*
(11). *What are you doing these days that's making you so busy?*
(12). *I've lost my senses looking after the baby these days.*
(13). *I stayed up all night in order to fix the car.*
(14). *Thank you so much for making the effort to come.*
(15). *I'm busy preparing for exams.*
(16). *Because I was so busy writing the report, I didn't have time to meet that person.*
(17). *I missed the bus since I slept in.*
(18). *What are you doing these days that's making you not even come to school?*
(19). *What are you doing to make yourself arrive late every day?*
(20). *What with proofreading the manuscript, I haven't had time to finish anything else.*

Exercise 9: English to Korean Translation

(1). 수업이 쉬우면 좋겠어요.
(2). 생선을 안 먹기로 했어요.
(3). 밤을 새기로 했어요.
(4). 시장님한테 다음 주까지 교정을 하기로 약속을 했어요.
(5). 학생들은 부지런하기도 하고 게으르기도 해요.
(6). 이 컴퓨터는 귀찮기도 하고 비싸기도 해요.
(7). 그 사람은 책을 읽기만 해요.

(8).   우리 개는 잠만 자요.
(9).   이 원고를 조금 늦게 제출해도 괜찮겠나요?
(10).   원고를 읽어 봤는데 다시 써야겠네요!
(11).   집에 돌아왔을 때 창문들이 다 열려 있었어요.

Lesson Thirty

Exercise 1: Convert to Plain Style

(1).   그 병원은 너무 작다.
(2).   내 방에 가방이 있다.
(3).   나는 모른다.
(4).   늦어진다.
(5).   그 사람은 자주 옷을 사(느)냐?
(6).   나는 친구를 기다렸다.
(7).   그 사람은 여기서 사(느)냐?
(8).   부산까지 오래 걸린다.
(9).   이렇게 할 수 있(느)냐?
(10).   나는 피곤하지 않다.
(11).   그 사람은 내일까지 낫겠다.
(12).   이것을 사자!
(13).   그 사람은 학교에 가겠(느)냐?
(14).   너무 다냐?
(15).   내 의사 선생님은 아주 친절하시다.
(16).   그 사람은 위험하게 운전한다.
(17).   그 사람의 부인은 내일 죽겠냐?
(18).   나는 낮에 안 눕는다.
(19).   그것은 15,000원 한다.
(20).   나는 오늘 오후에 학교에 있겠다.

Exercise 2: Convert to Quotations

(1).   우리 오빠는 나한테 왜 나가느냐고 물어봤어요.
        우리 오빠는 "왜 나가니?" 라고 물어봤어요.
(2).   우리 어머니는 우리한테 "오늘 밤에 놀러 와도 돼" 라고 했어요.
        우리 어머니는 오늘 밤에 놀러 와도 된다고 했어요.
(3).   그 사람은 우리하한테 같이 먹자고 했어요.
        그 사람은 "같이 먹자" 라고 했어요.
(4).   그 사람은 형이 유명한 가수라고 했어요.
        그 사람은 "형이 유명한 가수에요" 라고 했어요.
(5).   김 선생님은 늙은 여자들이 보통 뚱뚱하다고 생각해요.
        김 선생님은 "늙은 여자들은 보통 뚱뚱하다" 라고 생각해요.
(6).   남동생은 아버지가 책을 너무 많이 읽으신다고 해요.
        남동생은 "아버지는 책을 너무 많이 읽으신다" 라고 해요.
(7).   우리 아내가 친구한테 사과 좀 사 달라고 했어요.
        우리 아내가 친구한테 "사과 좀 사 줘요" 라고 했어요.
(8).   그 사람은 내일 방을 청소하겠다고 해요.

그 사람은 "내일 방을 청소하지요" 라고 해요.
(9).　나는 "이것이 김 선생님 댁이냐?" 라고 했어요.
　　　나는 이것이 김 선생님 댁이냐고 했어요.
(10).　그 사람은 나한테 더 열심히 공부하라고 했어요.
　　　그 사람은 나한테 "더 열심히 공부해요" 라고 했어요.

Exercise 3: Convert to Retrospectives

Using the Formal Style:
(1).　김 선생님은 오늘 아침에 전보를 보냈습디다. (보냈던데요)
(2).　화요일 날은 보통 비가 온다고 합디다. (하던데요)
(3).　그 사람은 그녀를 사랑합디까? (사랑하던가요?)
(4).　그 사람은 학교에 가기 전에 자전거를 고쳤습디다. (고쳤던데요)
(5).　다음 주는 장마철이 시작 되겠습디다. (시작되겠더군요)
(6).　그 맥주는 어떻습디까? (어떻던가요?)

Using the Plain Style:
(7).　그 사람은 어제 죽었다고 하더라.
(8).　아내는 지금 방에서 공부하더라.
(9).　내일은 춥겠더라.
(10).　언제부터 따뜻해졌더냐?
(11).　보석상에서 많은 귀중품을 누가 훔쳐갔더라.
(12).　그 여자는 그 신발을 시내에서 샀더냐?

Using the Polite Style (or *it's a fact that . . .*)
(13).　의사 선생님은 공항에 가고 있었데요.
(14).　그는 내일 안 가겠던데요.
(15).　그는 또 노래를 부르더라고요.
(16).　왕은 자기 아들이 가수가 되는 것을 원하지 않는데요.
(17).　어제 강의하셨던가요?
(18).　그 여자는 남자친구와 크게 싸웠데요.

Exercise 4: Convert to Questions in . . . 가요 and . . . 나요

(1).　그 사람이 읽고 있는 것은 잡지인가요?
(2).　저녁에 먹을 게 많은가요?
(3).　그 자동차는 빠른가요?
(4).　그 화가는 유명한가요?
(5).　그 사람은 공부하나요?
(6).　오늘 밤에 늦겠나요?
(7).　우리 남동생은 다시 농담을 하나요?
(8).　그 음악가가 연주하는 것을 몇 번 봤나요?
(9).　지난 여름에 영국에 가뭄이 있었나요?
(10).　그 방이 네가 책을 읽었던 방인가?

Exercise 5: Korean to English Translation

(1). *The person who ate dinner with us last night was our father.*

(2). *I like expensive watches, too.*

(3). *I couldn't wear my new shoes because it rained.*

(4). *It's vacation, so tomorrow I'm going to go home.*

(5). *Here comes the person who will sit beside me.*

(6). *While 영미 reads the paper, I will finish my homework.*

(7). *I couldn't hear what 영미 said.*

(8). *Today I'm not going to eat out; I'm going to eat at home.*

(9). *The person who is sitting next to Mr. Kim is a famous musician.*

(10). *According to the weather forecast, the weather's going to be nice.*

(11). *The person who planted flowers in our field also planted flowers in Mr. Kim's field.*

(12). *That nurse is very unkind to patients.*

(13). *Shall we go to a tabang together and have some tea?*

(14). *How nice it would be if it were to snow tonight.*

(15). *Have you ever seen such a tall mountain?*

(16). *Listen to the weather forecast. I do listen to the weather forecast, but it's not very accurate.*

(17). *When I was at the playground, I saw students doing sports.*

(18). *I want to finish this work quickly, but do you think you could help me before you leave?*

(19). *There is someone who brings the letters to the post office every day.*

(20). *When I was eating dinner yesterday, a guest came.*

(21). *The days are very cold, so I prefer staying at home.*

(22). *I will do my best in order to graduate next year.*

(23). *I can't read Japanese very well, but I can read a little Chinese.*

(24). *Even though that child can't even walk, she is trying to run.*

(25). *While we were playing tennis, it started to rain.*

(26). *It would be nice if our team were to win the soccer match tomorrow.*

(27). *Because I was so busy in the morning, I didn't have time to go to the bank.*

(28). *Let's not walk to the concert; shall we take a taxi instead?*

(29). *That store has both expensive and cheap clothes.*

(30). A. *In your view, these two colours are the same, right?*
B. *No, they're different.*

(31). *The person who teaches us English also teaches Mr. Kim.*

(32). *That person is neither lazy nor diligent.*

(33). *If a guest comes while I'm eating breakfast, tell them I'm not here.*

(34). *Can I listen to Mr. Pak's tape recorder?*

(35). *That woman doesn't like singing, and neither does she like playing the piano.*

(36). *Last night I saw Mr. Kim riding a bike.*

(37). *Instead of going to the theatre after eating dinner, shall we go before eating dinner?*

(38). *The movie I watched yesterday was not good.*

(39). *It was a very interesting talk, was it not?*

(40). *Have you ever heard such an interesting story?*

(41). *The person you heard singing last night is a famous vocalist.*

(42). *It's not good to just make excuses.*

(43). *Can you hear the wind blowing?*

(44). *Who is the person sitting behind that teacher over there?*

(45). *I saw Mr. Kim when I was eating dinner in the restaurant.*

(46). *The suit I want to buy is very expensive.*

(47). *If I do your homework for you, will you clean my room for me?*

(48). *I've never been to England, but I've been to America.*

(49). *I was born in America, but I came to Korea when I was young.*

(50). *I'm saving money for the sake of travelling to Europe next summer.*

Exercise 6: English to Korean Translation

(1). 이 서점에 있는 책들은 꽤 비싸겠지요?

(2). 부산에 사시는 미스터 김의 이모를 아시나요?

(3). 이렇게 아팠던 적이 없었어요.

(4). 저 산에 있는 크고 푸른 나무들이 보이나요?

(5). 그 사람은 이야기를 해 줬지만, 이해할 수가 없었어요.

(6). 저와 테니스 치는 게 어떨까요?

(7). 오늘 저녁은 밖에 나가지 않기로 결심했어요.

(8). 어제 저녁에 먹은 음식이 맛있었어요.

(9). 너는 먹기만 하는군!

(10). 한국에 사는 사람들은 밥을 많이 먹어요.

(11). 그 사람은 야구도 잘 하고, 피아노도 잘 쳐요.

(12). 저희 집 뒤에 있는 집은 파란색이에요.

(13). 넌 음악을 좋아하지? 당연하지!

(14). 축구하러 가기전에 좀 쉬자.

(15). 저쪽 낮은 건물 안으로 들어간 남자를 보셨어요?

(16). 저는 공부하는 게 싫지만, 좋은 점수를 받으려면 해야지요.

(17). 시험 기간이라서 요즘은 놀 수가 없어요.

(18). 저는 비 오는 날을 좋아하지 않아요.

(19). 너는 고등학교를 졸업한 뒤에 무엇을 할 계획이니?

(20). 어제 저녁 네가 아프고 콘서트에 가지 못해서 (나는) 속상했어.

(21). 네 시계를 훔친 도둑놈이 대문 쪽으로 도망쳤나?

(22). 은행 앞에 서 있는 저 남자는 누구에요?

(23). 눈이 내리기 시작하는 것 같은데요.

(24). 식사하는 동안 저랑 얘기하는 게 어떨까요?

(25). 어떤 날씨를 좋아하세요?

저는 날씨가 맑은 날도 좋아하고 구름이 낀 날도 좋아해요.

(26). 의자 위에 있는 교과서는 누구거예요?

(27). 비가 올 때 산보하는 걸 좋아하세요?

(28). 이 서점은 크고 좋죠?

(29). 제 생각에는 이 드레스는 매우 싼 거에요.

(30). 어두워지기 전에 우리 게임을 끝마칠 시간이 없을 것 같은데요.

(31). 내가 숙제를 하고 있는 동안에 그 사람들은 테니스를 치고 있었어요.

(32). 원하시면, 축구경기에 친구를 데리고 와도 돼요.

(33). 저희 팀이 축구경기에서 이기면 좋겠어요.

(34). 저 남자 보이지? 유명한 소설가야.

(35). 영화관이 여기서 너무 머니까 택시를 타고 가는 게 낫겠어요.

(36). 우리 남동생은 테니스도 잘 치고, 공부도 열심히 해요.

(37). 비가 오기 전에 택시를 타고 집에 가야겠네.

(38). 내년에 테니스를 배우면 좋겠어요.

(39). 잘 시간이 되기 전에 이 책을 읽으려고 노력하고 있어요.

(40). 영어를 읽을 수 있지만 러시아말은 못 읽어요.

(41). 테니스장에 또 가니? 테니스만 항상 치는군!

(42). 어머니가 푸른 드레스를 사 주겠다고 약속을 했어요.

(43). 아침을 침대에서 먹어 보는 적이 있어요?

(44). 비가 올 것 같아서 시내에 안 가기로 했어요.

(45). 신문에 의하면 그 유명한 가수가 아파서 내일 우리 학교에 못 와요.

(46). 이 책을 왜 안 읽지? 읽기는 읽었는데 이해를 못 했지.

(47). 해가 나려다가 날이 흐려졌어요.
(48). 그 학생은 태도가 좋지만 게으른 것 같아요.
(49). 아침에 일찍 일어나기가 싫지요?
(50). 우리가 자는 동안에 눈이 왔어요.

About the Authors

Ross King is Associate Professor of Korean at the University of British Columbia. He completed his B.A. in Linguistics at Yale in 1983 and his doctorate in Linguistics (Korean) at Harvard in 1991. Dr. King taught Korean language and linguistics at the School of Oriental and African Studies, University of London, from 1990 to 1994, before accepting his current position. He also serves as Dean of the Korean Language Village at Concordia Language Villages, a Korean language and culture summer immersion program for young people ages 7–18.

Jae-Hoon Yeon is Lecturer in Korean at the Department of Languages and Cultures of East Asia, and Chair of the Centre of Korean Studies, University of London, SOAS (School of Oriental and African Studies). Dr. Yeon received his B.A. and M.A. in Linguistics at Seoul National University in Korea and his Ph.D. in Linguistics at SOAS, University of London. He is the co-author of *Teach Yourself Korean* and *Integrated Korean: Advanced*. He has published many articles on Korean grammar and linguistics. He has been lecturing in Korean language, linguistics, and literature at SOAS since 1989.

Insun Lee is Senior Instructor of Korean at the University of British Columbia. She received her B.A. in English Language and Literature from the Sacred Heart College for Women, Korea. She also has a Graduate Diploma in TESL (Teaching English as a Second Language) from the University of Alberta, and an M.A. in Language Education from the University of British Columbia. Since 1986, she has taught Korean at a number of institutions, including UBC, Simon Fraser University, and Harvard University.